Christian Approaches to Other Faiths

SCM CORE TEXT

Christian Approaches to Other Faiths

Edited by

Paul Hedges

and

Alan Race

scm press

British Library Cataloguing in Publication data

A catalogue record for this book is available
from the British Library

978 0 334 04114

First published in 2008 by
13–17 Long Lan
London ECIA 9P

www.scm-canterburypress.co.uk

SCM Press is a division of
SCM-Canterbury Press Ltd

Typeset by Regent Typesetting, London
Printed in the UK by CPI William Clowes
Beccles NR34 7TL

Contents

Part 2 Christian Responses to Individual Faiths

Section A: Abrahamic Traditions

Section B: Indic Traditions

Section C: Chinese Traditions

Section D: Further Traditions

Preface

The purpose of this textbook in an already crowded market is validated by three key elements:

1 The importance of the subject matter.
2 The particular relevance for understanding in this area.
3 To address a lack in the existing range of texts.

First, Christians have always lived in a pluralist world, a place where many different faiths coexist. If, as Christians believe, the world is part of a divine creation, then Christians are faced with the theological necessity of answering the question, 'Why are there other faiths?' Moreover, the relationship of Christianity, or the Christian world, with other faiths, or the non-Christian world, is a matter of increasing importance. The events of recent history have shown us that we live in a world where conflict between blocs – understood as being on separate sides of an ideological faith divide – exist. Therefore, it is of absolute importance that Christians reflect upon and understand their relationship to the other faiths of the world, in both theoretical and practical terms.

Second, and very much related to our first point, is the need for understanding. This means several things. As we have said, it is of the utmost importance that Christians reflect upon their relationship to other faiths for practical and theoretical ends. However, this cannot occur in an isolated Christian context. Today's situation of plurality means we live in a world not just where we are aware of blocs of faith communities in different parts of the world, but where our friends, neighbours and colleagues will, increasingly, very often be of a different faith and cultural tradition to our own. We therefore need to develop a sympathetic and empathetic understanding and relationship with the other faiths, and to recognize their needs, desires and aspirations alongside our own. It is not, therefore, enough to think of the issue as important, so that simply holding a theoretical position about it seems all that is required; instead, it is a matter of integral and immediate concern in the daily lives of many Christians. Moreover, the needs and problems of these other faiths should also be seen as relevant to Christians when they ask who is their sister, brother or neighbour.

Finally, this textbook (and the accompanying Reader) is written, in part, simply with the hope of filling a lacuna in the field. There have been many recent works discussing the issues of the theology of religions, interreligious dialogue and engagement, including some books written as introductions to the area. However, these tend to focus separately on either the theoretical aspects, or approaches to particular faiths, or groups of faiths, or to provide a set of readings (often of a theoretical nature). We have therefore sought here to provide an introduction to the theology of religions that does all of this. A first section on theoretical dimensions is matched by a second section on approaches to individual faiths, each written by a particular expert in that area, while a carefully balanced selection of contemporary and classical readings is available in the Reader. Also, in its approach it has added to the standard 'classical' typology to consider feminist and postmodern approaches, as well as moving beyond relationships with the 'great world religions' to such things as indigenous faiths and New Religious Movements. It is hoped that this approach will be of use to both teachers and students and interested educated people beyond academia. For students and teachers, it is hoped that it will provide a textbook which can be used for courses and modules in the subject area. For the interested reader, it introduces a spectrum of views and approaches that won't be found elsewhere in onc volume.

It is our belief that it is imperative that Christians come to realize the very real importance of how Christian faith might respond creatively to our world's religious plurality through theological reflection as well as interreligious engagement. Our hope is that this book will stimulate involvement in all aspects of the new world which is opening up before us all.

Paul Hedges and Alan Race

Contributors

K. P. Aleaz is Professor of Religions at Bishop's College and Professor and Dean of the Doctoral Programme at the North India Institute of Post-Graduate Theological Studies, Kolkata, India. He also guides doctoral candidates of the South Asia theological Research Institute, Bangalore, India. Author of 20 books and more than 105 articles, he was William Patton Fellow of the Selly Oak Colleges, Birmingham, in 1977, Visiting Professor at Hartford Seminary, USA, and the University of South Africa, Pretoria, in 2002, and Teape Lecturer, in the Universities of Cambridge, Birmingham, Bristol and Edinburgh, UK, in 2005.

Martin Bauschke is Director of the Global Ethic Foundation's office in Berlin. He researches, lectures and provides educational materials in the fields of the Global Ethic Project and in the dialogue between the three Abrahamic religions. His publications include *Jesus in Koran* (2001, 2007), and *Gemeinsam vor Gott. Gebete aus Judentum, Christentum und Islam* (2004, 2006).

David Cheetham is Senior Lecturer in Theology and Religion at the University of Birmingham, UK, and specializes in the philosophy and theology of religions. He is the author of *John Hick* (2003) and numerous articles in journals, including *The Heythrop Journal*, *Sophia*, *New Blackfriars* and *Theology*. He is currently completing a new book entitled *Ways of Meeting and the Theology of Religions*.

Elizabeth Harris is Senior Lecturer in Religious Studies at Liverpool Hope University, with a specialism in Buddhism. Previously, for 11 years, she was the Secretary for Inter-Faith Relations for the Methodist Church in Britain. She is on the advisory group of the European Network of Buddhist–Christian Studies and of Voies d'Orient, Belgium. She has written widely on Buddhist–Christian relations, and her recent books include *Theravada Buddhism and the British Encounter* (2006) and *What Buddhists Believe* (1996). She is a Reviews Editor for the journal *Interreligious Insight*.

Paul Hedges has taught for universities in the UK (Winchester, Lecturer, 2005–present), Canada (Queen's, ISC campus) and China (2000–03). His Ph.D. (University of Wales, Lampeter, UK) is published as *Preparation and Fulfilment* (2001). He has published articles in journals including the *Journal of Religious History*, *Interreligious Insight* and the *International Review of Mission*. Broad research interests include: the theology and history of religious encounter (India, China, postmodernism, Global Ethic); modern and contemporary Christian thought (critiquing Radical Orthodoxy, modern/postmodern debates, contemporary liberal theology); theory in the study of religion (defining religion, Orientalism, death, sacred space).

Jeannine Hill Fletcher is an Associate Professor of Theology at Fordham University, Bronx, New York. Her research asks whether and how women's interfaith encounters offer new resources for theology. Publications include *Monopoly on Salvation? A Feminist Response to Religious Pluralism* (2005); 'As Long as We Wonder: Possibilities in the Impossibility of Interreligious Dialogue', *Theological Studies* 68 (2007); 'Women's Voices in Dialogue: A Look at the Parliament of the World's Religions', *Studies in Interreligious Dialogue* 16.1 (2006); and 'Shifting Identity: The Contribution of Feminist Thought to Theologies of Religious Pluralism', *Journal of Feminist Studies in Religion* 19.2 (2003).

Pan-chiu Lai graduated from the Chinese University of Hong Kong and King's College London (Ph.D., 1991). He is now Professor and Chairman of the Department of Cultural and Religious Studies at the Chinese University of Hong Kong. Research interests include interreligious dialogue, Christian theology and environmental ethics. In addition to publications in Chinese, he published in English *Towards a Trinitarian Theology of Religions: A Study of Paul Tillich's Thought* (1994) and numerous articles in various academic journals. He delivered the Edward Cadbury Lectures 2005/6, Birmingham, UK, on 'Experiments in Mahayana Christian Theology'.

J. Gordon Melton is the Director of the Institute for the Study of American Religion in Santa Barbara, California, and a research specialist with the Department of Religious Studies at the University of California, Santa Barbara. He was ordained an elder in the United Methodist Church in 1968. He is a fellow with the Western Institute for Intercultural Studies, a Christian association focused in studies of religious pluralism. Publications include more than 30 reference and scholarly texts on contemporary religion and modern religious history, including *American Religion: An Illustrated History* (2000), *Encyclopedia of Protestantism* (2005), and *Nelson's Handbook of Denominations* (2007).

Ronald H. Miller is a Professor of Religion at Lake Forest College, Illinois, USA. Recent publications include *The Hidden Gospel of Matthew* (2004), *The Gospel of Thomas: A Guide to Spiritual Practice* (2004), *Healing the Jewish–Christian Rift*, with Laura Bernstein (2006) and *The Sacred Writings of Paul* (2007). He is Vice President of Interreligious Engagement Project 21, on the board of 'Hands of Peace', an organization bringing young people from the Middle East into dialogue with American Jewish, Christian and Muslim teenagers, and a Reviews Editor of *Interreligious Insight*.

John Parry is Lecturer in World Faiths and Missiology at Northern College, which is part of the Partnership for Theological Education, Manchester. He is a Presbyter of the Church of Bangladesh and currently a United Reformed Church Minister in the UK. His research area is the encounter of Sikhs and Christians and he has contributed to numerous books on interfaith dialogue, particularly with the Sikh tradition. He is presently working to produce a volume on the history of the theological implications of the encounter between Sikhs and Christians.

Alan Race is Dean of Postgraduate Studies, St Philip's Centre, and Vicar of St Philip's Church, Leicester, and an Honorary Canon of Leicester Cathedral. He has written two major books, the classic work *Christians and Religious Pluralism: Patterns in the Christian Theology of Religions* (1983 and 1993 revised and enlarged) and *Interfaith Encounter* (2001), and edited several texts, including *Religions in Dialogue*, with Ingrid Shafer (2002). He is Editor-in-Chief of the international journal *Interreligious Insight: A Journal of Dialogue and Engagement*. He has been involved in Christian theological education and training for many years and is also a respected conference speaker around the world.

Perry Schmidt-Leukel earned a doctorate in Buddhist–Christian dialogue (1990), and a habilitation (University of Munich, 1996) on the theology of religions. He has taught at the Universities of Munich, Innsbruck, Salzburg, and Glasgow, where he is Professor of Systematic Theology and Religious Studies ('Chair of World Religions for Peace'), and founding Director of the Centre for Inter-Faith Studies. Publications include over 20 books and 100 articles in Buddhist studies, Buddhist–Christian dialogue, interfaith studies and systematic theology. Recently edited publications include *War and Peace in World Religions* (2004), *Buddhism and Christianity in Dialogue* (2005), *Understanding Buddhism* (2006), *Islam and Inter-Faith Relations* (2007). A monograph, *God Without Limits*, is forthcoming.

Daniel Strange is Lecturer in Culture, Religion and Public Theology at Oak Hill Theological College, London. His doctoral work (University of Bristol, supervisor Gavin D'Costa) is published as *The Possibility of Salva-*

tion Among the Unevangelised: An Analysis of Inclusivism in Recent Evangelical Theology (2002). He has published articles and chapters in the area of the theology of religions and systematic theology. He co-edited a series for theology undergraduates, *Keeping Your Balance* (2001), *Getting Your Bearings* (2003) and *Encountering God's Word* (2003), and most recently is co-editing *Engaging with Barth: Contemporary Evangelical Critiques* (2008).

Garry W. Trompf is Emeritus Professor in the History of Ideas, University of Sydney. He was formerly Professor of History at the University of Papua New Guinea, and Visiting Professor to the Universities of California, Utrecht and Edinburgh. He is currently engaged with Sydney's Centre for Peace and Conflict Studies and the Institute of Ethnology and Cultural Anthropology, University of Warsaw. His books include *The Idea of Historical Recurrence in Western Thought* (1979); *Early Christian Historiography* (2000) and (on indigenous cultures) *Melanesian Religion* (1991); *Payback: The Logic of Retribution in Melanesian Religions* (1994); and *Religions of Melanesia: A Bibliographic Survey* (2006; with F. Tomasetti).

This book is dedicated to
my mother, Sheila Anne Hedges, in memoriam (PH)
Christine, Nick, Georgina, Madeleine (AR)

Part 1

Theoretical and Methodological Issues

Section A: Mapping the Terrain

1

Theology of Religions in Change: Factors in the Shape of a Debate

ALAN RACE

Today's Context

The celebrated historian of religion Wilfred Cantwell Smith, who helped to pioneer the study of religion as a disciplined enquiry in its own right, famously made the observation:

> I would simply like to suggest that from now on any serious intellectual statement of the Christian faith must include, if it is to serve its purposes among men [*sic*], some doctrine of other religious ways.[1]

That was in 1972. The task to which Smith alluded has become known as the 'Christian Theology of Religions' and is the subject of this book. Yet it is also pertinent to ask: Are we any closer today to this goal or does Smith's 'suggestion' remain still a distant aspiration? Driving home the urgent necessity of the task, he offered a reason for his call:

> We explain the fact that the Milky Way is there by the doctrine of creation, but how do we explain the fact that the Bhagavad Gita is there?[2]

If it is the task of Christian theological reflection to be as all-embracing as possible in its desire to comprehend the religious dimensions of our being human then the very fact of religious plurality surely cries out for interpretation.

Of course, it is far from obvious what the shape of that theology should be. Since Smith's provocation the amount of theorizing and speculation in this field has increased exponentially. This is partly because the fact of plurality has become a pressing existential concern for many and partly because, once Smith's question has been asked, it becomes impossible to ignore its force. At least what has transpired is the recognition that any serious statement of Christian belief is woefully inadequate if reflection on religious plurality is ignored. To this extent Smith has been prophetic.

Why be Interested in Religious Others?

Prior to the issue of a theology of religions is the question 'Why be interested in religious others?' 'Because they are there' is insufficient as a full response, for other religions offer pathways of transformation either in competition or, in some sense, comparable with the Christian cause itself. It is the salvific or transformative potential in other religious ways which compels Christians to be interested in religious others, and therefore in the need for a theology of religions.

Let me suggest at least three reasons why Christians might be interested in other religions. First has been the missionary motivation. This is probably among the oldest of motivations, for it has often been recognized that the simple condemnation of other religions undermines missionary strategy itself. Often what has transpired is a process we have come to call 'inculturation', which is the phenomenon of Christian critical adaptation to local culture. For example, when Augustine of Canterbury (not Hippo) was sent by Pope Gregory the Great in 596, to convert the English people, he was charged with the need to discern how old religious festivals and sites could be sanctified or adapted to suit Christian aims, a strategy which required some knowledge of the local religions. Or when the Jesuit missionaries entered China in the sixteenth century they began by adopting the dress and habits of Buddhists, only eventually to realize that the garb of Confucian scholar-officials would gain them better access to the imperial court. In the contemporary context, the necessity for inculturation is fully accepted as an integral dimension of missiology.[3]

In relation to the theology of religions a good case can be made for seeing the roots of the modern movement for interreligious dialogue in missionary activity. Expectations on the part of many missionaries in the modern period of encountering 'outer darkness' were not fulfilled. The discovery of personal religion, spirituality, transforming ethics and impressive religious philosophy in contexts where the opposite was assumed to be the case led many missionaries to reassess their easy assumption that 'God' was alive in the Church but nowhere else.[4] Missionary interest in 'others' leads directly to the theology of religions debate.

A second reason for being interested in other traditions is felt more urgently in the context of the twenty-first century. I refer to the assumption that the religions are often accused of being responsible for many of the ills of the world, and in particular for the violence associated with religious rivalry or religious extremism. This is a common theme since the attacks on the central institutions of the USA, dramatically symbolized by the destruction on the World Trade Centre in New York in September 2001 (the so-called 9/11 attacks). But the accusation itself is an old theme.

If the religions feel any responsibility at all for the future shape of the world it seems obvious that any sense of rivalry-leading-to-violence will need to be addressed most urgently. When we consider the current tensions within and between nations, cultures and religions in many parts of the world, this point cannot be gainsaid. Moreover, it can be less than honest to claim that 'real' or 'true' religion bears no responsibility and that it is religious extremists who must be condemned. Most religious traditions have their 'texts of terror' which demonize the religious other as a first step on the way to their recommended destruction. Of course the situation is immensely more complex than the idea of rivalry between religious outlooks suggests, and violence in the world erupts for many reasons. Nevertheless, a quick glance down the corridors of history lends credibility to Hans Küng's much-cited aphorism that there can be no peace in the world without peace between the religions.[5]

Religions coming together for the sake of justice and peace in the world is certainly one highly laudable aim of interreligious dialogue. But there may be a connection between the task inherent in the theology of religions and the threat of violent interreligious competition. It has been pointed out that the elimination of other religious perspectives by violent actions could well spring directly from exclusivist attitudes in the theology of religions.[6] While this is not necessarily the case, history is littered with examples where the desire to eliminate the religious other is experienced as a divine command. As with mission, the Christian interest expressed in the concern for a peaceful world through shared ethical practice contains within it ramifications for the Christian theology of religions.

Third, Christians are interested in religious others as a theological concern. The biblical affirmation that God cannot be without witnesses in other cultures and religions; the theological belief in the expansive creativity of God expressed universally through the created order in nature, conscience, ethical impressiveness and examples of religious piety alive in other forms; the philosophical observation that all our language about God is necessarily indirect and limited by the historical/cultural processes of human mediation – all add up to a significant expectation that there is 'more' to the reality of God than can be glimpsed through any one tradition alone. The spirit which informs the outward forms of other religious practices – such as worship/meditation, architecture, community, scriptures, and so on – is what stimulates theological enquiry and leads us to the theology of religions questions. Perhaps the sharpest form of those questions was asked by the Indian Christian theologian Stanley Samartha, as follows: 'Can it be that it is the will of God that many religions should continue in the world?' To be drawn into that question is to be drawn to the heart of the theology of religions debate.

Taking other religions *qua* religions seriously arises from critical thinking in religious understanding. That is to say, it arises because we recognize that to welcome another religious human being is also to welcome the religion which has shaped them. Moreover, if we are not de-contextualized beings, neither are we incapable of transcending the conditioning that has shaped us to date. Religions are not fixed reifications, but have evolved over time, shaping and being shaped by the culture around them. Giving full reign to this outlook entails that we are bound to honour the forms of religious expression which have nurtured human beings as well as individual human piety itself. To echo Wilfred Cantwell Smith again, we might ask what God was up to through the matrix of what we have called Islam or Buddhism or indigenous religion, and so on.[7] As with missionary evangelism and working together for peace, justice and sustainability, the theological interest in other traditions means being open to the awareness of the reality of God in other places and through unfamiliar means. How to account for this in terms of a Christian understanding is the theology of religions' task.

Sources for Christian Reflection

As with any theological topic, it is important to be clear about the methodology for Christian reflection on religious plurality. Are we to be exegetical, either biblically and/or doctrinally, or responsive to new experiences which are imagined to provide, in some sense, new data for theological work? Do we consider 'Christian truth' to be constant through history, with perhaps some degree of adaptability in the face of cultural change, or is 'Christian truth' to be renegotiated with each new generation? Those who lean to exegesis and deductive methodology are likely to seek solutions in past provisions; but those who relish renegotiation are more relativistic in relation to past formularies.

So, for example, it has often been noted that the New Testament writers generally advocate a theology whereby Judaism's dreams of a kingdom of justice and peace are said to have been fulfilled in the person of Christ, with the intention that Judaism is thereby superseded. By extension, this positioning of Judaism in God's plan of salvation is then applied to 'other religions', which consequently come to occupy the same theological space assigned to Judaism. The exegesis of Scripture thus determines the outcome for every historical period thereafter. Let the author of the Epistle to the Hebrews, from the end of the first century CE, sum up this approach (expressing himself in the process in christological terms):

> Long ago God spoke to our ancestors in many and various ways by the prophets, but in these last days he has spoken to us by a Son, whom he appointed heir of all things, through whom he also created the worlds. (Heb. 1.1–2)

For many this assessment provides the framework for a Christian theology of religions. The contrast between a time before and after the appearing of the Son, coupled with the absorption of other religions into the category of former-time 'prophets', who subsequently assume a preparatory role in the divine plan of salvation prior to the revelation in Christ, determines the outcome. In terms of the theology of religions, this is what I am calling an exegetical methodology.

In contrast, those who favour a renegotiation methodology, under the influence of critical historical thinking, would note the inappropriateness of applying this scheme to other religions, for what can it mean outside of the connection with Judaism? And, furthermore, what does it mean for an historical figure to be also the creator of worlds? For renegotiators, the religious centre of what is revealed through the Christ figure can be retained, but it is to be expressed differently outside of the historical conditioning of the first century. There is nothing privileged about the first-century context.

The role of exegesis is not immediately obvious in the theology of religions debates. The Finnish New Testament scholar Heikki Räisänen draws an unfashionable sharp distinction between exegesis and hermeneutics in formulating the role of New Testament texts for making theological judgements today. Exegesis depends on placing texts in their historical contexts and this might be far removed from the experience of contemporary life. Therefore biblical texts are necessarily indirect in their impact. The Apostle Paul's view of relations with pagans, for example, in his writings, tells us little about our relationships today with Buddhists or Sikhs or others. As Räisänen says:

> The exegete may be needed in the global village as the 'historical conscience' in the dialogue, as one who warns of attempts to make too direct a use of the texts.[8]

This is a sobering judgement, both for those who would accord high hermeneutical value to such texts as John 14.6 ('Jesus said, "I am the way, and the truth, and the life. No one comes to the Father except through me"') for their theology of religions, and also for those who would shun proof-texting as such but favour, nevertheless, an overall biblical message which tends towards accepting Christ as the unsurpassable saviour of the world. This is not to say that the Bible has nothing to contribute in the theology of religions; that would indeed be an odd position to advocate. But it does mean that it is not the sole determiner of our theological judgements.

I have alluded to the tension between exegetical and renegotiated approaches, and used a biblical debate to illustrate what is at stake. A similar illustration from the world of Christian doctrine could have been employed. On the one hand, there are those who stand by the Christian Fathers as having set the parameters for any future theological work, and, on the other hand, there are those for whom the Fathers represent a chorus of voices from a particular period (designated 'classical') but should not be seen as the final arbiters of theological truth for all time. Examples of the former would be those theologians who accept the classical doctrines of the divine Christ and the view of God as Trinity as bedrock categories for interpreting religious plurality. In this scheme, apart from strict exclusivists, usually some balance is sought between the uniqueness of Christ as the origin of salvation and the work of God as Spirit throughout the world beyond the impact of Christ.[9] Examples of the more relativizing latter group would be those theologians for whom the impact of critical thinking pushes the boundaries of classical Christian doctrine and thereby creates openings for the interpretation of other faiths which does not 'trump' their experience with the absoluteness of the Christ figure and Christian experience.[10]

It is important to be aware of these different methodological stances, for confusion often arises between methodological issues and what we imagine the scope of a Christian theology of religions to be.

Three Ways in which Theological Study Reflects an Interest in Religious Plurality

Precisely how the knowledge of world religions and the encounter with religious others through friendship or dialogue affects Christian theological reflection is varied. If Christian theology is a process of reflection on experience – as in the famous Anselmian definition of theology as 'faith seeking understanding' – then we might ask about what constitutes the data of experience. The theology of religions debate assumes that data to be both the legacy of Christian history and also the context of our present world, which is a plural world. If that is correct then one might put the issue like this: What level of impact might the data of other religious experiences and convictions have? There are broadly three possible responses to this question.

First, Christian theology of religions might be confined to the final chapter of the doctrinal textbook. That is to say, after the unfolding of the meaning of Christian experience, there is then a kind of afterthought about plurality and its place in the Christian understanding of God's desires for the world. Most previous-generation systematic theology textbooks functioned in that manner, if they considered the issues of plurality at all. But today this is becoming rarer as plurality deepens its impact. The Catholic theologian Roger Haight sums up the recognition of this change aptly when he writes of Christology: 'Many theologians now acknowledge that the narrow christological problem must be addressed within the framework of an estimation of the place of Jesus Christ among other religions.'[11] For some, this sentiment might beg the question, for it already assumes that religious plurality is a positive context in which other religions are accorded value. Yet this seems to be the momentum that arises from either taking plurality seriously or entering into interreligious dialogue. The relation of Christian faith's central revelatory figure to other religions must nowadays be, as Haight insists, more than 'an addendum or corollary'.[12]

Second, the interest in religious plurality might be manifest in theological works which express a desire to learn from or make some measure of adaptation to perceived truths not fully explored hitherto in Christian thought. For example, *Christian Systematic Theology in a World Context*, by Ninian Smart and Steven Konstantine, seeks to present Christian faith self-consciously in full view of the world's religions and to a degree be modified by them. The authors are prepared to portray their Christian distinctiveness sometimes in contradistinction to, and sometimes in readiness to learn from other religions. As they state it:

> Every movement is in the minority in the one world in which we now live and may perish. So Muslims without a good theory of other faiths, or Marxists without a grasp of the history of religions, or Buddhists without an analysis of the great religious alternatives, are all out of date. And so are those Christians who neglect world culture and world history.[13]

Smart and Konstantine are not relativists, if by this is meant that all religions are equal or the same, whatever that might mean. They affirm the Christian vision but do not claim it as the only or necessarily the superior vision. But they present it in line with due attention being paid to other religions and worldviews as serious phenomena of world history and therefore worthy of respect. They are prepared to look for overlapping features or analogous representations between religions, without surrendering the specific features of a largely classical Christian faith. This all calls for a shift in Christian imagination away from purely deductive presentations of Christian faith. A similar project, though with more concentration on representative figures from different traditions, can be traced in the British Christian philosopher Keith Ward, in his series of writings dubbed 'comparative theology'.[14]

A third form of interest in the world's religions by Christian theology takes the form of specific interreligious dialogue. In this regard, a good example would be *Religious Feminism and the Future of the Planet: A Buddhist–Christian Conversation*, by Rita M. Gross and Rosemary Radford Ruether. Here two authors set out their views in critical conversation with one another, aware of their differences yet celebrating one another's validity and authenticity even as they offer mutual criticism.

It is instructive to note how deep the dialogue unveils the overlap between the two voices. Taking the Christian author, for our purposes, Ruether expresses her appreciation for the Buddhist view of reality as follows:

> Buddhism does not believe in a literal God of any gender who exists as an ontological being outside of the world. Their vision, as I understand it,

> sees reality as arising mysteriously from an ultimate Void and ultimately returning to this Void . . . This view to a large extent, corresponds with my own intuitive sense of the nature of reality. Whatever I call God is not some ontological being, some ultimate Mind, existing invisibly in a disembodied form beyond the world. Rather, what exists is this very creativity of interdependent co-arising . . .[15]

The degree of resonance expressed here between Christianity and Buddhism is quite unusual and would most likely represent a minority Christian viewpoint. Yet its power for disturbing settled Christian patterns of thought resides in precisely the sense in which an 'alien' perspective has been received into the heart of Christian understanding. Not all Christian participants in Buddhist–Christian conversation would concur with Ruether's assessment at this point, but neither would they dismiss it out of hand. More than the other two strategies outlined above, it remains an example of how far-reaching the demand for reinterpreting Christian conceptual frameworks potentially might become in the light of taking religious plurality very seriously.

The Structure of this Book

There are two major parts to this book. Part 1 accepts the validity of seeking for an overview of how Christian faith interprets the fact of religious plurality and explores various responses in the Christian theology of religions. It refers to what has been described as the classical typology in this field, but is aware also of viewpoints which claim to break the bounds of this style of categorizing the responses. The classical approaches are described under the labels 'exclusivisms', 'inclusivisms' and 'pluralisms', and it is hoped that the reasons for using the plural form of those terms will become apparent: each is diverse in its formulations. The other three approaches canvassed here extend the classical typology and may even sit very loose to its three-fold schema. There are different opinions about this, but it seemed to the editors best to retain what has proven to be of considerable analytical worth, while also acknowledging both the critiques that have been made of the classical typology and also the alternative proposals that have been submitted.

In this regard, approaches under the descriptor 'Particularity' draw on tendencies and themes from postmodernism, a loose current of thought which maximizes differences between religions and presumes the classical typology to rest on certain assumptions derived from European Enlightenment philosophy, assumptions which themselves have become questionable for many. Feminist approaches, on the other hand, explore the opposite tendency, often contesting the assumption that the religions should be imagined as tightly bounded communities of radical difference. Perhaps resting on a certain cognitive difference between the genders, or simply given a different methodology governing interreligious conversation and encounter, the experience of some women (though not exclusively women) has led them to experiment with multiple identities. It will be obvious how this pushes at the boundaries of the usual kinds of discussion in this field.

Some Christian writers are close to abandoning the whole project of a theology of religions, believing that such an exercise is bound in some way to distort the self-perceptions of the religions, thus rendering the attempt at an overview an act of hubris.[16] However, I believe that this is not a sustainable position, for it would be tantamount to a retreat from a proper Christian concern for understanding the nature of reality as a diverse whole. Yet these voices need to be heeded, and they are discussed mostly in the chapter on 'Particularities'.

As I have already stated above, the array of different viewpoints in this field has become overwhelming. At one level, this is evidence of vigorous interest and debate and is to be welcomed. But the array can also be experienced negatively, as though there were no patterns to be discerned among the many writers. This book takes the view that there are patterns which follow certain lines of enquiry and which can be grouped roughly together. The whole of this discussion is carefully explored in the chapter reflecting on the worth of typologies.

Positioned at the end of Part 1 is a discussion of the nature and impact of interreligious dialogue. In one sense this is not an 'alternative' approach, for representative theologians of all categories might pursue dialogue, albeit for varied reasons. Yet dialogue is more than a process of neutral conversation and is generating its own 'rules of engagement', expectations and desires. Certainly those involved in dialogue operate from assumptions, hidden or open. This chapter therefore explores dialogue and its connections with differing Christian theological outlooks. Its positioning at the end of Part 1 is also a kind of bridge to the second part of the book.

The second part of this book considers a number of Christian responses to individual religions. This is an important complement to the search for a theological overview and is generally not included in usual introductory works in the field. One reason for including these responses is that it critiques the theological strategy of placing 'other religions' in the 'Judaism position'. That is to say, if the Christian theology of religions has largely been shaped by Christianity's historically negative relationship with Judaism then this needs to be deconstructed if we are to do justice to the very different bilateral relationship, say, with Hindu habits of thought and life.

A further reason for including Part 2 as integral to the theology of religions is that, given that bilateral dialogues between Christianity and another faith often highlight certain issues not prominent in other bilateral discussions, this can only add to the depth of the theology-of-religions project as a whole. For, if it is the case that 'ultimate reality' is best pondered as a rich mystery then a dialogue emerging from Christian responses to Hinduism will yield different interests from that with Islam, and this is to be expected. The ramification of this is as follows: if different concerns occupy the exchanges of different bilateral dialogues, then this ought to be reflected in the search for a viable Christian theology of religions in general terms.

If bilateral relationships (or other clusters of relationships) enhance the search for an overview theology of religions then the question arises which faiths are to be included. In this decision a number of parameters have been set. In terms of numerical importance and geographical spread, the major traditions of Hinduism, Islam and Buddhism classify for inclusion. Also, even though it is hard to judge current numbers, a similar assessment can be made for native Chinese religions, which are demonstrating their considerable resilience after years of communist neglect or oppression. Given that Christianity emerged out of first-century Judaism, it is scarcely possible to exclude this historic faith. Then, in order not to be limited to the so-called 'great world religions', it was thought that the inclusion of indigenous traditions was necessary as an antidote to their former evaluation as 'primitive'. Although Sikhism has small numbers globally, Sikhs have played a prominent part in interfaith activities worldwide in their diaspora and therefore Sikhism warrants proper consideration. Finally, given the scholarly interest in New Religious Movements and their attraction for many in the Western world as an alternative spirituality, these too have been included. No doubt other choices could have been made, but we consider that the faiths which have been included represent the spread of the many forms of religious consciousness experienced by most of our globe.

Theology of Religions as *Via Media*

In his award-winning novel, *The Life of Pi*, the author, Yann Martel, sets up a tension between the official guardians of religious tradition and the all-absorbing interest of his central character, Pi, in a number of religious faith visions. Pi, who is Indian, comes to describe himself simultaneously as Hindu, Christian and Muslim – 'I just want to love God,' was his cry – and he supposed that this essence of religious belief was found in each tradition. But of course this breaks all of the usual boundaries of religious identity and practice, if we suppose religions to be strongly bounded communities.[17] In response to Pi, the religious official guardians express their alarm and rehearse their caricatures of one another, their standard disagreements and thinly veiled disdain of any religious practice not their own. 'He can't be a Hindu, a Christian *and* a Muslim. It's impossible. He must choose,' says the pandit, on behalf of all three guardians.[18] The tension between the universal summons 'to love God' (speaking theistically), recommended as the transformative highpoint of all religious ethics, and the particular historically grounded nature of separate traditions is here depicted. The task of a Christian theology of religions, it might be claimed, is to negotiate the *via media* between the universalism of religious truth and the particularity of its diverse glimpsing. The religions are neither 'all the same' nor are they 'all different'.

This tension between Christian experience and the recognition of potential authentic practice outside of the Christian revelation, in fact has always existed in Christian history from the beginning. It is present in the Apostle Paul's wrestling in Romans 9–11 with the impact of Jesus and the need to honour God's faithfulness towards his own Jewish people. It is there in the synoptic tradition when we compare Mark's openness with Matthew's hardening of attitude, in their shaping of the words of Jesus:

> Whoever is not against us is for us. (Mark 9.40)
>
> Whoever is not with me is against me. (Matt. 12.30)

It is there also in the Johannine tradition where the writer of John's Gospel celebrates the logos-light of God as being responsible for the creation of the world (John 1.1–5), while also claiming Jesus as *the* light of the world (John 14.6).

This tension continues through the Christian tradition. Whether or not solutions to the tension from the past are applicable in the contemporary world, either directly or with minor adjustments, is a moot point. This is the contextual challenge facing a Christian theology of religions today and to which this book makes its own contribution. The editors make no claim to an overall solution to the problems, but we do hope to have canvassed the very vigorous debate now taking place in both church and academy.

Study Questions

1. Do you think that the impressiveness of spirituality in other religions ought to make a difference in the theological interpretation of them?
2. Outline how you think the contemporary hermeneutical recognition of the importance of context in theological work has an effect in the theology of religions debate.
3. Is it possible to hold allegiance to more than one religion?

Further Reading

Dupuis, Jacques, SJ, 1997, *Toward a Christian Theology of Religious Pluralism*, Maryknoll: Orbis.
Heim, S. Mark, 2001, *The Depth of the Riches: A Trinitarian Theology of Religious Ends*, Grand Rapids: Eerdmans.
Hick, John, 2004, *The Fifth Dimension: An Exploration of the Spiritual Realm*, Oxford: Oneworld.
Newbigin, Lesslie, 1989, *The Gospel in a Pluralist Society*, London: SPCK.
Plantinga, Richard J. (ed.), 1999, *Christianity and Plurality: Classic and Contemporary Readings*, Oxford: Blackwell.

Notes

1 Smith, Wilfred Cantwell, 1972, *The Faith of Other Men*, New York: Harper Torchbooks, p. 133. Reprinted as 1998, *Patterns of Faith Around the World*, Oxford: Oneworld, p. 138.

2 *Ibid.*

3 Examples are Bosch, David J., 1991, *Transforming Mission: Paradigm Shifts in Theology of Mission*, Maryknoll: Orbis; Sanneh, Lamin, 1991, *Translating the Message: The Missionary Impact on Culture,* Maryknoll: Orbis; Schreiter, Robert, 1985, *Constructing Local Theologies*, Maryknoll: Orbis.

4 Cf. Cracknell, Kenneth, 1995, *Justice, Courtesy and Love: Theologians and Missionaries Encountering World Religions 1846–1914*, London: Epworth Press.

5 Küng, Hans, 1991, *Global Responsibility: In Search of a New World Ethic*, London: SCM Press.

6 Schmidt-Leukel, Perry, 2007, 'The Struggle for Peace: Can Religions Help?', *Interreligious Insight*, vol. 5, no. 2, pp. 49–63.

7 Smith, Wilfred Cantwell, 1981, *Towards a World Theology: Faith and the Comparative History of Religion*, London: Macmillan.

8 Räisänen, Heikki, 1997, *Marcion, Muhammad and the Mahatma*, London: SCM Press, p. 15.

9 This strategy is best illustrated by the standard inclusivist Catholic response to other faiths. Francis A. Sullivan, 1992, *Salvation Outside the Church? Tracing the History of the Catholic Response*, London: Geoffrey Chapman, provides an excellent overview here: the formula is retained but interpreted subtly over a long period of historical change. More recently, and in similar ways, it is a given among theologians of the 'particularist' persuasion (see Chapter 2 in this book) that the Trinity is a *sine qua non* for the Christian response to other faiths, though with the additional emphasis borrowed from postmodern influences.

10 John Hick's *The Metaphor of God Incarnate*, London: SCM Press, 2005, 2nd and enlarged edn, is probably the best example of Christian doctrines being reworked self-consciously for a religiously plural context.

11 Haight, Roger, 1999, *Jesus Symbol of God*, Maryknoll: Orbis, p. 395.

12 *Ibid.*

13 Smart, Ninian, and Konstantine, Steven, 1991, *Christian Systematic Theology in a World Context*, London: Marshall Pickering, p. 18.

14 In the 1990s Keith Ward embarked on writing Christian theology in critical dialogue with other religions and modern scientific understanding. See his books published by Oxford University Press: *Religion and Revelation* (1994), *Religion and Creation* (1996), *Religion and Human Nature* (1999), and *Religion and Community* (2000).

15 Gross, Rita M., and Ruether, Rosemary Radford, 2001, *Religious Feminism and the Future of the Planet: A Buddhist–Christian Conversation*, London: Continuum, pp. 150–1.

16 For example Fredericks, James L., 1999, *Faith among Faiths: Christian Theology and Non-Christian Religions*, New Jersey: Paulist Press.

17 Cf. Buck, Harry, 1997, 'Beyond Walls, Fences, and Interreligious Dialogue', *Journal of Ecumenical Studies*, vol. 34, no. 4, pp. 521–30.

18 Martel, Yann, 2003, *The Life of Pi*, Edinburgh: Canongate Books, p. 69. Originally published, Canada: Alfred Knopf, 2001.

2

A Reflection on Typologies:[1] Negotiating a Fast-Moving Discussion

PAUL HEDGES

Introduction

The best known typology for the theology of religions was that introduced by Alan Race in 1983 in his groundbreaking work, *Christians and Religious Pluralism*.[2] This set out a three-fold typology of exclusivism, inclusivism and pluralism as three basic categories into which Christian responses to other faiths could be fitted. It has been widely used, although sometimes with a modification of terminology, or with the inclusion of other categories.[3] I shall address some of these alternatives below. Moreover, it has also had a number of critics, some of whom have called the entire categorization into question, a matter which I also address below. In this textbook, we (the editors) have decided both to retain the basic structure of the typology as a way of honouring the stimulus it has provided and to explore further categories of approach as a way of recognizing the emerging broad range of discussion that has ensued since it was first published. I propose, therefore, some positive reasons for continuing to employ it as a basis: (1) this typology is the most widely used and known; (2) most books which reject the typology or use modified versions either still employ it as their basis of analysis or simply change the names – for instance, Gavin D'Costa and others use it despite expressing reservations,[4] and Paul F. Knitter employs a four-fold system that adds a new category very close to the approach here labelled 'Particularities';[5] (3) it seems necessary in a study such as this to give some academically systematized account of different approaches; and (4) I would suggest that the various criticisms either misconstrue the original typology and its intention, or can be met and answered.

For those unfamiliar with the original typology, briefly, it may be stated that the terms were intended as descriptive of the kind of approaches found within different parts of the Church and at different times. Exclusivism, therefore, refers to those systems that excluded non-Christians from salvation. That is to say its advocates believed that unless one expressed a personal faith in Jesus, or belonged to the correct wing of the Church, the only alternative was damnation and hellfire. Generally, for an exclusivist, God only revealed himself through one means (Jesus) and through one tradition (Christianity). Inclusivism refers to those who wished to include believers from other religious traditions among the ranks of those who could be saved. Therefore, if someone obeyed the moral laws and norms of their community they knew of a 'natural law' that God had made available in the hearts of all people, and therefore was being led in the right direction, coming to salvation through their own tradition while in this life, and being confronted with Christ, perhaps, at the Last Judgement. Pluralism, however, holds that no one tradition has a monopoly on revelation or salvation, and that we have no way to adjudicate between the claims to be 'saved' by people of any faith, all of whom deeply and wholeheartedly adhere to their own tradition. Pluralists therefore suggest that each religion knows transcendent reality ('God') yet in partial perspective. Obviously, this is a highly simplified account, which does not reflect the many nuances and variations within each position. Moreover, in his original exposition, Race described it as a 'broad typological framework', where the differences were classified as 'largely a matter of emphasis on the part of the particular writers'.[6] It should not be imagined, therefore, that it was employed as a framework into which any position or tradition could be neatly fitted.

I will now set out a defence of the typology, before setting out some alternative versions and finally concluding with some reflections on how I think the typology is best understood.

Criticisms of the Typology

The fullest response to the criticisms of the typology has been made by Perry Schmidt-Leukel, who reaffirms the original categories and seeks to provide a basis for them in what he sees as logical necessity.[7] He lists what he sees as eight major criticisms and offers replies to all of them.[8] I do not intend to set out a full defence of the typology here, but will instead seek to answer the main criticisms, an exercise which will partly mirror Schmidt-Leukel's responses, and in the process refer to my own understanding of the typology, which will be set out more clearly at the end.[9]

The typology misconstrues the diversity of religions

Two principle objections arise here. First, there is what is seen as a misplaced wrong focus on salvation. That is to say, the typology focuses around issues of who is saved, whereas some would suggest that differences of *religiouspractice* should be our key concern. However, the typology is not prescriptive but descriptive; historically, most theologies of religions have raised questions of salvation as central, and therefore this is how they are classified.

Second, as Terrence Tilley expresses it: 'the typology . . . obscures another basic issue: the need to recognize the religious other as *other*, not as a mere outsider to, reflection of, extension of, or unwitting member of one's own tradition'.[10] I fully concur with Tilley here, but nevertheless this does not get round the point that Rahner, for instance, understands observant members of other faiths as 'anonymous Christians',[11] and, as far as the typology is concerned, there is no getting away from this.

In so far as these kinds of critiques necessitate a different approach, the chapter on particularities will address some alternative standpoints that are being canvassed in the literature.

More or less options exist

According to Schmidt-Leukel there are only three logical possibilities evinced in the classical typology. So, with regard to the idea that there are more options, he dismisses the idea that someone such as S. Mark Heim proffers us a convincing alternative; indeed, as Schmidt-Leukel reminds us, Heim is a self-confessed inclusivist – though he does have affinities to particularity.[12] Further, Schmidt-Leukel rightly, in my view, points out that Schubert Ogden's suggestion – that pluralism should be envisaged both as a reality and as a potential – seems meaningless, and Grünschloß's 'inferiorism', he believes, is simply 'inclusivism' from a different angle.[13] However, while Schmidt-Leukel's logical approach clearly defines three options, I suggest that a more phenomenological and heuristic approach to the typology allows us to be more flexible about the options, as I will suggest below.

The alternative, that fewer options exist, argues that everything is a type of inclusivism or exclusivism. This may seem strange, as a certain commonsense approach suggests that these three are different; nevertheless, a good logical case exists. However, even if this argument is correct, it does not undermine the typology. To explain, I will briefly outline the arguments and counter-arguments. Probably the most sophisticated proponent of this view in the English-speaking world is Gavin D'Costa. Originally one of the typology's greatest defenders, he came to believe that pluralism is really a form of exclusivism.[14] Basically, his argument is that pluralism's claim that all religions are heading to the same soteriological end entails that the truth-claims of every religion, to be the one true religion, are superseded by a pluralist meta-claim which positions all religions within its own interpretive framework. That is to say, the 'real' religious truth is pluralism, not what other religions say, and, therefore, by overriding their claims, it is a form of exclusivism as it says only its claims are correct. In short, according to D'Costa, by saying that it has the correct interpretation, and that other interpretations are wrong, all positions, especially pluralism, are actually covert forms of exclusivism, precisely because they exclude other truth-claims. It could also be argued, probably more convincingly, that pluralism is a form of inclusivism, as it puts other faiths in a position related to your own beliefs – that is to say they are included within your religious worldview. For instance, Knitter suggests that 'we are all inclusivists'.[15]

It is not clear that the criticism of pluralism does hold in all cases. However, even if it does, this does not invalidate the typology. Real and substantial differences exist between the options, meaning that they should be distinguished. The claim that salvation comes only through my tradition alone and others will not be saved, differs from the claim that every religion offers a pathway to salvation though this must ultimately come from being incorporated into my faith, and the claim that every religion is its own legitimate pathway to salvation. Certainly, in one sense they are all exclusive, in so far as every truth-claim excludes certain others[16] but they are not identical, and need to be described, as it is meaningless to put them all within one heading. Moreover, as I will suggest below, the typology is not a tool to critique these options, but is rather a descriptive one.

The categories are incoherent

Joseph DiNoia claims that inclusivism is incoherent, because it assumes that every religion is seeking the same goal of 'salvation'. Moreover, according to him and others, not only is the category 'religion' flawed (there is no common genus that can be identified cross-culturally), rather, every faith tradition is following its own set of goals and ideals, which are, in fact, very diverse. The common translation of terms from the religious cultures that use Sanskrit, Arabic, Chinese, and so on, as 'salvation' in English obscures a vast diversity of conceptions. Therefore, to say, with the inclusivist, that every religion is diversely systematizing the idea of salvation, or God, and that the Buddhist, for instance, is coming to Christ through their tradition, is simply based on a misguided understanding of that faith, which subsumes its ideals and goals to one's own. This amounts to a general critique of the typology as focusing upon 'salvation'. However, as noted below, in so far as the typology describes the way people have developed theologies of religions, most of these have focused upon the notion of salvation, as to who is, or who is not, within the boundaries of the saved community. Also, arguments claiming that there is no such category as 'religion', or no cross-cultural comparison, are not closed and decided, with strong counter-arguments existing.[17]

It cannot cope with the varieties of positions that exist

Any typology must, of necessity, aim to simplify and codify a considerable amount of nuanced, slippery, multi-faceted and varied data into simpler segments with common characteristics. If it were therefore presented as the be-all-and-end-all of everything that could be said, then I would concur with this critique. However, as a gently guiding analytic tool, seen to have hazy edges, and used primarily for heuristic purposes, to get to grips with the complexity of the subject area, then, I believe, the typology has a place.

A further extension of this is the claim that many individuals cannot be fitted within one category. For instance, Karl Barth is claimed by some of his advocates to be both an exclusivist and an inclusivist, while also being a 'universalist'.[18] Meanwhile, Lesslie Newbigin proclaims himself to be both an inclusivist and an exclusivist.[19] My response to this is 'Yes, that's correct'. It was never the point of the typology to make everyone fit within it; the categories are fluid approaches, with permeable membranes, rather than restrictive and closed essences. Many people will undoubtedly fit more easily into one, while others will be at the edges, or even fit over several categories. The categories are not mutually exclusive. I therefore think such criticisms have missed the point of this typology.

A more radical claim is that certain people's ideas actually transcend the typology. That some approaches certainly see themselves as branching out beyond it is acknowledged by the inclusion of further approaches. Indeed, certainly new approaches have arisen since Race first propounded the typology, though whether they actually go beyond it is something that will be discussed in due course. Certainly, it is intellectually fashionable to claim to be outside these categories, but this in itself does not prove anything. For instance, the Church of England report, *The Mystery of Salvation*, proudly proclaims itself to have bypassed the old inclusivist category, before going on to advocate a return to the classic inclusivist paradigm of fulfilment theology.[20] I think this is partly due to the success of the original typology, that it has helped show that the old-style inclusivist approaches were, in certain ways, quite patronizing to other faiths, and, as such, if new approaches arise beyond the typology, it could be said to have been extremely successful.

A final critique, which is worth attending to, is that of the feminist writer Jeannine Hill Fletcher, who has argued that the fixed parameters of exclusivism, inclusivism and pluralism suggest that we should envisage a situation where something called 'Christianity' can be accurately positioned against something else called 'Islam', 'Buddhism', and so forth. Instead, she suggests that rather than being monolithic entities, each faith system is actually an internally diverse network of different positions.[21] While I would agree with the essence of her critique – that we cannot simply say the Christian faith should view other faiths in such and such a way – I think it does not prevent either the usage of the typology here, or that of Schmidt-Leukel. In terms of the usage here, in so far as it is primarily descriptive and heuristic, rather than prescriptive, it simply reflects the fact that most theorists have seen the debate in this way. Meanwhile, the philosophical ultimacy of Schmidt-Leukel's model is not affected either, as it simply outlines certain borders for the debate in soteriological terms. Nevertheless, I believe that Hill Fletcher's insights are important for developing the future direction of theory in this area, and build on some notions inherent in the particularist approach.

The terms are polemical

This charge is especially levelled against the use of the term 'exclusivism'. In reply to this, I can do little better than largely repeat Schmidt-Leukel's response. He says all these words can have positive or negative overtones, such as exclusive shops or services, while inclusiveness can equal a welcoming openness. Indeed, he notes some exclusivists are happy with the terms.[22] Furthermore, we should note that every use of language is rhetorical to some degree, and that no neutral language exists. Perhaps the most common change to the typology is the substitution of 'particularity' for 'exclusivism' while the other two categories are kept.[23] For instance, McGrath suggests we use this 'neutral' term in place of the 'polemical' 'exclusivism', or, more recently, he has proposed a new term 'parallelism' – which equates to my own use of particularities.[24] However, this ignores the polemical rhetoric of 'particularity', which suggests that the position so described respects the individuality of each faith, in its own particular manifestation, seeing each as an individual particular. The term is therefore just as charged, and while, for reasons of political correctness, some modern-day exclusivists may wish to say that they are not actually insisting upon their own correctness and seeing others as inferior, merely seeing each as particular, this is not really a fair indication of the exclusivist type approach. Again, 'parallelism' would suggest a pluralist type approach, with many parallel religious truths, whereas the actual claim is that only one is ultimately correct. Approaches which emphasize the particularity of faiths do exist, and, indeed, herein, are labelled 'particularities'; traditional forms of exclusivism are somewhat different in nature, character and approach. If we may employ a common advertising phrase, 'it does exactly what it says on the tin', then exclusivism excludes from salvation other faiths and their members and so should be termed as such. It is not the job of academic description to whitewash approaches and paint them in the best possible light that will keep their exponents happy.

Other Typologies

As has been mentioned, despite its perceived problems, many people have used this typology, or just adjusted it with a slight renaming of the 'exclusivist' category. However, a number of different typologies, or versions of the typology, have been used, which it would be worthwhile discussing. Those to be discussed are the formulations of Perry Schmidt-Leukel, Veli-Matti Kärkkäinen, Paul Knitter and Owen Thomas. We will also mention the 'Comparative Theology' approach of James Fredericks and Francis Clooney.

Schmidt-Leukel's logical-necessity typology

Schmidt-Leukel's ideas are a noteworthy reworking of Race's original typology, which he sees as a way to show why the original typology must be upheld. I would suggest, however, that he responds to the criticisms by transforming a descriptive, phenomenological typology into a 'logically precise and comprehensive classification'.[25] To this end he outlines the following options, where 'P' = mediation of salvific knowledge of ultimate/transcendent reality:

1 P is not given among the religions.
2 P is given among the religions, but only once.
3 P is given among the religions more than once, but within only one singular maximum.
4 P is given among the religions more than once and without a singular maximum.

This, he says, is logically comprehensive: option (1) is atheism; option (2) is exclusivism; option (3) is inclusivism; and, option (4) is pluralism. While acknowledging the logical consistency within its own terms of reference, I would not wish to use this version of the typology.[26] There are several reasons for this. First, the original typology allowed for the application of the typology to individuals and their theologies or religions, but Schmidt-Leukel argues that his version does not address the individual, but rather sets limits to the discussion.[27] Second, related to the last point, Schmidt-Leukel's logical schema does not allow for a clear distinction between the groups in terms of actual positions held. For instance, many Christians, who we would normally acknowledge as inclusivists, would agree with statement (2) above, yet would see many faiths as leading towards 'P'. Third, as already noted, some thinkers believe that salvation should not be the main focus of the theology of religions debate, and so a purely logical approach does not properly address the concerns of those who do not raise salvation as a main issue. Schmidt-Leukel is no doubt right to say that this question has an 'ultimate inevitability'.[28] However, it may not be the best way to provide a clearly structured division of the positions.

Kärkkäinen's three-fold typology

Veli-Matti Kärkkäinen offers his own three-fold typology, utilizing the terms 'ecclesiocentric', 'christocentric' and 'theocentric'.[29] He describes them, respectively, as those which have the focus of salvation: (1) on members of the Church; (2) based around Christ (who may reach out beyond the Church); or (3) in deity, which allows other faiths to be equally salvifically potent. He says this differs from the original typology as the three form concentric circles of inclusion within the soteriological realm. However, it is difficult to see why the original typology does not do the same. Also, it seems hard to see what else is different, apart from the names, within this framework, except, perhaps, that it has harder borders, thus suggesting that individuals must fit within one category. I would therefore suggest that this typology simply offers a renamed version of the original.

Knitter's four models

Knitter has recently offered his own framework which adds a fourth category, or as he terms them, 'models'.[30] I would equate his categories to those of the classical typology in the following way: Replacement Model = exclusivisms; Fulfilment Model = inclusivisms; Mutuality Model = pluralisms. Knitter, indeed, seems to see his first three models as, more or less, analogues for the categories of Race's original typology. It is also notable that his usage and interpretation of it is closer to a broad heuristic interpretation I am suggesting here, rather than Schmidt-Leukel's. As Race's terms are better known, it seems simplest to use his, as they are already widely used, and also, I would suggest, are clearer.[31] For instance, if we take Farquhar's fulfilment theology, it was envisaged by Farquhar that Christianity, or Christ, 'replaces' Hinduism in its fulfilment of it; yet it was inclusive of Hinduism as a way that may lead to belief in Jesus rather than excluding it as a realm or system of false belief.[32] Knitter's fourth category, the 'Acceptance Model', however, offers an extension of the classical typology. This embraces both what may be termed the post-liberal or particularity viewpoint as well as the Comparative Theology concept of Fredericks and Clooney. As such, it encompasses one of the further approaches offered here, that of particularities. If we accept the descriptive and heuristic nature of typological thinking, then the inclusion of a further category is permitted; indeed, I have previously argued that particularity should be seen as a fourth category.[33] Whether it is actually a position that lies beyond the three 'classical' options of the typology is something open to debate, but I believe that Knitter is right to include this extra category, which he sees as grounded in a post-modern respect for the 'Other'. Some reasons for accepting particularity as an extra category will be discussed below, which, as mentioned, differs from his Acceptance Model. Some of the reasons for this will be discussed below when we consider the 'Comparative Theology' position.

Thomas's typology

Owen Thomas probably made the first formal distinction of theologies of religions into different types.[34] He outlined various attitudes into seven types, and surveyed ten different figures and classified each as taking a different approach. While fully recognizing the differences, this framework also makes it difficult to recognize similarities. Also, especially today, with an increasing discussion of these ideas, it would be very difficult to follow such an approach, even if we counted most people under one of his types, and perhaps introducing a few new ones. Quite simply, as this typology is mainly heuristic, it seems best to limit the typology to a few readily identifiable categories, which may then, within themselves, have various subdivisions. It is perhaps useful, though, to draw attention to the seven attitudes he canvasses. These are: (1) 'Truth–Falsehood', where Christianity is true and other faiths false; (2) 'Relativity', where each religion is an expression of its own culture; (3) 'Essence', which asserts that all religions have a common mystico-experiential core; (4) 'Development-fulfilment', where other faiths are seen as leading towards Christian truths; (5) 'Salvation History', a similar position to the previous one, but suggests that the whole has a place within a grand plan of salvific development; (6) 'Revelation–Sin', suggests God has a natural revelation available in creation, but human sinfulness corrupts the reception of it; (7) 'New Departures', actually encapsulates two views – 'Christian presence', which essentially relates to being in dialogue as the primary means of engagement, and 'Christian secularity', which suggests that Christian faith is antithetical to the world while, simultaneously, accepting that secularism is a relative good, as it can liberate human beings from those elements of superstition which lie within the religious systems of other faiths.[35]

Comparative Theology

Scholars such as Michael Barnes, James Fredericks and Francis Clooney expound a position they call Comparative Theology, which suggests that we should engage with other faiths before we can know how we should grade or relate to them. Certainly, I think they have a very important case to make, and much will come from dialogue that the typological classifications may not be able as yet to imagine or describe. However, this approach does not supersede or invalidate the typology for a number of reasons. First, the typology describes approaches that have been taken, and therefore need in no way interfere or prescribe what outcomes will occur from dialogue. Also, they are both engaged in slightly different areas. One is the first-order meeting and interrelationship of religions, the work of primary theology, the other is the second-order analysis and comment on the experience of encounter and dialogue, an exercise in analytic theology and understanding. However, theological analysis may also inform first-order encounter, a point which brings me to my second point, which is that it is not clear why *praxis* and *theoria* should be so divided in this way.[36] To act requires some basis upon which it is done, even if only at a very minimal level. It is therefore important to see the two working in tandem: it is simply not possible to say that encounter precedes conceptualization and that when this is finished then conceptualization begins. For is there a prescribed endpoint at which dialogue stops? This brings me to the next point concerning the place of comparative theology. It is better imagined as a *praxis* which already operates within a conceptual framework, that is, one which accepts that engagement with other religions can be meaningful and purposive, and as such it has already predetermined (the proponents may deny this, but the way they engage seems to contradict such a denial) that the other faiths are not demonic or satanic perversions but have insights from which Christianity can learn. Therefore, I would suggest that they are not beyond or outside the possibility of typological classification.

Typologies: Classical Categories and Beyond

An understanding of the typology

As we have discussed, there seem to be good reasons for continuing to use the categories of Race's original typology. They provide a useful framework into which to consider different types of approaches, which is neither too narrow nor too wide. However, as already indicated, we should not see these as the limits of the debate. In relation to this, both Knitter and I have separately suggested the inclusion of an extra category, extending the original three-fold one to a four-fold one. While, in this book, we have also taken account of the distinctive voice of feminist approaches and interfaith dialogue; none of these should be seen as mutually incompatible.

I will now go on to explain an understanding of the typology that will help make sense of its usage within this text, and as a viable phenomenological and heuristic approach to categorizing various approaches to other faiths. Importantly, as just mentioned, the separate categories are not wholly discrete and incompatible. Rather each represents a different emphasis of approach. Some people may, quite easily, fit within two or more of the approaches, while others may clearly fit neatly within one.[37] They define not so much an essence as a disposition. Also notable is that each category is named in the plural, exclusivisms–inclusivisms–pluralisms, and also particularities and feminisms. Thus, rather than there being a fixed type of approach that we can label 'inclusivism', there are a great many 'inclusivisms', which may vary across a spectrum of thought from those which are closer to the variety of exclusivisms, pluralisms or particularities. It is intended that this will point to the open and fluid nature of the typology as a framework which can be used to explore a range of ideas, rather than as a straitjacket containing fixed or determined essences. As I noted above, they are fluid categories with permeable membranes. A more cumbersome phrase, such as 'exclusivism-inclined' or 'inclusivism-inclined' may have done this too, but I consider this to be less elegant and unwieldy, and besides, in general usage, people would no doubt simplify to 'exclusivism', 'inclusivism', and so on. Therefore, the addition of the plural is probably the best option.[38]

This brief description has suggested that the typology should be seen as descriptive (it tells us what positions have been taken, not what the positions should be), heuristic (it gives guidelines to help understand the complexity of ideas and their relationships), multivalent (each category is not a single approach, but a spectrum of related approaches), and permeable (people may express ideas that spill over several of the categories), rather than as prescriptive, normative, defining, and closed.

Particularities

I will now briefly outline what is meant by particularity and its relationship to the previous categories within the 'classical' typological framework. As the term 'particularity' implies, this approach derives its emphasis from the distinct or *particular* nature of each faith. The orientation of particularity has affinities with exclusivist type approaches, in that it sees each faith as being 'tradition-specific', which is to say, it speaks its own unique language about its own unique goals and purposes. It also has affinities with inclusivisms, in that many particularists allow that the Holy Spirit may be at work in other faiths. It might also move towards some measure of overlap with pluralisms, for a number of particularists hold that other faiths display some purpose within the divine mystery and may hold truths from which Christianity can learn. However, as defined here, particularity is grounded in post-modernism, and it is this which provides its distinctive character.

We must therefore explore how I am using the term 'post-modern' here.

This much-disputed, and often contradictorily defined, term, has two facets: post-modern philosophy (hereafter post-modernism) and post-modern culture (hereafter post-modernity). The former refers to a variety of somewhat connected, though also contradictory, trends in continental philosophy and hermeneutics, which have questioned the hegemony of Western rationalism and science, and which view the 'Enlightenment quest' for progress in human affairs, brought about through an autonomous human reason, to be over. The latter, on the other hand, is a complex set of relations in contemporary Western society, such as multiculturalism, communication technology, consumerism, which affect the way we live. In this sense, we may all be said to live within post-modernity, even if we have not embraced post-modernism. It is hoped that this brief description will help orientate the reader to how the term is employed here.[39]

Post-modernism relates to the theology of religions by disputing basic (modern) assumptions. One of these is the question of whether all 'religions' are pursuing the same goal, even granting that such a category termed 'religions' exists at all. It also emphasizes the need to respect the religious 'Other', rather than fit other faiths within a grand overarching (Western, rational, controlling) metanarrative. This approach is found especially in post-liberal traditionalist theologies, which see it as a strong critique of pluralism. Essentially, it asserts that Christian truth-claims need to be based in traditional Christian belief systems, and that these systems are inherently different from those of other faiths, and from this it follows that we should not seek to relate them to Christianity directly. For example, Christians should not assume that terms such as 'salvation' carry a universal meaning because the reality inherent in the experience and concept of salvation carries very different connotations in other language and religious systems: Theravada Buddhism, for instance, does not conceive of 'salvation' in anything like the Christian sense. Therefore, particularists assert that a typical inclusivist claim, that another faith is really oriented on Christianity if only their adherents could see it truly (or properly, or fully), is absurd; or, to suggest, with a pluralist, that it is a different response to the same transcendent reality is simply naive. In some ways then, particularity seems closest to exclusivism, but it differs from exclusivism in so far as traditional exclusivism tends to brand other religions as 'false religions', whereas, for the particularist, they are simply other forms of discourse which do not fall within any broad category such as this. For particularists, therefore, other faith systems are not anti-Christian because they are not opposed religious systems. As can be seen, particularist approaches stand on the same grounds that see the categories of any typology as incoherent. To include them, therefore, within an extended typology might be simply wrong-headed, as well as, perhaps, not doing justice to their claim to be beyond the categories. However, as I have outlined the typology above, the classical three categories may or may not be coherent, but they do identify approaches that have been taken, and so may still be usefully employed. Therefore, an approach beyond the classical categories may also be included as another category. Of course, this would not apply to Schmidt-Leukel's account, which is why I have avoided its usage, as it does not allow other approaches beyond its logical limits to the discussion. However, many particularists would be wary of specifying where they stand in relation to it, and so would be hard to comprehend under this usage.

However, a more fundamental problem exists, which is that some scholars doubt whether particularity exists as a separate category. As noted above, there is no place for it in the Schmidt-Leukel approach to the typology. Probably the major doubt results from the failure to see any distinction between it and an inclusivist position, although a number of those we are including here as particularists have also been classed as exclusivists.[40] Nevertheless, proponents of particularity might typically respond that those who complain in this manner have failed to grasp the distinctively post-modern position they are proposing, and would maintain it transcends the distinction of exclusivist or inclusivist. In part, there would be a post-modern rejection of the controlling metanarrative of exclusivism–inclusivism–pluralism. Another reason is that particularist type thinkers will often speak of an 'unknowability', in contrast to traditional exclusivist or inclusivist writers, who have presumed to know how Christianity relates to other faiths or how the Holy Spirit operates within them. While inclusivism defines the way in which God works through other faiths, particularists opt for a post-modern indeterminacy in this matter.[41] By stressing the particularity and value of other faiths, it sees itself as being more than merely a mediating middle way between exclusivism and inclusivism. Moreover, particularists refuse Christian mastery of other faiths by suggesting that Christianity's exclusive claims to truth lie only in a future realization, and that, for the time being, it just narrates another story. Indeed, D'Costa has argued that it bypasses such arguments altogether, as they are discussing the relationship between 'religions', but, by introducing the concept of 'revelation', the Christian story is playing a different game.[42] That is to say, we cannot have a 'theology of religions' in terms of one religion discussing other religions, for, in Barthian terms, that would imply comparing different ways human beings speak of God; instead they see God's Word as a separate form of narrative, not simply another religion. It would also, as has been noted, reject claims that such things as common cross-cultural categories – for example, 'religion', 'mystical experience' or 'salvation' – either exist or have any significant meaning. This, it is claimed, undermines claims that the various faiths are aiming at similar goals, or are speaking analogously about essentially unified ideas, and, as a consequence, this renders the traditional classifications, which often seem to make these kinds of assumption, either obsolete or inapplicable.

Conclusion

As we have seen, there are many ways in which people have suggested we can categorize various approaches to the theology of religions. Within this it has been argued that the most widely known and used approach, the three-fold typology of exclusivisms–inclusivisms–pluralisms has a secure and useful role, and that many of the criticisms of it do not apply to a phenomenological and heuristic usage, advocated here. Moreover, I have suggested that there is scope for seeing the typology under a four-fold categorization of exclusivisms–inclusivisms–pluralisms–particularities. However, this is not to say that this defines the possible limits of the discussion, for, as I have suggested, some feminist writers, such as Jeannine Hill Fletcher in this book, make a valid case for rethinking the boundaries of the discussion from a feminist standpoint,[43] while a variety of approaches can be identified. Within this, there is nothing to stop anyone from working across different paradigms – perhaps being a feminist-particularist-pluralist![44] I leave it, however, to the reader to decide for him- or herself the validity and applicability of these categories to the current discussion.

Study Questions

1 Explain, in your own terms, what you think are the most significant criticisms of the classical typological framework, and how you would seek to answer them.

2 Do you think it makes sense to include 'particularities' as a fourth category in the typology?

3 Do you think the typology would most usefully be seen as a set of logical parameters or as a descriptive heuristic tool?

Further Reading

D'Costa, Gavin, 1996, 'The Impossibility of a Pluralist View of Religions', *Religious Studies*, vol. 32, pp. 223–32.

Knitter, Paul F., 2002, *Introducing Theologies of Religions*, Maryknoll: Orbis.

Markham, Ian, 1993, 'Creating Options: Shattering the Exclusivist, Inclusivist and Pluralist Paradigm', *New Blackfriars*, vol. 74, no. 867, pp. 33–41.

Race, Alan, 1993, *Christians and Religious Pluralism*, 2nd edn, London: SCM Press.

Schmidt-Leukel, Perry, 2005, 'Exclusivism, Inclusivism, Pluralism: The Tripolar Typology – Clarified and Reaffirmed', in Knitter, Paul F. (ed.), *The Myth of Religious Superiority: A Multifaith Exploration*, Maryknoll: Orbis, pp. 13–27.

Thomas, Owen C., 1969, *Attitudes Toward Other Religions: Some Christian Interpretations*, London: SCM Press.

Notes

1 My thanks go to Alan Race for his suggestions on an earlier draft of this chapter.

2 Race, Alan, 1983, *Christians and Religious Pluralism: Patterns in the Christian Theology of Religions*, London: SCM Press (enlarged 2nd edn, 1993).

3 It was subsequently taken up and used by Gavin D'Costa, who helped popularize it (D'Costa, G., 1986, *Theology and Religious Pluralism*, Oxford: Blackwell), and who, even after rejecting it, spoke of its dominance (D'Costa, G., 2000, *The Meeting of Religions and the Trinity*, Edinburgh: T&T Clark).

4 D'Costa, Gavin, 1989, 'Theology of Religions', in Ford, D. (ed.), *The Modern Theologians*, Oxford: Blackwell, and also in subsequent editions of this work in 1996 and 2005. Other critics who also mention its usefulness include DiNoia, J. A., 1992, *The Diversity of Religions: A Christian Perspective*, Washington DC: Catholic University of America Press, and Markham, I. S., 2008, *Understanding Christian Doctrine*, Oxford: Blackwell, pp. 190–3.

5 Knitter, Paul F., 2002, *Introducing Theologies of Religions*, Maryknoll: Orbis.

6 Race, *Christians*, p. 7.

7 His account will be set out in the section on alternative typologies.

8 See Schmidt-Leukel, P., 2005, 'Exclusivism, Inclusivism, Pluralism: The Tripolar Typology – Clarified and Reaffirmed', pp. 13–27 in Knitter, Paul F. (ed.), *The Myth of Religious Superiority: A Multifaith Exploration*, Maryknoll: Orbis, pp. 14–16. His list of eight criticisms may briefly be listed as: (1) The typology is inconsistent in structure, because the positions do not address the same questions; (2) The typology has a wrong focus for the theology of religions: either, on salvation rather than religious practice; or, it just makes members of other faiths subsets of one's own; (3) More than three options exist; (4) There are fewer than three options; everything is a type of inclusivism or exclusivism; (5) The typology cannot deal with the nuances of actual theologies and is too abstract, while many people will not neatly fit one category; (6) It fails to take account of the vast diversity of religions; (7) It is an offensive polemic used by pluralists, especially the use of the term 'exclusivism'; (8) We cannot choose these options yet, as such positioning should come after dialogue not before it.

9 For those wanting a full discussion of all the criticisms, refer either to Schmidt-Leukel's original defence, or to my own (forthcoming) 2009, *Controversies in the Theology of Religions*, London: SCM Press.

10 Tilley, Terrence W., 1999, '"Christianity and the World Religions": A Recent Vatican Document', *Theological Studies*, vol. 60, pp. 318–37, at p. 323.

11 See the chapter on inclusivism.

12 Heim, S. M., 2001, *The Depth of the Riches: A Trinitarian Theology of Religious Ends*, Grand Rapids: William B. Eerdmans, p. 8, see Schmidt-Leukel, 'Pluralisms', herein, as well as the chapters on 'Inclusivisms' and 'Particularities' for further discussion on Heim.

13 Schmidt-Leukel, 'Exclusivism', p. 24.

14 D'Costa, Gavin, 1996, 'The Impossibility of a Pluralist View of Religions', *Religious Studies*, vol. 32, pp. 223–32.

15 Knitter, *Introducing*, p. 217. D'Costa also notes this possibility.

16 Schmidt-Leukel, 'Exclusivism', p. 24.

17 These are addressed in the chapter on particularity, where a fuller account of both sides is given. However, the reader may also wish to consult Clarke, J. J., 1997, *Oriental Enlightenment*, London: Routledge, and Hedges, P., 2002, 'The Interrelationship of Religions: Some Critical Reflections on the Concept of Particularity', *World Faiths Encounter*, vol. 32, pp. 3–13.

18 This term is used of someone who believes, or hopes, that all people will be saved.

19 See Race, A., 2001, *Interfaith Encounter: The Twin Tracks of Theology and Dialogue*, London: SCM Press, pp. 37ff., for a discussion of some such cases and a reason why they fall between.

20 Doctrine Commission of the Church of England, 1996, *The Mystery of Salvation* (A Report), London: Church Publishing House. Indeed, given that Farquhar's position is a rather 'negative' form of fulfilment theology, this seems somewhat strange – see footnote 37 below.

21 Hill Fletcher, J., 2006, *Monopoly on Salvation: A Feminist Approach to Religious Pluralism*, London: Continuum.

22 For example, Netland, Harold, 1991, *Dissonant Voices: Religious Pluralism and the Quest of Truth*, Grand Rapids: Eerdmans; Eddy, Paul, 2002, *John Hick's Pluralist Philosophy of World Religions*, Abingdon: Ashfield.

23 McGrath, A., 2006, *Christianity: An Introduction*, 2nd edn, Oxford: Blackwell, p. 165, and Netland, Harold, 2001, *Religious Pluralism: The Challenge to Christian Faith and Mission*, Downers Grove: InterVarsity Press, pp. 46ff.

24 McGrath, A., 2007, *Christian Theology: An Introduction*, 4th edn, Oxford: Blackwell, pp. 462–3. He names DiNoia and Heim as two principal exponents of this view.

25 Schmidt-Leukel, 'Exclusivism', p. 18.

26 It should be noted, though, that Race has much sympathy with this reworking and restating of his typology.

27 Schmidt-Leukel, 'Exclusivism', p. 24.

28 *Ibid.*

29 Kärkkäinen, Veli-Matti, 2003, *An Introduction to the Theology of Religions: Biblical, Historical, and Contemporary Perspectives*, Downers Grove: InterVarsity Press.

30 Knitter, *Introducing*.

31 Knitter made a similar point when he advocated following the 'neat classification' of the classical typology as a way of negotiating the diversity of views in his 1995 book, *One Earth Many Religions: Multifaith Dialogue and Global Responsibility*, Maryknoll: Orbis, p. 25.

32 See, Hedges, Paul, 2001, *Preparation and Fulfilment: A History and Study of Fulfilment Theology in Modern British Thought in the Indian Context*, Bern: Peter Lang, ch. 7.

33 Since I first proposed particularity as a fourth category (Hedges, 'Interrelationship'), to my knowledge, only Knitter and McGrath have offered similar

extensions to the typology. There are, I would suggest, two main reasons why this change has been slow: (1) most post-modern particularist figures reject the typology (for the reasons discussed herein) and therefore would not want there to be an extra category; (2) most 'liberal/modernist' users of the typology don't recognize the post-modern turn and see particularists within the previous categories.

34 Thomas, Owen C., 1969, *Attitudes Toward Other Religions: Some Christian Interpretations*, London: SCM Press.

35 *Ibid.*, pp. 19–28.

36 Race also makes a distinction between what he calls the 'spirit of dialogue' and the 'theoretics of dialogue', yet without separating their close interrelationship. The spirit of dialogue harbours expectations of learning and receiving from the other, while the theoretics of dialogue has the potential to disclose new data and insights for integrating into theological thinking. See Race, *Interfaith*, ch. 5, pp. 85–104.

37 A case in point might be Farquhar, who we have mentioned above, whose exposition of fulfilment theology was more suggestive of the 'death' of Hinduism than its fulfilment; indeed 'death' and 'rebirth' may be said to be his paradigm's controlling tropes, which makes his version of the typically inclusivist fulfilment theology closer to exclusivism (see, Hedges, *Preparation*, especially pp. 334–40).

38 Alan Race must be credited with the suggestion to provide a plural.

39 A longer discussion and references for further reading are included in the chapter on particularities.

40 Kärkkäinen, Veli-Matti, 2004, *Trinity and Religious Pluralism*, Basingstoke: Ashgate, classifies D'Costa as an inclusivist, while D'Costa would also fit Netland's definition of inclusivism (*Dissonant*, pp. 51–2). However, Josef Lössl suggests D'Costa is now an exclusivist (Lössl, J., 1998, Review of 'Gerth, Andre A., *Theologie im Angesicht der Religionen. Gavin D'Costa's Kritik an der pluralistischen Religionstheologie John Hicks*', in *Religious Studies*, vol. 34, p. 357). Meanwhile D'Costa, although eschewing the term, discusses Lindbeck and DiNoia under the category of exclusivism ('Theology', pp. 630–1), and Markham, another critic of the typology, again uses it to define Lindbeck as 'a highly sophisticated exclusivist' (Markham, *Understanding*, p. 188).

41 According to Knitter, they 'don't offer any clear-cut, sure-fire directions' (*Introducing*, p. 218). Although Knitter's claim here is arguable – many of them offer very clear directions, generally of absolutist Christian supremacy, but then try to cloak this in more moderate rhetoric and claims to post-modern indeterminacy and openness.

42 D'Costa, Gavin, 2001, in 'Roundtable Review' of his *The Meeting of Religions and the Trinity*, in *Reviews in Theology and Religious Studies*, p. 246.

43 The reader is also directed to her chapter on feminist approaches herein.

44 Personally, I would suggest that the most fruitful grounds for further reflection in this area would benefit from working at the intersections of these approaches, perhaps with an eye to such classical approaches as the fulfilment paradigm.

Section B: The 'Classical' Approaches

3

Exclusivisms: 'Indeed Their Rock is Not like Our Rock'

DANIEL STRANGE

Introduction: Defending the Indefensible?

Whether at the level of popular conversation or academic discourse, to continue to defend and propound a metanarrative for the uniqueness, particularity and exclusive truth of the Christian faith (or any faith for that matter), in contradistinction to other 'faiths', would appear to be both intellectually and morally not only naive and offensive but simply an inconceivable impossibility. While it is incontrovertible that the weight of historical theology recognizes the hegemony of something like Christian exclusivism, surely, in our post-Kantian, post (late) modern, post-Christendom, postcolonial, post-Holocaust, post 9/11, 7/7, multi-ethnic and multicultural context, such exclusivity is precisely that, a relic of 'history'. It is forever an uncomfortable memory now reinterpreted as the times of ignorance and infancy when Christians did not know any better because they did not know the religious Other any better.[1] Therefore, in liberal Western culture generally there would appear to be a deep implausibility structure regarding exclusivism, with 'defeaters' against exclusivism being legion.[2] To put it another way, in the world we are told we all want, which lauds inclusive plurality, equality, tolerance and peace, and in the story that we tell ourselves about who we are, where we have come from and where we are going, an exclusivistic Christianity at best is given the role of the villain, or worse, is given the role of the pantomime villain (because a militancy based on Islam has taken the part of the real villain), or even worse still, is not even deemed worthy to have a part in the story, even a bit-part. Within such a context, it is a gargantuan challenge not simply to describe but persuasively to prescribe a robust exclusivist Christian approach to other faiths against its cultured despisers. This though is the task before us.

As we begin to trace historically support for exclusivism, we must first make a definitional remark concerning what we mean by 'exclusivism', or rather 'exclusivisms', for descriptively the category encompasses many different variations on a broad theme. Harold Netland helpfully gives us the outline of the theme which we will use as a working definition:

1 The Bible is God's distinctive written revelation; it is true and fully authoritative; and thus where the claims of Scripture are incompatible with those of other faiths, the latter are to be rejected.
2 Jesus Christ is the unique incarnation of God, fully God and fully man [*sic*], and only through the person and work of Jesus is there the possibility of salvation.
3 God's saving grace is not mediated through the teachings, practices or institutions of other religions.[3]

The Exclusivist tradition (most often found within Lutheran and Calvinist circles) is fundamentally concerned to affirm two central insights. The first is that God has sent his Son, Jesus Christ, to bring salvation into the world and that this salvation is both judgement and mercy to all human beings who are deeply estranged from God. Salvation comes from faith in Christ alone – *solus Christus*. In this respect, many exclusivists share this affirmation. Second, this salvation won by Christ is only available through explicit faith in Christ which comes from hearing the gospel preached (*fides ex auditu*), requiring repentance, baptism and the embracing of a new life in Christ.

If a truly comprehensive Christian theology of religions includes not only questions pertaining to salvation, but questions pertaining to truth, and questions pertaining to the phenomena of human religiosity, then two observations need to be made with regard to the category of 'exclusivism'. First, exclusivism is a broad enough category to posit a number of different configurations and interpretations concerning soteriological and alethic issues. As will be seen, for example, being an exclusivist does not necessarily entail a parsimony or restrictiveness regarding who eventually will be saved. Indeed, depending on other theological decisions, it is possible that inclusivists and pluralists could be more soteriologically parsimonious than exclusivists. Second, because of the organic, systemic, connectedness of Christian doctrine, a truly accurate description of any example of 'exclusivism' is formed and fashioned within a particular tradition-specific framework recognizing that the theology of religions is a parasitic discipline dependent on other *a priori* theological commitments. While the pedagogical usefulness of all typologies and taxonomies is recognized, there is no real 'generic' exclusivism, and if such a generalization is made it must be recognized as a rather blunt analytical tool.

Exclusivisms: An Historical Sketch[4]

The history of Israel and the early Church

In claiming 'variations on an exclusivist theme' as being 'the historical position' or 'the traditional position' of the Church, I do not wish to drown out historical testimony which both inclusivists and pluralists have used in support of their respective positions, testimony they will no doubt cite in their own defences. That said, there is something approaching a consensus that historically the dominant theme regarding Christian approaches to other religions has been an exclusive one. As Race himself notes, 'undoubtedly, the predominant attitude of the church through Christian history has been to regard the outsider as in error or darkness, beyond the realms of truth and light'.[5] What is more, Race acknowledges (citing texts like Acts 4.12 and John 14.6)[6] that such a view is based upon the absolute and final claims of the New Testament itself. Such a linkage is significant, for while philosophical and socio-cultural factors have played their part, the foundational authoritative basis for historical affirmations of exclusivism has been the strongly exclusivistic tenor of the Bible (both Old Testament and New Testament), which exclusivists have understood to be a true and unified revelation of God's works and words in history. Not to start with biblical history in a historical survey of exclusivism, therefore, would seem somewhat perverse.

First, from Genesis to Revelation and the corresponding history it encompasses, exclusivists argue that the surrounding context of the people of God was one of philosophical and religious diversity, not just a factual pluralism but often a cherished pluralism, be it henotheism, polytheism, or syncretism.[7] This makes any claims to Christian exclusivity all the more self-conscious and stark. Second, and positively, the constant theme throughout the history of Israel and in the founding of the Christian Church is both the incomparability (none like him) and transcendent uniqueness (no other God)[8] of YHWH and Jesus Christ who is God incarnate. Concerning both who the triune God is (in terms of metaphysics), what the triune God says (in terms of epistemology and revelation), and what the triune God does (in terms of his sovereignty over both creation and redemption), there is no one like him. Consequent on the nature and activity of God is a secondary affirmation of the incomparability and uniqueness of both Israel and the Church. There is no other covenant community like them, and there is no other community with a history like theirs, because the incomparable and unique God has covenanted with them alone and intervened salvifically on their behalf alone. Note though that with such strong default themes of particularity also come complementary themes of universality, inclusion, diversity and tolerance (for example, attitudes towards the alien and stranger; attitudes towards ethnic diversity, including the eschatological hope of Christians being drawn from all nations and languages; God's universal care and sustaining of creation; the universal scope of the gospel and the universal mandate to take the gospel to the nations, and so forth). Such exclusivity should never lead to vainglory or malice, for both Israel and the Church are chosen by the sheer grace of God to display his glory, and have a unique responsibility and calling to be a light for the nations in both word and deed. To neglect and abuse such a calling is an abuse of this delegated authority and power and leads to greater culpability.[9]

Third, and negatively, if principially[10] the loci of truth, salvation and goodness are only to be found in God, God's word and God's community, then principially all people outside of these boundaries are in error, cannot be saved, and are under the power of sin. The denouncement of idols and idolatry pervades both Old Testament and New Testament, remembering that idolatry is not simply worshipping 'another' god but (mis)representing the triune God in any way other than that in which he has freely revealed himself. In this sense idols are both nothing (for there is only one Creator God) and something (for all idols are human creations, whether of the mind or of the external world).[11]

The early Church Fathers

The exclusivist mood of the biblical testimony continued into the early Church and was soon to be consolidated, remembering too the substantial change in social and cultural dynamics as Christianity moved from minority sect to majority religion. Against this exclusivist monopoly, the writings of some of the early Fathers, such as Justin, Irenaeus, Origen and Clement of Alexandria, are often cited as indicating an important exception indicating an openness to non-Christian beliefs especially on the issue of soteriology.[12] Such examples cannot be ignored, and there is certainly a willingness by these Fathers to speculate on the relationship between Christianity and other philosophies. Equally, though, it is unacceptable to 'romanticize' this period as an oasis of inclusivism or pluralism in the vast desert of exclusivism. As the secondary literature suggests, there appears to be an ambivalent ambiguity among these Fathers regarding Christianity's relationship to non-Christian religions.[13]

One theological tradition which shows something of both this innovative construction and ambiguity concerning other religions is the *prisca theologia* (ancient theology), 'developed first by Clement of Alexandria, Origen, Lactantius, and Eusebius to show that the greatest philosophers have borrowed from the Chosen People'.[14] As McDermott writes:

> Typically it alleges that all human beings were originally given knowledge of true religion (monotheism, the Trinity, *creation ex nihilo*) by the Jews or by traditions going back to Noah's good sons (Shem and Japheth) or antediluvians such as Enoch or Adam. This knowledge was subsequently passed down to Zoroaster, Hermes Trismegistus, Brahmins and Druids, Orpheus, Pythagoras, Plato and the Sybils.[15]

We will return to the *prisca theologia* later in this chapter.

'Extra Ecclesiam Nulla Salus' and the Catholic Church to Vatican II[16]

It is Cyprian (200–58) in *The Unity of the Catholic Church* who is responsible for the slogan most often associated with exclusivism, '*extra ecclesiam nulla salus*' ('outside the Church there is no salvation'), remembering his focus was on schismatics and heretics rather than other religions *per se*. With Augustine (354–430), whose influence on the Church and its subsequent teaching cannot be overestimated, the axiom was strengthened. Augustine's teaching on original guilt, predestination, God's sovereignty and efficacious grace, gave a far more substantial theological and philosophical basis and reinforced Christian particularity. Fulgentius of Ruspe (468–533) widened the *extra ecclesiam* to include Jews and pagans, and the axiom is evidenced in Pope Innocent III's letter to the bishop of Tarragona (1208) regarding the return of a believer to the Catholic Church from the Waldensians and in the Fourth Lateran Council (1215). Most importantly the axiom was formalized officially at the Council of Florence in 1442:

> The Council firmly believes, professes and proclaims that those not living within the Catholic Church, not only pagans, but Jews, heretics and schismatics, cannot participate in eternal life, but will depart into everlasting fire which has been prepared for the devil and his angels, unless before the end of life the same have been added to the flock . . . No one, whatever almsgiving he has practiced, even if he has shed blood for the name of Christ, can be saved, unless he has remained in the bosom and unity of the Catholic Church.[17]

Moving once again from soteriology to the phenomena of other religions, there are some interesting nuances to note. Peter Leithart reminds us that in a work like Dante's *Inferno*, Muhammad is in the subcircle of hell reserved for schismatics rather than among the pagans.[18]

Within Roman Catholic teaching, exclusivistic interpretations of *extra ecclesiam nulla salus* (albeit with some modifications[19]) continued until the Second Vatican Council (1962–5), when many acknowledge that in terms of our three-fold typology, Roman Catholic teaching shifted from the exclusivist paradigm into the inclusivist paradigm.[20] However, interpretations of the conciliar documents have varied. While there appears to be more agreement as regards the possibility of salvation among non-Christians, it is more disputed as to whether other religious traditions play an instrumental/preparatory role in salvation.[21] There are post-Vatican II Roman Catholic theologians like H. Van Straelen who have persisted in interpreting the axiom in a far more exclusivist way.[22]

The Reformation heritage

As heirs of the Augustinian tradition and with the Bible as their supreme authority, the Protestant Reformers largely continued the exclusivist heritage,[23] not so much under the banner of *extra ecclesiam nulla salus* but rather under their five '*solas*': *sola Scriptura*, *solus Christus*, *sola fide*, *sola gratia*, *sola Deo Gloria*. In his *Larger Catechism*, Martin Luther wrote: 'For where Christ is not preached, there is no Holy Spirit to create, call and gather the Christian Church, and outside it no one can come to the Lord Christ . . . But outside the Christian Church (that is where the gospel is not) there is no forgiveness, and hence no holiness.'[24] John Calvin affirmed a universal natural revelation of God in all humanity, a *sensus divinitatis*[25] or *semen religionis*,[26] but claimed that because of the sinfulness of man, such knowledge was always twisted and distorted away from God: 'But all the heathen, to a man, by their own vanity either were dragged or slipped back into false inventions, and thus their perceptions so vanished that whatever they had naturally sensed concerning the sole God had no value beyond making them inexcusable.'[27] For Calvin, what is needed now for mankind is not only true knowledge of God the Creator, but true knowledge of God the Redeemer:

> For even if many men once boasted that they worshiped the Supreme majesty, the Maker of Heaven and Earth, yet because they had no Mediator it was not possible for them truly to taste God's mercy, and thus be persuaded that he was their Father. Accordingly, because they did not hold Christ as their Head, they possessed only a fleeting knowledge of God. From this also came about that they at last lapsed into crass and foul superstition and betrayed their own ignorance. So today the Turks, although they proclaim at the top of their lungs that the Creator of heaven and earth is God, still while repudiating Christ, substitute an idol in the place of the true God.[28]
>
> All the more vile is the stupidity of those persons who open heaven to all the impious and unbelieving without the grace of him whom Scripture commonly teaches to be the only door whereby we enter into salvation . . . Christ answered the Samaritan women: 'You worship what you do not know; we worship what we know; for salvation is from the Jews.' In these words he . . . condemns all pagan religions as false . . . No worship has ever pleased God except that which looked to Christ. On this basis, also, Paul declares that all heathen were 'without God and bereft of hope and life.'[29]

The missionary movement

For those coming under its sway, the Enlightenment, with its own ultimate commitment to autonomous human reason, signalled a paradigm shift in the theology of religions: the death knell for exclusivism but the breeding ground for what would become inclusivism, pluralism and the scientific study of religion (religious studies).[30] Changes in fundamental doctrinal *loci* would mean changes in the Christian attitude towards the religious other:

> A host of traditional Christian, especially Christological, doctrines came to be reconsidered and reshaped in light of this new outlook: the two natures of Christ, especially his divinity; the possibility of miracles, including the resurrection of Christ; original sin; the Trinity; divine revelation and so on. The Christianity that emerged out of this process looked quite different from the Christianity of the past and had to reconsider its relation to other religions, too. Moreover, not only Christianity but also other religions came under the scrutiny of this new independent reason.[31]

However, not all were influenced by Enlightenment presuppositions, and the early modern missionary movement continued to be propelled by an exclusivist engine fuelled on the uniqueness of Christ and the uniqueness of the Christian message. While the relationship between missions, colonialism and imperialism is a notoriously complex and agenda-laden debate, the motives of a Hudson Taylor, a William Carey, or a D. L. Moody were 'gospel' motives: 'a primary motive of most missionaries was a genuine feeling of concern for others, they knew that the love of God had been shed abroad in their hearts and they were willing to sacrifice themselves for the sake of him who had died for them'.[32]

In his own account, Netland regards the following statement by Judson Smith of the American Board of Commissioners for Foreign Missions in 1896, as being representative of the early missions mentality:

> Missionaries do not aim to Americanise or Europeanise the people of the Orient, or to bring them under the political control of the great powers of the West or to impose our type of civilization on them . . . They have a deeper aim and address a more vital need; they seek to Christianize these peoples, to penetrate their hearts and lives with the truth and spirit of the Gospel, to enthrone Jesus Christ in their souls . . . There is no faith which Christianity is not worthy to replace, which it is not destined to replace. It is not to share the world *with* Islam, or *with* Buddhism, or *with* any other religious system. It is the true religion for man in the Orient and in the Occident, in the first century and in the twentieth century and as long as time shall last.[33]

Increasingly, though, the missionary movement itself began to show internal theological tensions as various inclusivist models of fulfilment began to emerge and vie for supremacy.[34] This culminated in intense debate at the first three world missionary conferences of Edinburgh (1910), Jerusalem (1928) and Tambaram (1938), where a wide range of missiological issues were discussed, underlying which was the relationship of Christianity to the world religions. One exclusivist scholar inextricably linked to and towering over these conferences, in particular Tambaram, was the Dutch missiologist Hendrik Kraemer (1888–1965), whose multidisciplinary approach combined theological, missiological, linguistic and phenomenological insights.[35] Employing a dialectical methodology, Kraemer argued for the 'radical difference' of all religions (contra, fulfilment models), and the discontinuous and *sui generis* nature of the revelation of Jesus Christ:

> I propose to set the religions, including Christianity, in light of the Person of Jesus Christ, who is the Revelation of God and alone has the authority to criticise – I mean, to judge discriminately and with complete understanding – every religion and everything that is in man or proceeds from him.[36]

Kraemer's main works, *The Christian Message in a Non-Christian World* (1938), *Religion and the Christian Faith* (1956), and *World Cultures and World Religions* (1960), remain some of the most detailed, nuanced and sophisticated statements within the exclusivist paradigm, and have influenced (though not without criticism) subsequent generations of exclusivist missiologists from the Reformed tradition, most importantly J. H. Bavinck, Johannes Verkuyl and Lesslie Newbigin.[37]

Meanwhile, in the world of academic theology and in a parallel to these developments within missiology, Karl Barth's own interpretation of the Reformed tradition led to a stinging attack on the 'from below' method and content of theological liberalism, and a defence of a thoroughly 'from above' Trinitarian and Christocentric theological method and content.[38] The implications for Barth's understanding of other religions can be viewed as a further extension and reformulation of the Reformer's exclusivistic outlook. Most famously this is seen in 'paragraph 17' of *Church Dogmatics* 1/2, 'The Revelation of God as the Abolition of Religions', where God's revelation in Christ and human religion are seen to be antithetical to one another, such that religion is unbelief:

> From the standpoint of revelation religion is clearly seen to be a human attempt to anticipate what God in His revelation wills to do and does do. It is the attempted replacement of the divine work by human manufacture. The divine reality offered and manifested to us in revelation is replaced by a concept of God arbitrarily and wilfully evolved by man. 'Arbitrarily

> and wilfully' means here by his own means, by his own human insight, constructiveness and energy.[39]

For Barth such exclusivisty does not lead to a parsimony regarding salvation, for other *loci* in his theological project come into play, leading to what many regard to be a 'quasi-universalism' in Barth's theology. Consequently, and in contrast to the motives behind much of the historical missions movement, for Barth the 'missionary mandate' is refracted in a new way. As Race notes:

> As the locus of true religion (only as and when it lives by grace of course) the task of the church is to declare to all people that Jesus Christ has died and been raised for them, that they already stand in the light of life: 'In each and every man to whom it is directed it is concerned, not with an actual, but certainly with a virtual or potential Christian, with a *christianus designatus*, with a *christianus in spe*. It is concerned with a creature ordained to know and realise his membership of the body of Christ.[40]

The contemporary scene

I wish to finish this short historical survey by briefly noting the state of 'exclusivisms' within the contemporary scene. While there may be some familial similarities, all current articulations of exclusivism come coated in their own tradition-specific flavours claiming historical continuity and precedence for their positions.

First, there are those exclusivisms which continue to be influenced by neo-orthodoxy and the dialectical method, especially the teaching of Barth. Second are those exclusivisms under the banner of 'post-liberalism' which argue for the incommensurability between different religious traditions. George Lindbeck argues that doctrine is not to be understood as either exclusively 'cognitive' (that is, in terms of propositional content) or 'experientially expressive' (that is, in terms of symbolic expression of religious experience), but rather, 'becoming a Christian is a process of being included into a cultural-linguistic practice'.[41] Applying this soteriologically, Lindbeck claims that 'there is no damnation – just as there is no salvation – outside the church. One must in other words, learn the language of faith before one can know enough about its message to reject it and thus be lost.'[42] Lindbeck still wishes to retain the principle of *fides ex auditu* (faith by hearing) while realizing that not everyone has the opportunity to be included cultural-linguistically in the Christian faith. His proposal 'is that dying itself be pictured as the point at which every human being is ultimately and expressly confronted by the gospel, by the crucified and risen Lord. It is only then when the final decision is made for or against Christ . . . All previous decisions, whether for faith or against faith are preliminary.'[43]

Third, and by far the biggest grouping both in terms of theological scholarship and confessional community, are those 'exclusivisms' which come from within Protestant (yet trans-denominational) 'evangelical' Christianity.[44] Despite there being some scholarly disagreement among evangelicals over a plethora of issues regarding soteriological, alethic and missiological questions (and that several prominent evangelicals more naturally fit into the inclusivist paradigm), evangelicalism is still largely a confessionally exclusivistic movement, stressing the authority of the Bible, the uniqueness of Christ and the necessity of faith in Christ. Three important international symposia have articulated exclusivist themes in their official statements: the Frankfurt Declaration (1970), the Lausanne Covenant (1974) and the Manilla Manifesto (1992), and several evangelical theologians and missiologists have articulated nuanced and constructive exclusivist positions, as for example Harold Netland,[45] Don Carson,[46] Chris Wright,[47] Vinoth Ramachandra,[48] Gerald McDermott[49] and Terrance L. Tiessen.[50]

Exclusivism: A Contemporary Defence

In order to gain a deeper understanding of exclusivism, a particular tradition-specific 'evangelical' version of exclusivism will be outlined, noting again that in the twenty-first century this is largely where exclusivism is to be found. However, given the confusion over the term 'evangelical', I further define this variation as 'Reformed Evangelical Presuppositional Exclusivism' (REPE). Admittedly, such a title sounds convoluted. However, I trust it describes clearly the character and context of this variation of exclusivism. The terms 'Reformed' and 'Evangelical' place this defence in continuity with those historical movements, traditions and communities that I have outlined in the previous section, and it builds methodologically and substantially from those doctrinal raw materials. That is to say that such a defence seeks to be faithful to biblical revelation (supremely), but also the Ecumenical Creeds,[51] the five *solas* of the Reformation,[52] and the creedal affirmations of Reformed orthodoxy.[53] The term 'presuppositional' is important and contains within it two related arguments revolving around the area of ultimate commitments.

The tradition-specific nature of all positions

The first argument, and an argument found in the majority of contemporary exclusivist defences, not just this one, seeks to clear the ground and level the playing field by arguing for the impossibility of epistemological neutrality and the tradition-specific nature of all positions within the theology of religions. This applies not simply to non-exclusive Christian positions regarding other faiths, but rather goes deeper to the foundation on which the debate has taken place, the typology which has generated such paradigms of thought. It is argued that there is an inbuilt prescriptive bias in the way the typology has been construed, a bias against exclusivism often portrayed in overly emotive and 'sensationalistic' terms, and for pluralism (and to a lesser extent inclusivism) portrayed not only as more enlightened and tolerant than the other positions but most significantly religiously and epistemologically 'neutral'. Here the work of Alvin Plantinga and Gavin D'Costa have been especially important and insightful.[54]

From the discipline of analytic philosophy, Plantinga deals not with the truth of exclusivism but rather with the propriety or rightness of exclusivism against claims that such a position 'is irrational, or egotistical and unjustified, or intellectually arrogant, or elitist, or a manifestation of harmful pride, or even oppressive and imperialistic'.[55] He groups such charges into two categories: moral objections (that exclusivism is arbitrary and arrogant) and epistemic objections (that exclusivism is irrational and unjustified). In both cases, Plantinga shows that these common objections to exclusivism are not necessary objections and even if they are valid then they equally apply to other positions with the result that so-called non-exclusive positions become guilty of self-referential incoherence. Plantinga writes of someone who holds exclusivistic beliefs:

> she must also believe that those who believe something incompatible with them are mistaken and believe what is false. That's no more than simple logic. Furthermore, she must also believe that those who do not believe as she does . . . fail to believe something that is true, deep, and important, and that she does believe. She must therefore see herself as privileged with respect to those others . . . They are ignorant of something – something of great importance – of which she has knowledge.[56]

But does this make her arrogant? Plantinga says no:

> I think the answer must be no. Or if the answer is yes, then I think we have here a genuine moral dilemma; for in our earthly life here below . . . there is no real alternative; there is no reflective attitude that is not open to the same strictures. These charges of arrogance are a philosophical tar baby: get close enough to them to use them against the exclusivist, and you are likely to find them stuck fast to yourself.[57]

D'Costa's argument is set firmly within the theology of religions itself. Examining the pluralisms of Hick, Knitter and Cohn-Sherbok, D'Costa's thesis is that 'pluralism' is itself a 'myth' and in reality a covert form of exclusivism:

> 'pluralism' represents a tradition-specific approach that bears all the features of exclusivism – except that it is liberal modernity's exclusivism . . . in so much as they are Enlightenment exclusivists, I shall argue they fail in terms of their own stated intentions: to facilitate better interreligious conversation. Unwittingly they stifle religious differences within the grand narrative of liberal modernity so that no religion, not even their own, is allowed to speak with its full force. One might say, polemically, that they are hard-line exclusivists.[58]

Far from enabling tolerance and diversity, pluralism does the opposite for it 'privileges liberal modernity as a mastercode within which all the religions are positioned and neutered'.[59] His conclusion is that 'pluralism' becomes something other than Christian:

> First, that when Christian theologies of religion have assimilated themselves to modernity rather than the triune God, they end up representing modernity's gods: agnosticism (in the case of Hick) and a form of neo pagan-unitarianism (Knitter). Second, in so much as their positions actually advance modernity's project, rather than Christianity's engagement with difference, they deny or obliterate difference and Otherness. In Hick's case, he mythologises the differences away so that religions can be fitted into his system. In Knitter's case, the religions are all judged by allegedly self-evident criteria that are found in the eco-system. Both Hick and Knitter know the full truth and what is ethically required of the religions independently of any of the religions. Third, and as a consequence, their pluralism turns out to be a strong form of Kantian exclusivist modernity. It cannot succeed in its claims to be more tolerant and open than other forms of Christian Trinitarian theology.[60]

To put it another way, far from demonstrating epistemic humility, pluralism is epistemologically arrogant in its claims. Newbigin made the same point regarding the 'pluralist' illustration based on the ancient fable of the blind men and elephant:[61]

> In the famous story of the blind men and the elephant, so often quoted in the interest of religious agnosticism, the real point of the story is constantly overlooked. The story is told from the point of view of the king and his courtiers, who are not blind but can see that the blind men are unable to grasp the full reality of the elephant and are only able to get a hold of part of the truth. The story is constantly told in order to neutralise the affirmation of the great religions, to suggest that they learn more humility and recognize that none of them can have more than one aspect of the truth. But of course, the real point of the story is exactly the opposite. If the king were also blind there would be no story. The story

> is told by the king, and it is the immensely arrogant claim of one who sees the full truth which all the world's religions are only groping after. It embodies the claim to know the full reality which relativizes all the claims of the religions.[62]

Such an argument is not intended to be a form of theological mud-slinging, merely a recognition that in the way the academic debate has been set up, the playing field has not been level, and that pluralism is no less 'tradition-specific', 'neutral' nor presuppositional (in terms of having ultimate epistemological commitments) than exclusivism. The 'religion' of pluralism is an exclusivistic faith.[63]

Scripture as ultimate authority

The term 'presuppositional' not only reiterates the impossibility of a neutral confession-less stance regarding one's assessment of other religions, but also conveys the Christian's ultimate presupposition as resting upon the authority of God and his authoritative word.

> Presuppositional apologists claim that there is no neutrality, invoking Jesus' saying that 'one cannot serve two masters' (Matt. 6.24). There can be no compromise between the wisdom of God and the wisdom of the world. Unbelief leads to distortion of the truth, exchanging the truth for a lie (Rom. 1.25). Only by trusting God's Word can we come to a saving knowledge of Christ (John 5.24, 8.31, 15.3, Rom. 10.17). And trusting entails presupposing: accepting God's Word as what it is, the foundation of all human knowledge, the ultimate criterion of truth and error (Deut. 18.18–19, 1 Cor. 14.37, Col. 2.2–4, 2 Tim. 3.16–17, 2 Pet. 1.19–21). So the apologetic argument, like all human inquiries into truth, must presuppose the truths of God's Word.[64]

REPE seeks to apply this apologetic method and apply it to the theology of religions, arguing for the exclusivity of Christianity, both soteriologically and alethically. Concerning the epistemological authority for such a position, REPE argues that while the triune God has revealed himself through his work in the natural world, in terms of an ultimate religious authority, it is God's totally truthful revelation of himself and his works in divinely inspired (or rather God-breathed) Christian Scripture that is the ultimate authority in all metaphysical, epistemological, ethical and soteriological issues,[65] and like all claims to ultimate authority (Enlightenment rationalism included) such a claim is made on the Bible's self-attestation, for to go outside of Scripture for Scripture's justification would be self-referentially incoherent.[66]

Moving from theological method to theological content, the following features of REPE can be outlined, features which delineate elements of both discontinuity and continuity between Christianity and other religions.

Principial[67] discontinuity

In a variety of ways, Christian Scripture describes there to be principially a fundamental discontinuity between the truth of the Christian faith, built on the foundation of God's revelation, and the falsity of all other worldviews/philosophies/pseudo-gospels, built on the foundation of human imagination. Indeed the exclusive truth of Christianity means the impossibility of the contrary. In other words, on closer inspection of these other non-Christian worldviews and according to their own presuppositions, we can show their instability and futility, a move which is an important apologetic strategy.

Scripture attests an extreme opposition or 'antithesis'[68] between belief and unbelief, light and dark, death and life, those who are blind and those who can see, covenant keepers and covenant breakers, those in Adam and those in Christ. As Jesus says, 'Whoever is not with me is against me, and whoever does not gather with me scatters' (Matt. 12.30) and 'No one can serve two masters . . .' (Matt. 6.24). This 'fundamental, everlasting and irreconcilable antithesis between the regenerate and unregenerate is found in the observation that this antithesis applies just as much to the mental life and conduct of men as it does to their other affairs. The "enmity" between Satan's seed and God's seed which is seminally spoken of in Genesis 3.15 is intellectual in nature, as well as social, or familial, or economic, or military, or political, or what have you.'[69]

What must be stressed, is that this antithesis must not be seen as simply between religious 'faith' as opposed to 'unbelief'. Rather it is drawn between 'true faith' (according to the triune God's revelation of himself in word and deed) and what the Reformed scholastic Turretin calls 'false faith',[70] all beliefs/worldviews (both those demarcated as 'religious' and those not) which do not cohere with God's own revelation of himself, including all 'other religions', worldviews and philosophies within which we must subsume the 'other religion' of Enlightenment pluralism with its unitarian deity. All of these are subsumed under the biblical category of idolatry.

Under the heading 'Principial discontinuity', let me now delineate the uniqueness of the Christian faith in a number of ways.

In metaphysics

First, Christianity offers a unique metaphysics. In contrast to other religions, the Christian God reveals himself to be absolutely independent (*a se*) and self-contained, and yet absolutely personal, both transcendent and immanent, both 'other to humanity' (we are not like him) and like humanity (we are made in his 'image').[71] There is therefore a fundamental and unique distinction between Creator and creature. Cornelius Van Til, the 'father' of Reformed presuppositional apologetics, stressed this point constantly to his students, as John Frame outlines:

> As Van Til put it, the Christian worldview involves a 'two-level' concept of reality. Van Til used to walk into class and draw two circles on the board, one under the other, connected by vertical 'lines' of communication. The larger upper circle represented God; the smaller, lower circle represented the creation. All non-Christian thought, he argued, is 'one circle' thought. It either raises man to God's level or lowers God to man's. In any case, it regards God, if it acknowledges him at all, as man's equal, as another part of the 'stuff' of the universe.[72]

Finally, God reveals himself to be triune, both one and many,[73] neither Unitarian, henotheistic, nor polytheistic but Trinitarian: One God, Father, Son and Spirit. Again this understanding of triunity is unique among the major world religions, 'and even in the Christian heresies there is little of the Trinity. Indeed, in these heresies the doctrine of the Trinity is often first to be denied.'[74]

In summary we can say:

> Christianity offers the triune God, the absolute personality . . . as the God in whom we believe. This conception of God is the foundation of everything else that we hold dear. Unless we can believe in this sort of God, it does us no good to be told that we may believe in some other sort of God, or in anything else. For us everything depends for its meaning upon this sort of God. Accordingly we are not interested to have anyone prove to us the existence of any other sort of God but this God. Any other sort of God is no God at all.[75]

In epistemology

Such a metaphysic has implications for epistemology. In contrast to modernist pluralistic hubris and late-modern relativistic despair, Christians claim that the triune God originally created us to know things truly (because God has revealed himself) but not exhaustively (because we are not God). There is a difference between archetypal knowledge (God's exhaustive knowledge of himself) and ectypal knowledge (knowledge God gives us of himself). God has revealed himself both through his works and through his words. However, God's revelation in nature lacks the specificity of worded revelation. God's words have always been needed to interpret, supplement and therefore complement his work. These two modes of revelation were never meant to be separated from one another or to work independently of each other.

This is not all, though, for this objective epistemological insufficiency of natural revelation becomes intensely more acute after the Fall. First, there is an increased complexity and potential hermeneutical ambiguity in the objective external revelation; for what is revealed now is not only God's glory and goodness but his wrath and judgement as well (Rom. 1.18). Second, this revelation of wrath is revealed both externally in the world and internally within mankind. Here we must keep in mind both God's original judgement in linear history from the Fall of Adam and Eve, and also the present continuing cyclical nature of God's wrath in his 'giving up' of sinful humanity (Rom. 1.24, 26). For those with eyes to see, both blessing and wrath reveal God, but for those dead in sin, the wicked suppression and substitution of God's blessing and wrath in natural revelation means that they do not truly know God – even as Creator. After the Fall what sinners need is the regenerating power of the gospel to know God as Creator and Redeemer, and natural revelation is an inappropriate vehicle because knowledge of the gospel of our Lord Jesus Christ is not contained in it: 'Man the sinner, as Calvin puts it, through the testimony of the Spirit receives a new power of sight by which he can appreciate the new light given in Scripture. The new light and the new power of sight imply one another. The one is fruitless for salvation without the other.'[76] Johnson echoes this:

> Special revelation is needed because special grace is needed. An intense knowledge of one's own unworthiness and a determination to do better, even with the gospel is not salvific. Faith must be consciously placed in the gospel of Jesus. The difference here is the difference between knowing the standard for which man was made and receiving God's provision for the standard breaker. It is the difference between law and gospel.[77]

In ethics

The above quotation takes us into the area of ethics. In ethics, again we see a radical difference between Christianity and other systems. Frame classifies (and internally critiques) the ethical approaches of other religions into three broad types: those based on fate; those as self-realization; and, those as law without gospel. For Frame all of these options presuppose an impersonalistic deity and a soteriological works-righteousness as opposed to Christianity's personal God who reveals himself to be the supreme standard of right and wrong and where for the Christian, 'good works' are not understood to be a cause of salvation but rather a willing and faithful response to God's free gift of grace and salvation in the propitiatory death of Christ and his vindicating resurrection from the dead.[78]

In redemptive history and the gospel message

Distinguishing Christian uniqueness by isolating metaphysics, epistemology and ethics is somewhat artificial and atomistic. All these separate elements are necessary interconnected strands of a unique and unified system of thought, or more correctly, a unique historical and eschatological story/metanarrative, which places all humanity within an epic cosmic drama of creation–fall–redemption–consummation with a particular focal point. This history of redemption and redemptive history is thoroughly Christocentric – it is the good news of Jesus Christ which is both the message of Christianity and the heart of the Christian worldview and philosophy. It is the person and work of Christ that distinguishes Christianity from all other 'faiths' and gives Christianity its exclusive or particular claims. This gospel message can be simply summarized as described by the Reformed exclusivist Tim Keller:

> Why we are here. The one God is a community – a Trinity of three persons who each perfectly know and defer to one another and therefore have infinite joy and glory and peace. God made a good, beautiful world filled with beings who share in this life of joy and peace by knowing, serving and loving God and one another.
>
> What went wrong. Instead, we chose to centre our lives on ourselves and on the pursuit of things rather than on God and others. This has led to the disintegration of creation and the loss of peace – within ourselves, between ourselves, and in nature itself. War, hunger, poverty, injustice, racism, bitterness, meaninglessness, despair, sickness, and death are all symptoms.
>
> What puts the world right. But though God lost us he determined to win us back. He entered into history in the person of Jesus in order to deal with all the causes and results of our broken relationship with him. By his sacrificial life and death he both exemplifies the life we must live and rescues us from the life we have lived. By his resurrection he proved who he was and showed us the future – new bodies and a completely renewed and restored new heaven and new earth in which the world is restored to full joy, justice, peace and glory.
>
> How can we be part of putting the world right. Between his first coming to win us and his last coming to restore us, we live by faith in him. When we believe and rely on Jesus' work and record (rather than ours) for our relationship to God, his healing power comes upon us and begins to work through us. Christ gives us a radically new identity, freeing us from both self-righteousness and self-condemnation. This liberates us

> to accept people we once excluded, and to break the bondage of things (even good things) that once drove us. He puts us into a new community of people which gives a partial, but real, foretaste of the healing of the world that God will accomplish when Jesus returns.[79]

In summary, what REPE argues for is the 'all or nothing' systemic and *solus Christus* character of Christianity in matters of both salvation and truth:

> From the point of view of the sinner, theism is as objectionable as Christianity. Theism that is worthy of the name is Christian theism. Christ said that no man can come to the Father but by him. No one can become a theist unless he becomes a Christian. Any God that is not the Father of our Lord Jesus Christ is not God but an idol. It is therefore the Holy Spirit bearing witness by and with the Word in our hearts that alone effects the required Copernican revolution and makes us both Christians and theists.[80]

Practical continuity

The picture I have sketched so far is stark, as the antithesis must be. However, only to emphasize the antithesis is simplistic and lacking theological sophistication. Biblically and experientially any 'theology of religions' has not only to answer questions of salvation but to account for the phenomena of other religions and human religiosity. Metaphysically, epistemologically and ethically we appear to see similarity and commonality between various religious traditions; adherents of other religions often appear to do 'good' works and have a belief system like those of the Christian. REPE is able to give such an explanation while still upholding the principle of the antithesis. That is to say, within an overarching pattern of discontinuity between Christianity and other faiths, there can be seen elements of continuity also.

The antithesis between Christianity and other religious traditions is what one might call its 'pure' state or consistent state. In terms of 'principle', that is 'principially', the antithesis between Christianity and other religions is total. However, life is more messy than this because both believers and unbelievers for various reasons are inconsistent and don't live according to who they truly are. This is often noted by critics of Christianity, but of course it is a profound theological truth. Principially Christians are described as new creations, and yet daily they struggle with indwelling sin.[81] Similarly there are various reasons why those who are not Christians are inconsistent in their unbelief.

> The natural man 'sins against' his own essentially Satanic principle. As the Christian has the incubus of his 'old man' weighing him down and

therefore keeping him from realizing the 'life of Christ' within, so the natural man has the incubus of the sense of Deity weighing him down and keeping him from realizing the life of Satan within. The actual situation is therefore always a mix of truth with error. Being 'without God in the world' the natural man yet knows God, and, in spite of himself, to some extent recognizes God. By virtue of their creation in God's image, by virtue of the ineradicable sense of deity within them and by virtue of God's restraining general grace, those who hate God, yet in a restricted sense know God, and do good.[82]

REPE argues that there are several theological factors which cause such inconsistency. First is the Reformed doctrine of 'common grace'.[83] This variegated non-salvific work of the Holy Spirit restrains sin and the consequences of sin in the non-Christian and excites non-Christians to perform acts of 'civic righteousness' and culture building. These may be solid enough grounds for Christians to engage in co-belligerence with other faiths.[84] Second are implications arising from the Christian doctrine of creation. While the non-Christian may be epistemologically autonomous from God, metaphysically all humanity relies on the triune God for their very being. Despite their rebellion, all humanity is made in the image of the triune God, a finite replica built to worship its Creator. Such an image can never be erased and is there as a constant reminder of the true God to be worshipped. We have already mentioned Calvin's *sensus divinitatis*, and a *semen religionis*. This universal religious consciousness accounts for the religiosity of human beings, and all other religious traditions. It is what the Reformed missiologist J. H. Bavinck called the '*thatness*' to humanity's religious quest. Bavinck noted 'five magnetic points'[85] which humanity cannot evade, fundamental questions which humans have always asked:

1 *'I and the cosmos'* ('A sense of belonging to the whole; an awareness of cosmic relationship'[86]).
2 *'I and the norm'* ('A sense of transcendent norms'[87]).
3 *'I and the riddle of my existence'* ('A sense of the governance of existence by a providential or destining power'[88]).
4 *'I and salvation'* ('A recognition of the need for redemption'[89]).
5 *'I and the Supreme Power'* ('A sense of relatedness to a Superior or Supreme power'[90]).

However, and *contra* inclusivism, even though we assert the '*thatness*' of a universal religious consciousness, there is almost immediately in sinful humanity a suppression and substitution of this knowledge of God, what Bavinck calls the '*whatness*' of religion: 'the sparse, totally decontextualised elements deriving from it that do manage to stick in the conscious mind form nuclei around which conceptual complexes of a totally deviant nature crystalise'.[91]

At this point the frequent biblical teaching on idols and idolatry becomes a sophisticated analytical tool. Idols are not created *ex nihilo*, for they are created things made to replace the Creator. These creations are not simply physical objects but can be creations of the mind. In other words, all beliefs about the triune God which do not conform to the way God has revealed himself in Scripture are idolatrous creations of the sinful mind. As worshipping beings, we must worship something, but what we worship are distortions and perversions of the unique triune God and his unique attributes. Idols are counterfeits, designer deities to avoid our responsibilities before the living triune God. So we observe religious traditions which overstress God's transcendence and otherness, or God's immanence and closeness, religions which teach law and works-righteousness rather than grace and forgiveness. As I noted above, something like the *prisca theologica* means that many religious traditions are distortions and derivations not just of God's revelation in nature but rather God's specific worded revelation.[92] Because idols are distortions and perversions of truth and so 'related' to truth, like Kraemer one might cautiously say that Christianity is the 'contradictive or subversive fulfilment' of the human religious quest.[93]

REPE and other exclusivisms

Finally, and synthesizing the above characteristics of REPE, we are able to distinguish this version of exclusivism from other versions, particularly concerning the question of soteriology, where REPE could be called 'instrumentally restrictive'. Like Barth, REPE affirms the sovereignty of God and the Christocentric nature of salvation; but, unlike Barth, REPE is highly critical of his tendency towards universalism which itself arises from other problematic elements within Barth's theology as a whole.[94] Like Lindbeck, proponents of REPE stress the *fides ex auditu*[95] but would also note the exegetical flimsiness concerning a post-mortem encounter with Christ, and the exegetical weight pointing to the instrumentality of salvation being ordinarily through a human messenger in this life.[96] Unlike Lindbeck, REPE can affirm that outside of Christianity there is damnation, because of the necessity of repentance and faith in the person and work of Christ which has been revealed in the apostolic gospel message, and the claim that God is perfectly just in his condemnation of non-Christians, for no one is ever 'ignorant' of God and their responsibilities before their Creator. All humanity is universally guilty of rejecting the knowledge of God they have been given in revelation and will be judged for this rejection.[97]

Conclusion

This chapter began by noting exclusivism's dissonance with contemporary culture but recognized the historical hegemony of such a position. This historical support was then summarized noting especially Roman Catholic and Protestant formulations. Finally a contemporary and tradition-specific version of exclusivism was described, a version which argues *for* the uniqueness of the Christian faith and *against* the idolatry of all other faiths. 'Indeed their rock is not like our Rock.'[98]

Study Questions

1. What do you think are the main reasons for: (a) the hegemony of exclusivism throughout much of Christian history?; (b) the rise and popularity of other non-exclusivist positions within the theology of religions?
2. What is the relationship between exclusivism and the authority of Scripture and its interpretation?
3. Discuss the claim that the analytical tool of 'idolatry' can account for both discontinuity and continuity between Christianity and other religions.

Further Reading

Bavinck, J. H., 1966, *The Church between Temple and Mosque: A Study of the Relationship between the Christian Faith and Other Religions*, Grand Rapids: Eerdmans.

Calvin, John, 1960, *Institutes of the Christian Religion*, McNeill, John T. (ed.), Philadelphia: Westminster Press.

Carson, D. A., 1996, *The Gagging of God: Christianity Confronts Pluralism*, Leicester: Apollos.

Netland, Harold, 2001, *Encountering World Religions: The Challenge to Christian Faith and Mission*, Leicester: Apollos.

Perry, Tim, 2001, *Radical Difference: A Defence of Hendrik Kraemer's Theology of Religions*, Ontario: Wilfrid Laurier University Press.

Plantinga, Alvin, 1995, 'Pluralism: A Defense of Religious Exclusivism', in Senor, T. (ed.), *The Rationality of Belief and the Plurality of Faith*, London: Cornell University Press.

Notes

1 Notwithstanding another uncomfortable and stubborn fact, that millions of Christians throughout the world today remain firmly entrenched in some version of exclusivism.

2 A 'defeater belief' is a philosophical term to say that if Belief-A is true then Belief-B *cannot* be true.

3 Netland, Harold, 2001, *Encountering World Religions: The Challenge to Christian Faith and Mission*, Leicester: Apollos, p. 48.

4 For a more detailed description and analysis of the historical data, see Kärkkäinen, Veli-Matti, 2003, *An Introduction to the Theology of Religions: Biblical, Historical and Contemporary Perspectives*, Downers Grove: IVP.

5 Race, Alan, 1983, *Christians and Religions Pluralism: Patterns in the Christian Theology of Religions*, London: SCM Press, p. 10.

6 Acts 4.12: 'There is salvation in no one else, for there is no other name under heaven given among mortals by which we must be saved'; John 14.6: 'Jesus said to him, "I am the way, and the truth, and the life. No one comes to the Father except through me."'

7 See, for example, Hess, Richard S., 1991, 'Yahweh and His Asherah? Epigraphic Evidence for Religious Pluralism in Old Testament Times', in Clarke, A., and Winter, B. (eds), *One Lord One God: Christianity in a World of Religious Pluralism*, Cambridge: Tyndale House, pp. 5–33; Winter, Bruce, 1991, 'In Public and in Private: Early Christians and Religious Pluralism', in Clarke and Winter (eds), *One*, pp. 125–48.

8 See Wright, Christopher J. H., 2006, *The Mission of God: Unlocking the Bible's Grand Narrative*, Nottingham: Apollos, p. 82. Wright refers to numerous biblical texts to evidence this claim, e.g. 2 Sam. 7.22; Ps. 86.8, 10; Isa. 46.9; 1 Kings 8.23, 60.

9 See, for example, Wright, *Mission*, pp. 90–92; Kaiser, Walter C. Jr, 2000, *Mission in the Old Testament: Israel as a Light to the Nations*, Grand Rapids: Baker.

10 That is most basically or fundamentally.

11 The Bible contains hundreds of references to idols and idolatry. Some representative passages include: Isa. 44; Ps. 115; Hos. 8.4; Acts 17; Rom. 1.18–32; 1 Thess. 1.9. See Wright, *Mission*, ch. 5, 'The Living God Confronts Idolatry'; Ovey, Mike, 2002, 'Idolatry and Spiritual Parody: Counterfeit Faiths', *Cambridge Papers*, vol. 11.1 (March).

12 For a survey of these views see Kärkkäinen, *Introduction*, ch. 5; Tiessen, Terrance L., 2004, *Who Can Be Saved? Reassessing Salvation in Christ and World Religions*, Downers Grove: IVP, pp. 48–52.

13 See Sigountos, James G., 1991, 'Did Early Christians Believe Pagan Religions Could Save?', in Crockett, William, V., and Sigountos, James G. (eds), *Through No Fault of Their Own? The Fate of Those Who Have Never Heard*, Grand Rapids: Baker, pp. 229–44; Bray, Gerald, 1997, 'Explaining Christianity to Pagans', in Vanhoozer, Kevin J. (ed.), *The Trinity in a Pluralistic Age: Theological Essays on Culture and Religion*, Grand Rapids: Eerdmans, pp. 9–26.

14 McDermott, Gerald, 2000, *Jonathan Edwards Confronts the Gods: Christian Theology, Enlightenment Religion and Non-Christian Faiths*, Oxford: Oxford University Press, p. 93.

15 *Ibid.* McDermott notes that the *prisca theologia* is later developed in the Renaissance by Ficino and Mirandola, and in the seventeenth and eighteenth centuries by the 'Jesuit Figurists' and Jonathan Edwards, who was influenced by writers such as Chevalier Ramsay and Philip Skelton.

16 For a more detailed account of this period see, Sullivan, Francis A., 1992, *Salvation Outside the Church? Tracing the History of the Catholic Response*, London: Geoffrey Chapman, pp. 3–140.

17 Quotation taken from Sullivan, *Salvation*, p. 66.

18 'In treating Mohammed as a Christian schismatic, Dante was not inventing a new perspective (he rarely did), but presenting views widespread of his time. Many in the Western medieval world believed that Mohammed himself was apostatized from Christianity, and some even believed he had once been a cardinal.' Leithart, Peter J., 'Mirror of Christendom', Mars Hill Audio Resource Essay, p. 1. Accessed: 9/11/07. Posted at: http://www.marshillaudio.org/resources/pdf/Leithart.pdf. Similarly, Judaism was seen to have similar apostate status.

19 For example, the categories including the 'invincibly ignorant', 'implicit faith' and the 'baptism of desire' as seen in documents such as Pope Pius IX's *Singulari Quadem* (1854) and *Quanto Conficiamur Moerore* (1863). See Tiessen, *Who*, pp. 52–6; Sullivan, *Salvation*, chs 7 and 8; and Eminyan, Maurice, 1960, *The Theology of Salvation*, Boston: St Paul.

20 Netland notes 'inclusivism' is a very broad category with the following characteristics: '1) There is a sense in which Jesus Christ is unique, normative or superior to other religious figures and in some sense it is through Christ that salvation is made available; 2) God's grace and salvation, which are somehow based on Jesus Christ, are also available and efficacious through other religions; 3) Thus other religions are generally to be regarded positively as part of God's purposes for humankind.' Netland, *Encountering*, pp. 52f.

21 For a description of Vatican II's teaching regarding the salvation of non-Christians see Sullivan, *Salvation*, ch. 9. For a summary of differing interpretations of Vatican II's understanding of the role of religions in salvation see Kärkkäinen, *Introduction*, pp. 117–19. Kärkkäinen believes D'Costa's cautious interpretation best represents the majority Catholic opinion. D'Costa writes: 'it is difficult to read the Conciliar documents as giving a positive answer to the question: can other religions *per se*, in their structures be mediators of supernatural revelation and supernatural grace. While it is true that there is no explicit negative answer, there is certainly no positive answer . . . It may well be the case that the documents' silences are intentional and could be read, as I would suggest, as prohibiting any unqualified positive affirmation of other religions as salvific structures or as containing divine revelation. This is all held, while holding at the same time, without contradiction, that supernatural grace is operative in other religions and that in those other religions there is much that is true, good, and holy, and much to be admired and learned by the church' (D'Costa, Gavin, 2000, *The Meeting of Religions and the Trinity*, Maryknoll: Orbis, p. 105). For another conservative interpretation, see Ruokanen, Miika, 1992, *The Catholic Doctrine of Non-Christian Religions According to the Second Vatican Council*, New York: Brill.

22 Van Straelen, H., 1966, *The Catholic Encounter with World Religions*, London: Burns & Oates.

23 Sullivan points out that the counter-Reformation documents of Trent did not

see a need to repeat the *extra ecclesiam nulla salus* axiom, 'perhaps because the Reformers were as insistent as the Catholic Tradition had been that there was no salvation to be had outside the church', Sullivan, *Salvation*, p. 82.

24 Luther, Martin, 1959, *Large Catechism*, trans. Robert H. Fischer, Philadelphia: Fortress, II.45, 56.

25 For 'sense of the divine', see Calvin, John, 1960, *Institutes of the Christian Religion*, McNeill, John T. (ed.), Philadelphia: Westminster Press, 1.3.1.

26 For 'seed of religion', see Calvin, *Institutes*, 1.3.1–2; 5.1.

27 Calvin, *Institutes*, 1.10.3.

28 Calvin, *Institutes*, 2.6.4.

29 Calvin, *Institutes*, 2.6.1.

30 For a history of this transition see D'Costa, Gavin, 2005, *Theology in the Public Square: Church, Academy and Nation*, Oxford: Blackwell, chs 1–3.

31 Kärkkäinen, *Introduction*, p. 92.

32 Bosch, David, 1991, *Transforming Mission: Paradigm Shifts in Theology of Mission*, Maryknoll: Orbis, p. 287; quoted in Netland, *Encountering*, p. 28.

33 Smith, Judson, 1896, 'Foreign Missions in the Light of Fact', *North American Review* (January), quoted in Netland, *Encountering*, p. 29.

34 See Netland, *Encountering*, pp. 32–8; Kärkkäinen, *Introduction*, ch. 10, 'The Fulfillment Theory of Religions'.

35 For an excellent monograph on Kraemer's life and work see Perry, Tim, 2001, *Radical Difference: A Defence of Hendrik Kraemer's Theology of Religions*, Ontario: Wilfrid Laurier University Press.

36 Kraemer, Hendrik, 1938, *The Christian Message in a Non-Christian World*, New York: Harper & Row, p. 15.

37 Bavinck, J. H., 1960, *An Introduction to the Science of Mission*, Freeman, David H. (trans.), Phillipsburg: P&R; 1966, *The Church between Temple and Mosque: A Study of the Relationship between the Christian Faith and Other Religions*, Grand Rapids: Eerdmans; Verkuyl, Johannes, 1978, *Contemporary Missiology*, Grand Rapids: Eerdmans; Newbigin, Lesslie, 1989, *The Gospel in a Pluralist Society*, Grand Rapids: Eerdmans.

38 For example, 'The doctrine of the Trinity is what basically distinguishes the Christian doctrine of God as Christian, and therefore what already distinguishes the Christian concept of revelation as Christian, in contrast to all other possible doctrines of God or concepts of revelation' (Barth, Karl, 1956, *Church Dogmatics* 1/1, Bromiley, G., and Torrance, T. (eds), Bromiley (trans.), Edinburgh: T&T Clark, p. 301).

39 Barth, *Church* 1/2, pp. 299f. Barth described the religion of Muhammad as a judgement of God Almighty, in Barth, Karl, 1960, *Community, Church and State*, New York: Doubleday, p. 46.

40 Race, *Christians*, p. 15.

41 D'Costa, Gavin, 1997, 'Theology of Religions', in Ford, David. F. (ed.), *The Modern Theologians*, 2nd edn, Oxford: Blackwell, p. 630.

42 Lindbeck, George, 1984, *The Nature of Doctrine: Religion and Theology in a Postliberal Age*, London: SPCK, p. 59.

43 Lindbeck, *Nature*, p. 59.

44 For an overview of evangelical approaches to the theology of religions see Strange, Daniel, 2001, *The Possibility of Salvation Among the Unevangelised*,

Carlisle: Paternoster, pp. 3–32, 294–331; Kärkkäinen, Veli-Matti, 2007, 'Evangelical Theology and the Religions', in T. Larsen and D. J. Treier (eds), *The Cambridge Companion to Evangelical Theology*, Cambridge: Cambridge University Press, pp. 199–212.

45 Netland, *Encountering*, pp. 248–309.

46 Carson, D. A., 1996, *The Gagging of God: Christianity Confronts Pluralism*, Leicester: Apollos, pp. 141–370.

47 Wright, *Mission*.

48 Ramachandra, Vinoth, 1996, *The Recovery of Mission: Beyond the Pluralist Paradigm*, Carlisle: Paternoster.

49 McDermott, Gerald, 2000, *Can Evangelicals Learn from World Religions*, Downers Grove: IVP; 2007, *God's Rivals*, Downers Grove: IVP.

50 Tiessen, *Who*.

51 The Apostle's Creed, the Nicene Creed, the Athanasian Creed, and the Creed of Chalcedon.

52 As described above.

53 The Thirty-Nine Articles (1571, Anglican); the Westminster Confession of Faith (1643–6, Presbyterian); the so-called 'Three Forms of Unity' which consist of the continental creeds (The Heidelberg Catechism (1563), The Belgic Confession (1561) and The Canons of Dordrecht (1618–19)); the New Hampshire Baptist Confession (1833, Baptist), and the Baptist Faith and Message (1925/1963).

54 Plantinga, Alvin, 1995, 'Pluralism: A Defense of Religious Exclusivism', in Senor, T. (ed.), *The Rationality of Belief and the Plurality of Faith*, London: Cornell University Press, pp. 191–215; D'Costa, *Meeting*.

55 Plantinga, 'Pluralism', p. 194.

56 Plantinga, 'Pluralism', p. 197.

57 Plantinga, 'Pluralism', pp. 197f.

58 D'Costa, *Meeting*, p. 22.

59 D'Costa, *Meeting*, p. 91.

60 D'Costa, *Meeting*, p. 39.

61 John Hick uses the illustration in 1973, *God and the Universe of Faiths*, Oxford: Oneworld, p. 140.

62 Newbigin, *Gospel*, pp. 9–10.

63 What about 'inclusivism'? Like pluralism, D'Costa argues that inclusivism is yet another form of exclusivism for it still claims the ultimate truth of a tradition-specific Christian metanarrative which explains all other religious traditions. Then there are the similarities between inclusivism and exclusivism in that both 'hold to the inseparability of ontology, epistemology and ethics such that truth cannot be separated from the Mediator: Christ and his church' (D'Costa, *Meeting*, p. 22). Finally, and not unlike Kraemer, D'Costa questions the logical coherence of the inclusivist claim: 'If religious traditions are properly to be considered in their unity of practice and theory, and in their organic interrelatedness, then such "totalities" cannot be simply dismembered into parts (be they doctrines, practices, images, or music) which are then taken up and "affirmed" by inclusivists, for the parts will always relate to the whole and will only take their meaning in this organic context. Hence, what is thus included from a religion being engaged with, is not really that religion *per se*, but a reinterpretation of that tradition in so much as that which is included is now included within a different paradigm, such that its meanings and

utilization within that new paradigm can only bear some analogical resemblance to its meanings and utilization within its original paradigm.' D'Costa, *Meeting*, pp. 22f.

64 Frame, John, 2006, 'Presuppositional Apologetics', in *New Dictionary of Christian Apologetics*, Leicester: IVP, p. 576.

65 For contemporary defences of an evangelical doctrine of Scripture see Jensen, Peter, 2002, *The Revelation of God*, Leicester: IVP; Carson, D., and Woodbridge, J. (eds), 1983, *Scripture and Truth*, Leicester: IVP; 1986, *Hermeneutics, Authority and Canon*, Leicester: IVP; Mathison, Keith A., 2001, *The Shape of Sola Scriptura*, Idaho: Canon Press.

66 Of course such an argument will be called 'circular' but this is unavoidable when talking about ultimate commitments.

67 The term principial originates in the sixteenth century and is defined by the OED as: '2. Chiefly *Theol.* and *Philos.* Constituting a source or origin; primary, original; basic, fundamental.'

68 The term 'antithesis' as used here does not refer to Hegelian thinking but is rather a technical theological term associated with Reformed theology and referring to the difference between believer and unbeliever.

69 Bahnsen, Greg, 1990, 'At War with the World: The Necessity of Biblical Antithesis', *Antithesis*, vol. 1.1, p. 3.

70 Turretin, Francis, 1992, *Institutes of Elenctic Theology*, vol. 1, Phillipsburg: P&R, Topic 9. Q. 6. IX.

71 See Frame, John, 2007, 'Divine Aseity and Apologetics', in Oliphint, K. Scott, and Tipton, Lane G. (eds), *Revelation and Reason: New Essays in Reformed Apologetics*, Phillipsburg: P&R, pp. 115–30.

72 Frame, John, 1994, *Apologetics to the Glory of God*, Phillipsburg: P&R, pp. 43f.

73 . . . and the only solution to that perennial philosophical conundrum.

74 Frame, *Apologetics*, p. 47.

75 Van Til, Cornelius, 1967, *The Defense of the Faith*, Phillipsburg: P&R, pp. 29f.

76 Van Til, Cornelius, 1953, 'Nature and Scripture', in Stonehouse, N. B., and Woolley, Paul (eds), *The Infallible Word: A Symposium*, Phillipsburg: P&R, p. 281.

77 Johnson, Greg, 2008, 'The Inadequacy of General Revelation for the Salvation of the Nations', quoted in Strange, Daniel, 'General Revelation: Sufficient or Insufficient' in Peterson, Robert A., and Morgan, Christopher W. (eds), *Faith By Hearing: A Response to Inclusivism*, Nottingham: Apollos. Posted at: http://gregscouch.homestead.com/files/Generalrev.html.

78 Frame, John (forthcoming), 'Ethics and the Religions', in *Doctrine of the Christian Life*. Posted at: http://reformedperspectives.org/newfiles/joh_frame/dcl5,_ethics_and_the_religions.doc. Accessed: 10/09/07.

79 Keller, Tim, 'Deconstructing Defeater Beliefs', available at: http://www.greentreewebster.org/Articles/Deconstructing%20Defeater%20Beliefs%20(Keller).pdf. Accessed: 10/09/2007.

80 Van Til, 'Nature', p. 280.

81 Gal. 5.7.

82 Van Til, Cornelius, 1974, *An Introduction to Systematic Theology*, Phillipsburg: P&R, p. 27.

83 For a classic exposition of this doctrine, see Murray, John, 1977, 'Common Grace', in *Collected Writings*, vol. 2: *Systematic Theology*, Murray, J. (ed.), Edinburgh: Banner of Truth.

84 See Strange, Daniel, 2005, 'Co-belligerence and Common Grace', *Cambridge Papers*, vol. 14.3 (September).

85 Bavinck, *Church*, p. 32.

86 Visser, Paul J., 2003, *Heart for the World: The Life and Thought of a Reformed Pioneer Missiologist Johan Herman Bavinck (1895–1964)*, Eugene: Wipf & Stock, p. 158.

87 Visser, *Heart*, p. 158.

88 Visser, *Heart*, p. 159.

89 Visser, *Heart*, p. 159.

90 Visser, *Heart*, p. 160.

91 Bavinck, J. H., 1948, *Religieus besef en christelijk geloof*, Kampen: Kok, p. 179, quoted in Visser, *Heart*, p. 146.

92 Islam and Judaism would be important examples here.

93 Kraemer, Hendrik, 1939, 'Continuity or Discontinuity', in Paton, G. (ed.), *The Authority of Faith*, London: Oxford University Press, p. 5. Can REPE speak of 'truth' in other religions? Here the answer is somewhat complex, though again Visser articulates it as well as any: 'The residues of revelation never lie hidden as petrified fossils in the soil of pseudo religion. False religion always presents itself as, and in actual fact invariably constitutes, a monolithic aggregate. Consequently, all ideas it absorbs become amalgamated with and deformed by the whole. In other words, it is not possible for isolated elements of verity, sparks of divine truth to exist in the midst of falsehood and error – in fact, if such sparks were present, they would lead to friction in and destruction of the very essence of pseudo religions' (Visser, *Heart*, p. 172).

94 For example, Crisp, Oliver, 2008, 'Karl Barth and Jonathan Edwards on reprobation (and hell)', in Gibson, David, and Strange, Daniel (eds), *Engaging with Barth: Contemporary Evangelical Critiques*, Leicester: IVP, pp. 300–22. All the essays in this book compare and critique aspects of Barth's theology to Evangelical orthodoxy. On the doctrine of hell within a Reformed theological framework see, Strange, Daniel, 2003, 'A Calvinist Response to Talbott's Universalism', in Parry, Robin, and Partridge, Chris (eds), *Universal Salvation: The Current Debate*, Carlisle: Paternoster, pp. 145–68.

95 For example, Rom. 10.9–10; Acts 4.12; John 14.6. For a detailed study of this issue see Strange, *Possibility.*

96 See Strange, 'General'.

97 It must be remembered that the judgement and punishment of unbelievers is always according to the revelation they have received. Those who have suppressed both general and special revelation will be judged more harshly than those who have received only general revelation. This appears to be the meaning behind texts like Luke 12.47–8 with its 'few blows' and 'many blows', and also Jesus' words in sending out the seventy-two in Luke 10.12, 'I tell you, on that day it will be more tolerable for Sodom than for that town.'

98 Deut. 32.31.

4

Inclusivisms: Honouring Faithfulness and Openness

DAVID CHEETHAM

Introduction

Christian inclusivism seeks to make sense of two vital features of the Christian faith: (1) the commitment to Christ as the unique and normative revelation of God, and (2) God's universal salvific will. The fact that these two aspects are crucial is an important feature of inclusivism. In this sense, it is not properly understood as a half-hearted version of pluralism or a watered-down exclusivism, rather it claims to represent a definite position that seeks to take proper account of the available evidence: biblical, experiential, historical, missiological and so on. Put simply, it represents a commitment to both the revelation of God and the heart of God. Locating inclusivism between exclusivism and pluralism in the 'classic' typology means that arguments for it tend to derive from those against the other options. The potential danger is that exclusivism and pluralism can seem to be the real alternatives, while inclusivism appears to be a brand of agnosticism. I do not think that this should be the case at all. Instead, I would argue that inclusivism includes the strengths of the other positions while addressing their respective weaknesses. Thus, exclusivism and pluralism actually represent extreme locations that typically overstress certain aspects of the debate: whether it is the 'guarding' of revelation or an 'openness' to all religions.

It is probable that inclusivism represents the mainstream view among the majority of Christians today. Statistically this is probable if only because the groundbreaking statements of Vatican II in the 1960s have meant that an inclusivist approach has achieved a normative theological status in the Roman Catholic Church. Moreover, various versions of inclusivism find expression in many denominations and Christian movements. For example, inclusivist perspectives have been adopted by a number of evangelicals, including John Sanders,[1] Clark Pinnock,[2] Gerald McDermott,[3] and the Pentecostal theologian Amos Yong.[4] Further, other famous figures in Christian history who have expressed some version of inclusivism include: Justin Martyr, Charles Wesley, John Stott and C. S. Lewis, to mention but a few.

Biblical Testimony

Without an appeal to the biblical testimony it is unlikely that any theology of religions will have much attraction for Christians themselves. Indeed, it is questionable that we can speak of a theology of religions as being properly 'Christian' if its theological proposals neglect to show their biblical credentials. Nevertheless, things are not always that clear-cut. Even if we were to seek to undertake a solely 'biblical' theology of religions then there would still be a considerable amount of debate to be had. It would be incorrect to assume that on the basis of such obvious verses as 'I am the way, and the truth, and the life. No one comes to the Father except through me' (John 14.6); or '. . . there is no other name under heaven given among mortals by which we must be saved' (Acts 4.12), that the biblical viewpoint is wholly exclusivistic. There is, of course, a very particular and unique revelation that the Bible contains; however, there is also a much richer testimony to be discerned within its pages. A complete reading of the biblical testimony seems to stress simultaneously both the particularity and the universality of God's revelation. There are the covenants addressed to the whole world – the Noahide covenant, for example – but there are also the covenants to Israel in particular. There are examples given in the Bible of the knowledge of God outside of Israel and, in the New Testament, outside the Church. Moreover, people with such knowledge are sometimes instrumental in bringing revelation to pivotal biblical characters, such as Abraham or Peter. For example, we read in Gen. 14.17–24 the story of Melchizedek, King of Salem, who blesses Abraham and receives from Abraham a tithe. Historically speaking, it is clear that Melchizedek was operating from within his own Canaanite context, with its religion and culture, and therefore referred to God as *El Elyon* ('God Most High'). Yet Abraham happily tithes to him. Moreover, in Heb. 7.17, Jesus himself is called a high priest 'in the order of Melchizedek'. Other examples of revelation 'outside' of Israel might include the striking statement issued by Darius the Mede following the deliverance of Daniel in the lions' den:

> I make a decree, that in all of my royal dominion people should tremble and fear before the God of Daniel. For he is the living God, enduring for ever. His kingdom shall never be destroyed, and his dominion has no end. He delivers and rescues, he works signs and wonders in heaven and on earth; for he has saved Daniel from the power of the lions. (Dan. 6.26–7)

How are we to interpret this and other similar statements coming from pagan rulers in the Bible? Is it a kind of 'forced' acknowledgement or is it something that represents a true revelation of God imparted by the Spirit? There may be little controversy that Darius is speaking the 'truth' here;

however, what is disputed by theologians is whether or not the kind of knowledge displayed by Darius constitutes 'salvific' knowledge of God.

A brief survey of the biblical evidence indicates another common theme: that God wants his glory to be displayed to all the peoples of the earth, not just Israel or the Church. A few examples can be found in Ex. 14.4, Isa. 37.20 and Ezek. 38.16. Although the context of such passages is speaking of God's judgement and the destruction wrought on his enemies, often the purpose is to reveal God's character to the nations and bring glory to his name. This may simply be a matter of God justly promoting his own fame, or it could also be an insight into the divine heart that desires all to understand his character and cause them to turn to him. Indeed, when Isaiah 55 speaks of the divine will to satisfy 'everyone who thirsts' (v. 1) and to '. . . call nations that you do not know' (v. 5), God reminds the hearer that: '". . . my thoughts are not your thoughts, nor are your ways my ways," says the Lord' (55.8).[5]

In the Gospels we see Jesus doing and saying things that stretch the religious boundaries or expectations of his hearers and critics. While denigrating the 'legitimate' religious authorities of his day, he deliberately praises the better moral display of the foreign Samaritan in the story of the Good Samaritan (Luke 10.25–37). He singles out the faith of a Canaanite woman, saying 'Woman, great is your faith!' (Matt. 15.28). Following his dramatic reading from Isaiah in the synagogue, Jesus declares that a prophet is never accepted in his home town and he then makes a point of reminding his hearers that Elijah was sent not to the widows of Israel but to the widow of Zarephath in Sidon, and it was only Naaman the Syrian who was cleansed of his leprosy (Luke 4.24–7). Moreover, when confronted with the faith of a Roman centurion, Jesus declares: 'I tell you, not even in Israel have I found such faith' (Luke 7.9). Of the ten who were healed of leprosy, only the Samaritan returned to give thanks (Luke 17.11–19). And so on. If anything is revealed by Jesus' earthly ministry it is his strong dislike for a form of religious correctness that draws a legalistic line around God's sovereign right to communicate with whoever he chooses.

When we consider the narratives of Acts, we see further evidence of a more inclusivistic picture. The non-Christian Gentile Cornelius is singled out as 'an upright and God-fearing man' (Acts 10.22). Cornelius and his family are used to help Peter realize that 'God shows no partiality, but in every nation anyone who fears him and does what is right is acceptable to him' (Acts 10.34, 35). In Acts 17, Paul addresses the people on the Areopagus in Athens and, while recognizing the idolatry that surrounds him, draws attention to one particular altar with the inscription: 'To an unknown God'. He then declares: 'What therefore you worship as unknown, this I proclaim to you' (17.23). Here, the inference seems to be that there is continuity between the unknown deity of the Greeks and Paul's understanding of God. Paul sees his task as providing further knowledge (salvific knowledge) about the God they already worship. Moreover, this appears to be consistent with Paul's writing in Rom. 1.18–32, where he makes it clear that 'what can be known about God is plain' (19), so much so that 'they are without excuse' (20). Here Paul is speaking about what he sees as self-evident about creation itself. In other places, we read about the desire of God to reach all people, in the New Testament. For example: '. . . God our Saviour, who desires everyone to be saved and to come to the knowledge of the truth' (1 Tim. 2.3–4); or, 'The Lord . . . is patient with you, not wanting any to perish, but all to come to repentance' (2 Peter 3.9).

Logos and Fulfilment

Perhaps the most significant passage – certainly one of the most referenced – in the New Testament for the theology of religions is the prologue of John's Gospel. 'In him was life, and the life was the light of men' (John 1.4). 'The true light, which enlightens everyone, was coming into the world' (v. 9). It is this passage that inspires one of the earliest church fathers, Justin Martyr (c. 100–165 CE), to formulate a view that has become a precursor to much subsequent inclusivistic thought.[6] Justin interpreted the *logos* as something that was dispersed like 'seed' into the world – such that wherever reason[7] was exercised, this was the work of the *logos*. In one place, he writes in such a way that strongly prefigures the thinking of the Roman Catholic inclusivist thinker Karl Rahner, in the twentieth century. Thus, according to Justin:

> We are taught that Christ is the first-born of God, and [. . .] he is the Word of whom all humanity has a share, and those who lived according to the Logos (*hoi meta logou biosantes*) are therefore Christians, even though they were regarded as atheists; among Greeks, Socrates, and Heraclitus; and among non-Greeks, Abraham, Ananias, Azanus, and Misad, and Elias, and many others.[8]

This use of the term *logos* in early Christian thinking at once connected Christian philosophy to Greek concepts and showed a sense of continuity with the broader intellectual context of the times. This also highlights something that is so obvious that it is often overlooked: Christians throughout history have been actively involved in situating or incarnating the Christian message within the different cultural and intellectual contexts in which they find themselves. This is not so much a question of 'selling-out' to a particular culture's agenda (although there are dangers for theologians here), but rather involves a sort of intellectual and cultural inclusivism or appropriation. We see this clearly, for example, in two of the greatest figures in Christian intellectual history: Augustine (354–430) with his substantial absorption of Neoplatonism, and Thomas Aquinas (1225–74) with his great synthesis of Christian and Aristotelian thinking. In such cases, prevailing philosophies have been essentially 'baptized' and have helped to sharpen the articulation of Christian thought and shape its systematic development. In later European Christian history we see this again in the way that humanism and the Renaissance spirit in the fifteenth and sixteenth centuries influenced the Reformers. Without beginning to exhaust possible examples, we might also think of a whole range of other intellectual developments and movements such as scientific rationalism, existentialism, Marxism, postcolonialism or postmodernism which have been used to develop Christian discourse. Related to this, of course, is the appropriation of the literature, poetry, art and music of particular cultures to help in the expression of the gospel. Drawing inspiration from sources outside the explicitly Christian 'text' is something that has been and is routinely carried out by Christian thinkers (and preachers) from across the theological spectrum.

In the eighteenth century, the founder of the Methodist movement, John Wesley (1703–91), adopted a seemingly inclusivist (or tolerant) attitude that stemmed from a combination of Arminian theology, notions of prevenient grace and the emphasis on a life of holiness. Wesley would often hold up the examples of virtuous behaviour in non-Christian religions in order to shame Christians into living more holy lives.[9] This attitude produced some interesting statements from Wesley: 'I believe the merciful God regards the lives and tempers of men more than their ideas. I believe He respects the goodness of the heart rather than the clearness of the head.'[10] This does not mean that Wesley was engaging in a full-blown inclusivist theology of religions, rather it inspired in him a certain agnosticism with regard to the place of other faiths. In a significant passage, he says:

> According to that sentence, 'he that believeth not shall be damned,' is spoken to them whom gospel is preached. Others it does not concern; and we are not required to determine anything touching their final state. How will it please God, the judge of all, to deal with them, we may leave to God himself. But this we know, that he is not the God of Christians only, but the God of the heathens also; that he is rich in mercy to all that call upon him, according to the light they have and that 'in every nation he that feareth God and worketh righteousness is accepted of him.'[11]

Such a broad and generous view stems from Wesley's rejection of the separation of nature from grace in Reformation theology. Instead, Wesley emphasizes prevenient grace. This is grace that has 'gone before', that is present and working everywhere, and which prepares people to receive the gospel. Moreover, this is a grace that is the power behind all good works – even those found among the 'virtuous pagans'.

Long before the development of the 'theology of religions' as a discipline in the twentieth century, we see a diversity of approaches taken by Christian missionaries to the issue of contextualization and indigenization. Some took an uncompromising stance and only drew attention to idolatry and error in the religions they encountered. Others sought to adopt methods of inculturation. For example, in the sixteenth century, the Italian Jesuit Matteo Ricci (1552–1610) served as a missionary in China and sought to present his message in Buddhist and Confucian garb; similarly, Roberto di Nobili (1577–1656) hoped to appeal to the brahminical Hindus and employed sanskrit terms in his apologetic – even dressing in the saffron robes of a high caste Hindu priest.

Later on in the nineteenth century, the increased attentiveness to indigenous cultures and the encounter with devout Hindus, Muslims and Buddhists meant that the place of other faiths in the scheme of salvation became an important issue. At the same time, there was a desire to maintain a commitment to the uniqueness and finality of Christ. The combination of these concerns gave rise to the idea of 'fulfilment'. Fulfilment theology, although not his invention, became particularly associated with the Scottish missionary and indologist J. N. Farquhar (1861–1929). Farquhar's book *The Crown of Hinduism* (1913) has become a classic in inclusivist literature.[12] His thought in this book reflects the dominance of the evolutionary paradigm at the beginning of the twentieth century. Thus, Christ was portrayed as the pinnacle of religion: the 'crown of Hinduism'. In saying this Farquhar was being consistent with his evolutionary and 'science of religion' approach. It wasn't just that Christianity was implicitly present in Hinduism; rather Christianity supremely solved a universal religious impulse. All religions contain comparative elements found in all other religions, but these elements are wholly satisfied in Christianity. Thus, Christianity could fulfil all religions (not just Hinduism) by fulfilling the 'universal' human religious need.[13] Methodologically, Farquhar was following a 'science of religion' or a 'history of religions' approach. Thus, Christianity is presented as

> the fulfilment of all that is aimed at in Hinduism, as the satisfaction of the spiritual yearnings of her people, as the crown and climax of the crudest form of her worship as well as those lofty spiritual movements which have so often appeared in Hinduism but have always ended in weakness [. . .] The theory [of fulfilment] thus satisfied the science of religion to the uttermost, while conserving the supremacy of Christ.[14]

Farquhar was not developing a deep *logos* theology. Paul Hedges points out that Farquhar was not a sophisticated theologian as such and in fact had a 'straightforward faith'.[15] Nevertheless, in a classic theological statement, he says that: 'In Him [Christ] is focussed every ray of light that shines in Hinduism.'[16] His work had an important influence on missionary thought in the few decades after the publication of *The Crown of Hinduism*; however, by the time of the world missionary conference in Tambaram (1938), his fulfilment approach had been eclipsed by the exclusivistic perspective of the Dutch theologian Hendrik Kraemer (1888–1965). Kraemer's thesis presents a fundamental challenge to fulfilment and inclusivist theologies in general because it stresses the 'discontinuity' between religions and their basic intratextuality. In an important passage, he writes:

> Every religion is a living, indivisible unity. Every part of it – a dogma, a rite, a myth, an institution, a cult – is so vitally related to the whole that it can never be understood in its real function, significance and tendency, as these occur in the reality of life, without keeping constantly in mind the vast and living unity of existential apprehension in which this part moves and has its being.[17]

Thus, the idea of trying to distil universals in the phenomenon of religion, or trace some common themes, is undermined by Kraemer's reasoning. However, even if he is correct that we must take the contexts of beliefs and their systems into account, we might question whether his emphasis on discontinuity really eliminates the possibility of some commonalities between traditions being discerned. To draw absolute distinctions between traditions is unlikely given our common humanity. Nevertheless, there is also the question of whether or not Farquhar's fulfilment ideas, in particular, have created an idealized form of Hinduism that has been shaped by his prior Christian and 'evolutionary' allegiances. Has Farquhar ended up creating, in the words of one Hindu critic, a 'monolithic and homogenized Hinduism'?[18]

Vatican II and Karl Rahner

The most pivotal event in the twentieth century for relations between the Roman Catholic Church and other religions was the Second Vatican Council (1962–5). The following quote from *Nostra Aetate* (NA) ushered in a new era:

> The Catholic Church rejects nothing that is true and holy in these religions. She has a high regard for the manner of life and conduct, the precepts and doctrines which, although different in many ways from her own teaching, nevertheless often reflect a ray of that truth which enlightens all men. (NA 2)

Echoing Justin Martyr eighteen centuries earlier, another document *Ad Gentes* (AG) spoke of the 'seeds of the Word' (AG 11, 15) in the world's religions. This leads to the following practical consequences for Christians: 'Let Christians, while witnessing to their own faith and way of life, acknowledge, preserve and encourage the spiritual and moral truths found among non-Christians, also their social life and culture' (NA 2). Nevertheless, in *Nostra Aetate* an important proviso is added: 'Yet she [the Church] proclaims and is in duty bound to proclaim without fail, Christ who is the way, the truth and the life (John 14.6)' (NA 2). Taking his inspiration from such statements, the inclusivist evangelical Clark Pinnock categorizes them as a 'cautious inclusivism'.[19] The reason is that the Vatican II documents, despite their positive reading of other faiths, do not necessarily endorse the view that non-Christian religions provide the structure of salvation in their traditions or possess a 'salvific' status. Rather, the documents stop short of affirming this. As Paul Knitter puts it, these 'rays of truth' are not 'ways of salvation'.[20] Instead, the conciliar statements merely praise whatever is true and holy – similar to Paul's exhortation to dwell on 'whatever is true, whatever is noble, whatever is right, whatever is pure, whatever is lovely, whatever is admirable . . .' (Phil. 4.8).

Vatican II was influenced by the contribution of the German Jesuit Karl Rahner (1904–84) (although the Council did not go as far as Rahner when it came to seeing other religions as being capable of saving their members). In order to understand the approach of Rahner, it is important to grasp something of his anthropology. It is a rich anthropology that is quite unique in terms of its theological and intellectual development. First, Rahner thinks that all of humanity is related to God because the presence of God is already deep within the unconscious. Paradoxically, it is more natural for a human person to be 'supernatural' than it is for them to be purely natural. The Spirit of God is already in close communion with every human being. Rahner writes: 'God . . . has already communicated himself in his Holy Spirit always and everywhere and in every person as the innermost center of his existence.'[21] Additionally, God's presence in a human person is already ahead of the person's self-awareness. The Rahner scholar Karen Kilby puts this very well when she writes:

> On Rahner's account we are, whether we realize it or not, already related to God [. . .] Being related to God is so much part of our structure, if Rahner is to be believed, that it is not possible properly to describe what it is to love, or what it is to will or even to think, in a perfectly ordinary, human way, without bringing God into the description.[22]

In an analogy that Rahner uses himself, it is as if God is the 'horizon' that is the point of reference that guides our understanding and apprehension of the world. It lurks at the background of our perceptions, even in the encounter with everyday things. Our 'supernature' naturally reaches beyond our perception of ordinary things. This natural 'supernature' is intimately connected to God's universal presence. Rahner's word for this presence is 'grace', by which he means God's 'self-communication'. He writes: 'Grace

[. . .] always surrounds man, even the sinner and the unbeliever, as the inescapable setting of his existence.'[23] With such anthropology, it is hardly surprising that Rahner's perspective is an open one with regard to human religiosity in general. However, it is important to see that Rahner's understanding has emerged from his reflection on what it is to be a human being rather than his encounter with other religions in particular.

Nevertheless, as well as seeking to present the universal aspect of God's revelation, Rahner wishes to stress the particular aspects. Although he wants to reconcile the exclusivistic expression of Christianity with God's universal love for all humankind, he is clear that this universal aspect is explicitly revealed in Christ. He is committed to a Trinitarian perspective: thus, the God encountered in other religions is not the God of the philosophers which is an abstract deity; rather, it is the Christian God.

In the fifth volume of his *Theological Investigations*, Rahner organizes his thinking around four 'theses' which set out his inclusivist position. In the first thesis, he states his foundations: 'Christianity understands itself as the absolute religion intended for all men, which cannot recognize any other religion beside itself as of equal right.'[24] As with the Protestant thinker Karl Barth (1886–1968), Rahner begins by clearly stating his commitment to Christianity as 'absolute'. This is an important starting point for Rahner because it identifies that his theology of religions, however expansive and universal in other respects, remains rooted in a firm commitment to the normativity of the Christian revelation. However, Rahner adds the caveat that we must also consider the fact that Christianity has a historical starting point. Thus, he writes: 'Nevertheless, the Christian religion as such has a beginning in history; it did not always exist but began at some point in time.'[25] Despite Christianity's absolute status, those who lived before Christ as well as those who are currently outside the historical or geographical scope of the proclamation of the gospel are not necessarily understood to reside in total darkness. Thus, Christianity is a 'historical quantity'.[26] Although the revelation of Christ is absolute, this revelation is set in the context of time and place.

Rahner's second thesis contains the most important details concerning his inclusivism:

> Until the moment when the Gospel really enters into the historical situation of an individual, a non-Christian religion (even outside the Mosaic religion) does not merely contain elements of a natural knowledge of God, elements, moreover, mixed up with human depravity which is the result of original sin and later aberrations. It contains also supernatural elements arising out of the grace which is given to men as a gratuitous gift on account of Christ. For this reason a non-Christian religion can be recognized as a lawful religion (although only in different degrees) without thereby denying the error and depravity contained in it.[27]

In order to appreciate the significance of what Rahner means by lawful religion, it is important to understand that, for Rahner, religion takes on a social form. Being religious is not an isolated individual act, rather it includes a 'social constitution'. In fact, Rahner is clear that religion 'can exist only in a social form'. Moreover, human beings are compelled (or 'commanded') to 'seek and accept a social form of religion'.[28] Thus, he describes lawful religions as legitimate institutional forms that can be used by people at certain periods of time and represent a 'positive means' of entering into a relationship with God. Rahner goes as far as to state that lawful religions are vehicles 'for the attaining of salvation, a means which is therefore positively included in God's plan of salvation'.[29] Thus, as we indicated earlier, he sees religions as salvific and it is this that separates his inclusivism from other more cautious types which, while acknowledging that people may obtain salvation despite being members of other religions, hesitate when it comes to recognizing the religious structures themselves. However, although he does not (as Barth might) draw attention to stark contrasts between Christian revelation and human religion, we see in the second thesis that Rahner does not embrace non-Christian religions in an undiscerning way. In this sense, he is only suggesting that salvation in other religions is possible, not necessarily guaranteed. Thus, he is clear about the mixture of light and darkness, grace and sin that exist in religion. However, his anthropology means that he is not as adamant as Barth about religion being 'unbelief'. As religions possess 'grace-filled' elements they are recognized as already containing the presence of God and the gospel encounters them in that condition. Thus, in a now famous phrase, Rahner's third thesis argues that we should see a member of a non-Christian religion as an 'anonymous Christian'.[30] This anonymity is connected to Rahner's ideas about our basic humanity as supernatural. Thus, as we said a moment ago, it is important to recognize that he is not making a direct phenomenological observation or judgement on other religions as such.

If 'grace' is present in all of creation and anonymously in other religions, then we might think that this makes the Church redundant in Rahner's inclusivist scheme. Nevertheless, consistent with his picture, Rahner sees the Church as the peak of the grace that is already present everywhere. So, in his fourth thesis, he speaks of the Church as the 'historically tangible vanguard and the historically and socially constituted *explicit* expression'[31] of the full revelation of God. Indeed, once the fullness of the gospel is heard, anonymous Christianity should be transformed into an explicit profession of Christian faith. Rahner does not consider anonymous Christianity to represent an adequate substitute once the gospel has been encountered and understood.

Criticisms of Rahner's position have come from both exclusivist and pluralist positions. First of all, from the exclusivist side, has Rahner safeguarded the uniqueness of salvation in Christ? The criticism here is that the distinctive historical and concrete picture of grace as evidenced in Jesus of Nazareth is abstracted beyond recognition in Rahner's view of 'graced nature'. Despite Rahner's desire to uphold a high Christology, its fullness is muted in his universal scheme. He has reduced the particularity of the presence of the Christian God into an abstracted subjectivity. In fact, Hans Küng wonders if Rahner has just elegantly swept all those of 'good-will' through the back door and into the Church. If this is the case, Küng argues, then we are faced with the problem of 'making the Church equivalent to the world'.[32] Moreover, if the 'light' is said to be everywhere then there is the potential for this to diminish the impact of the Church which is said to bring the light.[33]

Furthermore, if we consider soteriological questions, we might ask: What is the connection between salvation 'in Christ' and the 'salvation' experienced anonymously in other contexts? This concerns the uniqueness of salvation in Christ and the need for an explicit 'new birth'. Is there any need to experience Christianity at all if it is already anonymously present in other religions? Rahner seeks to address this issue when he speaks of a distinction between incomplete and complete revelation. A moment ago, in his fourth thesis, we saw that the Church was seen as the 'explicit expression' of Christianity. So, we can see that anonymous Christianity is not something that Rahner is advancing as a wholly satisfactory state. In fact, Jacques Dupuis describes Rahner's attitude as follows: 'anonymous Christianity remains a fragmentary, incomplete, radically crippled reality'.[34]

This obscuring of the particularity of Christ makes Rahner's inclusivistic picture vulnerable not just to an exclusivist critique but also to the pluralist's call to move away from inclusivism and towards a full-blown pluralism. Put simply, is it worth holding on to an abstracted Christ at all? It is questionable that there is any meaning to be found in determining that all religious experience, despite its diversity, is somehow ontologically rooted in 'grace'. Such an inclusivist strategy may be weak (or presumptuous) when it comes to a phenomenological description or explanation of the varieties of religious experience. In this connection, the pluralist philosopher John Hick compares the Christian inclusivist hermeneutic with the futile attempts in sixteenth-century Europe to compatibilize a discredited Ptolemaic view with the astronomical data when the Copernican view would have been a much better explanation.[35] Thus, the pluralist urges us to step beyond our allegedly 'Ptolemaic' theological commitments and speak in what might be called proper abstracts like 'inner reality', 'common spirituality', 'depth experience', 'cosmic feeling', 'the Real' . . . or whatever. Nevertheless, is this really an advance beyond inclusivism at all? Ostensibly, the pluralist has escaped the gravity of particular religions in order to gain an overall perspective on the universe of faiths that does not privilege any particular religious tradition. However, is such an 'overall' perspective attainable and don't we just end up occupying a particular location ('the view from above/outside') after all? In fact, the idea of standing above the action, so to speak, has been severely criticized and it seems possible to argue that the main exponents of pluralism are really just expressing another kind of perspective in their own right. Following a postmodern critique, some scholars have sought to identify this perspective as 'liberal modernism', which, rather than reflecting a more neutral stance, actually betrays a commitment to the ideals set out in the European Enlightenment.[36] Whether this is correct or not, the crucial point being made is that even the pluralist has a 'history' and a set of 'commitments'. In addition, it seems clear that in order for the pluralist perspective to have a tangible consequence in the world of religion it is forced to reinterpret various truth-claims in religions that conflict with each other. This should indicate very clearly that a pluralist position, like the inclusivism it rejects, must impose its own hermeneutical strategy onto the religious landscape.

Inclusivism and Difference

Rahner was more concerned with making sense of an *a priori* commitment to Christ and the universal grace of God than with interpreting 'difference'. In addition, his inclusivism is clearly not intended as a viewpoint to further interreligious dialogue as such, rather it is a conversation between Christians themselves. Nevertheless, Rahner gets into trouble over his tendency to assume that a similar kind of (anonymous) religious experience is going on in all religions. It is highly problematic to talk of a generic kind of salvation. Instead, salvation is a Christian-specific notion. For example, St Paul, rather than talking of some kind of abstract transcendent state, speaks of Christians 'being transformed into the same [Jesus'] image' (2 Cor. 3.18). There is also the broader point that when we look at the sheer diversity of religions in the world, we can observe that the goals appear to be different. This is one of the criticisms that inclusivist theologians have sought to address in the decades following Rahner's landmark contribution.

One strategy has been to try to concentrate less on ideas of the hidden Christ, or the *logos*, and develop theologies of the Spirit instead. Here the intention is to move toward more open interpretations of 'other' religious experiences that do not depend so heavily on christocentric formulations. This resolution is quite tricky as it is not so easy (certainly not for the 'Latin' Church with its *filioque* commitment) to view the Spirit and the Word as distinct 'economies' (along the lines that St Irenaeus described as the 'two hands of God'). In the final analysis, most theologians who have sought to develop the potential of a pneumatological approach (however nuanced) have decided to interpret the Spirit's activity as working within a single economy of salvation.

A Roman Catholic theologian, Gavin D'Costa prefers to speak of 'fulfilment' as a two-way process rather than being a matter of one religion 'crowning' all the aspects of the other.[37] The Spirit pervades all the creation and 'the wind blows wherever it pleases' (John 3.8); thus we should expect that the Spirit moves in other religions. D'Costa maintains that this will lead to 'surprising' new insights from the Spirit in our encounter with people of different faiths, and Christians should therefore be faithful by listening attentively to what the Spirit says in these contexts.[38] Moreover, the priority should be given to a religion's 'auto-interpretation' (self-interpretation) before any legitimate 'hetero-interpretation' can take place, and this can lead to genuinely new insights.[39] Nevertheless, he adds the caveat that what the Spirit reveals, however surprising, will not ultimately be contrary to the revelation in Christ.[40]

Stretching inclusivism to its limits (some think too far), another Roman Catholic figure, Jacques Dupuis, does not wish to place a hermeneutical straitjacket onto other faiths. Similar to D'Costa, he prefers to speak of 'mutual complementarity'; he also seeks to extend the autonomy of the Spirit. Thus, he argues that although 'Pneumatocentrism and Christocentrism cannot . . . be construed as two separate economies of salvation',[41] the Spirit might be involved in very different 'revelations' in addition to (but not contradicting) the revelation of Christ. Although he thinks that we cannot separate the Spirit and the Word and make them responsible for two distinct economies of salvation, one must not forget that the Christian trinitarian picture is also meant to reveal the distinctiveness of the divine persons. Thus, in an important passage, he suggests that other religions are not just 'stepping stones' towards the Christian revelation, but 'represent additional and autonomous benefits'. Furthermore, he claims that 'more divine truth and grace are found operative in the entire history of God's dealings with humankind than are available simply in the Christian tradition'.[42] Although Dupuis's suggestions are among some of the most refined and carefully nuanced that one can find, some critics still feel that he has not gone far enough in developing a pneumatology which allows the Spirit a greater autonomy from a christocentric foundation.[43] In fact, there are passages in his major work, *Towards a Christian Theology of Religious Pluralism* (1997), where he explicitly cautions against the idea of devising distinct economies for the Spirit and the Word.[44] Thus, does he really succeed in speaking about the 'autonomous benefits' of other religions?

Within the evangelical/charismatic traditions, two theologians have attempted to develop inclusivist theologies of religions which have a pneumatological focus. They are Clark Pinnock and, more recently, Amos Yong. Pinnock's theology is deeply concerned to convey the 'wideness of God's mercy' and it is this that provokes his inclusivist perspective. If we view the Spirit as the universal 'presence' of God in creation (within the context of the distinctive roles assigned to persons in the Trinity), then Pinnock expects the Spirit to be 'present and make himself felt (at least occasionally) in the religious dimension of cultural life'.[45] Thus, he expresses the hope that other religions may have also been touched by the Spirit. Amos Yong, seeking to exploit a distinctively Pentecostal perspective, argues that the main 'impasse' in the theology of religions has been its concentration on purely christocentric points of departure. Instead, while ultimately respecting christological criteria, he develops a pneumatological theology that gives a greater emphasis on the discrete economy of the Spirit. He seeks to place the spiritual practice of 'discernment' at the centre of the theology of religions. Discerning the work of the Spirit in other religions (before returning to a christological base) will lead to a 'thoroughly reconstructed Christian theology that will have passed over onto the other faiths and returned home transformed in such a way as to be able to speak the gospel more effectively in a world context'.[46] Yong attempts to go further than some others with the possibilities for a pneumatological theology of religions. He suggests that a 'robust sense of discernment' is required in order to take account of the 'interconnectedness' and 'complexity' of human experience: something he calls the 'hermeneutics of life'.[47] His criteria for discernment are divine presence (truth, goodness, beauty and holiness . . .), divine absence (evil, falseness, ugliness and the demonic . . .) and divine activity (the continuous or evolving historical movement of things either towards or away from their 'divinely instituted reason for being').[48] Some critics have suggested that such criteria might be a little too vague;[49] however, although Yong is seeking to 'stretch' his criteria, he also makes it clear that he is concerned to remain faithful to the gospel of Christ.

Even though his thinking is ultimately underpinned by a trinitarian ontology, the North American theologian S. Mark Heim presents his thesis as a more authentic 'pluralistic' view. He seeks to highlight the 'plenitude' that originates in the relations between members of the Trinity and reflects the divine fullness. The expression of this fullness is a 'plenitude that results when creation's freedom is worked out in the realization of a variety of religious ends'.[50] Thus, as well as communion with the triune God, there are many different ways of relating to God – impersonal as well as personal – and this should cause us to recognize the real possibility of alternative religious ends. This is in contrast to the stark labelling of other religious goals as simply 'wrong' or anonymously the same. He argues that when 'humans choose less than all God offers, it does not mean they choose nothing that God desires. This is the extraordinary mystery and wonder of the divine providence.'[51] The result is a theology of religions that, while seeking to hold on to a Christian trinitarian perspective, highlights the differences between traditions.

Heim argues that the basic mistake made by some more pluralistic theologies of religions is to assume that 'salvation' is some kind of constant. He notes: 'In expositions of pluralist theologies of religion by their primary advocates, one word never appears in the plural: salvation.'[52] Thus, rather

Kiblinger remarks that if the interpretation of the other religion 'is no longer recognizable to its home members, what is going on is no longer really inclusivism, for something foreign is remade so that it is no longer very foreign . . . only a pretense of interest in what is different remains'.[57]

Rather than this kind of objection representing an embargo on 'inclusivist' interpreting, it suggests that dialogue must become an essential activity where authentic 'voices' can be heard and conversations between faiths developed. It is extremely important when meeting people of other faiths to allow them to be understood – to the fullest extent possible – on their own terms before attempting to reflect on things from within a Christian perspective. Kiblinger, again, rightly speaks of an 'engaged inclusivism': learning the other's experiences and texts on their own terms before seeing where they fit in one's own schema or how they might nourish one's own religion. Thus, '*Respect*, for . . . [engaged] inclusivists, is less about acceptance than it is about sincere open consideration and the pursuit of accurate understanding.'[58]

Nevertheless, although having an 'accurate understanding' is important, this does not mean that such understanding should be definitive or, even, rigid. Sometimes it is important for people to hear other readings of their beliefs – perhaps viewed through the particular lenses of 'outsiders'. This means that we should not always rely on interpretations that are the guarded products of 'closed communities' or our own isolated belief structures. Instead of being a form of hermeneutical 'violence', being able to give and receive different readings of each other's texts and traditions can be a healthy activity. In addition, rather than being patronizing, one might even view inclusivism as an act of generosity instead. Drawing attention to Donald Davidson's 'principle of charity',[59] Bruce Marshall seeks to apply this to Christian interpretations of the other:

> Charity about truth shapes the interpretation of whatever discourse the Christian community encounters; the goal of interpretation is to find a way of understanding that discourse which allows it to be held true, that is, to find a place for it within the world or 'domain of meaning' opened by the scriptural text.[60]

Thus, the effort to find ways of affirming and including the 'rays of truth' in other religions is to exercise charity towards them. It is an open gesture that seeks out the best in the other (and the other's well-being) within one's own narrative. The point is that, even if an interpretation of the other is being made, the motivation is not to condescend but to embrace. Furthermore, is it possible that the accusation of being patronizing to others emerges from a sort of cultural-identity politics that presents cultural authenticity or 'sovereignty' as one of the highest (and most sacrosanct) of virtues? But, given the fluid dynamics that govern how cultural identities are actually formed and how different traditions have historically interacted with each other, this seems a rather restrictive kind of objection. It is surely the case that cultures and traditions have always been cross-fertilizing, interpreting, dialoguing and criticizing each other as a matter of course. Moreover, one suspects that the dynamism behind this particular criticism of inclusivism stems from a commitment to the kind of religious epistemology that privileges a more experiential model of religious knowledge. Of course, if our religious knowledge is largely the product of our experiencing, or as one pluralist writer puts it – human responses to the transcendent[61] – then seeking to include the other in one's own perspective is bound to appear somewhat patronizing. However, if other more 'revelatory' models of religious knowledge are adopted then it is entirely appropriate to seek to work out our theologies in accordance with these models.

Humanly speaking, it seems unrealistic to suppose that people are not going to bring some sort of *a priori* interpretation and commitment to their conversations with the other. This is something that occurs in most religious traditions: it occurs when Muslims speak of a person 'reverting' to Islam, it occurs when Pure Land Buddhists speak of the buddha-nature as a potentiality in all beings, it occurs when Advaita Vedantic Hindus say something like 'all rivers flow into the same ocean'. This author can remember attending an interfaith group in Birmingham when the new Sikh chairperson introduced his inaugural speech by magnanimously welcoming all those present as fellow 'Sikhs'! If we acknowledge that this kind of perspective is adopted by many religions and reflects human epistemic limitation, then it is hard to understand what exactly is the nature of the offence.

As we have said, a listening process is crucial if we are to gain an accurate understanding of other religions. Nevertheless, although one may be encouraged to aim to listen to others and respect difference, it can never be realistically assumed that our knowledge of the other is entirely value-free or disinterested. As one writer puts it: 'There is no theological helicopter that can help us to rise above all religions and look down upon the terrain below in lofty condescension.'[62] Furthermore, it is surely a questionable educational practice to give the impression that one could obtain an unreachable (and impractical) epistemological location. Instead, combined with the acknowledgement of human limitation, we should encourage a realistic learning narrative of 'positive inclusion'. Our learning objectives might be motivated by a desire to understand, organize and assimilate towards a positive or constructive purpose. It is important that we recognize our own standpoints, allegiances and loyalties in order that, rather than seeking to conceal or dispel them, we may learn to handle them positively and responsibly – with others in mind.

Conclusion

As we said at the beginning of this chapter, Christian inclusivism is not just about successfully performing a theological balancing act. Nor is it just a kind of theological compromise designed to help its advocates maintain friendships in both exclusivist and pluralist camps! Rather, Christian inclusivism is about giving a full account of the Christian message and vision: sustaining a commitment to the normative revelation of Christ as well as making sense of God's universal loving purposes. Moreover, because it seeks to utilize a particularly Christian discourse it can release the imagination of those within the Christian tradition in order to provoke the kind of gift-love required to meet those of other faiths in a generous and self-sacrificial spirit. This is about finding the narrative resources from within one's own religious tradition and about how one might view oneself viewing other religions. So, from within the Christian tradition, knowing the relational God of love allows one to see others as God sees them: as made in his image, as loved from eternity, as part of God's plan of salvation. Moreover, for the Christian, it is Christ who exemplifies the self-emptying attitude that seeks to submit to others and consider others greater than oneself. Rather than attempting to exercise an abstract and sterilized 'good will', one is compelled to engage generously with religious others knowing that relating to them in self-emptying love is ontologically necessary because it is rooted in the relating God.

Study Questions

1 John 1.9: 'The true light, which enlightens everyone, was coming into the world.' Discuss the significance of this verse for the theology of religions.

2 Think about Rahner's four theses. Do you think that his ideas are useful for interreligious encounter?

3 Some recent attempts to respect the differences between religions within an inclusivist framework have attempted to utilize the concept of the Trinity (for example, Dupuis, D'Costa, Pinnock, Yong, Heim). What do you think are some of the problems associated with these strategies?

Further Reading

Dupuis, Jacques, 1997, *Toward a Christian Theology of Religious Pluralism*, Maryknoll: Orbis.
Farquhar, John Nicol, 1930 [1913], *The Crown of Hinduism*, London: Humphrey Milford and Oxford University Press.
Hedges, Paul, 2001, *Preparation and Fulfilment: A History and Study of Fulfilment Theology in Modern British Thought in the Indian Context*, Bern: Peter Lang.
Heim, S. Mark, 2001, *The Depth of the Riches: A Trinitarian Theology of Religious Ends*, Grand Rapids: Eerdmans.
Kärkkäinen, Veli-Matti, 2004, *Trinity and Religious Pluralism: The Doctrine of the Trinity in Christian Theology of Religions*, Aldershot: Ashgate.
Panikkar, Raimundo, 1981, *The Unknown Christ of Hinduism*, rev. edn, Maryknoll: Orbis.
Pinnock, Clark, 1992, *A Wideness in God's Mercy: The Finality of Jesus Christ in the World of Religions*, Grand Rapids: Zondervan.
Rahner, Karl, 1966, 'Christianity and Non-Christian Religions', *Theological Investigations*, vol. 5: *Later Writings*, Kruger, K. H. (trans.), London and New York: DLT and Seabury Press.
Rahner, Karl, 1979, 'Anonymous and Explicit Faith', in *Theological Investigations*, vol. 16, Morland, David (trans.), London: DLT.
Yong, Amos, 2003, *Beyond the Impasse: Toward a Pneumatological Theology of Religions*, Grand Rapids: Baker Academic.

Notes

1 See Sanders, John, 1994, *No Other Name? Can Only Christians be Saved?* London: SPCK.

2 See Pinnock, Clark, 1992, *The Wideness of God's Mercy: The Finality of Jesus Christ in the World of Religions*, Grand Rapids: Zondervan.

3 See McDermott, Gerald, 2000, *Can Evangelicals Learn from World Religions? Jesus, Revelation and Religious Traditions*, Downers Grove: IVP.

4 See Yong, Amos, 2003, *Beyond the Impasse: Toward a Pneumatological Theology of Religions*, Grand Rapids: Baker Academic.

5 John Sanders makes a similar point: 1995, 'Inclusivism', in Sanders, John (ed.), *What About Those Who Have Never Heard? Three Views on the Destiny of the Unevangelised*, Downers Grove: IVP, p. 26.

6 Even if the notion of 'inclusivism' as a specific designate within the theology of religions has emerged recently, it certainly appears that the broad ideas associated with inclusivism have been present since patristic times. Wolfhart Pannenberg goes so far as to suggest that exclusivism 'looks more like a later constriction imposed upon an originally broader attitude': 1992, 'Religious Pluralism and Conflicting Truth Claims: The Problem of a Theology of the World Religions', in D'Costa, Gavin (ed.), *Christian Uniqueness Reconsidered: The Myth of a Pluralistic Theology of Religions*, Maryknoll: Orbis, p. 99.

7 In Greek thinking, *logos* is usually associated with rationality or logic. For example, the Stoics associated *logos* with the source of rationality.

8 Justin, *Apologia*, I.xlvi.2–3, in 1987, *Saint Justin: Apologies*, Wartelle, Andre (ed.), Paris: Etudes Augustiniennes, 160.1–10, cited in McGrath, Alistair, 1995, *The Christian Theology Reader*, Oxford: Blackwell, p. 320.

9 He laments: 'Are Christians any better than other men? Are they better than Mahometans or Heathens? To say the truth, it is well if they are not worse; worse either than Mahometans or Heathens' (1996, 'Sermon 116', in *The Complete Works of John Wesley*, The Ages Digital Library Collections, vol. 7, Albany: Ages Software, p. 317, cited in Miles, R. L., 2000, 'John Wesley as Interreligious Resource: Would you Take This Man to an Interfaith Dialogue?', in Forward, Martin, *et al.* (eds), *A Great Commission*, Bern: Peter Lang, p. 70). Miles's piece provides an excellent overview of Wesley's viewpoint.

10 'Sermon 130', in Outler, Albert (ed.), 1987, *The Works of John Wesley*, Nashville: Abingdon Press, vol. 4, p. 175.

11 'Sermon 91', in Outler, Albert (ed.), 1986, *The Works of John Wesley*, Nashville: Abingdon Press, vol. 3, pp. 295–6.

12 This work has often been compared with another important later work by Raimundo Panikkar, 1981, *The Unknown Christ of Hinduism*, rev. edn, Maryknoll: Orbis.

13 See the discussions in Hedges, Paul, 2001, *Preparation and Fulfilment: A History and Study of Fulfilment Theology in Modern British Thought in the Indian Context*, Bern: Peter Lang, esp. ch. 7; and Sharpe, Eric, 1986, *Comparative Religion: A History*, 2nd edn, London: Duckworth, pp. 151–4.

14 *Report of the Conference of the World's Student Federation held at Oxford, England, 1909* (Farquhar was speaking), p. 72, cited in Sharpe, Eric, 1965, *Not to Destroy but to Fulfil: The Contribution of J. N. Farquhar to Protestant Missionary Thought in India before 1914*, Uppsala: Gleerup, pp. 255–6.

15 See Hedges, *Preparation*, pp. 331–2.

16 Farquhar, John Nicol, 1930 (1913), *The Crown of Hinduism*, London: Humphrey Milford/Oxford University Press, p. 458. As we have said, Farquhar was hardly expressing an original idea. For example, earlier, Indian theologians like Keshub Chunder Sen, had said the following: 'You will find on reflection that the doctrine of divine humanity is essentially a Hindu doctrine [. . .] The doctrine of absorption in the Deity is India's creed, and through this idea I believe, India will reach Christ. Will he not fulfil the Indian scripture?', in Sen, Keshub Chunder, 1979 (1879), 'Lectures: India Asks: "Who is Christ?"' (9 April 1879)', in Scott, D. C. (ed.), *Keshub Chunder Sen*, Madras: Christian Literature Society, p. 214.

17 Kraemer, Hendrik, 1938, *The Christian Message in a Non-Christian World*, London: Edinburgh House Press, p. 135.

18 Sugirtharajah, Sharada, 2003, *Imagining Hinduism*, London: Routledge, p. 93.

19 See Pinnock, Clark, 1995, 'Inclusivism', in Okholm, D. L., and Phillips, T. R. (eds), *More Than One Way?* Grand Rapids: Zondervan, pp. 98–100.

20 See Knitter, Paul, 2002, *Introducing Theologies of Religions*, Maryknoll: Orbis, pp. 76–8.

21 Rahner, Karl, 1982, *Foundations of Christianity*, New York: Crossroad, p. 139.

22 Kilby, Karen, 1997, *Karl Rahner*, London: Fount, p. 2.

23 Rahner, Karl, 1966, *Theological Investigations*, vol. 4, Smyth, K. (trans.),

London: DLT, p. 181.

24 Rahner, Karl, 1966, *Theological Investigations*, vol. 5, Kruger, K. H. (trans.), London and New York: DLT and Seabury Press, p. 120. Immediately following this statement, Rahner – in Barthian mode – makes it clear that such a belief is held dogmatically: 'This proposition is self-evident and basic for Christianity's understanding of itself. There is no need here to prove it or to develop its meaning.'

25 Rahner, *Theological* 5, pp. 118–19.

26 Rahner, *Theological* 5, p. 119.

27 Rahner, *Theological* 5, p. 121.

28 Rahner, *Theological* 5, p. 120.

29 Rahner, *Theological* 5, p. 125.

30 Rahner, *Theological* 5, p. 131.

31 Rahner, *Theological* 5, p. 133. Emphasis mine.

32 Küng, Hans, 1978, *On Being a Christian*, Glasgow: Collins/Fount Paperbacks, p. 98.

33 Küng, *Being*, p. 99.

34 Dupuis, Jacques, 1997, *Towards a Theology of Religious Pluralism*, Maryknoll: Orbis, p. 146.

35 Thus, he argues that maintaining a christocentric interpretation of other religions amounts to 'epicycles added to a fundamentally absolutist structure of theory in order to obscure its incompatibility with the observed facts'. Hick, John, 1985, *Problems of Religious Pluralism*, London: Macmillan, p. 52. For Hick's analogy, the Copernican revolution in astronomy is suggestive of a possible pluralist 'revolution' in theological thinking.

36 For example, see Milbank, John, 1992, 'The End of Dialogue', in D'Costa, *Christian*, pp. 174–91. See also MacIntyre, Alasdair, 1985, *After Virtue*, 2nd edn, London: Duckworth; also, 1988, *Whose Justice? Which Rationality?* London: Duckworth.

37 D'Costa, Gavin, 2000, *The Meeting of Religions and the Trinity*, Edinburgh: T&T Clark, p. 132.

38 Thus, he writes: 'Without listening to this testimony [of the Spirit in other religions], Christians cease to be faithful to their calling as Christians, in being inattentive to God' (1992, 'Christ, the Trinity, and Religious Plurality', in D'Costa, *Christian*, p. 23).

39 See D'Costa, *Meeting*, pp. 100, 115–16.

40 He writes: 'There is no independent revelation through the Paraclete, but only an application of the revelation of Jesus', *Meeting*, p. 122.

41 Dupuis, *Towards*, p. 197.

42 Dupuis, *Towards*, p. 388.

43 For a good critique, see Kärkkäinen, Veli-Matti, 2004, *Trinity and Religious Pluralism*, Aldershot: Ashgate, pp. 61–6. See also Knitter, *Introducing*, esp. chs 5 and 6.

44 See Dupuis, *Towards*, pp. 195–8.

45 Pinnock, Clark, 1996, *Flame of Love: A Theology of the Holy Spirit*, Downers Grove: IVP, p. 201.

46 Yong, *Beyond*, pp. 190–1.

47 Yong, *Beyond*, p. 165.

48 See Yong, *Beyond*, pp. 165–6.

49 See Dale Irvin's 2004 review of Yong's *Beyond the Impasse*, in *Journal of Pentecostal Theology*, vol. 12.2, pp. 277–80.

50 Heim, S. Mark, 2001, *The Depth of the Riches: A Trinitarian Theology of Religious Ends*, Grand Rapids: Eerdmans, pp. 254–5.

51 Heim, *Depth*, p. 269.

52 Heim, S. Mark, 1994, 'Salvations: A More Pluralistic Hypothesis', *Modern Theology*, vol. 10, no. 4, p. 341.

53 Heim, *Depth*, p. 44.

54 Hick's comments are taken from a review article of Heim's book that appears on his website: http://www.johnhick.org.uk/article6.html. Accessed: 11/8/2007.

55 See Kärkkäinen's critique: *Trinity*, pp. 145–8.

56 Kärkkäinen, *Trinity*, p. 146.

57 Kiblinger, Kristen Beise, 2005, *Buddhist Inclusivism: Attitudes Towards Religious Others*, Burlington: Ashgate, p. 24.

58 Kiblinger, *Buddhist*, p. 28. Emphasis mine.

59 This concerns Davidson's philosophy of language.

60 Marshall, Bruce, 1990, 'Absorbing the World: Christianity and the Universe of Truths', in Marshall, Bruce (ed.), *Theology and Dialogue: Essays in Conversation with George Lindbeck*, Notre Dame: University of Notre Dame Press, p. 75. This issue, as well as Davidson and Marshall, is raised by Kiblinger, *Buddhist*, p. 24.

61 Hick, John, 2004, *An Interpretation of Religion: Human Responses to the Transcendent*, 2nd edn, Basingstoke: Palgrave.

62 Samartha, Stanley, 1981, *Courage for Dialogue*, Maryknoll: Orbis, p. 97.

5

Pluralisms: How to Appreciate Religious Diversity Theologically

PERRY SCHMIDT-LEUKEL

The Pluralist Option in the Theology of Religions

'Pluralism' or 'religious pluralism' – as used here – does not signify the fact of religious diversity but refers to a specific option within the Christian theology of religions and to analogous options within the respective discourse of other religious traditions. 'Theology of religions', in this wider sense, deals with the self-understanding of one's own religion in relation to other religions, and with the understanding of these other religions in relation to the self-understanding of one's own. Therefore it is rooted, on the one hand, in the beliefs and doctrines of one's own tradition and, on the other hand, is based on the concrete knowledge of and acquaintance with other religions.

'Theology of religions' becomes an inevitable task once one begins to take other religions and their truth-claims seriously. In one way or another, each of the major religious traditions claims to teach a path of 'salvation', that is, beliefs, attitudes and practices which are considered essential in order to reach the highest goal of human existence in relation to an ultimate reality. Consider, for example, the following selection:

from the *Torah* (Deut. 5.33):

> You must follow exactly the path that the Lord your God has commanded you, so that you may live, and that it may go well with you . . .

or from the *Qur'an* (1.6f.):[1]

> Show us the straight way, the way of those on whom Thou hast bestowed Thy Grace, those whose (portion) is not wrath, and who go not astray.

or from the Daoist *Dao De Jing* (16.40):[2]

> . . . returning to one's destiny is known as constancy.

> To know constancy is called 'enlightenment'.
> Those who don't know constancy wantonly produce misfortune . . .
> To be Heavenly is to embody the Way.

or from the Hindu *Upanishads* (Brhadāranyaka-Up. 1.3.28):[3]

> From the unreal (. . .) lead me to the real (. . .)!
> From darkness lead me to light!
> From death lead me to immortality!

or from the Buddhist *Dhammapada* (vv. 273f.):[4]

> Of paths, the eightfold is the best.
> Of truths, the four statements. (. . .)
> Just this path, there is no other
> For purity of vision.

or from the *New Testament* (John 14.6) where the Gospel writer summarizes the meaning of the divine Word (*logos*) embodied in Jesus as:

> I am the way, and the truth, and the life. No one comes to the Father except through me.

If through interfaith encounter religions become fully aware of their respective claims, they have the moral and intellectual obligation to reply to each other's claims and consider whether these might be true or not. This is the central task of any theology of religions. The price of refraining from this challenge is simply to deafen one's ears and harden one's heart against the witness of one's neighbour.[5]

So, is the claim of the religions to mediate a salvific knowledge of an ultimate transcendent reality true? One possible answer is an outright 'No': none of them is true, because an ultimate, transcendent reality, on which our salvation depends, does not exist. This is the position of atheism or naturalism. Or the answer is 'Yes'. Then the question is whether only one religion, or more than one, is right in this claim. If the answer is 'Only one' we have the position of exclusivism, and the religion considered to be uniquely true will be naturally one's own. If the answer is 'More than one', the question arises, whether among the various religions which indeed mediate salvific knowledge of a transcendent reality, one surpasses all others. If the answer to this question is 'Yes' we have the position of inclusivism, that is, the claim that one religion (one's own) is superior to all others in its mediation of salvific knowledge. But if the answer is 'No' we finally arrive at the position of pluralism. Pluralism entails that at least some religions, not necessarily all of them, are equally right or equally valid as paths of salvation. Note that this classification, due to its strictly disjunctive character, comprehends all possible answers to the question: 'Does any religion mediate salvific knowledge of transcendent reality?' The answer is either 'No' or 'Yes'. If 'Yes', then there is either only one, or more than one, which does so. And if there is more than one, then either one is superior in this to all others or none is superior so that at least some do so equally well. The 'No'-answer, being the position of naturalism, might be true (and needs to be taken seriously), but it is not a theological or religious option. Thus theologians of the various religious traditions have to choose between the remaining three: Will they understand the relation between their own tradition and the others either along the lines of the exclusivist, the inclusivist or the pluralist option? For logical reasons no further choice is left.

Throughout the more recent debates over this tripolar classification a range of interpretations were produced which confused rather than clarified the case.[6] A major reason for this is that the terminology in itself – regardless of the positions to which the terms refer – can carry a range of disparate meanings. This necessitates some further clarifications. First, 'exclusivism', as used here, does not refer to the epistemological fact that each proposition, if true, excludes the truth of its logical opposite.[7] In this sense, all of the three or four positions would be 'exclusivist'. But this formal feature does not tell us anything about the content of the propositions. Second, 'inclusivism', as used here, does not refer to something that could be called hermeneutical inclusivism, namely that theologians from one religion will express their assessment of other religions in the terms and concepts of their own religion. Again, this does not necessarily predetermine the content of this assessment. An assessment of other religions expressed in Christian terms (and thus hermeneutically 'inclusivist') can still be either exclusivistic (for example seeing them as demonic), or inclusivistic (for example seeing them as 'anonymous Christianity'), or pluralistic (e.g. seeing them as containing differently shaped but equally saving revelation). Third, 'pluralism', here, is not used in the sense of an 'anything-goes' mentality. Nor does it entail the relativism of radical incommensurability claims. These deny the existence of any universally valid norms and standards. From this perspective all religions are 'equal' in the sense that there is no justifiable norm by which they could be assessed as more or less genuine or as more or less salvific. In contrast, pluralism, as an option within the theology of religions, assesses at least some other religions as equally genuine and salvific on the basis of norms and criteria that are understood to be universally valid.[8] Fourth, 'pluralism', as used here, does not refer to the political or social concept of an 'open' or 'pluralistic society'. One does not need a pluralist theology of religions in order to establish the need for a society that is as open as possible to a large diversity of worldviews, convictions, lifestyles, and so forth. The justification of socio-political pluralism cannot be based on pluralism in a 'theology of religions' sense, for a truly pluralistic society must not be confined to those religions which a pluralistic theology would recognize as salvifically equal.

Finally, 'pluralism', as understood here, is not a religious position 'above' the existing religions. As such, it would be self-refuting, for it would turn into a new religion that claims for itself to be superior to all the others. Of course, a pluralist position suggests an overarching interpretation of religious diversity. But this does not distinguish it from exclusivism or inclusivism, which do exactly the same. What is important is that each of the three options is expressed from within a particular religious tradition. And it is from this specific perspective that other religions are judged either to lack any salvific potential, or to be salvific in some limited or partial sense, or to be salvific in a different but nevertheless equally genuine and efficient way.[9] A pluralist position from within the Christian tradition would thus entail that some other religions (at least one other religion, but usually the major world religions) are in a theological sense on a par with Christianity. They testify to the same ultimate transcendent reality despite the different forms this testimony takes, and they do so with the same authenticity and with an equal salvific potential.

The Emergence of the Pluralist Option

The biblical scriptures do not contain an elaborate theology of religions but a number of different verses which can and are in fact quoted in support of each of the three possible options. A Christian pluralist, for example, can refer to passages such as Amos 9.7, Matt. 8.11 or 1 John 4.7, the latter stating indiscriminately that 'everyone who loves is born of God and knows God'. During the patristic period various church fathers leaned towards an inclusivistic view while others developed exclusivistic positions, which gradually became harsher and, from the fourth century onwards, became the dominant strand in Christian theology. This has certainly to do with the fact that by then the classical Greek and Roman religions had nearly disappeared. The Jews were not perceived as a different religion but as the people of the old covenant who had deliberately rejected the new one. Islam was not understood as another religion either but as a Christian heresy that had arisen from a false prophet.[10] If one were to look for early signs of theological moves towards a pluralist understanding one would have to turn to those very small Christian minorities who lived among the major non-Christian religions, as for example the Nestorians in India and China. And indeed there are indications that at least something like pluralist leanings existed among them.[11]

In the Western churches theology of religions gained new attention in the later Middle Ages, when Judaism and Islam began to be perceived as religions in their own right, and in particular after the 'discovery' of the Eastern religions in early modernity. In the works of Nicolas Cusanus (1400/1–64), Herbert of Cherbury (1582/3–1648), Matthew Tindal (1657–1733), up to Enlightenment philosophers and theologians like Gotthold Ephraim Lessing (1729–81), Immanuel Kant (1724–1804), and the early Friedrich Schleiermacher (1768–1834), we find new attempts to interpret religious diversity, which point in a pluralist direction. However, by and large religious pluralism became an elaborated option in the Christian theology of religions only after the rapid improvement of knowledge about other religions from the late nineteenth century onwards[12] and in particular through increasing dialogical encounters with people from other faiths. Seven major lines can be distinguished along which religious pluralism emerged.

Pluralism as a result of interfaith dialogue

Several Christian theologians developed their version of a pluralist option in and out of a long, sincere and penetrating dialogue with people from other faiths. Some of the better-known examples from Hindu–Christian dialogue are Raimundo Panikkar and Stanley Samartha, as well as the two Benedictines Henri Le Saux (Swami Abhishiktananda) and Bede Griffiths, who both developed their reflections out of the spiritual practice of a Hindu–Christian synthesis.[13] Dialogue with Buddhism led theologians like Lynn de Silva, Aloysius Pieris, Seichi Yagi, and Paul Ingram to pluralistic conclusions.[14] Michael von Brück crafted his own version of pluralism out of his experiences in dialogue with Hinduism and Buddhism.[15] The encounter with Islam was the crucial impulse in Wilfred Cantwell Smith's development towards a pluralist position and more recently for Martin Bauschke.[16] For Rosemary Radford Ruether and Leonard Swidler it was the Christian–Jewish dialogue that played a decisive role.[17]

Pluralism as a hypothesis of comparative religion

Important impulses for the development of a pluralist theology of religions also emerged from the science of religions, in particular from comparative religion. Already the later writings of Friedrich Heiler and Gustav Mensching demonstrate pluralist tendencies and these are even stronger in the work of Helmut von Glasenapp or Willard Oxtoby. More recently Stephen Kaplan has opted for a polycentric version of pluralism (cf. the section 'Polycentric Pluralism?' below) as a possible hypothesis in the scholarly interpretation of religious diversity.[18] By far the most influential impact, however, came from the writings of Wilfred Cantwell Smith. With his major works on concepts and methodology in religious studies, alongside his already mentioned works on Islam and Muslim–Christian relations, and with his vision of a 'world theology', he is to be counted among the 'fathers' of a pluralist theology of religions.[19]

Pluralism as a hypothesis of systematic theology and the philosophy of religion

Comparatively early moves towards a systematic elaboration of a pluralistic approach are already found in the very last writings of Ernst Troeltsch and Paul Tillich.[20] But the main features of a consistent pluralistic hypothesis were, from the 1970s onwards, developed systematically by the philosopher and theologian John Hick.[21] Up until today his work exerts the major influence on the development and discussion of pluralism, although an impressive list of other systematic theologians and philosophers of religions made further contributions which partly build on Hick's ideas, or complement them or present alternative versions of pluralistic approaches. Among these are the Protestant theologians Gordon Kaufman, Langdon Gilkey and Glyn Richards,[22] the Anglican theologians Alan Race, Maurice Wiles and Keith Ward,[23] and the Roman Catholics Paul Knitter, Leonard Swidler and Chester Gillis.[24] The Anglican John Macquarrie and the Roman Catholic theologian Roger Haight have shown how contemporary Christology fits into and supports a pluralistic position.[25] Peter Byrne made important suggestions from a more philosophical point of view.[26] My own work in this field falls also primarily under the rubric of systematic theology, although it extends into religious studies and was triggered by my longstanding commitment to Buddhist–Christian dialogue.[27]

Pluralism as a metaphysical axiom of the 'perennial philosophy'

Vivid impulses, though not always easy to identify, came from a group of thinkers of diverse religious backgrounds which is frequently referred to as the 'traditional school' or 'perennial philosophy'. It is characterized by a strictly metaphysical position, drawing on the major forms of mysticism in the various religions, and often combined with a fierce anti-modernism. Among the intellectual fathers of this line are René Guénon, Frithjof Schuon and Ananda Coomaraswamy. Marco Pallis, Seyyed Hossein Nasr and Huston Smith developed their ideas further from within the Buddhist, the Muslim and the Christian tradition respectively.[28] Future research will have to clarify the exact extent to which this school exerted its influence on the formation of religious pluralism within the Christian theology of religions.

Pluralism as a guiding vision in ecumenical and missiological studies

As an inclusivist theologian, Karl Rahner had not only claimed that Christianity is superior to all other religions, he also made the same claim in relation to the position of his, the Roman Catholic Church, against all other Christian churches. In contrast, among Christian ecumenical circles the idea has become more widespread that the major Christian denominations could understand each other as different but nevertheless equally valid expressions of Christianity. Some ecumenically committed theologians have extended this sort of inner-Christian 'pluralism' to other religions as well. Many Christian theologians are nowadays prepared to understand Christian–Jewish relations as an ecumenical relationship, and some are prepared to see at least Judaism as being theologically on a par with Christianity.[29] Leonard Swidler, for many years the editor of the *Journal of Ecumenical Studies*, is a perfect example of a theologian who widened his ecumenical vision first to include Judaism and then other religions too. Out of similar motives the World Council of Churches opened the inner-Christian ecumenical dialogue towards an interreligious one. Major theologians who shaped this process were Stanley Samartha, Wesley Ariarajah and Hans Ucko, who all follow (to varying degrees) a pluralist paradigm.[30] This process resonated with certain developments in mission studies where some theologians sought to overcome supersessionist concepts of mission in favour of an ecumenical, and in the end pluralistic, understanding of the practical relationships between Christians and non-Christians. In this regard one can refer to the work of Eugene Hillman, Kenneth Cracknell and Diana Eck, and, of course, to William Ernest Hocking, who to some extent prefigured this development.[31]

Pluralism as a foundation for an interreligious theology of liberation

How can 'theology of liberation', with its concern for the poor, and its option for the poor as the proper subject of theology, be carried out in those parts of the Third World where the majority of the poor belongs to non-Christian religions? This question triggered intensive controversy and debate within the Ecumenical Association of Third World Theologians (EATWOT).[32] Some liberation theologians argued in favour of an exclusivist approach, criticizing non-Christian religions along the lines of Karl Marx as oppressive, and along the lines of Karl Barth as idolatrous unbelief in opposition to the uniquely liberating gospel. Others, however, opted for a pluralistic approach suggesting that the poor are God's people regardless of their religious affiliation, so that interreligious alliances can be formed in which the liberating elements from all religions should be employed in service of a common practice. Some of the more prominent representatives of this view are the Sri Lankan theologians, Aloysius Pieris and Tissa Balasuriya, and the Indian, Felix Wilfred.[33] Paul Knitter has also integrated central features of liberation theology into his own version of pluralism and given it a decisively practical-political orientation.[34]

Pluralism as a foundation for interreligious feminism

The principle concern of feminism, to unmask and overcome any socio-cultural structures confining women to an inferior role, has quite naturally an intercultural and hence interreligious dimension. Feminist theologians who do not reduce religion to a mere socio-cultural phenomenon are therefore interested to combine their feminist concern with a theological understanding of the relation between Christianity and non-Christian religions. Their sharpened sense for the ambivalences of Christianity has prepared a number of them to approach non-Christian religions with a similar attitude, that is, the readiness to discover comparable ambivalences in all the religious traditions. Feminist theologians who thereby arrived at a pluralist understanding are, for example, Ursula King, Marjorie Hewitt Suchocki, Manuela Kalsky, and the already mentioned Rosemary Radford Ruether.[35]

The development of a pluralist attitude towards other religions is by no means confined to Christianity.[36] The restrictions of this chapter do not permit of going into too much detail. But it is worth mentioning that a growing number of Muslim[37] and Jewish[38] theologians are developing pluralist approaches from within their own traditions. In the late nineteenth and early twentieth centuries some of the leading figures of Neo-Hinduism, like Ramakrishna, Vivekananda or Tagore, supported a kind of pluralist view, which, however, was often a sort of *primus inter pares* pluralism ('first among equals'), claiming that Hinduism stands out because it alone is capable of affirming the basic equality of all major religions. Sarvepalli Radhakrishnan,[39] who held a similar view, also exerted a considerable influence within Western religious studies. Buddhism, which is often falsely regarded as a kind of naturally pluralist religion, has, in fact, the least number of pluralist thinkers, but even here some are now transgressing the traditionally dominant exclusivistic and inclusivistic approaches.[40]

Theological Presuppositions of a Christian and Pluralistic Theology of Religions[41]

The paths of salvations taught by the various religions intrinsically depend on an ultimate reality to which they refer in different ways and by different concepts and names, as for example, the eternal dao; the 'deathless' and 'unconditioned' *nirvana*; the 'formless' *dharmakāya*; the divine brahman (either understood as a transcategorial [*nirguṅa*] reality or identified as a theistic deity, as Vishnu or Shiva); *Yahweh*, the 'Lord of the Lords'; Allah, the one who is highly exalted above all else; or the *Holy Trinity*. If religions, or their theologians, would hold that ultimate reality is something that human beings can accurately grasp by their thoughts and adequately describe by their words, a pluralist approach would become impossible. For then it would follow that among all the different names, concepts and doctrines one particular set is closest to the most adequate description of the ultimate while all the rest would be less accurate or false to the extent that they diverge from this best description.

This, however, is not in line with the traditional understanding of most thinkers of the major religions. Quite the contrary, we find the widespread conviction that ultimate reality necessarily transcends all human understanding,[42] and hence cannot be adequately described in human words.[43] The various names, concepts and teachings must therefore not be mistaken as literal descriptions of a divine, but in principle conceivable and comprehendible reality, but as metaphors, analogies, 'skilful means', symbols or pointers to an inconceivable and indescribable divine mystery. Their primary function is not to provide conceptual understanding but to relate crucial experiences with the ultimate and to orient humans towards it in a salvific and liberative way.[44] If this is how religious talk about the ultimate needs to be understood then there is space for the idea that different ways of talking about the ultimate – even if they would be mutually exclusive when (mis-)taken as accurate descriptions – can be compatible because they possibly refer to different experiences of and different but equally salvific attitudes towards the ultimate. They are not different expressions of the same experience,[45] but reflect different experiences with the same ultimate reality. According to this view a personal representation of the ultimate, for example as a divine Father or Mother, does not give us any information about the gender or generative function of the ultimate, but entails that the ultimate can be genuinely experienced as being like a merciful father or a loving mother and that humans can relate to it in this way. An impersonal representation of the ultimate, for example as the 'heavenly way', the 'deathless', the 'formless body of Buddhahood', does not reflect a higher or lower degree of insight but different historical experiences of how to be aware of and relate to the ultimate. Personal representations are neither superior to impersonal ones, nor *vice versa*. Both need to be understood as limited images pointing towards a reality that exceeds personal as well as impersonal categories. But this understanding can easily be, and has in fact often been, associated with both personal and impersonal forms of designating the ultimate.

Within the Christian tradition the vast majority of the church fathers affirmed the absolute transcendence and ineffability of God. To mention just a few examples: Anselm of Canterbury (1033–68) famously held that if 'God' refers to a reality 'than which nothing greater can be conceived', God must be necessarily 'greater than can be conceived'. For if God were conceivable, one could postulate a reality that is so 'great' that it is inconceivable. Hence 'God' necessarily refers to the latter.[46] According to Thomas Aquinas (1225–74) 'the utmost of human knowledge of God is to know that we cannot know God'.[47] 'For the divine substance, by its immensity, transcends every form that our intellect can reach; and thus we cannot apprehend it by knowing what it is.'[48] 'Apophatic' or 'Negative Theology' – that is, the conviction that God's nature necessarily and radically exceeds human words and understanding – has not been a minority position in classical Christian theology but reflects a broad consensus among the church fathers. For, as Nicholas of Cusa rightly stated, without 'negative theology' God would not be worshipped as the infinite God but would be reduced to the level of a finite creature, and our worship would become idolatry. We would give our images of God the honour that only befits the divine reality itself.[49]

However, 'negative theology' is not only the crucial antidote against intellectual or theological idolatry, it also provides an important foundation for the development of a pluralist theology of religions. This has not been seen by the Christian tradition, although there was the awareness that divine ineffability leaves room for a plurality of approaches and the respective images. The fact that our intellect is unable to grasp the divine nature explains – according to Thomas Aquinas – why so many different names need to be applied to God:

> Since we cannot name an object except as we understand it (for names are signs of things understood), we cannot give names to God except in terms of perfections perceived in other things that have their origin in Him. And since these perfections are multiple in such things, we must assign many names to God.[50]

A further important presupposition of a Christian and pluralistic theology of religion is that revelation is best not understood as propositional revelation (God revealing 'texts' in a specific human language and conceptuality) but as the divine self-communication to human beings which is perceived and expressed in human terms so that the 'revelatory' texts are the result of genuine religious experience. Any propositional theory of revelation is confronted by the insurmountable difficulty of distinguishing the divine from the human element in the purportedly revealed texts. For the language and concepts of these texts are of human origin, and hence always contain a human – fallible and limited – element, even if one assumes that these texts are verbally inspired. A non-propositional understanding of revelation presupposes that human beings can have a genuine experience of divine reality (this is what the idea of divine self-communication means, if seen from the human, that is the recipient, end), but that this experience is always shaped and structured by the concrete individual, social, cultural, historical and other conditions and limitations of the person who undergoes this experience. Divine infinity and ineffability do not exclude that ultimate reality can be experienced. They only exclude that it can be experienced in his/her/its infinite nature (that is, as it is in itself). The divine can be genuinely experienced but in those limited ways that reflect the specific limitations and conditions of the experiencing subjects. It is like someone standing at the shore and looking at the ocean. What she sees is really the ocean, but not in its oceanic wideness.[51] A Christian and pluralistic theology of religions can therefore assume that 'there is a plurality of divine revelations, making possible a plurality of forms of saving human response'.[52]

This, however, requires another presupposition, namely that the divine reality itself is the ultimate ground and constitutive cause of human salvation, not any particular historical event. If, for example, the life and death of Jesus were regarded as constitutive for human salvation, this would result either in an exclusivistic position, requiring the explicit acceptance of the salvation caused by Christ, or in an inclusivist position according to which someone can unknowingly receive Christ's grace. This would put Christianity in a superior position in so far as 'Christians know this through their faith, while others remain unaware that Jesus Christ is the source of their salvation' – as it was formulated in an official document of the Roman Catholic Church.[53] There are, however, serious theological reasons[54] which support the view – as Schubert Ogden expressed it – that Jesus Christ does not *constitute* salvation but *represents* it: 'The Christ event cannot be the cause of salvation because its only cause, and the cause of this event itself, is the boundless love of God of which this event is the decisive re-presentation.'[55] This understanding allows for the possibility that the constitutive role of ultimate reality for human salvation/liberation – the benign character of the Transcendent in its relation to us or, in theistic terms, 'the boundless love of God' – can also be, and has been represented in other ways, within other (for example impersonal) conceptualities, and through other media and mediators.

A Christian pluralist will therefore agree that Jesus is a unique representation, in his concrete individuality, and a special mediator of a saving relationship with God, but also propose that he is not the only one, as in Paul Knitter's words: 'The uniqueness of Jesus' salvific role can be reinterpreted in terms of *truly* but not *only*.'[56] This view does not necessarily conflict with a traditional two-natures Christology. The two natures would then refer to the medium and the mediated respectively. The nature of Jesus, as the mediator, is undiminishedly human and the nature of the reality that he mediates is undiminishedly divine.[57] This is, as Roger Haight has shown, in line with the basic idea of symbolic representation: 'A symbol is that through which something else is made present and known; a symbol mediates a perception and knowledge of something other than itself. . . . Since God is both present to and transcendent of any finite symbol, the symbol both makes God present and points away from itself to a God who is other than itself.'[58] But again, the idea of symbolic mediation, in particular the idea of finite symbols mediating an infinite reality, is open to the possibility of a plurality of such symbolic mediations and representations. This does not exclude that Jesus is, for Christians, the normative mediator. Any criteria to identify other possibly genuine mediations and representations of the divine must not be in essential conflict with the basic norms manifested in Jesus (cf. Mark 9.40). But at the same time it allows 'for the possibility of other savior figures of equal status . . . who may also reveal something of God that is normative'.[59]

John Hick has suggested as a general formula for an understanding of salvation that is in line with the normative traditions of the major religions: the 'transformation from self-centredness to Reality-centredness'; whereby 'Reality' signifies the ultimate, transcendent Reality and the crucial, but by no means only,[60] criterion being that this transformation 'shows itself, within the conditions of this world, in compassion (*karuňā*) or love (*agape*)'.[61] Characterizing 'salvation' as the orientation towards the Transcendent, away from self-centredness, manifesting itself in genuine love, is certainly in line with Jesus' message that the two basic signs of living under God's rule (kingdom) are to love God with all one's heart and one's neighbour as oneself (Matt. 22.37ff.). It may be worth pointing out that Josef Ratzinger once suggested a rather similar criterion in the assessment of other religions' claims to be paths of salvation:

> humans are not saved by a system or by the observation of a system, but they are saved by what is more than all systems and what represents the opening of all systems: love and faith, which are both the true termination of self-centredness and of self-destructive hubris. Religions assist in salvation to the extent that they induce this attitude; they are obstacles of salvation to the extent that they prevent humans from it.[62]

Polycentric Pluralism?

A criticism has been made suggesting that a pluralist theology of religions along the lines just sketched would not be sufficiently 'pluralist'.[63] A truly pluralistic approach would have to reckon not with just one but with a plurality of ultimates, and/or not just with one salvation, realized along different paths, but with several salvations. To use a picture: a truly pluralistic pluralism should not understand the religions as different paths to the same summit but as different paths to different summits.

As said before, 'pluralism', as an option within the theology of religions, must not be misunderstood in some more general sense of 'pluralism'. The question 'How pluralistic is a pluralistic theology of religions?' confuses the issue, for it is not the task of a pluralistic theology of religions to be as 'pluralistic' as possible, in the sense of admitting as wide a diversity of theories of religions as possible. Its task is to show whether from the standpoint of one religion other religions can be understood as genuinely and equally salvific. How, from this perspective, should we then assess the suggestions of reckoning with different ultimates or different salvations? Are these attempts – which can be referred to as 'polycentric pluralism' – forms of religious pluralism in the sense in which this term is used here?

Two major representatives of polycentric pluralism are John Cobb, Jr, and David Ray Griffin, both of whom are dependent on the process philosophy of Alfred North Whitehead.[64] Their suggestion is that there exist three 'ultimates': *first*, 'God' as the supreme being; *second*, pure 'creativity' or 'being itself', which finds its highest embodiment in God but is also embodied in the *third* ultimate, the universe or the 'totality of (finite) things'. 'Being itself' is co-eternal with God and is, like God, an uncreated ultimate reality (the idea of a *creatio ex nihilo* is rejected). The concrete cosmos, in its specific form, depends on the ordering and shaping activity of God (functioning as a demiurge), but the fact that there will always be some sort of cosmos is not contingent – it corresponds to the eternal activity of God and therefore constitutes the third ultimate of which God is the 'worldsoul'. These three 'ultimates' allow for three different types of religious orientation and experience: 'theistic, acosmic, and cosmic'. A particular religious tradition can be focused primarily on one of these, although all three orientations may also exist in a variety of different mixtures and combinations within the various traditions.[65]

The idea of several 'ultimates' seems to be to a significant extent counter-intuitive. If 'ultimate reality' refers to an 'unlimited' reality or a reality 'greater than anything else', it is even logically impossible that more than one such reality exists. For if there were a second 'ultimate', both would 'limit' each other and none of them would be 'greater than anything else'. Indeed, within process philosophy/theology God's power is regarded as seriously limited precisely by the fact that the existence of 'creativity' and of a 'cosmos' as such does not depend on God. Therefore the talk about 'different ultimates' seems to entail that none of these is truly ultimate, or 'ultimate' only in some limited sense. But the idea of a 'finite God', of an ultimate not being an unlimited ultimate, is, as John Hick once stated, 'metaphysically unsatisfying'.[66] Moreover, if God is understood as the 'worldsoul' of the cosmos (making the latter God's 'body') and if both are seen as co-actualizations of 'creativity' which does not exist in itself but only in its realization as God and some sort of cosmos (this is what process theologians emphasize in response to the accusation of polytheism!),[67] would it then not be more appropriate to speak of three different aspects of one complex ultimate reality instead of three ontologically distinct 'ultimates'?

The same question arises in relation to Stephen Kaplan's version of a polycentric pluralism.[68] Kaplan compares three different concepts of the ultimate – the theistic God, the Buddhist emptiness and the Advaitic brahman/atman – to the complex characteristics of a holographic picture. The three-dimensional holographic image can be compared to the 'graphic' or 'plastic' features of the theistic God, the two-dimensional film on which the image is stored lacks all features of the image itself and thus resembles the universal emptiness (everything lacking self-nature), while the fact that each part of the film contains the specific interference pattern that can (re-)produce the whole image is analogous to the non-dual unity of the totality as being present in each of its parts. However, in the end this analogy entails that the different concepts – as Kaplan understands them – do not really refer to ontologically separate ultimates, but to different simultaneous structures or aspects of one ultimate reality.[69] The differences consist in the fact that these aspects elicit different (and, as Kaplan assumes, incompatible) existential orientations, each one of which constitutes 'a different, yet equal, soteriological conclusion to human existence'.[70]

Kaplan, however, does not pursue the question on which criteria such a soteriological equality can be postulated. Not only in relation to Kaplan's model but even more so in relation to process theology one needs to ask whether each of the three 'ultimates' – or each of the three aspects of one complex ultimate – is soteriologically of equal significance. Do the different types of existential orientations which they elicit lead to different but equally salvific goals? This question takes us to the model suggested by S. Mark Heim.

In his work *Salvations*,[71] Heim not only proposed that the major religious traditions pursue essentially different kinds of 'salvations', that is different religious ends, but also that all of these different ends might factually coexist as ontologically and eschatologically distinct states. From a Christian point of view, some religious ends might equal complete lostness, but others might indeed represent different forms of penultimate fulfilment, while the Christian end would stand for the highest goal because of being 'more consistent with the nature of the ultimate'.[72] In *The Depth of the Riches*,[73] Heim provides the metaphysical basis for his multiple ends theory. If the Christian end is highest in being most consistent with the true, that is, Trinitarian nature of the ultimate, other ends can be real and salvific to the extent that they entail the awareness of some limited aspects of the Trinity, for example in Buddhism the selflessness or emptiness of each of the persons of the Trinity, in Advaitic Hinduism their non-dual relationship, in various monotheisms their inner unity in relation to the world, and so forth. But the Christian end of full communion with the Trinitarian God is the superior, most comprehensive goal – and Heim makes this crystal clear by now reserving the term 'salvation' strictly for the Christian end.[74] So the 'different' religious ends are in the end not so radically different. They are situated along the lines of a continuum, and the difference of the penultimate ends of other religions from the highest Christian end correlates with the degree of their fragmentary or inferior nature. This, of course, is not a pluralistic approach at all, but an inclusivistic one,[75] becoming still more apparent in Heim's further suggestion that even under eschatological conditions God might continue to drag the non-Christian from their eschatological 'ends' to the highest goal of fully taking part in the Trinitarian community.[76] From this perspective, Heim's 'multiple ends' turn out to be just multiple transition stages on the path to the single true end.

However, the idea of one ultimate reality with different aspects does not necessarily lead to the inclusivistic consequences as they are evident in S. Mark Heim's approach. If these 'aspects' are not reified (in some conceptual attempt to provide a comprehensive description of God) but understood as different impressions which human beings legitimately have and had in their various experiences of the ultimate, and if it can be established by suitable criteria that these different 'aspects' are capable of eliciting different, but nevertheless equally salvific responses, in that they equally well foster the transformation from self-centredness to a new centring in the divine exhibited in a loving attitude to one's fellow beings, we would have a genuinely pluralistic approach.

The Case for Pluralism

Why should Christians adopt a pluralistic position in relation to other religions? It is sometimes argued that only a pluralistic approach enables meaningful interreligious dialogue. The importance of such a dialogue in our religiously diverse world would therefore make a pluralist theology mandatory. But this is hardly a convincing argument. Why should it be a precondition of meaningful interfaith dialogue to accept, prior to the dialogue itself, the faith of one's partner in dialogue as displaying an equally salvific knowledge of transcendent reality? Such a view might very well be the outcome of the dialogue, but there is no need to demand it as its condition. In fact a number of pioneers of the pluralist approach developed their version of religious pluralism in and through dialogue, while they had entered this dialogue as exclusivistically (for example W. C. Smith) or inclusivistically (for example R. Panikkar, L. de Silva) minded theologians. What meaningful dialogue requires is the acceptance of one's dialogue-partner as someone who *might* have some truth to convey (not as someone who in fact does), the willingness to learn in and through dialogue (implying the understanding that one does not already possess in some infallible manner the fullness of truth) and a non-repressive context so that none of the dialogue-partners needs to fear any threats as a result of expressing themselves freely (unfortunately, not everywhere and not always are religious communities prepared to fulfil these conditions). Exclusivists, inclusivists and pluralists, however, will differ in the expectations and interests with which they enter dialogue. An exclusivist will not expect to discover any soteriologically significant truth in the faith of the other and will see the dialogue primarily as a good way to witness the gospel. The inclusivist will be prepared to discover the 'seeds of the logos' and the 'rays of the light' in the other's faith, but the major interest will also be to communicate the gospel in some optimal form. A pluralist will be open to find out whether the other's faith is one that contains the same soteriological potential as one's own or whether it might turn out to be essentially inferior. And while neither an exclusivist nor an inclusivist would expect to learn something new from the other's faith that is theologically essential, a pluralist can indeed harbour such an expectation. But still, all three are able to enter dialogue with the general epistemological openness to learn something that one would *not* expect given their respective theological background.[77] And this kind of openness is sufficient to carry out meaningful dialogue.

At other times it is argued that religious pluralism is necessary because it is the only approach that allows for genuine tolerance. This is a serious and potentially harmful confusion of *tolerance* with *appreciation*.[78] The concept of 'tolerance' or 'toleration' was developed during the Enlightenment (with some notable forerunners as, for example, Sebastian Castellio) in the sense of tolerating the existence (and activities) of people whose beliefs, values, practices one does not share or appreciate. It is recommended as the alternative to their extinction or serious sanctioning. Religious pluralism, as defined here, is not about tolerating what one does not like, but about the due theological recognition of what is appreciated as a different but equally valid path of salvation (of course, under the epistemological restraints of pre-eschatological existence which do not allow for infallibly certain knowledge). In a sense, tolerance presupposes an exclusivist or inclusivist approach not a pluralist one, although a pluralist will not regard *all* claims to salvation as equally valid. Thus in relation to those religious claims which a pluralist too would assess as false or deficient, tolerance is required. And a pluralist needs to be tolerant in relation to exclusivists or inclusivists of one's own religious tradition (and vice versa), otherwise pluralism too could become dangerously intolerant. There are important lessons to be learnt from some features of contemporary Indian politics where at times pluralist ideas are used to justify intolerant means against the presumed absolutist religions of Islam and Christianity. There always needs to be a discussion of the limits of tolerance, that is, whether some worldview might evidently have such evil implications that its toleration can no longer be justified. But if tolerance were restricted to only those views that we appreciate, we would have lost a crucial achievement of the Enlightenment. What would we then do with those who hold views that we don't approve of?

Now if religious pluralism cannot be established by the need for interfaith dialogue and religious toleration, what then is the case for pluralism? I think it rests basically on four points: First, there is an implicit leaning towards a pluralist position in a number of central Christian beliefs and their contemporary theological understanding. As has been shown above (the section 'Theological Presuppositions of a Christian and Pluralistic Theology of Religions') traditional belief in divine transcategoriality[79] corresponds to the insight that there can (and has to) be a legitimate diversity of approaches ('names') to the divine mystery. This consequence is spelled out fully in a pluralist theology of religions. Further, a non-propositional understanding of revelation as divine self-communication received in valid religious experience leans towards the idea of a legitimate diversity of such experiences. A Christology which dismisses the mythological, quasi-docetist view of a 'God come down taking on human flesh' and sees Jesus – in accordance with his self-understanding – as a genuine human being who distinguishes himself strictly from God but nevertheless mediates divine presence by the way in which he radically reflects and manifests divine love through his own life, allows and indeed suggests that there have been a range of other human beings who have in varying degrees (and some presumably in the same degree) reflected and mediated the divine through their concrete and unique lives. And a soteriology which abandons the highly problematic view that salvation had to be bought and caused by a cruel sacrifice and thus sees the soteriological significance of the 'Christ event' not as constitutive but as representative does also allow for a range of other meaningful representations of the ultimate reality as the sole ultimate source of our salvation. None of these doctrinal points was initially developed in order to establish religious pluralism. They evolved from the persuasive strength of various theological, philosophical and historical arguments. But they undermine the theological basis of Christian exclusivism and inclusivism, and thereby support pluralism.

A strong case for pluralism arises, second, from our, as compared to earlier periods', significantly improved knowledge of other religions and from the specific kind of understanding that flows from a dialogical encounter in the spirit of friendship and openness. If on the basis of such knowledge and understanding we look at the salvific potential of other religions, measuring this by the criterion of their fruits (the only criterion that Jesus himself recommended in order to distinguish the true from the false prophets; Matt. 7.15–20), we need to conclude, as John Hick convincingly argued, that Christianity has not proven more efficacious in bringing about these fruits than the other major religious traditions.[80] This, however, is what one would have to expect if exclusivism or inclusivism were correct. For if there is 'a strong correlation between the authenticity of the forms of religious experience and their spiritual and moral fruits', it would have to 'follow from the inclusivist position that there should be a far higher incidence and quality of saintliness in one tradition – namely, that in which contact with the Transcendent occurs in "its purest and most salvifically effective form"

– than in others. But this does not seem to be the case.'[81] This argument is sometimes misunderstood as if Hick would intend to establish the truth of religion or religions by practical criteria.[82] But this misses the point of the argument. Imagine the claim that the health system of a particular culture *A* is significantly superior to that of culture *B*. If it turned out that in fact life expectancy and life quality in culture *A* are not significantly higher/better than in culture *B* something would be wrong with the claimed superiority of *A*'s health system. Analogously, Hick's argument shows that the roughly[83] equal distribution of the 'fruits' among the religions – and the religions' inner potential to bring these about – is not in line with what one would expect if inclusivism (or exclusivism) were right and thus undermines their plausibility, while it is perfectly in accordance with a pluralist interpretation of religious diversity.

A third argument in favour of religious pluralism results from what can be called the 'benign' character of ultimate reality in relation to us. Theistic traditions express this by talking of God's universal or indiscriminate love or mercy; non-theistic traditions emphasize, for example, the universal Buddha-nature in and of everyone and everything, or the universal presence of the divine atman in everyone and everything. Such beliefs entail that nobody is excluded from the presence of the ultimate as the true source of our salvation. But if this is the case, should people from various religious traditions not expect to find signs of this universal saving divine presence all over the globe and throughout human history? And would it not appear to be a rational expectation that the signs of this presence and its reflections in human religions are in various places and at various times, despite the diversity of their forms, nevertheless of equal goodness and intensity? The idea that the saving presence of the divine is restricted to just some place, some period or some people is clearly at variance with the belief in its comprehensively and indiscriminately benign character.

A fourth and final point in support of religious pluralism is that neither exclusivism nor inclusivism is able to see any genuine value in religious diversity. If one is honestly convinced that one's own religion is in an objective sense uniquely true or uniquely superior, and if one honestly wishes one's neighbour only the best, one will inevitably harbour the wish that ideally all people in the world should embrace this uniquely true or uniquely superior religion. In fact, it would be immoral to wish that others should remain satisfied with having a false or inferior religion, thereby losing or reducing their chance of salvation. But if ideally all people should join the one and only true or superior faith, all other religions would disappear.[84] For someone who is a convinced exclusivist or inclusivist, religious uniformity – a global religious monoculture – will thus be quite naturally the religious ideal. In contrast, a religious pluralist can and does appreciate, within limits, the value of religious diversity.

Diversity, however, is certainly not a value in itself. A diversity of evils does not make evil any better but even worse. On the other hand, a diversity of goods will make them even better. Diversity seems to operate as a kind of intensifier and so the crucial question is whether religion is understood as something fundamentally good or as something fundamentally evil. If it is seen as being basically good – because it is, existentially, about the saving relation to the ultimate transcendent reality – it would be counter-intuitive to support a theology that is hostile to the idea of religious diversity. To a religious pluralist the diversity of religions is, in the end, a reflection and a result of the diversity of humankind. It is as ambivalent as humans can be ambivalent. But within this ambivalence there is more than one way in which different human beings can orient their lives towards the eternal source and goal of all life.[85]

Study Questions

1. Can religions accept other religions as different but nevertheless equally valid and equally salvific?
2. Many sacred texts and traditional religious thinkers affirm that divine reality is beyond human understanding and description. At the same time religions frequently presuppose that their own doctrines about divine reality are superior to those of other religions. Is this a contradiction?
3. How do you think about the idea that there might be several ultimate realities and that different religions relate to different ultimates?
4. Is the Christian belief in God's revelation through Jesus an insurmountable obstacle to the development of a Christian and at the same time pluralistic theology of religions?

Further Reading

Coward, Harold, 2000, *Pluralism in the World Religions: A Short Introduction*, Oxford: Oneworld.

D'Costa, Gavin (ed.), 1990, *Christian Uniqueness Reconsidered*, Maryknoll: Orbis.

Hick, John, 1989, *An Interpretation of Religion: Human Responses to the Transcendent*, Basingstoke: Macmillan.

Hick, John, and Knitter, Paul F. (eds), 1987, *The Myth of Christian Uniqueness: Toward a Pluralistic Theology of Religions*, Maryknoll: Orbis.

Knitter, Paul F. (ed.), 2005, *The Myth of Religious Superiority: Multifaith Explorations of Religious Pluralism*, Maryknoll: Orbis.

Schmidt-Leukel, Perry, (forthcoming), *God Without Limits: A Christian and Pluralistic Theology of Religions*, London: SCM Press.

Notes

1 'Alī, Àbdullah Yūsuf, 1989, *The Meaning of The Holy Qur'ān*, Beltsville: Amana, p. 15.

2 Ivenhoe, Philip J., and Van Norden, Bryan W. (eds), 2001, *Readings in Classical Chinese Philosophy*, 2nd edn, Indianapolis: Hackett, p. 170.

3 Goodall, Dominic (ed. and trans.), 1996, *Hindu Scriptures*, London: Phoenix, p. 47.

4 Carter, John Ross, 2000, *The Dhammapada*, Mahinda Palihawadana (trans.), Oxford: Oxford University Press, p. 49.

5 James Fredericks has suggested that we should refrain from any theology of religions and instead replace it with 'comparative theology'. Rightly understood, however, 'comparative theology' is a form of interreligious dialogue which leads directly into the kind of questions dealt with in the theology of religions. Cf. Fredericks, James, 1999, *Faith among Faiths: Christian Theology and Non-Christian Religions*, New York: Mahwah; Schmidt-Leukel, P., 2007, 'Limits and Prospects of Comparative Theology', in Hintersteiner, N. (ed.), *Naming and Thinking God in Europe Today: Theology in Global Dialogue*, Amsterdam and New York: Rodopi, pp. 493–512.

6 For a defence of the tripolar classification in face of various criticisms cf. Schmidt-Leukel, P., 2005, 'Exclusivism, Inclusivism, Pluralism: The Tripolar Typology – Clarified and Reaffirmed', in Knitter P. (ed.), *The Myth of Religious Superiority: Multifaith Explorations of Religious Pluralism*, Maryknoll: Orbis, pp. 13–27.

7 This confusion lies at the bottom of one of Gavin D'Costa's major objections against religious pluralism. Cf. D'Costa, G., 2000, *The Meeting of Religions and the Trinity*, Maryknoll: Orbis, pp. 19–52.

8 Through the dialogical process the set of suitable criteria might change and expand. As Ninian Smart once rightly stated: 'If faith F presents C as a criterion of truth, then faith T may turn out to do well or badly by that criterion. If well, then that is a ground for respecting criterion D put forward by T, and so something like an inter-system consensus about criteria cannot be ruled out' (Smart, N., 1995, 'Truth, Criteria and Dialogue between Religions', in Dean, T. (ed.), *Religious Pluralism and Truth*, Albany: SUNY Press, pp. 67–71, at p. 68).

9 John Hick, who is often charged with pretending a 'bird's eye view', has in fact rejected the idea that anyone could assume a 'vantage-point from which one can observe both the divine Reality and the different limited human standpoints from which that Reality is being variously perceived'. According to Hick, the 'advocate of the pluralist understanding cannot pretend to any such cosmic vision. . . . The pluralist hypothesis is arrived at inductively' – that is, by starting from the religious experience of one's own tradition and then proceeding to a tentative assessment of those of others (Hick, J., 1985, *Problems of Religious Pluralism*, Basingstoke: Macmillan, p. 37).

10 In addition to the chapter in this book, see for a brief summary of traditional Christian understandings of Islam: Bauschke, Martin, 2007, 'A Christian View of Islam', in Schmidt-Leukel, P., and Ridgeon, L. (eds), *Islam and Interfaith Relations*, London: SCM Press, pp. 137–55. A revised version of this chapter appears in this work as the chapter 'Islam'.

11 The famous Nestorian stele of Xi'an (erected in 781) quotes with approval an imperial proclamation that displays pluralist tendencies (cf. Saeki, P. Y., *The Nestorian Documents and Relics in China*, Tokyo: Academy of Oriental Culture, 1951). In India, the Portuguese synod of Diamper (1599) condemned the view of the Nestorian Indian Thomas Christians that 'everyone may be saved in his own law; all which are good and lead men to heaven'. Cf. Aleaz, K. P., 2005, 'Pluralism Calls for Pluralistic Inclusivism', in Knitter (ed.), *Myth*, pp. 162–75, at p. 163.

12 As one rather early example one might quote the Theosophists who, on the basis of their experiments in multi-religious experiences, start displaying some features of a pluralist interpretation of religious diversity.

13 See, for example, Panikkar, R., 1981, *The Unknown Christ of Hinduism*, rev. and enl. edn, Maryknoll: Orbis; Samartha, S., 1991, *One Christ – Many Religions*, Maryknoll: Orbis; Teasdale, W., 2003, *Bede Griffiths: An Introduction to his Interspiritual Thought*, Woodstock: Skylight Paths; Boullay, S. Du (ed.), 2007, *Swami Abhishiktananda: Essential Writings*, Maryknoll: Orbis.

14 See, for example, Silva, L. de, 1982, 'Buddhism and Christianity Relativised', *Dialogue*, N.S. 9, pp. 41–73; Pieris, A., 1988, *Love Meets Wisdom*, Maryknoll: Orbis; Yagi, S., and Swidler, L., 1990, *A Bridge to Buddhist–Christian Dialogue*, New York: Paulist Press; Ingram, P., 1997, *Wrestling with the Ox*, New York: Continuum.

15 See, for example, Brück, M., 1991, *The Unity of Reality*, New York: Paulist; Brück, M., and Lai, W., 2001, *Christianity and Buddhism*, Maryknoll: Orbis.

16 See, for example, Smith, W. C., 1967, *Questions of Religious Truth*, London: Victor Gollancz; 1981, *On Understanding Islam*, The Hague: Mouton; Bauschke, 'Christian'.

17 See, for example, Ruether, R., 1974, *Faith and Fratricide*, New York: Seabury; Swidler, L., 1990, *After the Absolute*, Minneapolis: Fortress.

18 Cf. Heiler, F., 1959, 'The History of Religions as a Preparation for the Co-Operation of Religions', in Eliade, M., and Kitagawa, J. (eds), *The History of Religions: Essays in Methodology*, Chicago: University of Chicago Press, pp. 132–60; Mensching, G., 1971, *Tolerance and Truth in Religion*, Alabama: University of Alabama Press; Glasenapp, H. von, 1963, *Die fünf Weltreligionen*, Düsseldorf: Diederichs; Oxtoby, W., 1983, *The Meaning of Other Faiths*, Philadelphia: Westminster; Kaplan, S., 2002, *Different Paths, Different Summits*, Lanham: Rowman & Littlefield.

19 Cf. Smith, W. C., 1963, *The Meaning and End of Religion*, New York: Macmillan; 1979, *Faith and Belief*, Princeton: Princeton University Press; 1981, *Towards a World Theology*, Basingstoke: Macmillan.

20 Troeltsch, E., 1980 (1923), 'The Place of Christianity among World Religions', in Hick, J., and Hebblethwaite, B. (eds), *Christianity and Other Religions: Selected Readings*, London: Fount Paperbacks, pp. 11–31; Tillich, P., 1966, 'The Significance of the History of Religions for the Systematic Theologian', in *The Future of Religions*, New York: Harper and Row, pp. 80–94.

21 See, for example, Hick, J., 1973, *God and the Universe of Faiths*, Basingstoke: Macmillan; 1982, *God Has Many Names*, Philadelphia: Westminster; 1985, *Problems of Religious Pluralism*, Basingstoke: Macmillan; 1989, *An Interpretation of Religion*, Basingstoke: Macmillan; 1993, *The Metaphor of God Incarnate*, London: SCM Press. In 1995, *The Rainbow of Faiths*, London: SCM Press, and

2001, *Dialogues in the Philosophy of Religion*, Basingstoke: Palgrave, Hick engages in critical discussions with a range of objections against his theology/philosophy.

22 Kaufman, G., and Gilkey, L., 1987, in Hick, J., and Knitter, P. (eds), *The Myth of Christian Uniqueness*, Maryknoll: Orbis; Richards, G., 1989, *Towards a Theology of Religions*, London: Routledge.

23 See, for example, Race, A., 1993, *Christians and Religious Pluralism*, 2nd enl. edn, London: SCM Press; 2001, *Interfaith Encounter*, London: SCM Press; Wiles, M., 1992, *Christian Theology and Interreligious Dialogue*, London: SCM Press; Ward, K., 1991, *A Vision to Pursue*, London: SCM Press.

24 See, for example, Knitter, P., 1985, *No Other Name?* Maryknoll: Orbis; 1995, *One Earth Many Religions*, Maryknoll: Orbis; 1996, *Jesus and the Other Names*, Maryknoll: Orbis; 2002, *Introducing Theologies of Religions*, Maryknoll: Orbis; Swidler, *After*; Gillis C. , 1993, *Pluralism*, Louvain: Peeters.

25 Cf. Macquarrie, J., 1990, *Jesus Christ in Modern Thought*, London: SCM Press; 1995, *The Mediators*, London: SCM Press; Haight, R., 1999, *Jesus Symbol of God*, Maryknoll: Orbis; 2005, *The Future of Christology*, New York: Continuum.

26 Byrne, P., 1995, *Prolegomena to Religious Pluralism*, Basingstoke: Macmillan.

27 See, for example, Schmidt-Leukel, P., 1992, *'Den Löwen brüllen hören' – Zur Hermeneutik eines christlichen Verständnisses der Buddhistischen Heilsbotschaft*, Paderborn: Schöningh; 1997, *Theologie der Religionen*, Neuried: Ars Una; 2005, *Gott ohne Grenzen*, Gütersloh: Gütersloher Verlagshaus (English translation: 2009, *God Without Limits*, London: SCM Press).

28 See, for example, Guénon, R., 2004 (1921), *Introduction to the Study of Hindu Doctrines*, 2nd rev. edn, Hillsdale: Sophia Perennis; Schuon, F., 1984 (1948, 1979), *The Transcendent Unity of Religions*, Wheaton: Quest Books; Coomaraswamy, R. P. (ed.), 2003, *The Essential Ananda K. Coomaraswamy*, Bloomington: World Wisdom; Pallis, M., 2004, *A Buddhist Spectrum*, new edn, Bloomington: World Wisdom; Nasr, S. H., 1989, *Knowledge and the Sacred*, Albany: SUNY Press; Smith, H., and Griffin, D., 1989, *Primordial Truth and Postmodern Theology*, Albany: SUNY Press.

29 Cf. the overview in Pawlikowski, John, 1988, 'Judentum und Christentum', in *Theologische Realenzyklopädie*, vol. 17, Berlin and New York: de Gruyter, pp. 386–403.

30 See, for example, Samartha, S., 1981, *Courage for Dialogue*, Geneva: WCC (see also fn. 13); Ariarajah, W., 2005, 'Power, Politics and Plurality: The Struggles of the World Council of Churches to Deal with Religious Plurality', in Knitter (ed.), *Myth*, pp. 176–93; Ucko, H., 2002, *The People of God*, Münster: LIT.

31 See, for example, Hillman, E., 1989, *Many Paths*, Maryknoll: Orbis; Cracknell, K., 1986, *Towards a New Relationship: Christians and People of Other Faith*, London: Epworth; 2005, *In Good and Generous Faith: Christian Responses to Religious Pluralism*, London: Epworth; Eck, D., 1993, *Encountering God*, Boston: Beacon Press; Hocking, W. E., 1932, *Re-Thinking Missions*, New York: Harper & Brothers.

32 Cf. Balasuriya, T. (ed.), 1988, *Emergence of Third World Theology*, Voices from the Third World, XI.1, Colombo: Asian Theology Centre, pp. 152–71; (ed.), 1988, *Christologies in Encounter*, Voices from the Third World, XI.2, Colombo: Asian Theology Centre.

33 See, for example, Pieris, A., 1999, *An Asian Theology of Liberation*, Edinburgh:

T&T Clark; Balasuriya, T., 1984, *Planetary Theology*, Maryknoll: Orbis; Wilfred, Felix, 1993, *Leave the Temple*, Maryknoll: Orbis.

34 Cf. Knitter, P., 1987, 'Toward a Liberation Theology of Religions', in Hick and Knitter (eds), *Myth*, pp. 178–200.

35 See, for example, King, U., 1993, *Women and Spirituality*, 2nd edn, University Park, PA: Pennsylvania State University Press; (ed.), 1995, *Religion and Gender*, Oxford: Blackwell; Hewitt Suchocki, M., 1987, 'In Search of Justice: Religious Pluralism from a Feminist Perspective', in Hick and Knitter (eds), *Myth*, pp. 149–61; 2003, *Divinity and Diversity*, Nashville: Abingdon; Kalsky, M., 2000, *Christaphanien*, Gütersloh: Gütersloher Verlagshaus; Ruether, R. Radford, 1987, 'Feminism and Jewish–Christian Dialogue', in Hick and Knitter (eds), *Myth*, pp. 137–48.

36 For a selection of approaches to religious pluralism from different religious traditions see Knitter (ed.), *Myth*.

37 See, for example, Askari, H., 1991, *Spiritual Quest*, Pudsey: Seven Mirrors; Aydin, M., 'Islam in a World of Diverse Faiths – A Muslim View', in Schmidt-Leukel and Ridgeon (eds), *Islam*, pp. 33–54; Ayoub, M., 1997, 'Islam and Pluralism', *Encounters: Journal of Inter-Cultural Perspectives*, vol. 3, pp. 103–18; Engineer, Asghar Ali, 2005, 'Islam and Pluralism', in Knitter (ed.), *Myth*, pp. 211–19; Esack, F., 1997, *The Qur'an, Liberation and Pluralism*, Oxford: Oneworld; Sachedina, A., 2001, *The Islamic Roots of Democratic Pluralism*, Oxford: Oxford University Press.

38 See, for example, Cohn-Sherbok, D., 1994, *Judaism and Other Faiths*, Basingstoke: Macmillan; Hartman, D., 1990, *Conflicting Visions*, New York: Schocken Books; Solomon, N., 1996, 'Faith in the Midst of Faiths', in Ucko, H. (ed.), *People of God, Peoples of God*, Geneva: WCC, pp. 84–99; Kogan, M., 2005, 'Toward a Pluralist Theology of Judaism', in Knitter (ed.), *Myth*, pp. 105–18; and, to some extent, Sacks, J., 2002, *The Dignity of Difference: How to Avoid the Clash of Civilizations*, London and New York: Continuum.

39 See, for example, Radhakrishnan, S., 1948, *The Hindu View of Life*, London: Allen & Unwin; 1937, *An Idealist View of Life*, 2nd rev. edn, London: Allen & Unwin.

40 Cf. Schmidt-Leukel, P. (ed.), 2008, *Buddhist Attitudes to Other Religions*, St Ottilien: EOS.

41 In the following section I present my own view regarding the theological presuppositions of a Christian and at the same time genuinely pluralistic theology of religions. This is broadly in line with a number of pluralistic approaches by other Christian theologians but not with all of them. A major type of a different approach is dealt with in the section 'Polycentric Pluralism?' below.

42 As Holmes Rolston rightly states (having compared various religious concepts of the ultimate): 'The comprehensive ultimate is, almost analytically, incomprehensible. Comprehended by it, we cannot comprehend it' (Rolston, Holmes, III, 1985, *Religious Inquiry – Participation and Detachment*, New York: Philosophical Library, p. 136).

43 The assumption that there is (or might be) a reality which necessarily exceeds all human understanding cannot be blamed as irrational, although it does involve the kind of logical paradox that inevitably appears once one points by logical/rational/linguistic means beyond the limits of what logic/reason/language can encompass.

44 Of course, these teachings still need to entail some propositions which are

meant to be literally true, for example that the ultimate can be experienced, that it is the ground of our salvation, that it does exceed human understanding, and so on. But these propositions can be understood as referring to the relation between ultimate and penultimate reality and need not be seen as a description of ultimate reality as such. And on the level of these kinds of propositions, many apparently incompatible claims may turn out to be less, or not, contradictory.

45 This is a widespread misunderstanding of the pluralist position in general and of Hick's position in particular. As such it is probably due to George Lindbeck's description of what he calls the 'experiential-expressive model', according to which 'the various religions are diverse symbolizations of one and the same core experience of the Ultimate . . .' (Lindbeck, G., 1984, *The Nature of Doctrine*, Philadelphia: Westminster Press, p. 23). Before Lindbeck there had been a fairly long debate whether the striking structural similarities in the records of mystics from different religious backgrounds suggest that in the case of mystical experience a basically identical or similar experience is merely expressed in different forms. But this specific debate must not be confused with the epistemological implications of religious pluralism in general. Moreover, Hick in fact has sided with S. Katz and argued that even in the case of mysticism we should reckon with culturally conditioned and differently shaped experiences. Cf. Hick, *Interpretation*, pp. 292–6.

46 Cf. Anselm, *Proslogion* XV.

47 Cf. Thomas, *De potentia*, q. 7, a. 5.

48 Cf. Thomas, *Summa contra gentiles* 14.

49 Cf. Nicholas of Cusa, *De docta ignorantia* I, 26.

50 Cf. Thomas, *Compendium theologiae* 24, Cyril Vollert (trans.), http://www.diafrica.org/kenny/CDtexts/Compendium.htm#24.

51 This image was used by René Descartes in his response to Caterus.

52 Hick, *Problems*, p. 34.

53 *Dialogue and Proclamation*, No. 29. Cf. *Origins*, CNS documentary service, vol. 21.8 (4 July 1991), p. 127.

54 As, for example, the argument that a constitutive role of Christ would imply that the Christ event has caused some change in God, which contradicts divine immutability and perfection; or the argument that forgiveness which has been 'bought' by 'an adequate satisfaction' is no forgiveness at all (cf. Hick, *Metaphor*, p. 126); or that such a view would be in direct opposition to Jesus' own understanding and proclamation of God's unconditional love as the sole source of our salvation.

55 Ogden, S., 1992, *Is There Only One True Religion or Are There Many?* Dallas: Southern Methodist University Press, p. 93.

56 Knitter, P., 1997, 'Five Theses on the Uniqueness of Jesus', in Swidler, L., and Mojzes, P. (eds), *The Uniqueness of Jesus*, Maryknoll: Orbis, p. 7. See also Schmidt-Leukel, P., 2007, 'Uniqueness: A Pluralistic Reading of John 14.6', in O'Grady, J., and Scherle, P. (eds), *Ecumenics from the Rim*, Berlin: LIT, pp. 303–10.

57 Cf. Schmidt-Leukel, P., 2006, 'Chalcedon Defended: A Pluralistic Re-Reading of the Two-Natures Doctrine', *Expository Times*, vol. 118.3, pp. 113–19.

58 Haight, R., 1992, 'The Case for Spirit Christology', *Theological Studies*, vol. 53, pp. 257–87, at p. 263.

59 *Ibid.*, p. 281.

60 See his discussion of criteria in Hick, *Interpretation*, pp. 229–376.

61 *Ibid.*, p. 164.

62 Ratzinger, J., 1969, *Das neue Volk Gottes. Entwürfe zur Ekklesiologie*, Düsseldorf: Patmos, p. 356. My translation.

63 For example DiNoia, J. A., 1990, 'Pluralist Theology of Religions: Pluralistic or Non-Pluralistic?', in D'Costa, G. (ed.), *Christian Uniqueness Reconsidered*, Maryknoll: Orbis, pp. 119–34; Heim, S. Mark, 1995, *Salvations: Truth and Difference in Religion*, Maryknoll: Orbis, pp. 7f., 129f.; Griffin, David, 2005, 'Religious Pluralism', in Griffin, D. (ed.), *Deep Religious Pluralism*, Louisville: Westminster John Knox, pp. 3–38, at pp. 24ff.

64 Cf. Cobb, John, Jr, 1999, *Transforming Christianity and the World: A Way beyond Absolutism and Relativism*, Maryknoll: Orbis; Griffin, *Deep*.

65 Cf. the excellent account of the process approach to religious diversity in D. Griffin, 2005, 'John Cobb's Whiteheadian Complementary Pluralism', in Griffin, *Deep*, pp. 39–66.

66 Hick, John, 1981, 'Critique' (of D. R. Griffin), in Davis, S. (ed.), *Encountering Evil*, Edinburgh: T&T Clark, pp. 122f.

67 Cf. Griffin, 'John', pp. 47f.

68 Kaplan, Stephen, 2002, *Different Paths, Different Summits: A Model for Religious Pluralism*, Lanham: Rowman & Littlefield. Kaplan's approach has been to some extent prefigured by Burch, George Bosworth, 1972, *Alternative Goals in Religion*, Montreal: McGill–Queen's University Press.

69 This has also been pointed out by Hick, J., 2006, *The New Frontier of Religion and Science*, Basingstoke: Palgrave Macmillan, p. 158.

70 Kaplan, *Different*, p. 47.

71 Heim, *Salvations*.

72 Cf. *ibid.*, pp. 163–6.

73 Heim, S. Mark, 2001, *The Depth of the Riches: A Trinitarian Theology of Religious Ends*, Grand Rapids: Eerdmans.

74 Cf. *ibid.*, pp. 19, 179, 289, etc.

75 Cf. Heim's confession: 'I am a convicted inclusivist' (*ibid.*, p. 8).

76 Cf. *ibid.*, pp. 268, 279.

77 An exclusivist, for example, will (due to his/her exclusivism) not expect to discover something of theological relevance in the belief of his dialogue partner from another religious tradition. But the exclusivist too can entertain an epistemological openness, that is, he or she might hold that the truth of exclusivism is not infallibly certain and could turn out to be wrong (without expecting this). This kind of formal, epistemological openness is sufficient for entering into a meaningful dialogue. This has rightly been emphasized by Stenmark, M., 2006, 'Exclusivism, Tolerance and Interreligious Dialogue', *Studies in Interreligious Dialogue*, vol. 16, pp. 101–14.

78 Cf. Schmidt-Leukel, P., 2002, 'Beyond Tolerance: Towards a New Step in Interreligious Relationships', *Scottish Journal of Theology*, vol. 55, pp. 379–91; 2005, 'Tolerance and Appreciation', *Current Dialogue*, vol. 46, pp. 17–23.

79 This helpful term has been suggested by John Hick (cf. Hick, *Dialogues*, p. 76).

80 Hick points this out frequently; see, for example, Hick, J., 1987, 'The Non-absoluteness of Christianity', in Hick and Knitter (eds), *Myth*, pp. 16–36; 1988, 'Religious Pluralism and Salvation', *Faith and Philosophy*, vol. 5, pp. 365–77.

81 Hick, *Problems*, p. 38.

82 For example, Vroom, Hendrik, 1993, 'Right Conduct as a Criterion for True

Religion', in Kellenberger, J. (ed.), *Interreligious Models and Criteria*, Basingstoke: Macmillan, pp. 106–31.

83 This judgement needs to take into account the full picture, being aware 'that in some respects, or in some periods or regions, the fruits of one tradition are better than, whereas in other respects or periods or regions inferior to, those of another. But as vast complex totalities, the world traditions seem to be more or less on a par with each other. None can be singled out as manifestly superior' (Hick, 'Non-Absoluteness', p. 30).

84 This tendency to (ideally) replace all other religions by one's own is a central aspect of the religious potential for violent conflicts. For due to this tendency religions are inclined to perceive each other as threats against which they need to protect themselves. Cf. 2004, '"Part of the Problem, Part of the Solution": An Introduction', in Schmidt-Leukel, P. (ed.), *War and Peace in World Religions*, London: SCM Press, pp. 1–8.

85 I am grateful to Magdalen Lambkin and John Hick, who made helpful suggestions on earlier drafts of this essay.

Section C: Other Approaches

6

Particularities: Tradition-Specific Post-modern Perspectives

PAUL HEDGES

Introduction

While the term 'particularity' is becoming increasingly widespread, there is no agreement on its usage. Some have used it as a virtual synonym for exclusivism, suggesting we should follow a typology of particularity–inclusivism–pluralism.[1] Other thinkers, classed here as 'particularists', use other terms – for example, Gavin D'Costa defines his approach as 'tradition-specific'.[2] Therefore, I will begin with an overview of how particularity is understood here.

To give a generalized expression: particularity is a post-modern theological approach to other faiths. It rejects the idea that such things as 'religion', 'reason' or 'religious experience' exist as cross-cultural and universal categories. Rather, each culture has its own particular structure, discourse and expression, for which these terms may not be valid. It rejects pluralism, which it sees as speaking of universals; regards inclusivism as incoherent, because it tends towards a view that every 'religion' is essentially similar in nature; and is not exclusivism, because that may not be what is within God's plans.

This generalized expression contains a host of diversity and multifarious expressions in the work of such theologians as Gavin D'Costa, George Lindbeck, Rowan Williams, Kevin Vanhoozer, Lesslie Newbigin, Joseph DiNoia, John Milbank, Alister McGrath, and others. S. Mark Heim also has affinities with particularity, although he is not, perhaps, truly representative, and has described himself as an inclusivist.[3] All these figures can, as theologians, be broadly termed 'conservative', 'postliberal' and/or 'postmodern'.[4] A great many differences separate them, some of which we will explore below. However, most would broadly agree on the following points, which may be said therefore to constitute a framework for particularity: (1) each faith is unique, alterity[5] is stressed over similarity, as seemingly common elements in religious experience or doctrine are regarded as superficial; (2) it is only possible to speak from a specific tradition, there can be no pluralistic interpretation; (3) the Holy Spirit may be at work in other faiths, requiring them to be regarded with respect and dignity; (4) no salvific potency resides in other faiths, though they are somehow involved in God's plans for humanity but in ways we cannot know; (5) particularity is based in a post-modern and postliberal worldview; (6) the orthodox doctrines of Trinity and Christ are grounding points from which to approach other faiths.

Background and Development

Various pathways lead into particularity, which it is useful to consider if we are to understand what it claims and why. These are both theological and philosophical, compounded by politico-socio undercurrents, and are far from univocal.

Many proponents of particularity have a theological antecedent in Karl Barth, who propounded a view of theology that places the biblical narrative in a position of centrality. Therefore that narrative, or at least an interpretation of it, becomes the central focus of attention. In contrast to the liberal tradition, which looks to correlation with 'the world', Barth established a pattern of looking inward to Christian resources alone. Also, by stressing the separation of religion and revelation, Barth made a case that within God's revelation in Christ something unique happened, which is absent from other faiths. Hendrik Kraemer extended and helped popularize this trajectory of thought, with his notion of 'discontinuity', within the context of Christian approaches to other faiths.

Another important figure is Hans Urs von Balthasar, whose thought is grounded in patristic learning. A Roman Catholic, with ties to Popes John Paul II and Benedict XVI, he was friends with Barth, and, despite radical differences, he, like Barth, emphasized God's own story, and the return to a biblical worldview. He has been used by, or has influenced, a number of significant postliberal thinkers, both Catholics and others, including Rowan Williams and John Milbank. Notably, while exercising an influence on particularity, von Balthasar is an inclusivist, his patristic background leading him to expound a form of fulfilment theology.[6]

Post-modernism[7] is a widely used but disputed term, with almost every commentator having their own definition. Part of the trouble comes from the fact that post-modern philosophy (hereafter post-modernism) and post-modern culture (hereafter post-modernity) are often not clearly distinguished. The former we will discuss below. The latter is a complex set of relations in contemporary Western society, such as multiculturalism, communication technology, consumerism, which affects the way we live. In this sense, we may all be said to live within post-modernity, even if we have not embraced post-modernism. It is, however, not a simple divide because post-modernism arises from the situation of post-modernity, and, partly at least, it describes (one way of being within) this situation.

While notoriously difficult to define, it is nevertheless possible to identify various ideas commonly associated with post-modernism. It is rooted in dissatisfaction with the modern world, especially the rational tradition of the Enlightenment (project), and such figures as Immanuel Kant and Friedrich Hegel. It seeks to reconstitute knowledge, or, at least, to challenge traditional forms of knowing. One significant factor in this is what Jean-François Lyotard termed a suspicion of metanarratives – totalizing theories, which subsume the local and particular to universal concepts – because any interpretative framework must come from somewhere and have inbuilt presuppositions. Another factor, highlighted by Michel Foucault, is the way that knowledge and power are entwined: to define something is, in some way, to claim control over it, to interpret it in *your* way. Meanwhile, perhaps the most famous post-modern philosopher, Jacques Derrida, challenged conventional linguistic usage and understanding. He is especially famous for saying everything is text, which he glossed elsewhere by saying everything is context: all we have is given to us through language, there is no external referent point. Everything we say, know and experience is embedded within our given and inherited conceptual systems.

Post-modernism also has various themes associated with it. One is respect for the Other; it decries the way in which the marginalized or repressed (or exotic) are either ignored or packaged and controlled by an elite (for example, Western, male, powerful, academic), and seeks to give them their own voice(s). Another theme is heteroglossy, which comes from Mikhail Bakhtin. This implies a multiplicity of voices, as opposed to monoglossy, or a single voice or narrative. Finally, there is the denial of fixed essences; that is to say, everything is seen as being a complex and changing set of relationships, in contrast to modernity's (claimed) 'essentialism', which tried to define the true and unchanging nature of things.

These strands lead into the various conservative post-modern schools of theology and have influenced an upsurge of particularist thinking within them. While not wanting to downplay the vast differences of thinking, the following gives some guide as to how this has occurred: post-modernism is seen to have severely damaged, if not destroyed, the Western modern liberal tradition. This has meant that many mini-narratives, including traditional Christianity, can reassert themselves alongside the discredited metanarrative of universal reason. Further, the heritage of Barth and Balthasar helps to provide a framework for this, so that the Christian narrative is also reasserted as the best possible of all narratives. For instance, Gerard Loughlin states:

> The postmodern work, according to Lyotard, is not governed by the past, and cannot be judged by present rules, precisely because it calls past rules

> into question. The rules that govern the work are made in its production. The writer or artist works 'without rules, and in order to establish the rules for what *will have been made*.'[8]

While not discussing particularity, it gives some background to these thinkers who believe that modernist ways of thinking have passed (interpretations, typologies, and so on) and so we must construct anew. We shall unpack some of the implications of this in due course.

The System of Particularity

A lot of particularist writing has come out of a critique of pluralism, so it would be useful to set out some oppositions in order to highlight its tenets and post-modern views. We can interrogate this by seeing the way they view three ideas:

1. Religion: for pluralism, all religions stem from one basic form, and are essentially compatible; for particularity, they are independent 'language games' and mutually incompatible.
2. Religious/mystical experiences: pluralism is seen as believing one core experience exists across religions, which is interpreted differently according to culture;[9] for particularity, each religion has its own core experience, and only superficial similarities exist.
3. Religious teachings/doctrines: for pluralism, these are cultural expressions of faith, an interpretation of the core mystical experience; for particularity, they are given, even fixed, as part of internally coherent systems which cannot be compared.

The contrast is often seen as between worldviews, with particularity claiming that the modern worldview has ended and is no longer tenable.[10] Notions that real similarities exist between religions, or that an individual can find truth in more than one, are dismissed:

> It seems reasonable to say that Greek Orthodoxy and Gelug Tibetan Buddhism are different religions just because it is performatively impossible to belong to both at once – in much the same way that it is performatively impossible simultaneously to be a sumo wrestler and a balance-beam gymnast, or natively to live in the house of English and the house of Japanese.[11]

The following will, in large part, flesh out these ideas. We will begin with the last point made here, about language.

One of the earliest, and most influential, expressions of particularity was

Lindbeck's contrast between his 'cultural-linguistic' and the 'experiential-expressive' theories of religion.[12] The latter model posits that we can speak of essences of religion across cultures. Whereas, for Lindbeck, all our experience, including religious experience, is organized by 'categorical patterns embedded in a language':

> experience (viz., something of which one is prereflectively or reflectively conscious) is impossible unless it is in some fashion symbolized and . . . all symbol systems have their origin in interpersonal relations and social interactions. It is conceptually confused to talk of symbolizations (and therefore experiences) that are purely private.[13]

That is to say, religious (mystical) experience is regarded as a formulation of our thought structures created on the basis of our linguistic/symbolic system. In very clear language, Lindbeck states: 'Adherents of different religions do not diversely thematize the same experience; rather they have different experiences.'[14]

Much of this is based in reference to Wittgenstein's language games, used explicitly by Lindbeck and McGrath, and implicitly by many other particularists. Wittgenstein used games as an example, asking what the various things we call 'games' have in common, for instance, what links chess to baseball, or board games to athletics? His answer was that while we can find some common family resemblances (they have rules, participants, and often spectators or special arenas/areas for play), nevertheless, we cannot viably interrelate them. For instance, it is meaningless to ask if an action, undertaken in a game of football, is licit in terms of the rules of chess. This is extended to language, so that any word has a meaning only within its context, making translation between systems impossible; then, by analogy, to religion. Lindbeck offers the analogy of love to explain this:

> The datum that all religions recommend something which can be called 'love' towards that which is taken to be most important ('God') is a banality as uninteresting as the fact that all languages are (or were) spoken. The significant things are the distinctive patterns of story, belief, ritual, and behaviour that give 'love' and 'God' their specific and sometimes contradictory meanings.[15]

Continuing to speak of love, Lindbeck says:

> Buddhist compassion, Christian love and – if I may cite a quasi-religious phenomenon – French Revolutionary *fraternité* are not diverse modifications of a single human awareness, emotion, attitude or sentiment, but are radically (i.e. from the root) distinct ways of experiencing and being orientated towards self, neighbour, and cosmos.[16]

Therefore, only by looking at tradition-specific usage of terms such as 'God' can we understand 'how the word operates within a religion and thereby shapes reality and experience rather than by first establishing its propositional or experiential meaning and reinterpreting or reformulating its uses accordingly'.[17] We must find the meaning of the word within its linguistic/religious context, rather than seeking for a meaning outside of this to give it meaning.

Various particularists, notably DiNoia, and those who display a strong kinship with particularists, such as Heim, have claimed, therefore, that to say all religions are aiming at the same goal, when they express very different ideas of the afterlife, is incoherent. The Hindu wishes to achieve *moksha*, the Christian to attain heaven, meanwhile the Buddhist seeks nirvana. The first is annihilation of the self in the absolute, the second is theistically orientated, while the last is the destruction of self, expressed as *anatman*. Indeed, Heim explicitly sets out the idea that not only may every religion be aiming at different goals, but that each may reach it, as a lesser aim, although the Christian goal of salvation remains the highest.[18]

Particularity and Other Faiths

For a Christian particularist, there must be certain unique and inviolable things in Christianity which do not have their equivalent in other faiths. These are, first and foremost, the doctrine of the Trinity and the person of Christ, understood in traditional Christological formulae. Indeed, for particularists, it is impossible to look at other faiths unless one's own Trinitarian faith is foregrounded. According to Vanhoozer: 'The Trinity . . . is . . . the transcendental condition for interreligious dialogue, the ontological condition that permits us to take the other in all seriousness, without fear, and without violence.'[19] This statement is so central to the particularist point of view that we should take some time unpacking the various presuppositions and implications of it.

First, the Trinity might seem to block interreligious dialogue, as has been claimed, for example, by Rabbi Dan Cohn-Sherbok, when he asked, 'What is the point of multifaith dialogue if Christ is the only way to God?'[20] However, we should see why it might be considered the only authentic starting place for Christian interfaith relations. For postliberal traditions, Christianity's rationale is found solely within the resources of the tradition itself; the Christian can start in no other place. Every understanding of other faiths must be based in what is already known of God from within a lived tradition, its teachings, scriptures, practices and social framework. To do anything else, they would argue, is not to truly approach other religions, for to do this with depth and seriousness requires that it is done from what you believe and from the heart of your own tradition. There is certainly much to commend in this position in terms of its honesty and depth of approach. It can also answer Cohn-Sherbok's reproachful question with the reply, 'What is the point of multifaith dialogue, if you don't assert your own truth-claims?'

Second, we turn now to the phrase, 'without fear'. The idea of 'fear' may be taken to refer to a (perceived) lack of concern for those who enter dialogue from a Trinitarian perspective. For many, the notion of interfaith dialogue is inherently worrying, just because it might necessitate abandoning one's own presuppositions and tenets of faith. However, for the particularist, this is not necessitated by dialogue. Rather, coming to it with a Trinitarian perspective, your own faith is not shaped by the encounter. Although, importantly, for the particularist, you do not 'shape' other faiths either – this would imply the imposition of modernist fixed frameworks – rather you are allowing the particular distinctiveness of each.

This brings us, third, to the words 'without violence'. For particularity, as for post-modernism, the principal concern with violence is not physical, but epistemological – the 'violence' of misinterpretation and misrepresentation of the Other. Basically summarized, from a postliberal perspective, the Christian worldview is that which best explains the world; therefore, interpretations within this schema ought not to distort or disrupt that which they are explaining. Also, they should not assert mastery over the Other. We can see this expressed through a quotation from Loughlin:

> It must be remembered, however, that the Christian story is provisional because not yet ended. It is performed in the hope that the one of whom it speaks will return again to say it. The last word is yet to be said; and when it is, the Church will also find itself positioned. Thus the Christian story resists mastery by being the prayerful tale of one who comes in the form of a servant and who will return as a friend.[21]

While not discussing particularity, Loughlin's comments are highly pertinent, for he offers a defence of the theoretical underpinning of particularity, utilizing compelling rhetoric, combined with subtle philosophical positioning. It seeks to avoid the assertion of Christian supremacy, as one system over and against other systems, as particularity sees exclusivist and inclusivist positions doing. Instead, it says such language is simply not appropriate, or possible, for the truth of Christianity is that which comes through a servant, not through a show of divine power.[22] Indeed, particularists would not be happy to say that they are upholding Christian supremacy. This idea, that Christianity cannot be seen as higher, but instead resides in a different ground, is asserted by D'Costa:

> I suspect Hick's use of 'superiority' is a category mistake. One can say, 'This English apple is *superior* to other apples', when one is judging things

> in the same category. However, when we come to 'revelation' we are dealing with a *sui generis* reality which therefore admits no comparison. My argument is that such a notion of revelation upsets the apple cart, in at least three ways. First, the Trinitarian doctrine of God, properly understood, refuses closure in history, such that it is only through engagement with other religions in history that the church comes to a fuller confession and witness to the truth, which it never possesses.[23]

For the next two points, he claims the Trinity allows a more 'tolerant' and 'open' approach, and that it justifies contact with other faiths, without, however, presupposing they are speaking of the same God, or relativizing beliefs.[24]

For D'Costa, two problems haunt inclusivist thinking: it suggests that salvation through other faiths occurs because the Holy Spirit is active within them; and, seeing the Spirit active in some circumstances, means, in Kärkkäinen's useful summing up of his position: 'inclusivism violates the rule according to which each tradition has to be treated as a totality; one cannot affirm only some aspects of another tradition'.[25] Yet, D'Costa believes the Spirit may be (indeed, he suggests, the Spirit *is*) working in other faiths. However, he raises another problem, pointing out that, in traditional Christological thinking, the action of the Spirit is closely linked to the reception and salvific locus of Christ, as he puts it simply, 'It is clear that the Spirit cannot be dissociated from Christ.'[26] This raises problems, as he believes we cannot say so simply that Christ is present in other faiths. Inclusivism, he believes, creates a metanarrative to explain other faiths, and places them in a too-simplistic relationship to Christianity. This, for particularity, is problematic; we cannot be sure of God's activity in other faiths, while it violates their Otherness. For particularity, the relationship of Christianity and other faiths remains a mystery. As DiNoia observes:

> other religions are to be valued by Christians, not because they are channels of grace or means of salvation for their adherents, but because they play a real but as yet perhaps not fully specifiable role in the divine plan to which the Christian community bears witness.[27]

While particularity sees Christianity as the only legitimate source of salvation, particularist writers often express a hope, if not belief, in the salvation of all people. In terms of the dynamics, while particularity admits that only Christianity has salvific potency, it doesn't mean others are damned, as Lindbeck has argued:

> there is no damnation – just as there is no salvation – outside the church. One must, in other words, learn the language of faith before one can know enough about its message knowingly to reject it and thus be lost.[28]

Therefore, as Lindbeck and DiNoia make explicit, there must be some post-mortem conversion experience. Whether this be purification in purgatory or an encounter with Christ is, however, for most particularists left an open question.

Finally, views vary widely in particularity about engagement with other faiths. D'Costa, after much protracted struggle with the question, suggests that Jesus' 'reckless' love calls us to undertake interreligious prayer:

> I have been suggesting that plunging into the love of the triune God may well call us to risk finding even greater love of God through interreligious prayer, and into discovering the darkness and mystery of God afresh. Our marriage to our Lord may itself suffer infidelity in an absolute resistance to the promptings of suffering love which might entail interreligious prayer. But equally, interreligious prayer may also be an act of irreverent infidelity. The church is called to pray fervently for those who engage in interreligious prayer for the sake of Christ.[29]

Others, such as Milbank, however, feel the principal approach should be one of conversion, with Christians having nothing to learn from the Other.[30] It is hard to say where most particularists stand on this, but among their number are some, like Paul Griffiths, who are highly engaged in the encounter with other faiths, while others, such as DiNoia, actively call for response; and S. Mark Heim specifically praises Raimundo Panikkar, who has sought to widen a constructive Christian encounter with other faiths.[31]

Critiques

Having given an outline of particularity, it is now time to address the critique. First, as this is seen as a distinctly post-modern worldview, we must address the question of what this entails.

Post-modernism

One distinct problem is that particularity assumes post-modernism has 'overcome' or replaced modernity. However, most contemporary perceptive critics of post-modernism have rejected this rather naive view, popular some while ago, that it has replaced modernity, and have opted instead for seeing it as some form of new twist within modernity.[32] That is to say, it is seen as an extension, or exaggeration, of certain facets of modernity, rather than something altogether new. Some examples of post-modernism's continued status as a further stage within modernity are: it needs metanarratives – the claim that there are no metanarratives is the greatest of all; in proclaiming modernity's end, it is essentializing modernity – claiming to know its essence and reducing it thereby to a monolithic entity and ignoring its nuances, especially those which interfere with its own reading of modernity; it manifests the will-to-power in its attitude to other claims to knowledge, asserting its own claims as superior or unsurpassable and capable of positioning the Other without reference to how other systems of thought operate; only by using and adopting modernity's norms of rationality and argument, can it construct its own claims to modernity's failings, which begs questions of whether it has begun a new phase of discourse, or whether it is merely an internal critique. Thus, Loughlin's claims, based upon Lyotard's authority, need more than their own self-assertion to be valid. One of the dangers of post-modernism is fundamentalist post-modern thinking, that is, assuming its tenets are the fundamental basis for thinking. However, this very move makes them quintessentially modernist, for they then fall prey to the very foundationalist, essentialist, metanarrative structure and claims to power, that post-modernism has rightly seen as problems inherent within the extremes of modernity. Only a nuanced and balanced approach to post-modernism allows one to be truly post-modern, but this requires keeping one's feet very much within modernity, although as modified by the post-modern turn.

We may note some examples of where such problems turn up within particularity. First, the 'radical' difference between faiths is just the sort of conceit within post-modernism that Terry Eagleton has exposed; like all post-modern discourses it is itself full of metanarratives and universals.[33] The narrative of difference is just as universalizing as the narrative of similarity. Only by standing beyond the narratives could we assert such radical difference – the neutral vantage point that post-modernism has, correctly, discounted. All particularity can legitimately postulate is methodological agnosticism – which is, arguably, pluralism's standpoint!

Particularity's further leap, that one narrative is better than the others, is also a reassertion of metanarrative. Both Loughlin and D'Costa make this move – seeking to position Christianity beyond debates about 'religions' by invoking 'revelation', after the manner of Karl Barth. However, it is unclear if this point is anything but rhetorical manoeuvring. As Gavin Hyman has argued, it merely reinstates the suggestion of dominance at a higher transcendent level, rather than bypassing it.[34] It also ignores other faiths, which also respond to what may loosely be termed 'transcendent' levels or 'revelation', and could make equally irrefutable claims.

Before moving on, it is worth noting that a form of particularity can be maintained without a post-modern worldview. The early twentieth-century missionary theologian Alfred George Hogg[35] manifested many facets of particularity, especially the alterity of faiths, within a modern worldview.

The inter-relationship of religions

Various problems surround particularity's claims for the utter difference between faiths and these are both theoretical and empirical. We will begin with the linguistic focus of these arguments, that each is a separate language game, to which a further critique will be made in due course.

We begin with Paul Knitter's threefold argument against what he terms the 'lingusitic prism', based around the notions of 'isolationism', 'relativism' and 'fideism'.[36] The first means that, if accepted, religions can only 'talk within', and are cut off from other faiths – the problem with which we will see below. The second means that if each is self-contained there can be no external criticism, a point which leads to absolute relativism, although, generally, postliberal theologies do claim to be able to support Christianity's superiority (though this is argued for from internal logic). This leads us to Knitter's charge of fideism, which is similar to my charge of circularity, that each faith uses its own religious language and tradition to support its own claims, thus making it entirely dependent upon blind faith alone: if you already believe 'a' then this proves 'a' alone is correct, and 'b' is therefore a false faith. In part, particularity's claims in this regard rely upon a rejection of the category 'religion' and the similarities between faiths, which they seem to believe helps justify their separation of Christianity into a distinct category; however, we will address these points below.

Particularity suggests that theories seeking to show the similarity between faiths are flawed, because they postulate a further language/system of knowledge outside of the two compared – an obsolete metanarrative. However, Bernard Williams argues that this is based upon a flawed assumption; if, for example, we wish to translate from Chinese to English we don't need a third 'meta-language'.[37] We no more need a religious meta-language to compare Buddhism and Christianity. Consider what might be thought a mundane example, but which tackles Lindbeck's analogy of love. When a person from China watches *Romeo and Juliet* there is no need for some extra leap to a universal ideal of love for the Chinese person to appreciate and understand the play. He/she can do so within his/her own language and experience. This suggests that languages, and as we shall see below, religions, are not closed systems.

To further critique Lindbeck specifically, yet with a point that extends to all forms of particularity, the rhetoric of the argument is important. 'Love', we feel, is subjective, differing between people. However, for Lindbeck, all mental experiences are the same. However, if we substitute 'pain' for 'love' the argument immediately loses much of its potency; are we ready to say that the African experiences pain differently from a Frenchman? Furthermore, Lindbeck uses Ockham's Razor to argue that religious experience is no different from other experiences, that is to say, culturally determined.[38] However, Ockham's Razor, correctly applied, should lead us to reject many types of love, or religious experience, seeing them merely as variations of one basic experience. One of post-modernism's successes has been to demonstrate how much logical argument is often not so much logic as rhetoric; however, we can also expose its rhetoric and subject it to persuasive logic.

As well as being flawed in its application of the linguistic analogy, we can also see problems at the empirical level. Particularity rests upon an outdated view of European isolation. As recent anthropological theory tells us:

> The focus on single, presumably isolated societies as pieces in an enormous mosaic, championed by nationalists and classical social anthropologists for decades . . . has become increasingly obsolete.[39]

Much anthropology, once a bastion of support for particularity, now rejects it. Boyer, for one, has observed that, 'although anthropology generally assumes that the systems of ideas grouped under the label "religion" are essentially diverse, a number of recurrent themes and concepts can be found in very different cultural environments'.[40] Furthermore, he argues that very strong evidence is needed to 'postulate that a same idea is not the same', on the basis that the principle of 'same effects, same causes' is an extremely strong one, stressing a common 'biological history of the species'.[41] According to Robert Torrance, the 'spiritual quest' is a common trait in humanity, for:

> skepticism concerning often dubious and sometimes ethnocentric affirmations of human uniformities . . . need not eventuate in a relativism that rejects the very possibility of meaningful common human denominators.[42]

Particularity is based upon the assumption of 'a closed, self-sustaining . . . system', which should give way to the idea of cultures as 'aspects of intersubjective meaning . . . rather than "objective" properties'.[43] This may be seen as part of a growing band of theory which stresses solidarity over alterity.

In relation to the previous point, the long interaction between East and West is a subject of growing interest; old notions of Western (Judaeo-Christian) religion, as having no relation to Eastern religion (Hinduism, Buddhism, and others) are becoming untenable.[44] For instance, it is suggested that the mystery religions that influenced early Christianity are held to have 'shared a common inheritance with the religions of India'.[45] Such contacts have occurred throughout history. J. J. Clarke, for instance, in a highly provocative book, *Oriental Enlightenment*, has examined the way Eastern thought has influenced Western thought since the seventeenth century.[46]

Again, we must consider the reality of cross-faith interpenetration. No faith is an isolated cultural unit, each has been shaped by contact with other faiths, philosophies and cultures. For instance, the 'Indian form of Islam is moulded by Hindu beliefs and practices'.[47] It is certainly undeniable that in many places across India shrines exist where Hindus and Muslims come together, and some holy men, such as Kabir, are revered by both faiths. If each faith has a wholly different path to salvation, and different notions of holiness, then we must ask the exponent of particularity if the devotees of these faiths are mistaken: was the 'saint' 'saved' by the Hindu route or the Muslim route, and, if so, are the devotees of the other faiths wrong to revere him? For the devotee, such questions make no sense. Again, Julius Lipner has argued, from the example of Keshub Chunder Sen and the Brahmo Samaj, that the fact of religious interpenetration demonstrates that the difference posited by the particularity thesis cannot be viably maintained.[48]

As we have seen, a specific claim of difference within particularity is that every religion is aimed at different salvific goals. However, Christian beliefs on salvation and the afterlife have various sources. One is the early Israelite Sheol, another the Zoroastrian, via the Babylonian captivity, beliefs in resurrection of the body, a future eschaton, and ideas of heaven as paradise and the fires of hell, while, by around Jesus' time, Hellenistic ideas of a spiritual afterlife had entered the mix. Along with the martyr ideal of the Maccabean Revolt, and concepts from the Roman world, especially the mystery religions, all of these fed into early Christian conceptions. Any attempt to posit such a thing as a pure Christian notion of the afterlife or salvation, especially based upon a Jewish model, is simply nonsense. Jewish, Islamic, Christian and Zoroastrian beliefs form a complex and interrelated web, with further influences from Egypt, the mystery religions and Greek philosophical sources. We cannot simply say there are Christian ideas, which are fundamentally different from, at least, Muslim or Zoroastrian ones.

Indeed, variety applies to all traditions, against the stereotyped approach which says Christian salvation means going to heaven or hell, whereas in Hindu *moksha* the individual soul leaves the wheel of karma and becomes, indistinguishably, one with God. Rather, each faith, Christian, Buddhist, Hindu, and so on, has many models. For instance, many Hindus belong to dualist or qualified dualist bhakti traditions, and reject the notion that God and the soul are identical, indeed, the bhakti tradition even carries the tradition that, 'at the utterance of the word *mukti* (*moksha*) hatred and fear arise in the mind [of the bhakta]',[49] and sees salvation in terms of something more akin to paradise or the beatific vision. Similar variety also exists in Buddhism, where we may contrast Theravadin and Pure Land traditions. As such, particularity's claims are, in post-modern terms, engaged in a modernist essentialist fallacy.

Another specific claim of particularity is that religious performance is not just based in belief but is also bound up with a complex set of behaviours and cultural patterns – as Griffiths states, for example, it is 'performatively impossible' to be both an Orthodox Christian and a Gelug Tibetan Buddhist. This belief rests, in part, upon the linguistic turn, which says that it is not apparently similar concepts, but rather specific ritual and cultural behaviour in context that determines religious belonging, making it impossible to be two or more at the same time. However, various problems attend this. From a 'Western' or Abrahamic tradition perspective, this seems reasonable, for religions such as Christianity or Islam demand adherence to certain fixed tenets or doctrines, which rule out belonging to other faiths. However, in China, and elsewhere in the Far East, it has been normative practice for most believers to inhabit a variety of faith practices, either at different times or for different reasons. For instance, in Japan, Shinto sees death and blood as polluting, and therefore, traditionally, Buddhism would provide rituals for the beginning and end of life, while many other rites of passage are marked by Shinto festivals. This suggests that while particularity wishes to speak of each faith as performatively different, it comes from a Western viewpoint that begins with a preconceived focus of doctrinal difference as marking discrete and essential boundaries between faiths. There are also problems of people brought up between cultures, such as Julius Lipner, who readily describes himself as a Hindu-Christian, while Peter Phan also considers the question of multiple religious belonging as a category for Christian thought.[50]

Moreover, many Christians, including monks and nuns, employ Buddhist meditation techniques. This begs the question of what is meant by performative impossibility? McGrath makes the point that doctrine and liturgy are closely interwoven, such that one would find it hard, if not impossible, to graft Buddhist notions of salvation onto a Christian liturgy.[51] Meanwhile, DiNoia points to the very distinct ideals pursued by Christianity and Theravada Buddhism, suggesting that unless reconciliation can be argued we should assume alterity.[52] This must certainly be acknowledged; however, it ignores certain grey zones. For instance, while McGrath does not say what he means by 'Buddhist notions of salvation', it is certainly the case that Pure Land Buddhist notions could more easily find a resonance with Christian understanding, while if DiNoia compared Mahayana and Christian conceptions more scope for empathy would be found. Of course, this is not to say that they are anything like the same. Yet, as Daphne Hampson has argued, Catholic and Calvinist views of salvation are equally irreconcilable,[53] something which creates problems for the particularist position in its assumption that difference means non-comparable and inequitable. Related to these points, O'Leary has suggested that Griffiths' stress on the need for assuming ontological difference based upon propositional differences ignores the actuality of religions as lived practice within 'human contexts', where all doctrinal statements are merely provisional approximations to the absolute reality and which are worked out in communities where intuitive meanings may allow for apparent paradoxes to be upheld.[54]

The intra-relationship of religions

Extending the previous point, particularities raise problems with the notion that 'meaning is constituted by the uses of a specific language rather than being distinguishable from it'.[55] If so, then each language will form its own internal system. However, a further corollary of this is that we can ask this question: Is Lindbeck's idea of 'God' different from that of Jesus and his disciples? Or, again, do English, French, or Polish Roman Catholics speak different religious languages? Although particularity is based around notions of differences of religions, its basic claim is that this is analogous to the differences between languages. If we can no more translate or equate ideas between French and Spanish, than between Hinduism and Islam, then the religion of the French-speaking Protestant is just as distant from the Spanish-speaking Catholic, as the Hindu's is from the Muslim's. Particularists could, of course, claim absolute lines lie around every religion, saying that they constitute a meaning system regardless of language. However, this is merely arbitrary, and not without its problems. We have noted that many different internal explanations exist within religions; indeed, they can be so great as to be, apparently, mutually exclusive. The difference between Nestorian or Chalcedonian Christians, or the traditionally Orthodox and Monophysite Christians would, for instance, be one such example. In Griffiths' terms it is just as 'performatively impossible' to be a Mennonite and an Ethiopian Coptic, as to be a Greek Orthodox and a Gelug Tibetan Buddhist. Are we to say that the two different forms of Christianity are actually different faiths, leading to different salvific consequences? This could be seen as a traditional Christian claim, for the great councils and debates of the early Church were arguing over precise definitions of Christ's nature and the Trinity, simply because they thought only a correct interpretation could ensure salvation! If this is the case, then recent ecumenical rapprochements between Orthodox, Protestant, Catholic, Syriac, Coptic and other churches are entirely ill-founded because those who lack the correct definition are not, in particularity's terms, really Christians at all; that is to say they are not included within the Christian cultural-linguistic salvational path. Particularity, strictly followed, seems to imply every linguistic or cultural variation of Christianity is a discrete entity.

If we accept this, then we could say that not just each cultural-linguistic grouping has its own language game, but, even, that every individual has their own distinct symbolic framework! As Paul Badham has observed, the understanding of God expressed between a Christian who believes that all unbelievers are sent to an everlasting torment in hell, and a Christian who sees God as aiming to save all mankind constitutes a vast conceptual difference, surely as great as that between two people from different cultures.[56] They might share religious stories, sit side by side on a pew, but the word 'God', to use Lindbeck's language, 'operates' very differently for them.

Secular agenda

Another point of contention is particularity's secular agenda. This point is something of a double-edged sword, for it is a basis of support for particularities, yet it also causes division between particularities, as well as helping undermine all forms. John Milbank has forcefully argued that there is an inherent secular agenda within the social sciences, which presumes that everything that can be said about a religion is contained within a cultural-linguistic framework. Milbank retorts that religion should be approached on its own terms.[57] If we accept Milbank's critique (and there is good reason to do so – it is supported by other recent critiques emphasizing the biased, rather than neutral, agenda of the social sciences[58]) and thereby undermine the supposed objective commentary on religion, then several points follow.

First, if linguistics is used to interpret religion, it subjects it to an inappropriate typology. In post-modern terms we are imposing an external metanarrative over and against various 'religions' to control their interpretation to our own purposes. Moreover, it is not at all clear-cut that 'languages' and 'religions' are similar.

Second, particularity assumes that differences can be taken to imply the utter alterity of religious systems. In many cases, however, this assumption stems, more or less, directly from the modernist secular bias of the social sciences.[59] This assumes that religions have no transcendent referent beyond their particular cultural manifestation; therefore, to claim that two disparate religions can have any connection is ruled out *a priori*. Conservative post-modern theologians, in adopting the ideology of post-modernism, have used this to support their notion. A particularist response to this critique would say that these ideas are inherent to Christianity, especially within a Barthian tradition; however, at least in terms of academic theology, it is the language of respect for the Other and the particularity 'found' within other disciplines that have been used to defend this position, especially against pluralism and other viewpoints. However, as we have seen, such assumptions of isolated cultural islands are becoming increasingly untenable.

Orientalism, respect and truth-claims

Our final critiques form a set of three points related to the way particularity treats the Other. As we have seen, this is a major concern of post-modernism, and it forms part of particularity's assault on pluralism. Thus, one reason suggested for adopting particularity is the claim that it respects the 'Other' rather than submerging it into an all-encompassing Western, liberal theory. Yet stressing 'otherness' is not, in itself, a virtue. Rather, casting the Orient, or other faiths, in terms of 'otherness', in order to distance it from ourselves, is one of the key themes of postcolonial criticism in its critique of Western orientalist discourse.[60] As Sara Suleri has noted, the theory of alterity of much postcolonial discourse only continues 'the fallacy of the totality of otherness', and so, 'reinforces the old binary essentialism of East and West'.[61] In deliberately excluding those culturally and linguistically different, this theory only isolates cultural and religious groupings. Indeed, as Eagleton has noted, distinguishing ourselves from the other is one way of ignoring criticism, and may even serve to defend a parochial Western insularity, for no valid criticisms can be made between utterly different value systems.[62] As such, it is no accident that many of the most conservative forms of theology are linked into the postliberal–particularist axis. We may suggest that particularities continue many of the fallacies and prejudices highlighted by critics of Orientalism, in particular its lack of respect for the Other.

We can see this critique actively realized in certain forms of particularity. To take an example, we will look at Vanhoozer, who, referring to Lévinas, tells us that, 'to protect the Other's otherness . . . [is] the prime ethical imperative'.[63] So, for him, it follows that we must recognize the utter difference of Christian and non-Christian religions. For Christians, he believes, it is necessary to hold fast to the Trinity to respect their own tradition. However, it is hard to see where the respect of other traditions enters in. Once they are seen as different they are then dismissed as being other than, and, therefore, inferior to Vanhoozer's own faith system, possessing, he tells us, only a 'relative adequacy'.[64] As we have observed, he uses the paradox that the Trinity is 'at once exclusivistic and pluralistic' and 'the ontological condition that permits us to take the other in all seriousness', so as to approach other religions 'without fear'. It is easy to see why he uses the phrase 'without fear'; for him, difference means being alienated from the Trinity and therefore wrong. It is hard to see how this takes 'the other in all seriousness'.

The tension between supremacy and respect is commonly found. For instance, McGrath quotes with approval the following, which he attributes to Paul Griffiths and Delmas Lewis:

> It is both logically and practically possible for us, as Christians, to respect and revere worthy representatives of other traditions while still believing – on rational grounds – that some aspects of their world-views are simply mistaken.[65]

Evidently, any such respect is far from complete if you believe the other to be mistaken, and mistaken not simply about some minor matter, but about the knowledge of salvation and God; for McGrath, the absolute value of human life. We see this point summed up by Paul Griffiths:

> Christians should say of religious aliens . . . that in so far as they do not attend to Christ they cannot become what God wishes them to be, which is to say they cannot be saved.[66]

In the light of this, McGrath's comment that, 'It is no criticism of Buddhism to suggest that it does not offer a specifically Christian salvation',[67] seems, at best, disingenuous. If his words were merely a 'neutral' descriptive matter of religious beliefs, then this could be the case. However, he is affirming this within the context of, in his case, an evangelical Christian commitment which assumes 'not Christian, not true'. McGrath might defend himself against my use of words, for 'true' is redolent of modernist essentialisms, while he claims to be playing on a different field, merely pointing out options. As he says: 'In a free market of ideas, the attractiveness and relevance of the Christian understanding of salvation will determine whether others wish to endorse this understanding of salvation, and by doing so become Christians.'[68] However, such openness exists only as rhetoric. If we were discussing, for instance, shirts, and whether we were attracted to one or another on an open market, where we may freely change and buy as the whim takes us with no other consequence than keeping up with fashions, his claims might hold true. McGrath, however, wants to claim more than this. The choice, for him, is one of absolute importance for the individual. It is not simply a free market where any option is as good as any other. His claim for Christianity is not simply that wearing Christian clothes today will make you look nicer, it entails a claim that all other clothes are not, transcendently speaking, correct clothes. They are, in effect, no better than the emperor's new clothes. To opt for Buddhist robes is, for him, to be naked. If particularity is to maintain its claim as being more open than pluralism, or inclusivism, then it must hide its true intentions, yet it clearly is not universally tolerant.

Alongside this, we often find a Western parochialism. Thus, advocates of particularity, such as the Radical Orthodoxy group, espouse a form of Christianity that equates to some, supposed, 'pure' patristic archetype.[69] Other exponents of particularity are equally insistent on a Western version of Christianity. Stephen Williams argues that the only correct Christian doctrine is that expressed in terms of Greek philosophy. Thus he explicitly rejects any attempt to formulate an Indian Christian theology, for example, using the principles of Hindu philosophy,[70] as he believes that this would be utterly antithetical to Christianity. This is not surprising, for as Eagleton has observed, post-modernism, despite claims at radicalism, is often a deeply reactionary and conservative force.[71] However, this is not true of all particularists, for as we noted some have great respect for other faiths.

Therefore, in claiming that every religion must be seen on its own terms, far from respecting other religions, many religious adherents of particularity use it to disparage other faiths. Difference can mean that only one is right, and this they feel sure is themselves.[72] It may be said that particularity serves to maintain Christian dominance far more decisively and ingeniously than any supposed liberal essentialist schema.

Finally, in endorsing religious difference, particularity proclaims that each religion must hang on to its own claim to truth.[73] Yet this imposes a particular viewpoint upon other faiths, assuming that alterity is a norm. For instance, Griffiths claims not only that, 'Exclusivism will tend to be offered by the religiously committed',[74] but also that pluralism 'is not a response of much importance to religious people'.[75] Whereas, certain faiths suggest the opposite; Sikhism being a case in point, teaching that all faiths speak differently about the same God, or are following different paths up the same mountain.[76] Notwithstanding such faiths, particularity ignores the heteroglossia within traditions, for not every religious truth-claim is a claim of absolute distinction. Within Christianity, for example, Justin Martyr claimed that non-Christian teachers were also inspired by the Logos,[77] a tradition which has continued throughout history.[78] Within Hinduism, Vivekananda proclaimed his religion the *sanatanadharma*, eternal teaching, in which other religions find their highest expression.[79] It is not a specifically Western liberal perspective that says all religions aim at the same transcendent goal. Even if it were, why does particularity assume that the liberal Christian pluralist viewpoint should not also be accorded the same respect as other religious positions, as it does in claiming that it is an affront to 'the' religious point of view? Exclusivism, still less particularity, cannot claim to be the original or authentic form of belief – forms of inclusivism are found throughout religion's history.

Overview and Conclusion

While particularity has much to commend itself, in terms of trying to negotiate with contemporary thought, the response it offers seems to raise more questions than it answers, and to be based upon a number of deeply questionable underlying assumptions. Despite this, the increasing popularity of the concept suggests that such an approach has struck a chord in our post-modern world. However, significant counter trends exist, feminism, for instance, offers a further counter to all particularities.[80] Nevertheless, particularity brings a number of important factors to discussions of other faiths: (1) it rightly criticizes theories which seek to impose a foreign and alien agenda upon other faiths by stealth; (2) it points to the need for post-modern insights to be incorporated into interfaith thinking, though this must be understood as a corrective rather than an alternative to modernism; (3) in seeking to provide a traditionally faith-based model that is critically reflective and respectful of other faiths it could provide an important tool for interfaith understanding if appropriately expressed; (4) it raises serious questions about assumptions of naive religious similarity. While I have, here, raised serious questions about its own assumptions of difference, it is not transparently clear which side has the stronger case on this point. Particularities raise questions that proponents of all paradigms must grapple with.

Study Questions

1 Do you think that particularities are genuinely respectful to other faiths, or a mask for an expression of Christian supremacy by stealth?

2 Explain why it is difficult to maintain the particularist style claim that every religion is a discrete language game and should be viewed as an independent system.

3 Outline what advantages you think there are in the particularist argument over and against those of the 'classical' approaches.

Further Reading

Clarke, J. J., 1997, *Oriental Enlightenment: The Encounter between Asian and Western Thought*, London: Routledge.

D'Costa, Gavin, 2000, *The Trinity and Religious Pluralism*, Edinburgh: T&T Clark.

DiNoia, Joseph Augustine, 1992, *The Diversity of Religions: A Christian Perspective*, Washington DC: Catholic University of America Press.

Griffiths, Paul, 2001, *Problems of Religious Diversity*, Oxford: Blackwell.

Hedges, P., 2002, 'The Interrelationship of Religions: Some Critical Reflections on the Concept of Particularity', *World Faiths Encounter*, vol. 32, pp. 3–13.

Knitter, Paul F., 2002, *Introducing Theologies of Religions*, Maryknoll: Orbis.

McGrath, A., 1996, 'A Particularist View: A Post-Enlightenment Approach', in Okholm, D. L., and Phillips, T. R. (eds), *Four Views on Salvation in a Pluralistic World*, Grand Rapids: Zondervan, pp. 151–80.

Notes

1 McGrath, A., 2006, *Christianity: An Introduction*, 3rd edn, Oxford: Blackwell, p. 165.

2 D'Costa, Gavin, 2000, *The Meeting of Religions and the Trinity*, Edinburgh: T&T Clark.

3 Heim, S. Mark, 2001, *The Depth of the Riches: A Trinitarian Theology of Religious Ends*, Grand Rapids: Eerdmans, p. 8.

4 A lot of loaded and slippery terminology has just been set out here. The term 'conservative' for one is problematic. Some listed here may be, generally, doctrinally 'conservative', but have 'liberal' (another problematic term when used broadly) views on such matters as 'homosexuality', 'ecclesiology', and so forth. I am using 'postliberal' here in a broad sense to mean all those theologians who have reacted to currents in contemporary (post-modern) thought, in various ways, to move beyond and reject 'liberal' theology. These include the often termed postliberal Yale tradition(s), many other Anglo-American conservative post-modern theologians and movements, such as Radical Orthodoxy. It could also be extended to include figures such as John Paul II and Benedict XVI, who are, however, more inclusivist than particularist. However, we must not overlook the separate claims, lineages and antagonisms that exist between these groups, which may, superficially, appear very close. 'Post-modern' I will discuss below. In using these terms, the reader is asked to recognize that they are neither written, nor should be read, in monolithic, essentialist ways, but as deeply nuanced terms, which regrettably must be used as shorthand for a more complex set of dynamic relationships.

5 A word frequently used in post-modern discourse, which may simply be read as difference – though various post-modern writers might give various sub-layers of meaning to it.

6 '[T]he idea of the Bodhisattva, analogously related but ultimately inadequate, forms a sort of spiritual background to the "thought of substitution which realizes its perfection in the Cross of Christ".' Gawronski, Raymond, 1995, *Word and Silence: Hans Urs von Balthasar and the Spiritual Encounter between East and West*, Grand Rapids: Eerdmans, p. 187 (quoting Hans Urs von Balthasar, *Epilog*, pp. 55–6).

7 See, Lakeland, Paul, 1997, *Postmodernity: Christian Identity in a Fragmented Age*, Minneapolis: Fortress Press; Vanhoozer, Kevin, 2003, 'Theology and the Condition of Postmodernity: A Report on Knowledge (of God)', in Vanhoozer, Kevin (ed.), *The Cambridge Companion to Postmodern Theology*, Cambridge: Cambridge University Press; Lyon, David, 1994, *Postmodernity*, Buckingham: Open University Press; Tester, Keith, 1993, *The Life and Times of Post-modernity*, London: Routledge; and, Clarke, J. J., 1997, *Oriental Enlightenment*, London: Routledge. I have chosen to use the hyphenated form to emphasize its dependence upon modernity (following Tester) – something I will expand upon in the critique.

8 Loughlin, Gerard, 1996, *Telling God's Story: Bible, Church and Narrative Theology*, Cambridge: Cambridge University Press, p. 25. Loughlin stands within the Radical Orthodoxy grouping and therefore represents a particular point of view, though one that has resonances with other post-modern theologies.

9 This is not the view of all pluralists, but is certainly how most critics of pluralism see *all* pluralists – see Schmidt-Leukel's chapter on pluralism herein on this.

10 See Milbank, J., 1990, 'The End of Dialogue', in D'Costa, G. (ed.), *Christian Uniqueness Reconsidered*, Maryknoll: Orbis, pp. 174–90; McGrath, A., 1996, 'A Particularist View: A Post-Enlightenment Approach', in Okholm, D. L., and Phillips, T. R. (eds), *Four Views on Salvation in a Pluralistic World*, Grand Rapids: Zondervan, pp. 151–80; and D'Costa, *Meeting*, pp. 3–4.

11 Griffiths, Paul J., 2001, *Problems of Religious Diversity*, Oxford: Blackwell, p. 13.

12 Lindbeck, George, 1984, *The Nature of Doctrine: The Church in a Postmodern Age*, Philadelphia: Westminster Press, pp. 31–3.

13 *Ibid.*, pp. 37–8.

14 *Ibid.*, pp. 39–40.

15 *Ibid.*, p. 42.

16 *Ibid.*, p. 40.

17 *Ibid.*, p. 114.

18 Heim, *Depth*, pp. 7ff., and p. 272.

19 Vanhoozer, Kevin J., 1997, 'Does the Trinity Belong in a Theology of Religions?', in Vanhoozer, Kevin (ed.), *The Trinity in a Pluralistic Age*, Grand Rapids: Eerdmans, p. 71.

20 Cohn, Sherbok, Dan, 'Strait is the Gate, and I Shan't Get Through', *Church Times* (26 January 1996), p. 8.

21 Loughlin, Gerard, 1996, *Telling God's Story: Bible, Church and Narrative Theology*, Cambridge: Cambridge University Press, p. 24.

22 We should bear in mind Kierkegaard's views on Christianity as an existential leap of faith into the unknown; while exclusivisms and inclusivisms create narratives of Christian triumphalism, particularities seek to suggest that the truth is only known through paradox and denial of power.

23 D'Costa, Gavin, 2001, 'Roundtable Review' of *The Meeting of Religions and the Trinity*, in *Reviews in Theology and Religious Studies*, p. 246. This review is particularly interesting as it presents three responses to this work, with D'Costa's reply to his critics.

24 See also, D'Costa, *Meeting*, p. 9.

25 Kärkkäinen, Veli-Matti, 2004, *Trinity and Religious Pluralism*, Aldershot: Ashgate, p. 78, referring to D'Costa, *Meeting*, pp. 22–3.

26 D'Costa, *Meeting*, p. 110.

27 DiNoia, J. A., 1992, *The Diversity of Religions: A Christian Perspective*, Washington DC: Catholic University of America Press, p. 91.

28 Lindbeck, *Nature*, p. 59.

29 D'Costa, *Meeting*, p. 166.

30 Milbank, 'End', p. 190.

31 See, Heim, *Depth*, pp. 148ff.

32 See, for instance, Lyon, *Postmodernity*, or, Tester, *Life*.

33 Eagleton, Terry, 1997, *The Illusions of Postmodernism*, Oxford: Blackwell, p. 28.

34 Hyman, Gavin, 2001, *The Predicament of Postmodern Theology: Radical Orthodoxy or Nihilist Textualism?*, Louisville: Westminster John Knox Press, pp. 73ff.

35 While we are treating him as a type of particularist here, he has been labelled an inclusivist. See Tennent, Timothy, 2002, *Christianity at the Religious Roundtable: Evangelicalism in Conversation with Hinduism, Buddhism and Islam*, Grand Rapids: Baker Academic.

36 Knitter, Paul, 2002, *Introducing Theologies of Religions*, Maryknoll: Orbis, pp. 225–6.

37 Williams, Bernard, 1985, *Ethics and the Limits of Philosophy*, Cambridge MA: Harvard University Press, p. 17.

38 Lindbeck, *Nature*, p. 38.

39 Eriksen, Thomas Hylland, 1993, 'Do Cultural Islands Exist', *Social Anthropology*, no. 1, (1993), at: http://folk.uio.no/geirthe/Culturalislands.html. Accessed: 30/01/2008.

40 Boyer, Pascal, 1994, *The Naturalness of Religious Ideas: A Cognitive Theory of Religion*, Berkeley: University of California Press, p. 4.

41 *Ibid.*, pp. 6f. and 295f.

42 Torrance, Robert M., 1994, *The Spiritual Quest: Transcendence in Myth, Religion, and Science*, Berkeley: University of California Press, pp. xi–xii.

43 Erikson, 'Cultural', p. 2 and p. 1.

44 See Clarke, J. J., 1997, *Oriental Enlightenment: The Encounter between Asian and Western Thought*, London: Routledge, pp. 3ff.

45 *Ibid.*, p. 38.

46 See especially part II.

47 Radhakrishnan, S., 1940, *Eastern Religions and Western Thought*, London: Oxford University Press, p. 339.

48 Lipner, Julius, seminar: 'Are Hinduism, Buddhism, and Christianity Compatible?', University of Wales, Lampeter, 17 March 1999.

49 From the Caitanya tradition, cited in Zaehner, R. C., 1990, *Hinduism*, Oxford: Oxford University Press, p. 145.

50 Phan, Peter, 2002, *Being Religious Interreligiously*, Maryknoll: Orbis. His discussion of such figures as Abhishiktananda, Bede Griffiths, Aloysius Pieris and others who have lived between faiths deeply undermines the simple propositional alterity that Paul Griffiths and DiNoia strongly argue for. Their case is compelling in black and white, but when we view the shades of grey it becomes unstable.

51 McGrath, 'Particularist', p. 171.

52 DiNoia, *Diversity*, pp. 45–6.

53 Hampson, D., 2001, *Christian Contradictions: The Structures of Lutheran and Catholic Thought*, Cambridge: Cambridge University Press.

54 O'Leary, Joseph Stephen, 1996, *Religious Pluralism and Christian Truth*, Edinburgh: Edinburgh University Press, pp. 90–4.

55 Lindbeck, *Nature*, p. 114.

56 Badham, Paul, 1980, *Christian Beliefs about Life after Death*, London: SCM Press, pp. 10–11.

57 Milbank, John, 1990, *Theology and Social Theory: Beyond Secular Reason*, Oxford: Blackwell, pp. 1f. Although he specifically argues against defining theory in terms of social theory, the same principle can be held to apply against attempts to define religion in terms of linguistic theory.

58 From a theological standpoint see Clouser, Roy A., 1991, *The Myth of Religious Neutrality*, Notre Dame: University of Notre Dame Press; from a feminist standpoint see Sherif, Carolyn, 1987, 'Bias in Psychology', in Harding, S. (ed.), *Feminism and Methodology: Social Science Issues*, Bloomington: Indiana University Press; Haraway, Donna, 1991, 'Situated Knowledges', in Haraway, Donna, *Simians, Cyborgs and Women*, New York: Routledge; Longino, Helen, 2001, *The Fate of Knowledge*, Princeton: Princeton University Press; or, from the social sciences, Peter Berger's work, developed since 1969, *A Rumour of Angels*, New York: Doubleday, has also questioned its bias in relation to religion.

59 Flood, Gavin, 1999, *Beyond Phenomenology: Reinterpreting the Study of Religion*, London: Cassell.

60 See, Said, Edward, 1985, *Orientalism: Western Conceptions of the Orient*, London: Routledge and Kegan Paul; Inden, Ronald, 1992, *Imagining India*, Oxford: Blackwell; Urban, Hugh B., 1990, 'The Extreme Orient: The Construction

of "Tantrism" as a Category in the Orientalist Imagination', *Religion*, vol. 19, pp. 123–46.

61 Suleri, Sara, 1992, *The Rhetoric of English India*, Chicago: University of Chicago Press, p. 13.

62 Eagleton, *Illusions*, p. 124.

63 Vanhoozer, 'Trinity', p. 44.

64 *Ibid.*, p. 70.

65 McGrath, 'Particularist', p. 158, quoting Arnulf Camps, 1983, *Partners in Dialogue*, Maryknoll: Orbis, p. 30. D'Costa also makes a very similar claim in *Trinity*, p. 9.

66 Griffiths, P., 1997, 'The Properly Christian Response to Religious Plurality', *Anglican Theological Review*, vol. 79, pp. 3–26, at pp. 23–4.

67 McGrath, 'Particularist', p. 174.

68 *Ibid.*, p. 176.

69 Milbank, John, Pickstock, Catherine, and Ward, Graham (eds), 1999, *Radical Orthodoxy*, London: Routledge, see 'Introduction' and ch. 1.

70 Williams, Stephen, 1997, 'The Trinity and "Other Religions"', in Vanhoozer, *Trinity*, pp. 35–6.

71 Eagleton, *Illusions*, pp. 40–1, 132–3 and *passim.*

72 See, for instance, Hart, Trevor, 1997, 'Karl Barth, the Trinity, and Pluralism', in Vanhoozer, *Trinity*.

73 Pannenberg, W., 1990, 'Religious Pluralism and Conflicting Truth Claims', in D'Costa, *Christian*, p. 103.

74 Griffiths, *Problems*, p. 159.

75 *Ibid.*, p. 150.

76 As Guru Nanak stated, 'There is one Supreme Being, the Eternal Reality' (cited in McLeod, Hew, 1990, *Textual Sources for the Study of Sikhism*, Chicago: University of Chicago Press, p. 86), meaning this to refer to the source and origin of all religions and beliefs.

77 Justin Martyr, *Apology* I. xlvi; II. x and xiii.

78 Hedges, Paul, 2001, *Preparation and Fulfilment: A History and Study of Fulfilment Theology in Modern British Thought in the Indian Context*, Bern: Peter Lang, p. 26.

79 Vivekananda, 1894, 'Hinduism', in Barrows, John Henry (ed.), *The World's Parliament of Religions*, vol. 2, Chicago: Parliament Publishing Company, p. 968.

80 See the chapter herein on feminist approaches.

7

Feminisms: Syncretism, Symbiosis, Synergetic Dance

JEANNINE HILL FLETCHER

Introduction

Few feminist theologians have constructed a systematic theology of religions. However, recognizing the interreligious dimension of the feminist social movement and its parallel in theology, the application of feminist theological themes to a theology of religions is easily undertaken. This chapter will offer a brief history of the feminist approach to theology and the key themes relevant to this method. It will then explore the work of several Christian feminists some of whose theologies have a classic pluralistic resonance while others offer a vision of our multiplicity that moves beyond pluralism.

History: Feminist Theology Emerges out of an Interreligious Social Movement

The feminist approach to theology has its roots in the movements for women's rights that emerged around the globe in the late nineteenth and early twentieth centuries. The suffrage movement for women's right to vote in Britain and protests for women's access to education in India are just two examples that characterize this first wave of feminism. At the turn of the century, international communication and travel provided venues for cross-fertilization of ideas and the sharing of strategies for the struggle. Thus, the global women's movement was often enacted across religious lines. This continued into the second wave of feminism in America where, for example, Christian women from across denominations worked with Jewish feminists and women with no religious affiliation in the women's movement of the late 1960s and 1970s.

In both the first and second waves of the feminist movement, Christian women who struggled for their rights in society began to see the negative role that religion played. Male images of God as father reinforced the restriction of leadership roles to men; and the androcentric (that is, male-centred) values and writings propagated in the pulpits spilled over to reinforce the structures of a male-dominated society. As women gained increased access to higher education in the second wave, feminists undertook an academic study of the relationship between religion and society. Now the critiques that showed the sexist constructions in society were turned to implicate religions as sources of inequality and oppression as well. The approach known as 'feminist theology' began to emerge. Feminist theology recognizes that the Christian tradition emerging from male-centred societies has been largely shaped by men, and that theology not only reflects primarily male experiences but further reinscribes social realities that have placed the male in a privileged position over women. The feminist approach begins from the experience of women and has as its first concern the well-being of women. Feminist theology critiques the patriarchal androcentrism that has characterized the Christian tradition and seeks theologies that encourage liberation from these patterns for the well-being of women. But 'women's well-being' is not sufficient to characterize the approach of feminist theology. Voices of feminism's third wave insisted that the struggle for human wholeness is not only against gender oppressions but also the many forms of oppression that dehumanize persons on the basis of race, class, sexual orientation, culture and more. By bringing in women's experience and the stories of the marginalized, the feminist approach seeks theologies that encourage the full humanity of women and men.

In many ways, feminist theology continued to cross religious boundaries just as the feminist movement in many parts of the world had done. This is evidenced, for example, in the ground-breaking work *Womanspirit Rising: A Feminist Reader in Religion* (1979), which included writings from Christian, Jewish, post-Christian and pagan feminists. *Weaving the Visions: New Patterns in Feminist Spirituality* (1989) continued the interreligious co-operation expanding also to include Native American spirituality and reflections from the perspective of African Traditional Religion. The editors of these texts envisioned the feminist theological project across religious lines, writing, 'we are engaged in a common project of working toward more just and humane religious and social institutions'.[1] The practice of thinking theologically with other faiths continued in the volume *After Patriarchy: Feminist Transformations of the World Religions* (1991), in which feminists from Christianity, Hinduism, Islam, Buddhism, Judaism and Native American traditions applied shared methods to their specific faith traditions. The interreligious co-operation of the women's movement encouraged the fruitful exchange of methods and strategies so that feminist theology emerged in many places as an interreligious approach.

This background to the feminist approach is important because very few feminist theologians have explicitly constructed a theology of religions. Although Christian feminists have engaged across religious lines and share a methodology with feminists of other faiths, the theology of religions employed in their writing often needs to be drawn out from work devoted to other subjects. There are themes inherent in a feminist methodology that are particularly applicable for a theology of religions. First and foremost, this is because feminist theology began from out of the experience of women who felt they had been 'othered' by their religious tradition. That is to say, feminist theologians from across the traditions recognized that when the experience or thoughts of 'their religion' were being expressed, it was most likely the experience or thoughts of 'men' within their religion that was being expressed. Men's experience within the tradition was the norm; women were 'other'. As Rita Gross articulates:

> Feminist theology was born from the experience of being excluded by patriarchal religions and the resulting convictions that the voices of the excluded deserve to be heard and that adequate theology cannot be done on the basis of erasing many voices and limiting the theological voice to the chosen few.[2]

Having experienced being measured as 'less-than' the norm, feminist theologians have tended to be sensitive to the othering of others. Because feminist theology is characteristically a liberation theology aimed at eliminating the thought-systems and social structures that compromise the dignity and humanity of women and men, it would be ironic for the movement to reinscribe its own version of superiority vis-à-vis other religions. As Christian feminists have struggled to name the variety of factors that limit their human becoming and claim themselves as subjects, they are increasingly sensitive that this recognition of subjectivity and agency needs to be given to women and men of other faiths as well.

Contemporary and Theoretical Comments

While few feminist theologians have presented a systematic theology of religions, Christian feminist theology is characterized by key themes that provide for a distinctive reading of religious diversity. These themes include: (1) a critique of God-talk; (2) a new understanding of Christ; (3) a liberationist reading of salvation; (4) a theology beyond the Bible; and (5) the criterion of women's well-being. Each of these will be introduced below before identifying the work of feminist theologians who employ these themes and develop – whether implicitly or explicitly – a theology of religions.

Critique of God-talk

The major thrust of feminist thought has been to illuminate the distinctive experiences of women as they have been impacted by gendered constructions of social norms and expectations. Thinking *from* this set of experiences, feminist writings are directed *toward* the aim of securing the well-being of women. When these general strategies are applied to theology, particular attention is given to the way religious thought and symbols ignore the experience of women and/or participate in the oppression of women. The earliest writings of second-wave feminism focused on the symbols of the Christian tradition that limit the full becoming of women; primary among them was the symbol of God as father. As feminists critiqued the way male God-language reinscribed the privileges of patriarchy, they simultaneously argued for the reclaiming of 'God' as a reality beyond human understanding. Whether adopting writing strategies of Jewish colleagues in writing G-d to remind readers of the limits of language (as was done by Elisabeth Schüssler Fiorenza), or re-imaging God in new metaphors (in the work of Sallie McFague), or reclaiming the gender-neutral appellation of God as Be-ing (as Mary Daly did), feminists challenged the way talk of God can seem to communicate certainties in male-centred language. Instead, feminist theology underscores the limits of human language and our uncertainties in light of God's mystery.

The extension of this insight and application to a theology of religions is evident. If God is not literally the male figure of the Hebrew Scriptures or Jesus' father from the New Testament, then the symbolic aspect of all language for God is called to mind. If Christian words for God communicate symbolically a reality beyond human understanding, perhaps the words and symbols used by the diverse faiths do likewise. The feminist critique of God-language and insistence on its symbolic rendering provides a foundation for building a Christian theology of religions. In her work *Divinity and Diversity* (2003), Marjorie Hewitt Suchocki employs this strategy in order to assert that the many ways of conceptualizing God across the religions are not due so much to one religion being correct and all others wrong, rather, all of the religious traditions abstract their concepts of God from a much more complex lived experience of the presence of God within the universe.[3]

A new understanding of Christ

A second major symbol that has been the site of feminist theological efforts is the person of Jesus Christ. Since Jesus' own humanity was lived in a male body, there were early feminists (notably, Mary Daly) who suggested that Jesus himself symbolically participates in the privileging of the male form over that of the female. But Rosemary Radford Ruether and later Christian feminists shifted the focus of Jesus from his maleness to his liberating care for the oppressed. From out of this shift, feminist theology has identified Jesus Christ as one whose concern for the marginalized included the women of his day and our own (see, for example, Elisabeth Schüssler Fiorenza's *In Memory of Her* (1983)). Jesus is seen as one who transgresses the boundaries of gender norms to liberate women and men.

The application of this feminist symbolic transformation to religious diversity has had divergent theological outcomes. For example, the identification of Jesus as liberator could be applied to the exclusion of other liberators. That is, the identification of Jesus as liberator does not have any inherent mechanism for guarding against exclusivism (Jesus is *the* liberator) or inclusivism (*all* liberation comes from Jesus). Yet, it is precisely because feminist theology has been an interreligious movement that feminist theologians have been criticized when Jesus as liberator has worked in these ways. From the perspective of Jewish feminists, the identification of Jesus as liberator too easily set Jesus over-and-against Judaism. Similarly, in identifying Jesus as liberator par excellence, the patterns of Christian missionary conversion could be read as liberating native peoples from their indigenous (and implicitly false or inferior) religions. In the emerging feminist theology of religions of Chung Hyun Kyung and Kwok Pui-lan, Jesus as liberator is situated pluralistically as one resource among many through which humans struggle for wholeness.

A liberationist reading of salvation

Rooted in a liberationist understanding of Jesus Christ is a new reading of salvation as liberation. There is, perhaps, no more radical articulation of this shift in the reading of salvation than that expressed in the work of Ivone Gebara as she writes of 'everyday resurrections'. In her own words:

> Salvation will not be something outside the fabric of life but will take place within the heart of it . . . the process of salvation is a process of resurrection, of recovering life and hope and justice along life's path even when these experiences are frail and fleeting. Resurrection becomes something that can be lived and grasped within the confines of our existence.[4]

When Gebara goes on to identify this 'fragile redemption' in the course of everyday life, she breaks the boundaries of explicitly Christian experience and encompasses the lives of non-Christians as well.

Gebara's theological vision is shared broadly by feminist theologians who conceive of religion as a vehicle for human well-being and stand to critique it when it is not. With salvation recast as liberation, and the recognition of the ambiguity of religion (that it sometimes does and sometimes does not create well-being), feminists approach the discourse of religious pluralism with different concerns in mind. In her study of women's engagement in interfaith dialogue, Helene Egnell reflects how this shift in the understanding of salvation is manifest when she writes: 'The women brought different questions to the conferences . . . Their questions were how to survive in male-dominated religious traditions, but also the survival of humanity and the planet in a world of war and injustice.'[5] The shift of focus from other-worldly salvation to encompass a present liberation gives feminist theology a distinctive approach to a theology of religions.

Theology beyond the Bible

The transformation of Christian themes introduced above has its foundation in the feminist rereading of Scripture. Feminists have argued that the writings of Scripture have been shaped by male perspectives and therefore reflect distinctively male experience. In many cases, women's experiences have been erased by the androcentric bias of the scriptural authors. Further, feminist theology uncovers the way women as actors in the Bible are often eliminated by the translator's hand or ignored by the assumptions an interpreter brings to the text. Developing out of this approach that sees the human hand in Scripture and its interpretation, feminist methods have argued for the necessity of critiquing the biblical text from the perspective of lived experience. That is to say that sometimes the sacred text is not salvific in that it does not always readily offer a vision of wholeness for all persons (see, for example, the work of Schüssler Fiorenza and Phyllis Trible). There are revelatory strands of the text, according to feminists like Rosemary Radford Ruether, but for many feminists these need to be supplemented with other sources that might allow us to include what was written out of the text itself. As Rosemary Radford Ruether writes, 'Women must be able to speak out of their own experiences . . . as places of divine presence and, out of these revelatory experiences, write new stories.'[6] What takes place in feminist methodology is what Rita Gross calls 'widening the canon' or 'rejecting the binding authority of the past and . . . searching for new traditions'.[7] Women's experience is incorporated as a source of theological thinking with the Bible and beyond.

It is when this feminist principle of expanded sources is applied to religious difference that a feminist approach to the theology of religions is most distinctive. As feminist theology emerged as an interreligious discourse and feminist theologians affirmed their own experience as a site of supplementing or critiquing the Bible, they opened the space to affirm the experiences of their colleagues of other faiths and the resources of their faith traditions. Nowhere is this more clear than when Christian feminist theologians in multi-religious contexts, such as Asia or Africa, do theology. As Kwok Pui-lan articulates: 'Given the pluralistic and diverse understanding of scripture in the Asian context, the idea of truth neatly contained within the covers of one single book, as in the case of earlier European Christian understanding of the Bible, is foreign to most Confucians, Hindus, Buddhists, and Daoists.'[8] The openness to diverse sources of truth in relation to the plurality of religious scriptures is a perfect match for the feminist critique of the Bible as the only source of truth. As the feminist theologian Rosemary Radford Ruether summarizes, both feminism and the reality of other religions 'represent challenges to the concept of a single universal biblical faith'.[9]

A criterion to resist relativism

The themes and methods of feminist theology, especially in opening the resources of theology beyond the Bible, lay the foundation for a feminist theology of religions that is open to the reality of religious diversity in a new way. Yet this openness to religious diversity clearly does not mean 'anything goes' precisely because the feminist criterion of women's well-being grounds the methodology. In this way, feminist thought provides a safeguard to respond to the fear of 'relativism' that lurks in many conversations on religious pluralism. As Marjorie Hewitt Suchocki writes: 'Because I am convinced that God calls us to inclusive well-being, and because the oppression of women violates inclusive well-being, I quite openly think that oppression of women in any system (including my own!) is wrong.'[10]

Traditionally, the challenge of religious pluralism is constructed along the principle of non-contradiction: if two religions assert contradictory realities, only one can be correct. This construction has meant that truth resides within one tradition to the exclusion of all others. The pluralist transformation of this assertion has been to say that all religions possess truth within them, in varied symbolic expressions and linguistic schemes. This has left pluralism open to the charge of 'relativism' which, whether truly feared or employed as a defensive strategy, has been a critique levelled at pluralist theologies. What the feminist criteria of women's well-being afford is a way of affirming the truth *and* contradictions, not among religions but *within* them. If religion is for the purpose of salvation as fullness of life, then whatever in a religion promotes well-being is affirmed while that which compromises well-being is critiqued. This provides for a criterion to be applied among the religions. As Kwok Pui-lan writes from the context of Asia:

> Although many Asian feminist theologians are critical of the discriminatory practices of Asian religions, they also look for liberating aspects in which women may have played more significant roles. For example, Korean feminists have emphasized the influences of shamanism on women's spirituality, and the important role of the female shaman in local communities. Filipino feminists point to a more egalitarian social structure and the higher status of women within their indigenous traditions during precolonial times as compared to Filipino women's experiences under Roman Catholicism. Others have pointed to the rich traditions of feminine symbolism in Hinduism, the establishment of nunneries as an

alternative to patriarchal family in Buddhism and the Islamic belief in human equality as liberative elements.[11]

Recognizing the ambiguities within religion provides for a new criterion to be applied among the religions.

As indicated in the themes explored above, feminist methods offer new patterns of thought to theology. Since women have traditionally been barred from leadership in many of the Christian denominations, they have not been selected or seen as 'spokespersons' of the tradition. This negative reality has brought forth new possibilities in that if one is not determined to speak 'for the tradition' and defend the tradition's 'traditional' understandings, one is in a freer place to rethink the tradition in light of new challenges. 'Women, by their very presence in interreligious discussions, often question the "official" stances of their traditions.'[12] Religious pluralism is one such challenge, that feminist thought – coming from the 'margins' – has distinctive potential for opening theology up to diversity in a new way.

Important also is the fact that feminist theology has been done so often in interreligious contexts. As feminists shared strategies and methodologies, they also shared their work, that is, their theologies. Christian feminists have drawn on the work of Jewish feminists. The work of the Buddhist scholar Rita Gross has been central to the development of feminist theology. Increasingly the audience of feminist writings includes Muslim and Hindu women as well. Women who have left institutional religion (such as those self-identifying as 'post-Christian') or reclaim earth-based spirituality (whether traditional forms such as Native American or revived pagan ones) are also among the audience. This means that feminist theologies of religion uniquely have had both interreligious sensitivity but also interreligious supporters and critics. The distinctive milieu in which feminist theologians have worked suggests something distinctive about the outcomes and achievements for a feminist approach to the theology of religions.

An Emerging Feminist Approach to Theology of Religions

While the themes central to feminist approaches to theology have evident extensions and implications for a theology of religions, only recently has there emerged a series of feminist responses to the reality of religious difference in theological reflection. Indeed, it is not at all unusual for overviews of 'Theologies of Religions' to have no feminist or women's voices represented in the collection. This led Ursula King to describe feminism as 'the missing dimension in the dialogue of religions'. Feminist theologians have only recently explicitly turned attention to constructing a distinctive response to religious diversity that could be considered an emerging feminist approach to the theology of religions.

Pluralistic feminist theologies

Drawing on the above-mentioned trends of feminist thought, many of the feminist approaches to a theology of religions lean in a theologically liberal direction toward pluralism. For example, the writings of Rosemary Radford Ruether, while emphasizing a liberative reading of Christ, have been shaped by Jewish–Christian and Buddhist–Christian dialogue, as well as a concern for the future of the planet. She presents a pluralist approach to other religions when she writes: 'Interreligious relationships speak of many different ways in which experience of the divine has been localized in human experience and the mutual recognition of these historico-cultural configurations by each other.'[13] This articulation aligns classically with pluralist theologies of religions.

When thinking of women engaged in the pluralistic endeavour, perhaps none comes to mind so readily as the scholar of religion Diana Eck, whose 'Pluralism Project' at Harvard University has studied and disseminated information on the many religious traditions in America. Although not a systematic theologian, as a comparative scholar of Hinduism rooted in the Christian tradition, Eck has had cause to reflect theologically on the reality of religious difference. Adopting a pluralist position she writes:

> In a Christian pluralist perspective, we do not need to build walls to exclude the view of the other, nor do we need to erect a universal canopy capable of gathering all the diverse tribes together under our own roof. We do not need to speak of 'anonymous Christians'. From a Christian pluralist standpoint, the multiplicity of religious ways is a concomitant of the ultimacy and many-sidedness of God, the one who cannot be limited or encircled by any one tradition. Therefore, the boundaries of our various traditions need not be the places where we halt and contend over our differences, but might well be the places where we meet and catch a glimpse of glory as seen by another.[14]

In Eck's rejection of exclusivism and inclusivism, we can see the trajectory of rethinking God-language explored above. Although Eck does not write as a feminist theologian, her work in interreligious dialogue has been explicitly concerned for the experiences, representation and well-being of women.

A further example of a pluralistic feminist approach to religions can be seen in the words of the Christian feminist Ursula King. In discussing the cosmic Christ and its parallels in Buddha-nature and the cosmic figure of Vishnu, she writes:

> The specificity of all these different visions relates always to a particular tradition and a particular way of conceptualizing the ultimate. These visions are not identical. Rather, they are alternatives, though not ex-

> clusively so, because they also share certain commonalities and point beyond themselves to a Reality we cannot grasp. In this sense different visions of faith are like different human languages – they all contain words and world views, but they conceptualize them very differently for human communication.[15]

Here again, the example of feminist thinkers finding a resource for religious pluralism in the limitations of God-talk is evidenced.

What might be noted at this point is that the examples thus far demonstrate an overlap between some feminist approaches to religious pluralism and other classic approaches to a theology of religions. In fact, in the citations above, there is nothing distinctively 'feminist' about the theology as such. This is also the case with the next two thinkers, in that the roots of theological thinking stem from traditional theology (the theology of men) but can be incorporated with the criterion of women's well-being to provide a distinctively 'feminist' approach.

Among the few feminists writing a systematic theology of religions, Marjorie Hewitt Suchocki, in her book *Divinity and Diversity* (2003), offers a vision rooted in process thought which identifies God incarnated in the universe and reflected differently in the many different religious traditions. In its theological resources, Suchocki does not employ feminist sources or methodologies explicitly. Instead, the classic writings of the Christian tradition – from Augustine and Aquinas through Luther to contemporary theologians – and twentieth-century psychology and philosophy – from William James to Alfred North Whitehead – are engaged in the discussion. There is nothing in this aspect of her method that would be characterized as a 'feminist approach' as such. However, it is when Suchocki employs the criteria of women's well-being (as discussed above) that she introduces a distinctly feminist interest into her theology of religions. It was Suchocki who wrote: 'Because I am convinced that God calls us to inclusive well-being, and because the oppression of women violates inclusive well-being, I quite openly think that oppression of women in any system (including my own!) is wrong.'[16] The application of this criterion gives Suchocki a distinctively feminist liberationist spin on the pluralist position.

A second systematic work that might be identified as a 'feminist theology of religions' is written by Pamela Dickey Young. In her book, *Christ in a Post-Christian World: How Can We Believe in Jesus Christ when Those Around Us Believe Differently – or Not At All?* (2005), Young seeks to construct a theological response to religious difference that addresses the gender imbalance of power and privilege within religions. In short, she seeks a theology of religions that is not imperialistic (with respect to non-Christian faiths) and non-patriarchal (addressing her feminist concerns). What is distinctively 'feminist' about Young's methodology, as she herself identifies, is the embrace of particularity – both of women's particular experiences and well-being, and of the particularity of the person of Jesus Christ. She sees this as standing in contrast to those pluralist theologies that would relinquish the particular distinctiveness of Jesus in favour of a more generic vision of God or human wholeness. Thus, Young begins by embracing particularity as a feminist and Christian starting point.

Emphasizing particularity, Young asserts that it is Jesus Christ who truly brings salvation. Characteristic of a feminist liberationist approach to Jesus and salvation, Young offers an 'existential' Christology focused on the present wholeness that persons experience in encountering Jesus. In addition, Young repeats the feminist insistence on the limits of our understanding of God, recognizing how our religious symbols are historically conditioned. She writes: 'our images of God are in part the result of our experience of God and in part the result of our social and historical location'.[17] Young therefore affirms the diverse ways of accessing the universal reality of God. Drawing these strands together she presents an understanding of Christ's role in salvation in which Jesus represents the salvation that is the work of God. In her words: 'Jesus as the Christ does not constitute salvation or contact with God's love or grace. Rather, he re-presents or embodies God's grace or revelation, and thus in him God offers a salvation that is universal and universally accessible.'[18] In the end, Young offers a pluralist position of theocentric inclusivism that applies God's concern for integral well-being to all persons and religions with particular interest in the well-being of women. The patterns of thought evidenced in Young's theology reflect many of the feminist approaches to theology. The discussion she offers is particularly attentive to the well-being of women – another key element of a feminist approach. Yet, her theology of religions does not substantially change those inherited and identifiable among other non-feminist theologies of religions.

In the examples offered above, the 'feminist' approach to a theology of religions seems to have to do with expanding the scope of concerns within a theology of religions such that women's well-being is incorporated along with the pluralist affirmation of non-Christian religions. As outlined above, it is clear that these theologies resonate with other pluralistic approaches to a theology of religions. While having feminist concerns, the theology being offered is not necessarily substantially transformed and might be shared by non-feminist theologies of religions across the spectrum of pluralist theologies.

Beyond pluralism

In the theology of religions embedded in the work of feminist theologians in the multi-religious contexts of Asia and Africa a new mode of theology seems to be emerging. Here, the hermeneutic principle of reading beyond the bounds of Scripture and Christian tradition to include women's experience draws in and on the experience of other faiths. In an extended reflection on the Good Samaritan story from Luke's Gospel, Mercy Amba Oduyoye gives an example of a feminist response to religious difference in Africa. She writes:

> The mutual suspicion between Christian and Muslim, Muslim and Hindu, and the contempt poured on primal religions by Christians and Muslims alike, have not made for dynamic learning and affirming neighbourhoods. Religious chauvinism, from whatever quarters, is not a recipe for good neighbourliness. It presupposes a monopoly of truth and of God and so undercuts the roots of our common humanity in a way that prevents our acting humanely toward the other. The practice of neighbourliness is anchored in a spirituality of care and respect for the other's spiritual resources.
>
> Sharing spirituality across religious boundaries will make us neighbours who honour each other's specificities while at the same time seeking mutual caring and sharing and learning together.[19]

Following through on the idea of 'sharing spirituality across religious boundaries', Oduyoye reflects on salvation as human flourishing from both Christian and native African religious perspectives. Her multi-religious context allows her to reflect on women in religion in Africa – 'whether speaking of Christianity, Islam, or African traditional religions'.[20] This explicit writing on other religions and their resources for spirituality and wholeness communicates implicitly a theology of religions that is both 'pluralistic' and 'particularistic'. It is pluralistic insofar as it recognizes that the many religions of the world have salvific resources for healing the brokenness of our world; it is particularistic insofar as it sees these resources as *different* in the many different traditions. This same pattern is reflected in the overview of feminist theologies in Asia by Kwok Pui-lan when she writes:

> In their encounter with people of other faith traditions, Asian feminist theologians have cautioned against a triumphant attitude that assumes Christianity to be superior to others. Living closely with their religious neighbors, they know that they have much to learn from the diverse experiences of the ultimate mystery and the manifold articulations of the divine in other faith traditions . . . With humility and open-mindedness, many Asian feminist theologians recognize that God's revelation is found not only in the Bible and the Christian tradition but also in other peoples' religious experiences rooted in their sacred scriptures, myths, stories, legends and symbols . . . But there is also a radical perspective arguing that the divine is a mystery, not to be pigeonholed or limited by languages and expressions, nor boxed by our religious systems.[21]

A similar challenge to the privileging of Christianity and impermeable religious boundaries can be found in the work of the Korean feminist theologian Chung Hyun Kyung. But this feminist thinker pushes further in recognizing the salvific efficacy of the many religions as she encourages a syncretism of the many strands toward symbols and rituals of human and earth-healing.

Just as salvation includes the messiness of everyday life, religion is also messy in its blurring of boundaries between the faiths in the life and writing of Chung. Her reflections exhibit the themes identifiable in the broader movement of feminist theology; and her work pushes the theology of religions beyond pluralism. First, in reflecting on God she writes:

> We [that is, Christians] believe that God is a creator. God created everything in the world and said, 'it is beautiful.' In this creation the other world religions are included. Therefore, other religions are also beautiful in God's eyes. I also want to pinpoint the tradition of mysticism in Christianity. In Christian mysticism, God is beyond our naming, beyond our form and imagination. God is pure emptiness, as Meister Eckhardt said. Talking about God is always speaking of the unspeakable in this tradition. We share the silence of this original emptiness. In this mystical union, silence and emptiness are the places for all other religions.[22]

To this mystical approach to the divine, Chung brings in a liberationist understanding of Jesus. In her *Struggle to be the Sun Again* (1990), she describes 'Jesus Christ as priest of *han*',[23] representing Christ in the form of an indigenous shaman who is concerned for the healing of women. Throughout her writings Chung exhibits the liberationist impulse of the feminist approach that sees the purpose of religion in the healing and well-being of women and explicitly identifies this as a criterion against relativism: 'At the center, there is a center criterion . . . it is based on women's survival and liberation.'[24] Identifying religion for the purpose of survival and liberation, and recognizing the Bible as one resource among many for implementing this liberative practice, the multi-religious context of Chung's Korea creates a distinctive theology of religions. In her own words:

> When I look at women's religiosity, I can see that it can be described with the metaphors of a medicine chest, a kaleidoscope, and alchemy, because women use the different drawers of this medicine chest to heal, to liberate and to survive. They also intermingle some part of their religions for their life, for their survival, through multiple colors and shapes of the kaleidoscope. It is also alchemy, as women mix and develop something new.[25]

The alchemy of women's well-being draws in the many different religious forms of her context. As she describes, Christianity, Buddhism, Daoism and Confucianism are not sanitized away from one another in neat packages.

Rather, 'When I look at our women's religious experience very critically, it is not a religious pluralism. It is sometimes syncretism, sometimes symbiosis, and sometimes a synergetic dance of many religions in our daily lives.'[26]

A distinctive theme sounds through Chung's writing and may well characterize the feminist approaches to theology of religions in the future. This theme is that of the messiness of religious identity in our everyday lives. In the academic discourse of theology of religions, each religion stands packaged away from the other ready for comparison, critique, organization and definition. Which ones are salvific? Which are 'as good as' or 'as effective as' Christianity? How does each compare with Christianity? Thus, in theologies of exclusivism, inclusivism, pluralism and particularism one's Christian identity stands radically separated from other religious identities *and* other sources of identity. But, in the lived experience of everyday life, these various sources of meaning are not separated out from one another. Our identities are mutually informed by the many stories that shape us. With a necessarily hybridized or 'multiple' identity, we cannot say that 'Christianity' alone provides the salvific resources of a life of wholeness.

In my own writing, I employ this construction of identity as hybrid as a way to think beyond the traditional theologies of religious pluralism. The problem is that theologies of exclusivism, inclusivism and pluralism – in one way or another – construct humanity and human religiosity on the basis of sameness, looking for the ideals represented in one's own tradition in the tradition of the other. Theologies of particularism, on the other hand, move in the opposite direction in order to insist on the radical differences between persons of different faiths. These commonly held options leave us with the simplistic choices of seeing either 'sameness' or 'difference' when Christians consider persons of other faiths. I suggest that the inclusion of a feminist construction of identity as 'hybrid' allows us to find aspects of ourselves that overlap with our neighbours of other faiths. My theology witnesses to the distinctive stories of the various religions (a particularist approach) while it also recognizes that each person is shaped by many stories, not just those related to his/her religion (therefore pluralism, or even syncretism, is within the individual). These diverse stories (some religious, some not religious) provide resources for thinking together about the common challenges faced among human beings struggling for wholeness.

While I underscore the hybridity of human identities as persons are shaped by their religion and other sources of meaning-making, Chung recognizes a hybridity of religions within her own identity. Like my own vision, there are many aspects of who we are; but Chung underscores that sometimes people are shaped by a variety of religions simultaneously. This necessarily breaks down the barriers between religions and dismantles the argument of one privileged religious form. As Chung describes: 'When people ask what I am religiously, I say, "My bowel is Shamanist. My heart is Buddhist. My right brain, which defines my mood, is Confucian and Taoist. My left brain, which defines my public language, is Protestant Christian, and overall, my aura is eco-feminist."'[27] This recognition of hybridity challenges the 'fact' of religious pluralism to which theologies of religious pluralism respond. The question is no longer which religion is salvific, but which aspects of the many traditions can shape a life of wholeness. As Kwok Pui-lan writes:

> Some Asian feminist theologians have found that the model of inter-religious dialogue in the ecumenical movement is not adequate in some situations. Within this model, believers of different religions enter into critical conversations with one another, and each is transformed in the dialogical process. But in Asia, the boundaries of religions are not clear cut: one can be a Shinto and a Buddhist in Japan, or a Christian who consults shamans during a crisis in Korea or a Confucian-Buddhist in Malaysia.[28]

As a Christian theologian, Chung actively embraces the syncretism that not only affirms diverse religions, but is willing to blend them.

The embrace of border-crossings by feminist thinkers is indicative of the creativity that might be found among those excluded from the centre of power. In much of Christian theology, those who write and are heard on the topic of religious pluralism speak from an authoritative position. As spokes-person of the religion, theologians are often 'defenders' of doctrine or protectors of the tradition. Theologies of religion can be seen as the attempt to offer a response to religious diversity from within the boundaries of church teaching and tradition. But feminist theologians have traditionally been on the margins of power in the respective denominations. Less concerned with the defence of tradition and more likely to be critical of the shortcomings of doctrine, feminist theologians may be embracing the fluidity of the margins in responding positively to the reality of religious difference. But this is not without its consequences. Especially as it is matched with another important theme of feminist work – the embodied and lived dimensions of our theologies.

On the positive side, the embodied dimension of lived theology has enabled feminist theologians to reach across the boundaries of traditions and experience themselves as collaborating for change with feminists of other faiths. As Carol Christ recalls, the academic encounter among feminist theologians was an enriching experience that crossed religious lines. She describes: 'I vividly remember the days when the religion section [of the American Academy of Religion] was a place where feminists in religion engaged in dialogue across religious boundaries. I believed that we were working together to transform and recreate religious traditions.'[29] Positively, the embodied dimension has encouraged feminist theologians to prescind from the strictures of inherited teaching and embrace the 'other' as neighbour and sister in the struggle.

On another front, however, the border-crossing of feminist theology has not been without its detractors, as evidenced in the response to some of the work of Chung Hyun Kyung. Chung not only has written about her syncretistic openness to whatever in religions can be employed for the well-being of the oppressed, she has publicly embodied these ideas in performative theology. At the World Council of Churches Assembly (1991), as council representatives discussed the Christian theme of the Spirit at work in the world, Chung gave the plenary presentation. As described by Kirsteen Kim, Chung:

> Dispensed with lectern, notes, and even shoes, appearing on stage as a Korean shaman (most Korean shamans are women) in the midst of Korean and Aboriginal dancers. Drawing on the symbolism of her shamanist ancestors . . . Chung led an exorcist's dance invoking the Holy Spirit and the spirits of suffering, oppressed individuals and created things . . . In her presentation, Chung explained the Holy Spirit as identifying with these spirits, weeping with them, and actively seeking their liberation in a greedy, divided world of death.[30]

In a theological world where boundaries are closely guarded – indeed, the possibility of salvation beyond those boundaries is even debated – it is not surprising that Chung's embodiment of a theology of religions was, for some, cause for alarm. But there were also those present who applauded her work as a necessary step forward away from endless theological debate toward the necessary healing that might boldly cross religious lines.

Criticisms and Suggestions

A critique has been raised to feminist theology that it has not been sufficiently engaged in the issues of religious pluralism. As evidenced by the very few feminist theologians who construct a theology of religions, this criticism seems to carry some weight. As indicated earlier, it is not uncommon for overviews of theology of religions to discuss exclusively male theologians, precisely because female theologians have not sufficiently entered the discourse. In order for the feminist approach to the theology of religions to be authentically a new option, feminist theologians must continue to attend in increasing depth to the reality of religious pluralism.

Simultaneously, however, those who seek alternative theologies to those offered by exclusivism, inclusivism, pluralism and particularism might consider new sites of finding such theologies. Feminist theologians concerned for the well-being of women may not be participating in the abstract discussions of theologians of religions, but instead may be actively engaged in the dialogue and struggles of interreligious gatherings. Theology is not only articulated in systematic writing but is also implicit in the kinds of actions Christians undertake.

Overview

This chapter has suggested that while a feminist approach to a theology of religions is not mainstream (yet), there are distinctive features of feminist theology that lend themselves to developing a theology of religions. These include: (1) the recognition of the limitations of God-talk; (2) Jesus as liberator; (3) salvation as embodied in human wholeness; (4) a recognition that the Bible is ambiguous as a religious resource and therefore is not the only resource; and (5) that there is a criterion to be employed among the religions: women's well-being. These themes can be found within the classic texts of feminist theology and are beginning to be applied to the question of religious plurality. While some applications of these elements produce feminist approaches to a theology of religions not very different from other pluralist approaches, others provide for a very different theology that challenges the borders of religions altogether. The future of feminist approaches to a theology of religions will be seen in the willingness of feminists to continue the interreligious work inherent in the movement, and in the more widespread insistence on the well-being of women (and men) as the whole point of religion itself.

Study Questions

1 Why has the feminist approach to theology had an implicit theology of religions even if feminist thinkers have not explicitly constructed a systematic response to religious difference?

2 What examples do you see of feminist approaches to a theology of religions that fit within the categories of 'pluralist' or 'particularist' as they have been outlined in earlier chapters of this book?

3 Although many feminist approaches resonate with pluralist theologies of religions, there are two particularities that challenge this categorization: the criterion that resists relativism and the use of the concept of 'hybridity'. Describe each and explain how these concepts disrupt standard assumptions within theologies of religions.

4 What is distinctive about a 'feminist' approach to religious pluralism?

Further Reading

Chung, Hyun Kyung, 1990, *Struggle to Be the Sun Again: Introducing Asian Women's Theology*, Maryknoll: Orbis.

Gross, Rita, 2002, 'Feminist Theology as Theology of Religions', in Parsons, S. (ed.), *The Cambridge Companion to Feminist Theology*, Cambridge: Cambridge University Press, pp. 60–78.

Hill Fletcher, Jeannine, 2005, *Monopoly on Salvation? A Feminist Approach to Religious Pluralism*, New York: Continuum.

King, Ursula, 1998, 'Feminism: The Missing Dimension in the Dialogue of Religions', in May, J. D'Arcy (ed.), *Pluralism and the Religions: The Theological and Political Dimensions*, London: Cassell, pp. 40–58.

Kwok, Pui-lan, 2000, *Introducing Asian Feminist Theology*, Cleveland: Pilgrim Press.

Oduyoye, Mercy Amba, 2004, *Beads and Strands: Reflections of an African Woman on Christianity in Africa*, Maryknoll: Orbis.

Ruether, Rosemary Radford, 1987, 'Feminism and Jewish–Christian Dialogue: Particularism and Universalism in the Search for Religious Truth', in Knitter, P., and Hick, J. (eds), *The Myth of Christian Uniqueness: Toward a Pluralistic Theology of Religions*, Maryknoll: Orbis, pp. 137–48.

Suchocki, Marjorie Hewitt, 1987, 'In Search of Justice: Religious Pluralism from a Feminist Perspective', in Knitter, P., and Hick, J. (eds), *The Myth of Christian Uniqueness: Toward a Pluralistic Theology of Religions*, Maryknoll: Orbis, pp. 149–61.

Young, Pamela Dickey, 1995, *Christ in a Post-Christian World: How Can We Believe in Jesus Christ when Those Around Us Believe Differently – Or Not At All*, Minneapolis: Augsburg Fortress Press.

Notes

1 Christ, Carol, 1989, 'Introduction', in *Weaving the Visions: New Patterns in Feminist Spirituality*, San Francisco: HarperSanFrancisco, p. 8.

2 Gross, Rita, 2002, 'Feminist Theology as Theology of Religions', in Parsons, S. (ed.), *The Cambridge Companion to Feminist Theology*, Cambridge: Cambridge University Press, p. 63.

3 Suchocki, Marjorie Hewitt, 2003, *Divinity and Diversity: A Christian Affirmation of Religious Pluralism*, Nashville: Abingdon Press, pp. 50–1.

4 Gebara, Ivone, 2002, *Out of the Depths: Women's Experience of Evil and Salvation*, Minneapolis: Fortress Press, p. 122.

5 Egnell, Helene, 2006, *Other Voices: A Study of Feminist Approaches to Religious Plurality East and West*, Uppsala: Studia Missionalia Svecana C, p. 168.

6 Ruether, Rosemary Radford, 1987, 'Feminism and Jewish–Christian Dialogue: Particularism and Universalism in the Search for Religious Truth', in Hick, J., and Knitter, P. (eds), *The Myth of Christian Uniqueness*, Maryknoll: Orbis, p. 147.

7 Gross, 'Feminist', p. 63.

8 Kwok, Pui-lan, 1995, *Discovering the Bible in the Non-Biblical World*, Maryknoll: Orbis, p. 23.

9 Ruether, 'Feminism', p. 137.

10 Suchocki, *Divinity*, p. 83.

11 Kwok, Pui-lan, 2000, *Introducing Asian Feminist Theology*, Cleveland: Pilgrim Press, pp. 47–8.

12 Young, Pamela Dickey, 1995, *Christ in a Post-Christian World: How Can We Believe in Jesus Christ when Those Around Us Believe Differently – Or Not At All?* Minneapolis: Augsburg Fortress Press, p. 30.

13 Ruether, 'Feminism', p. 142.

14 Eck, Diana, 1993, *Encountering God: A Spiritual Journey from Bozeman to Banaras*, Boston: Beacon Press, p. 186.

15 King, Ursula, 1997, *Christ in All Things: Exploring Spirituality with Teilhard de Chardin*, Maryknoll: Orbis, pp. 153–4.

16 Suchocki, *Divinity*, p. 83.

17 Young, *Christ*, p. 83.

18 Young, *Christ*, p. 137.

19 Oduyoye, Mercy Amba, 2004, 'The People Next Door: An Essay in Honour of Kosuke Koyama', in *Beads and Strands: Reflections of an African Woman on Christianity in Africa*, Maryknoll: Orbis, p. 54.

20 Oduyoye, 2004, 'Women and Ritual in Africa', in *ibid.*, p. 79.

21 Kwok, *Introducing*, p. 67.

22 Chung, Hyun Kyung, 1997, 'Seeking the Religious Roots of Pluralism', *Journal of Ecumenical Studies*, vol. 34.3, p. 400.

23 Chung, Kyung Hyun, 1990, *Struggle to be the Sun Again: Introducing Asian Women's Theology*, Maryknoll: Orbis, p. 66.

24 Chung, 'Seeking', p. 402.

25 Chung, 'Seeking', p. 402.

26 Chung, 'Seeking', p. 401.

27 Chung, 'Seeking', pp. 400–1.

28 Kwok, *Introducing*, p. 50.

29 Christ, Carol, 2000, 'Roundtable Discussion: Feminist Theology and Religious Diversity', *Journal of Feminist Studies in Religion* 16, no. 2, p. 79.

30 Kim, Kirsteen, 'Spirit and "Spirits" at the Canberra Assembly of the World Council of Churches, 1991', *Missiology: An International Review*, vol. 32, no. 3 (July 2004), p. 350.

8

Interfaith Dialogue: Religious Accountability between Strangeness and Resonance

ALAN RACE

> We can only see into each other's souls if we take the trouble – and sometimes the risk – to visit each other.[1]

Throughout most of their history Christians have been taught to look on other religions and their adherents variously, as: theologically wrong-headed, morally evil, ideologically uncivilized, politically threatening, or simply sub-human. This does not describe the whole of Christian history by any means, and much of this outlook has been a function of Christianity's entanglement with power and empire as it has been religiously motivated. But the shocking starkness of my language is intentional and designed to highlight characteristic attitudes and responses which have been all too prevalent beneath the surface of Christian culture, if not actually on it. Under contemporary pressures of globalization, this is changing. Thankfully, one advantage of globalization is that we do have to take the trouble to visit each other, as the celebrated anthropologist and Muslim scholar Akbar Ahmed recommends.

The Range and Definition of Dialogue

This chapter retains a focus for dialogue as an interreligious encounter between different worlds of religious identity. Indeed, interfaith dialogue itself means 'reasoning across worlds of religious difference', from the Greek 'dia' (across) and 'logos' (reasoning). It assumes, therefore, that something is to be gained from dialogical encounter which is both more than simply another context for self-assertion (which would be exclusivistic monologue) and more than simply observing differences (which would be relativistic incommensurability). Dialogue harbours an expectation that a religious understanding of life in its fullest sense requires both transcending the self-sufficiency of individual traditions and also refusing the fate of relativism or indifference.

Interfaith dialogue between people of different religious persuasions covers numerous types of encounter and involves participants in many different expectations and processes, depending on the context. It may include the following: (1) encounters at a rational level, where theologians and philosophers thrash out the implications of bringing religious beliefs and traditions into positive conversation with each other; (2) meetings at the level of experiential awareness, where spiritual seekers share their experiences of transcendent reality, noting both the strangeness and resonance between them as practitioners; (3) sharing among activists from different traditions working together on a common cause, centred, for example, on issues of 'justice', 'peace' or 'ecological sustainability'. Sometimes dialogue seems synonymous with the very elastic and neutral-sounding term 'interfaith relations', but strictly speaking dialogue is more deeply and mutually implicated than the language of 'relations' suggests.

Defining interreligious dialogue at a basic level, therefore, depends on many factors, including social setting and political context, religious identity and schools of interpretation within religious traditions. One veteran activist of dialogue, the East European Protestant theologian Paul Mojzes, offers a provisional definition of dialogue as:

> a way by which persons or groups of different persuasions respectfully and responsibly relate to one another in order to bring about mutual enrichment without removing essential differences between them. Dialogue is both a verbal and an attitudinal mutual approach which includes listening, sharing ideas, and working together despite the continued existence of real differences and tensions.[2]

Note how this definition incorporates a paradoxical sense of people and communities being bound together by virtue of their lasting differences. Dialogue assumes neither harmony between religions nor isolationist self-sufficiency, but mutual accountability. In this sense, the space between the assumption that 'we're all the same' and the insistence that 'we're all different' is where dialogue flourishes.

Historically, interfaith dialogue is not entirely new, but the extent to which past instances can be cited as role models for dialogue in our present global context is a moot point. For example, in a Christian context, the classic text from the Acts of the Apostles 17.22–31, which portrays the apostle Paul in discussion with Athenian philosophers on the Areopagus (Mars Hill), is sometimes cited as a New Testament example of dialogue. Paul notes the piety of the pagan philosophers, draws attention to the altar bearing the inscription 'To an unknown god', and then sketches a line of argument which seeks to make overlapping 'points of contact' with pagan beliefs – for example through the Stoic sense that in God 'we live and move and have our being'. However, the speech also follows immediately on from Paul's severe disapproval of pagan idols (Acts 17.16), notes that prior to the coming of Christ the world was in ignorance, and finally crowns his speech with reference to the resurrection of Jesus, which for him is the sign of God's action that ushers in the final 'age to come'. This ambiguity in Paul has inevitably led commentators to draw opposite conclusions: either Paul was in dialogue to draw lines of continuity between the gospel of Christ and the best of pagan philosophy or he was seeking to supplant their philosophy with a superior message of the risen Christ. Irrespective of whether or not the Acts of the Apostles reflects the authentic voice and experience of the apostle Paul, I am inclined to agree with the New Testament scholar Heikki Räisänen, whose judgement on this passage is direct: 'the reference to their [pagan] spiritual life is used as a point of contact with the missionary purpose of winning them over'.[3] But if this is the case, in what sense can Paul's encounter really be called dialogue? I raise this point, moreover, in spite of the fact that the Greek word *dialegomai* is used by the writer of the Acts at various places where Paul is in discussion with the philosophers of the ancient Greek world. The sense of the word is nearer 'disputation' or 'arguing with force', and this is different from the modern sensibility surrounding the notion of dialogue. As Cardinal Francis Arinze, former President of the Pontifical Council for Interreligious Dialogue at the Vatican, has made clear: 'Reciprocity is in the nature of dialogue.'[4]

A strong case can be made for saying that many of the characteristics of our present global context are new and these are having a profound effect on what dialogue entails and has become. I shall chart some of these characteristics under the headings of: (1) Reasons and Motivations for Dialogue; (2) Permission for and Tensions within Dialogue; (3) Contexts and Models of Dialogue; and (4) Fruits and Ambiguities of Dialogue. In the process, I shall bring out some historical background to current discussions and highlight some features of dialogue in different religious ethical, theological and spiritual contexts.

Reasons and Motivations for Dialogue

There are numerous reasons for engaging in dialogue between religions. First, as globalization continues to shape our world in so many ways, drawing cultures and religions closer together, we encounter the sheer impressiveness of spirituality and spiritually motivated action elsewhere. Given this experiential impressiveness the need arises for explanation and understanding. Does the experience of 'the other' break open the bounds of Christian theorizing about other religions hitherto? The Indian theologian Stanley Samartha once asked the challenging question, 'Can it be that it is the will of God that many religions should continue in the world?'[5] The question seems to imply the answer 'yes'. But if that is the expectation, then some serious theological questions for Christian self-understanding will need to be faced, questions of salvation and of truth. It would seem that dialogue is indispensable for clarifying the exact import of those questions.

Second, dialogue arises through practical necessity. Many of the problems facing the world require co-operation on so many fronts. As problems become 'global' so the need for tackling them on a global scale becomes more urgent. HIV/AIDS, international conflict, poverty, climate change and ecological sustainability, to name but a few problems, are no respecters of boundaries. Moreover, these problems are not simply technological in scope; they involve values, ethical judgements and beliefs about the nature of reality itself. At this point, it is generally assumed that religious and belief systems would do well to co-operate for the sake of a larger good than their own particularized perception of what the good is. Dialogue then becomes a medium for critically evaluating potentially shared values and actions that affect everyone no matter what their religious or philosophical aspirations might be. Moreover, the spectre of interreligious violence seems sufficient grounds alone for religions to co-operate seriously on how both to interpret plurality and to act in concert for the common good in a complex diverse world.

Third, the claim has been made that the philosophical shift in epistemology, deriving from the European Enlightenment, necessitates embracing a dialogical view of reality as such. This shift is characterized by the recognition of the role of the subject in perception and interpretation. The American Catholic theologian Leonard Swidler has termed this the 'de-absolutizing of truth', which he summarizes as follows:

> Where immutability, simplicity, and monologue had largely characterized our Western understanding of reality in an earlier day, in the past 150 years mutuality, relationality, and dialogue have come to be understood as constitutive elements of the very structure of human reality.[6]

If this is true, then the religions are invited to learn from one another for the sake of a greater perception of religious truth than they had hitherto imagined when left to themselves.

In fact, it could be argued that the religions have known this all along, as it is implied in the very notion of a transcendent sacred reality itself. This brings us to the fourth motivation for dialogue, which is more strictly theological. It is common to note that the so-called axial or world-transforming religions are motivated in life and thought by their universal aspiration rather than their particularistic roots. That is to say, what Christians would define as 'the creative presence of God in the world' is a presence that dwells at the heart of all reality. In this light, the religious spirit dwelling in the heart of other ways of spirituality is 'of God' in some sense. There will always be 'more' to God than one tradition's glimpse of God. It may be that the mystics of all traditions have been more open to this dimension of religious faith than the doctrinal defenders of it. This is not to say that the experience of transcendent reality is the same in all traditions – clearly that is unlikely to be the case as the contingencies of language, belief and history, which shape experience, argue against such an assumption. Nevertheless, the sense of the universal presence of transcendent reality, which takes the characteristic shape of tradition, refuses to be hemmed in by factors of particularistic finitude. When this is combined with the realization that the rational articulation of 'God' transcends our grasp of 'divine' fullness, it leads us to the prospect of glimpsing further truth about 'God' from beyond our own walls. This is explored further in the section 'Fruits and Ambiguities' below.

Permissions for and Tensions within Dialogue

The wider cultural and historical background, from which Christian permission for dialogue emerged, involved many factors, including: the ending of Western colonialism, the promotion of human rights and freedom of religious practice, and the appreciation of diversity as central to the development of shared responsibility for the future of 'one world'. Some writers in cultural studies advocate dialogue as part of an overall pattern of global cultural evolution.[7] Others have heralded dialogue as an awakening to a Second Axial Period, as momentous as the First Axial Period.[8] Specific Christian theological and institutional permission for dialogue was given a major fillip through the watershed period of Vatican II in the Catholic world and through the World Council of Churches' (WCC) development of 'Guidelines for Dialogue' in the Protestant world.

The seminal Catholic document from Vatican II, *Nostra Aetate*, classically affirmed: 'The Church, therefore, urges her sons to enter with prudence and charity into discussion and collaboration with members of other religions. Let Christians, while witnessing to their own faith and way of life, acknowledge, preserve and encourage the spiritual and moral truths found among non-Christians, also their social life and culture.' The reason for such openness is because, 'The Catholic Church rejects nothing of what is true and holy in these religions.'[9] The WCC was equally making its first steps towards dialogue: 'Dialogue helps us not to disfigure the image of our neighbours of different faiths and ideologies', and 'Dialogue, therefore, is a fundamental part of Christian service within community.'[10] Both of these tentative opening overtures towards interreligious dialogue have deepened over the period since these beginnings. So the encyclical *Redemptoris Missio* (1990) declares: 'Dialogue does not originate from tactical concerns or self-interest but is an activity with its own guiding principles, requirements and dignity. It is demanded by deep respect for everything that has been brought about in human beings by the Spirit who blows where he wills.'[11] And the WCC, in a meeting of theologians at Baar, Switzerland, in 1990, moved beyond its early concentration essentially on the notion of 'service within community' to affirm not only the 'seeking' but also the 'finding' of God within other religious traditions *qua traditions*.[12] The exploration of that 'deep respect' and 'finding' extends the permission for dialogue given decades earlier.

However, the embracing of dialogue has also led to a tension within Christian theology, and this tension is far from finding a resolution. Expressed in a theological-christological framework, the question arises whether or not dialogue undercuts the concept of the finality of Christ as the sole origin and goal of the world's salvation, however carefully that finality is qualified. For example, the Catholic International Theological Commission, in 1997, acknowledged the christological problem as follows: 'How can one enter into an interreligious dialogue, respecting all religions and not considering them in advance as imperfect and inferior, if we recognize in Jesus Christ and only in him the unique and universal Saviour of mankind?'[13] Having raised the question in such direct terms the Commission failed to address it at all adequately. The issue was compounded in 2000 when the declaration *Dominus Iesus* underlined that non-Christian traditions are 'gravely deficient' in salvation: 'If it is true that the followers of other religions can receive divine grace, it is also certain that *objectively speaking* they are in a gravely deficient situation in comparison with those who, in the Church, have the fullness of the means of salvation.'[14] What can dialogue mean in this context?

Further, in a missiological framework, dialogue raises the issue of conversion. The Vatican document *Dialogue and Proclamation* (1991), for example, taught that dialogue 'remains oriented towards proclamation in so far as the dynamic process of the Church's evangelizing mission reaches in it its climax and its fullness.'[15] Clearly, the tension between the new openness assumed by dialogue and the sense of Christian tradition as the more adequate, authentic or superior vehicle of transforming truth remains.

More recently, the churches have turned to the concept of 'hospitality' as a means for continuing with the dialogical journey while avoiding direct conflict with theological finality. Hospitality is a function of the host–guest dynamic. The host community, at its best, offers generous welcome to the stranger (the other) and values the differences between them with respect. It provides an orderly context for exchange and learning, and might even lead to change. The idea of hospitality is based on persons and not on systems; it speaks of 'open house' and not of 'closed doors'. So the WCC document *Religious Plurality and Christian Self-Understanding* (2005) believes that 'The grace of God shown in Jesus Christ calls us to an attitude of hospitality in our relationship to others.' And further: 'Practical hospitality and a welcoming attitude to strangers create the space for mutual transformation and even reconciliation.'[16] These sentiments are as open as any we are likely to find in the institutional Christian embrace of dialogue.

Yet the question remains: how far does the turn to hospitality resolve the issues of theological finality and Christian absoluteness in relation to dialogue? In the light of hospitality (essentially an ethical category) what does it mean to speak of 'mutual transformation' and 'reconciliation'? Does it intend to view other faith-traditions as theologically equal in some sense? There is no indication that the official Christian world has been willing to endorse that view thus far. Indeed, the trinitarian theological framework in which *Religious Plurality and Christian Self-Understanding* is couched simply repeats the earlier permission-giving theology for dialogue that was first elaborated in the mid-1970s. Stanley Samartha, the first WCC Director of the Sub-Unit on Dialogue with People of Living Faiths, had already made broad appeals to the universalist thrust of Christian themes – for example, generalist notions that 'The incarnation is God's dialogue with humanity.' Apart from knowing more precisely what such a belief really means, Samartha himself acknowledged that affirmations like this were intended as strategic stimuli for establishing dialogical relationships in the early stages of the Dialogue Sub-Unit. Might it be that 'hospitality' functions in a comparable manner for a later period: it maintains the momentum of relationship while keeping the theological struggle hidden?

Contexts and Models of Dialogue

Four types of dialogue

As I have already said, part of the difficulty in clarifying the discourse about interreligious dialogue is that it has come to embrace a number of meanings, and there is no generally agreed definition of it. In a seminal article, in 1974, the religious studies scholar Eric Sharpe noted that dialogue was in danger of degenerating into a cliché and that 'it is not always clear in what sense (or senses) the word is being used'.[17] Sharpe then distinguished between four types of dialogue, which he labelled as follows:

1 Discursive Dialogue
2 Human Dialogue
3 Secular Dialogue
4 Interior Dialogue

Let me offer a brief comment on each in turn.

First, by 'Discursive Dialogue' Sharpe envisaged reasoned discourse on an intellectual plane, comparing and seeking informed judgements about beliefs and theological propositions. But a problem is likely to remain over how one interprets what has been heard other than perceiving it through the lens of one's own prior convictions. Of the four types, Sharpe was least hopeful that this kind of exchange would yield any advance in mutual rapprochement between religious traditions.

Second, in 'Human Dialogue' Sharpe outlined a view of dialogue that values *people* over *beliefs*. It involves a readiness to listen to 'the other' as 'other' and not as a pre-formed stereotype. However, with its emphasis on persons as such, Sharpe was concerned that this approach might imply that the notion of tradition is being bypassed completely.

Third, with 'Secular Dialogue' Sharpe alluded to the call for religions to join forces in facing and tackling the world's many problems, such as poverty, justice, peace, and so on. It assumes that the religions share a common concern for social and political action to improve the world in order to render it a more habitable place. Again, Sharpe was not impressed by this type if it involved erasing the differences between traditions in their ethical interpretations of the nature of reality and injunctions to action.

Finally, by 'Interior Dialogue' Sharpe meant the sharing and mutual exchange between traditions at contemplative or mystical levels. This is a form of encounter that is impatient with intellectual systems and claims to go to the heart of spirituality which is claimed to be the essential purpose of religious commitment. Sharpe thought that the focus on the interior life alone represented only a partial grasp of what religion intended as a whole.

Clearly, for Sharpe, there are pluses and minuses regarding dialogue. Moreover, it could be argued that Sharpe's separating out of a category labelled 'Human Dialogue' is misplaced, as dialogue is always between human beings and is implied in all of the other three areas. These other three areas seem more theologically motivated in terms of theology, ethics and spirituality. That said, however, clearly there are advantages and disadvantages with any categorization of dialogue and with the distinctive proposals attached to any one approach to dialogue. What is striking is that, since 1974, the four types described by Sharpe have continued roughly to represent the parameters for dialogue thereafter. For example, a similar categorization was proposed by the Vatican document *Dialogue and Proclamation* (1991), as follows:

> a) The *dialogue of life*, where people strive to live in an open and neighbourly spirit, sharing their joys and sorrows, their human problems and preoccupations. [Cf. Human Dialogue.]
>
> b) The *dialogue of action*, in which Christians and others collaborate for the integral development and liberation of people. [Cf. Secular Dialogue.]
>
> c) The *dialogue of theological exchange*, where specialists seek to

deepen their understanding of their respective religious heritages and to appreciate different spiritual values. [Cf. Discursive Dialogue.]

d) The *dialogue of religious experience*, where persons, rooted in their own religious traditions, share their spiritual riches, for instance with regard to prayer and contemplation, faith and ways of searching for God or the Absolute. [Cf. Interior Dialogue.]

Of course, these categories are not wholly discrete, as they are capable of overlap in numerous ways. The Catholic theologian Donald W. Mitchell has portrayed the four kinds of dialogue as four stations in a continuous journey.[18]

Global ethic thinking

One model of interreligious dialogue has been developed as what is termed a 'Global Ethic'. In 1993 the centenary meeting of the Parliament of the World's Religions, held in Chicago, USA, adopted the document *Towards a Global Ethic: An Initial Declaration*.[19] The first draft of this document had been written by the Christian theologian Hans Küng and this was followed by major revisions through a long consultation process with many spiritual leaders and theological/philosophical intellectuals from numerous traditions around the world. The *Declaration* was intended as a stimulus to further dialogue – hence '*Towards*' in the title. It is worth reflecting a little on the global ethic thinking in order to indicate a number of perennial issues surrounding the discourse about dialogue in general.

The Global Ethic accepts globalization as a fact: the world exists as an interconnected unity, such that what transpires in one part affects the whole. This new context requires fresh and imaginative thinking if we are to solve the many deep-seated problems which confront us. It is important to note, however, that the framers proposed this 'ethic' not as an attempt at synthesis between traditions but as 'a minimal *fundamental consensus* concerning binding *values*, irrevocable *standards*, and *fundamental* moral attitudes' – in order to meet the demands of an emerging global community. It is work-in-progress.

The essential shape of the *Initial Declaration* can be represented diagrammatically as in Figure 8.1. This representation follows what can be considered to be a standard cycle of religious commitment: there is a diagnosis of need (1), followed by a disclosure of fundamental awareness (2), which gives rise to a disciplined pathway of active change (3), and which in turn envisages the transformation of reality (4). At the heart of the Global Ethic lie the Four Irrevocable Directives. They provide the bridge between the religious basis for ethical life and its practical outworking in dialogue and co-operation among the religions.

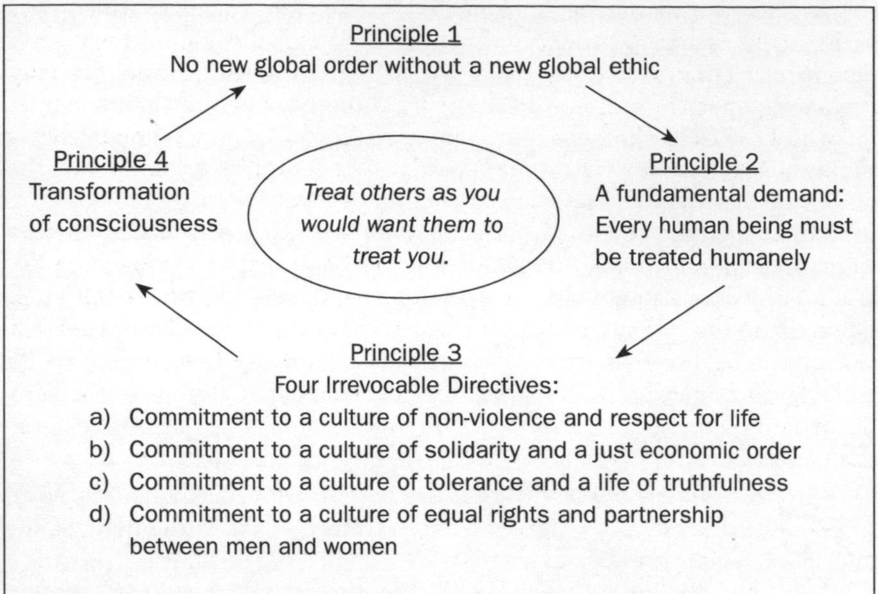
Principle 1
No new global order without a new global ethic
Principle 2
A fundamental demand: Every human being must be treated humanely
Principle 3
Four Irrevocable Directives:
a) Commitment to a culture of non-violence and respect for life
b) Commitment to a culture of solidarity and a just economic order
c) Commitment to a culture of tolerance and a life of truthfulness
d) Commitment to a culture of equal rights and partnership between men and women
Principle 4
Transformation of consciousness
Treat others as you would want them to treat you.

Figure 8.1

Let me now make two simple points concerning the Global Ethic as a document of dialogue. First, it is not an attempt at a universalist ethic in the sense of replacing the particularistic ethics of religious traditions. Certainly, it does claim that there is common ground among traditions – a 'minimal fundamental consensus'. In this respect, it assumes that in practice the meaning of different terms – for example love (*agape* in Christianity) and compassion (*karuna* in Buddhism) – lead to the same action. Those who stress the incommensurability between traditions may here warn against what appears to be a conflation of terms from very different traditions.[20]

The distinction made by the Princeton social scientist Michael Walzer, between what he called 'thick' and 'thin' morality, is sometimes cited at this point in order to provide some intellectual backing in the search for balancing the twin affirmations of unity and diversity. 'Thin' morality – or 'minimal morality' – depicts the unity when it refers to 'a whole set of elementary ethical standards, which include the fundamental right to life, to just treatment (including just treatment from the state), to physical and mental integrity'.[21] Furthermore, it seems to be the case that universal values do in fact arise when human beings are faced with oppression or unjust treatment, irrespective of the context in which such universalism is articulated. These values may be limited to fundamental values such as justice and truth, but nonetheless they are capable of being harnessed as 'a certain kind of universalism'.[22] On the other hand, 'thick morality' refers to the tradition-specific articulation of fundamental norms and principles which may vary widely according to cultural history and religious commitment, and therefore celebrates diversity. Moreover, these norms and principles may even be in opposition or contrast, but this need not militate against agreement at the level of 'thin morality'. The opposition or contrast then becomes simply an invitation to dialogue in order to discover whether or not the disagreements are real, apparent, or significant in any way.

Second, the 'Global Ethic' asserts that fundamental consensus emerges from 'ancient guidelines' within different traditions, so to speak 'from below'. Yet it has also clearly been influenced by modern critical thinking, especially in the framing of the Four Irrevocable Directives. Thus a certain tension can be discerned in the way the Four Irrevocable Directives provide a dialogical framework both for challenging religious traditions in the light of modern demands and also for testing modern demands against diverse ancient wisdoms in dialogue. Moreover, they provide an ethical direction for the pursuit of change in the following ways:

- The 'Commitment to respect for all life' is the basis for a critique of policies that fail to support environmental sustainability or that promote the militarization of international relations.
- The 'Commitment to a just economic order' intrinsically raises doubts about the long-term benefits of unbridled economic globalization and its capitalist engine.
- The 'Commitment to a life of tolerance and truthfulness' promotes human respect, celebrates the differences between histories and cultures, and embraces questions of truth as a function of new relationships.
- The 'Commitment to partnership between men and women' envisages a way of relating that refuses to lock men and women into prefigured roles and seeks to honour the full humanity of all genders.

These Commitments propel the religions and other worldviews into patterns of relationship that will transform the outlook of all of us. Given that it is in the details of particularistic traditions that the struggle to embody the four Commitments will be most keenly felt, sharing wisdoms in a new dialogical framework opens up the theological traditions to scrutiny from critical awareness arising from many analytical perspectives.

There will be those who see in this 'Global Ethic' project all of the ills of the enthusiasm for dialogue as such. Complaints may include: it already conflates religious differences; it is framed by an Enlightenment view of progress; and it is prescriptive about the outcome. These critiques can be overdrawn and are best received as warning shots rather than reasons for recommending closure on global ethic thinking as such. There is no reason why those matters usually thought to be derived from Western traditions alone – human rights, democracy, equality, and so forth – cannot also be rooted in ancient religious wisdoms.[23] To this extent, the Global Ethic, if it is to be fully acceptable, requires wide-ranging support from many traditions and movements.[24]

Fruits and Ambiguities of Dialogue

To the extent that interreligious dialogue candidly accepts the pluralism and diversity embodied in the diverse religious systems of the world, it has now gained a momentum of its own. One of its most elaborate forms has been devised by the Global Dialogue Institute (GDI), Philadelphia. It is worth citing their claim:

> Deep-Dialogue has emerged experimentally out of a wide range of Inter-World Encounters. When we live through the encounters of religious worlds, as we gain inter-cultural experience, as we struggle with the historic patterns of collisions of diverse philosophical world-views, as we creatively engage the powerful forces in civic life where ideologies and lifeworlds battle . . . this inter-world experience enables us to rise to a higher global perspective. As we attain this higher perspective we begin to see deeper patterns and pervasive dynamics evident in cultural evolution over the centuries.
>
> One remarkable discovery of these intensive inter-world experiments is that there must be, and is, a deeper common ground or source out of which diverse worldviews and perspectives arise. As we gain access to this deeper global source of all cultural life and experience it becomes more evident that we humans are in the midst of a profound self-transformation and maturation of our humanness.[25]

The aspirations represented by such an outlook are far-reaching indeed. However, the central 'discovery' that a 'deeper common ground' lies beneath the world religions is probably the most controversial aspect of this perspective. If there is such a common ground it is not at all obvious to everyone involved in the dialogical movement. For example, the veteran American process theologian of dialogue John Cobb disavows any reference to such common ground. Dialogue, Cobb believes, exists for the sake of mutual transformation, that is, a process of encounter which modifies traditions without disturbing their basic distinctive orientations. For Cobb, the aims and experiences of different religious traditions seem so diverse that the assumption of common ground is unwarranted. As he says, at this stage of human development all that can be affirmed is that 'the totality of what is, is very complex, far exceeding all that we can ever hope to know or think'.[26] This raises the prospect, paradoxically, of a metaphysical plurality of ultimates corresponding to the phenomenological plurality of religions in the world. But such a view, even if not provable, surely seems unsatisfactory by any standards.[27]

At the very least, dialogue generates a sense that the religions do share a family resemblance, even if our comprehension of that resemblance remains necessarily incomplete. Other trajectories of experience can be cited, however, in support of a notion of dialogue that draws the religions into some stronger relationship of mutual belonging and accountability. For example, let me highlight the well-known fruits of the Snowmass Monastic Interfaith Dialogue (1984–6). This was a dialogue among monastic representatives of various traditions, conducted over a period of time, and focused on a desire to discern the meaning of spirituality in a wider perspective. The results of their encounters, which incorporated Buddhist, Hindu, Jewish, Islamic, Native American, Christian (Russian Orthodox, Protestant, Roman Catholic) representatives, were published as an appreciation of 'Points of Agreement' or 'Similarity':

1 The world religions bear witness to the experience of Ultimate Reality, to which they give various names: Brahman, Allah, Absolute, God, Great Spirit.
2 Ultimate Reality cannot be limited by any name or concept.
3 Ultimate Reality is the ground of infinite potentiality and actualization.
4 Faith is opening, accepting and responding to Ultimate Reality. Faith in this sense precedes every belief system.
5 The potential for human wholeness – or in other frames of reference, enlightenment, salvation, transformation, blessedness, nirvana – is present in every human person.
6 Ultimate Reality may be experienced not only through religious practices but also through nature, art, human relationships, and service of others.
7 As long as the human condition is experienced as separate from Ultimate Reality, it is subject to ignorance and illusion, weakness and suffering.
8 Disciplined practice is essential to the spiritual life; yet spiritual attainment is not the result of one's own efforts, but the result of the experience of oneness with Ultimate Reality.[28]

This is a substantial list of points of agreement! However, even this degree of agreement at the phenomenological level of religious experience need not amount to the affirmation of common ground behind the different experiences associated with the different traditions. Given these fruits of dialogue, perhaps the most that can be said is that the 'points of agreement' provide a *prima facie* case for thinking that this could well be true. The Catholic Trappist and principal host of the dialogue, Thomas Keating, asks the question: 'Are there truths on which the religions of the world are in substantial agreement?'[29] Intriguingly, he answers: 'Having listened to the masters of other traditions, I am convinced that underlying the particular conceptual frames of reference is a unity that has never been sufficiently grasped.'[30] If there is credibility in this conviction born of experience, then it will not be a unity which is based on a naive view that the traditions are essentially 'experiencing the same experience'.

The fruits of dialogue have resulted, at least for some, in the invitation to theologians and philosophers to make reasoned sense of religious authenticity shared through dialogue. It is the question which dialogical encounter places firmly at the door of the guardians of religious tradition. The Christian philosopher John Hick has put this in the sharpest terms possible, when he asks why it is that the adherents of any religious pathway, which claims to be uniquely or eschatologically more authentically true or superior than other ways, do not manifest any superior fruits of their commitment as a matter of real historical achievement, personally or corporately.[31] Without such outcomes, what is the advantage of continuing with the claims of superiority?

In dialogue, a process which begins with the affirmation of respect for the one who is different, the discovery is often made that Christian identity is to be forged afresh. Christian identity is not to be seen as superior, patronizing, or antagonistic towards religious others. That has often been the way of history. In the emerging dialogical age, our expectation of insight from others, combined with a certain modesty or critical realism regarding our epistemological claims to religious truth, lead us to a different perspective. Should it not be that my/our religious identity is defined now by its proportionate relationship to others? That is to say, being Christian in the dialogical age entails, paradoxically, more than living out of the resources of Christian scriptures and tradition alone. As the Catholic writer Paul Knitter has put it:

> In dialogue one faces the utterly other and trusts that one can speak to, learn from, even work with that other. Within the heart of dialogue, therefore, there beats a deep act of faith and trust.[32]

One might add that Knitter has here highlighted something about dialogue which is in tune with basic religious commitment itself – it is 'a deep act of faith and trust'. Sadly, however, religiously committed people have often been educated in defensive ways with regard to interreligious encounter, and it is this that has generated mistrust between people of different traditions.

Concluding Remarks

We used to perceive the religious other as an object of suspicion or threat. Through dialogue, however, the religious other no longer becomes a dehumanized object but a living subject from and with whom we can learn.

Religious vision and the possibilities for making a difference in the world are enriched because they are shared.

Dialogue is both a process and a new way of articulating the varied transcendent vision and aims for human transformation that lie at the heart of the religious apprehension of life itself. As a process, dialogue depends on giving and receiving: we offer the wisdom, values and truth of 'our' tradition and we open ourselves to other articulations of the same. The process assumes at least the following attitudes and values:

- Listening for other articulations of religious authenticity.
- Respect for differences.
- Willingness to learn from one another and from all critical perspectives on reality.
- Self-criticism as a gateway to general criticism.
- Moving beyond absolutism and superiority.
- Leaving behind relativism and indifference.
- Forging criteria to distinguish between true and false religious belief and practice.

As a new way of pursuing religious truth, dialogue accepts that relationship between traditions assumes paramount importance. We are likely to welcome complementarities of vision over against the competition of visions associated with both absolutism and relativism. We give full reign to the recognition that no one tradition can comprehend the fullness of ultimate truth. The distinction between the hidden mystery of ultimate reality and the apprehension of that reality in historical forms is key to fruitful dialogical encounter. All traditions embody some version of this distinction.

In dialogue, partners articulate their basic experiences and developing traditions in conversation with one another. They will then learn about each other and in particular be challenged to overcome stereotypical images of one another. Such images are deep-rooted and only hard listening will lead to their removal. As trust grows, participants learn tolerance of one another, yet they may still maintain a respectful distance. We exist alongside one another in parallel lives; even so, the negotiation of similarities and differences begins in earnest. Eventually, dialogue leads to a deeper interaction whereby participants move beyond tolerance and learn to live within the space between different basic visions. This is a space that is vulnerable and risky, but its fruit is the mutuality of belonging: we become a community of communities.

Plainly, the religions are not all the same – we have different origins, histories and spiritualities. Yet neither are they all different, in the sense that no family resemblances can be discerned between them. We inhabit one earth and we have powers to exercise human empathy across many boundaries. Followers from many traditions seek transcendent vision and human transformation, no matter how variously these are shaped symbolically and worked out in practice. If we were all the same there would be no need to talk to one another; if we were hopelessly sealed in separate rooms there would be no possibility of talking at all!

The giving and receiving of dialogue is demanding spiritual work. For this reason, dialogue aims to embody relationships of trustful acceptance, critical friendship and mutual accountability. We are neither quick to judge nor uncritical in outlook. Worlds of difference really are strange to one another. Yet the ability to 'speak across' worlds of difference means that we are able to resonate with the authenticity of the subjective other. We are many communities yet one community; we are far apart yet belong together. In dialogue, we move between strangeness and resonance.

Dialogue cannot flourish in a decontextualized bubble. Traditions encounter one another on a global canvas. Religious truth is a transforming truth and therefore it exists for the sake of making a difference in the world. In this sense, a dialogical community of interreligious being and activity becomes a model community for the transformation of all life. Justice, peace, sustainability, compassion and community are articulated and lived out as a collective witness to the global future. The world needs religions in dialogue and not in competition.

Let us say that interreligious dialogue is both what the world yearns for from the religions and what the religions at their best do offer. It is more than a process and represents a paradigm shift in religious consciousness. Christians can embrace it without reserve.

Study Questions

1 Is interreligious dialogue a luxury or a necessity in today's context?

2 What are the Christian bases for the practice of interreligious dialogue? Are any bases needed?

3 What are the hopes for interreligious dialogue?

Further Reading

Barnes, Michael, 2002, *Theology and the Dialogue of Religions*, Cambridge: Cambridge University Press.

Cobb, John, Jr, 1999, 'Christian Universality Revisited', in Knitter, Paul F. (ed.), *Transforming Christianity and the World: A Way beyond Absolutism and Relativism*, Maryknoll: Orbis.

Forward, Martin, 2001, *Inter-religious Dialogue: A Short Introduction*, Oxford: Oneworld.

Küng, Hans, 1987, *Christianity and the World Religions: Paths of Dialogue with Islam, Hinduism, and Buddhism*, London: Collins.
Küng, Hans, 2002, *Tracing the Way: Spiritual Dimensions of the World Religions*, London and New York: Continuum.
Panikkar, Raimundo, 1978, *The Intrareligious Dialogue*, New York: Paulist Press.
Swidler, Leonard, 1990, *After the Absolute: The Dialogical Future of Religious Reflection*, Minneapolis: Augsburg Fortress Press.

Notes

1 Ahmed, Akbar, 2007, *Journey into Islam: The Crisis of Globalization*, Washington: Brookings Institute Press, p. 252.

2 Mojzes, Paul, 1989, 'The What and the How of Dialogue', in Bryant, M. Darrol, and Flinn, Frank (eds), *Inter-Religious Dialogue: Voices from a New Frontier*, New York: Paragon House, p. 203. Paul Mojzes is Professor of Religious Studies, Rosemont College, Rosemont, Pennsylvania, and Co-Editor of the *Journal of Ecumenical Studies*.

3 Räisänen, Heikki, 1997, *Marcion, Muhammad and the Mahatma: Exegetical Perspectives on the Encounter of Cultures and Faiths*, London: SCM Press, p. 12.

4 Arinze, Cardinal Francis, 1997, *Meeting Other Believers*, Leominster: Gracewing, p. 5.

5 Race, Alan, 2001, *Interfaith Encounter: The Twin Tracks of Theology ad Dialogue*, London: SCM Press, p. 21.

6 Swidler, Leonard, 1990, *After the Absolute: The Dialogical Future of Religious Reflection*, Minneapolis: Augsburg Fortress Press, p. 6.

7 For example, Kenney, Jim, 2004, 'Sea Change: Cultural Evolution in the Early 21st Century', *Interreligious Insight*, vol. 2, no. 3, pp. 26–34. Posted at: http://www.interreligiousinsight.org/July2004/July04Kenney.html.

8 Cousins, Ewert H., 1989, 'Interreligious Dialogue: The Spiritual Journey of Our Time', in Bryant and Flinn, *Inter-Religious*, p. 6.

9 *Nostra Aetate*, in Flannery, Austin, OP (gen. ed.), 1975, *Vatican Council II: The Conciliar and Post Conciliar Documents*, Northport and Dublin: Costello and Dominican Publications, p. 739.

10 WCC, 1979, *Guidelines on Dialogue with People of Living Faiths and Ideologies*, Geneva: World Council of Churches. Posted at http://www.wcc-coe.org/wcc/what/interreligious/77glines-e.html.

11 http://www.vatican.va/roman_curia/pontifical_councils/interelg/documents/rc_pc_interelg_doc_19051991_dialogue-and-proclamatio_en.html.

12 WCC, 1991, 'The Baar Statement', *Current Dialogue*, vol. 19. Posted at http://www.wcc-coe.org/wcc/what/interreligious/baar.html.

13 International Theological Commission, 1997, *Christianity and the World Religions*, Vatican, p. 15.

14 Congregation for the Doctrine of the Faith, *Dominus Iesus: On the Unicity and Salvific Universality of Jesus Christ and the Church*. Posted at: http://www.vatican.va/roman_curia/congregations/cfaith/documents/rc_con_cfaith_doc_20000806_dominus-iesus_en.html. Accessed: 31 July 2007.

15 http://www.vatican.va/roman_curia/pontifical_councils/interelg/documents/

rc_pc_interelg_doc_19051991_dialogue-and-proclamatio_en.html.

16 World Council of Churches, 2005, *Current Dialogue*, vol. 45, pp. 4–12.

17 Sharpe, Eric, 1974, 'The Goals of Inter-Religious Dialogue', in Hick, John (ed.), *Truth and Dialogue: The Relationship Between World Religions*, London: Sheldon Press, p. 78.

18 Mitchell, Donald W., 1993, 'A Revealing Dialogue', *Interfaith Spirituality, The Way Supplement*, vol. 78, pp. 42–53.

19 Küng, Hans, and Kuschel, Karl-Josef (eds), 1993, *A Global Ethic: The Declaration of the Parliament of the World's Religions,* London: SCM Press.

20 See the essay by Paul Hedges on 'Particularities' in this collection.

21 Cited by Küng, Hans, 1997, *A Global Ethic for Politics and Economics*, London: SCM Press, p. 95.

22 *Ibid.*, p. 97. See also the excellent article by Pedersen, Kusumita P., 2007, 'Universality of Moral Norms: A Human Rights Perspective', *Interreligious Insight*, vol. 5, no. 1, pp. 8–18.

23 Cf. Traer, Robert, *Faith in Human Rights: Support in Religious Traditions for a Global Struggle*, Washington, DC: Georgetown University Press, 1991; and Race, Alan, and Shafer, Ingrid (eds), 2002, *Religions in Dialogue: From Theocracy to Democracy*, Aldershot: Ashgate.

24 This support was already apparent in 1993, but it has been endorsed by many others since then. See: Küng, Hans (ed.), 1996, *Yes to a Global Ethic*, London: SCM Press; Swidler, Leonard, 1998, *For All Life: Toward a Universal Declaration of a Global Ethic*, Oregon: White Cloud Press; and Morgan, Peggy, and Braybrooke, Marcus, 1998, *Testing the Global Ethic: Voices from the Religions on Moral Values*, Oxford and Ada: IIC and WCF/CoNexus Press; Küng, Hans, 2002, *Tracing the Way: Spiritual Dimensions of the World Religions*, London and New York: Continuum. See also the website and online journal of the organization, Globalisation for the Common Good: www.commongoodjournal.com for a broadening of global ethic concerns.

25 http://astro.temple.edu/~dialogue/

26 Cobb, John, 1999, 'Christian Universality Revisited', in Knitter, Paul F. (ed.), *Transforming Christianity and the World: A Way beyond Absolutism and Relativism*, Maryknoll: Orbis, p. 135.

27 See the essay by Perry Schmidt-Leukel in this collection.

28 Keating, Thomas, 1993, 'Theological Issues in Meditative Technologies', *Interfaith Spirituality, The Way Supplement*, vol. 78, p. 56.

29 Keating, Thomas, 1989, 'The Search for Ultimate Mystery', in Bryant and Flinn, *Inter-Religious*, p. 23.

30 *Ibid.*

31 Hick, John, 2005, 'The Next Step Beyond Dialogue', in Knitter, Paul F. (ed.), *The Myth of Religious Superiority: A Multifaith Exploration*, Maryknoll: Orbis, p. 8.

32 Knitter, Paul F., 1990, 'Interreligious Dialogue: What? Why? How?', in Swidler, Leonard, Cobb, John B., Jr, Knitter, Paul F., and Hellwig, Monica K. (eds), *Death or Dialogue? From the Age of Monologue to the Age of Dialogue*, London: SCM Press, p. 19.

Part 2

Christian Responses to Individual Faiths

Section A: Abrahamic Traditions

9

Judaism: Siblings in Strife

RONALD H. MILLER

Striving from the Womb

> And the Lord said to Rebecca:
> 'Two nations are in your womb, and two peoples born of you shall be divided.'
> (Gen. 25.23)

Though often understood in the past as mother and daughter, Judaism and Christianity are more commonly regarded today as siblings.[1] Like Jacob and Esau struggling in Rebecca's body, these two religions emerged in strife from the womb of biblical Judaism. Whether one chooses to begin the history of biblical Judaism with Adam's family, with Abraham, or with Moses, a common denominator in all three of these narratives is animal sacrifice. 'The Lord had regard for Abel and his offering [the first-born sheep of his flock]' (Gen. 4.4b). Abraham learned that rams, not first-born sons, were the acceptable sacrifice to bring to God (Gen. 22). Moses sealed Judaism's most important covenant with God by sprinkling the people with the blood of sacrificed oxen (Ex. 24.8). When Solomon built God's Temple some three thousand years ago, this became the locus of an everlasting sacrifice to the Lord. A bull was sacrificed every morning and every evening as a whole burnt offering. After a brief hiatus following the destruction of this Temple (and of the city of Jerusalem itself) by the Babylonians, a Second Temple was dedicated in 516 BCE. The centrepiece of the Temple liturgy was the practice of animal sacrifice. This continued through the lifetimes of Jesus and Paul until the Romans destroyed the Temple in 70 CE.

In Search of a Hermeneutic

With the destruction of the Second Temple, biblical Judaism lost its heart, the priests their *raison d'être*. A hermeneutics was needed, an interpretation of this tragedy capable of opening a door to a viable future for this exiled people. The Pharisees were religiously observant and theologically liberal; there were about six thousand of them in a total Jewish population of some seven million in the first century BCE. It is the Pharisees, who become the rabbis, who offered a compelling hermeneutics securing a future for Jews and Judaism. They argued that the sacrificial system rested, ultimately, not on the blood of animals, but on the dedication of human beings to God symbolized by acts of animal sacrifice. And so the times of animal sacrifice were replaced by the times when the community gathered for formal prayer three times daily. And the holiness of the Temple's altar was replicated in the table in every Jewish home where the Sabbath was sanctified every week in a special meal and where the Exodus event was celebrated annually in the Passover meal, the *Seder*.

No less compelling was the hermeneutics put forward by a nascent group of messianic Jews, followers of *Jeshu ben Josef* (Joshua, the son of Joseph) whom they now confessed as *Jeshu ha Messiach* (Joshua the Messiah). And in the Greek language that carried their message he would be known by words closely resembling their English translation: *Jesus ho Christos*, Jesus Christ. What was the rival interpretation of this messianic sect? In his total obedience to God, Jesus was the ultimate sacrifice after which no other would ever be needed: 'Unlike the other high priests, he [Jesus] has no need to offer sacrifices day after day, first for his own sins, and then for those of the people; this he did once for all when he offered himself' (Heb. 7.27). Jesus the Messiah is both Priest and Sacrifice.

The Galilean *Hasid*

After a brief teaching career, largely to illiterate peasants, Jesus was executed by the Roman domination system. He left behind no writings. He was a Galilean *hasid* or holy man, a healer, and a wisdom teacher. In his own Jewish tradition, he would be known as a *moshel meshalim*, a master of parables. The *Gospel of Thomas*, discovered in its entirety only some fifty years ago, begins with the assertion that it is in the understanding of Jesus' teachings that immortality lies.[2] In other words, these teachings can lead to the transformation of consciousness, conscience and community central to all spiritual endeavour. Jesus reminds human beings of their deepest divine identity and encourages them to live from that source. His central image for this divine presence in human lives is God's reign.

Saul/Paul

The name of Thomas was by no means the only one evoked as carrier of Jesus' authentic message. Some Christians heard the voice of Jesus in his brother Jacob (James in English) or in his close companion Mary Magdalene, or in the fisherman Shimon, whom Jesus had dubbed Cephas (Peter/Rock). And then there is the man who never knew Jesus during his earthly career, Saul/Paul of Tarsus.[3] Fourteen of the 27 books of the Christian Testament are attributed to him, and the book that is supposed to be a history of all twelve apostles (Acts of the Apostles) is in fact largely a biography of Paul. In the development of normative Christianity, his voice virtually becomes the voice of Jesus. A contemporary biographer of Paul states: 'I shall argue that what Paul meant was not something other than or contrary to what Jesus meant, but that we can best find out the latter by studying the former.'[4] This is a thesis with which a large number of current Pauline scholars, myself included, would strongly disagree.

Paul exemplifies marvellously the type of personality categorized by William James as 'a sick soul'. James writes: 'Wrong living, impotent aspirations; "What I would, that do I not; but what I hate, that I do," as Saint Paul says; self-loathing, self-despair, an unintelligible and intolerable burden to which one is mysteriously the heir.'[5] The propensity of such a soul is to feel deeply the pain of the world (what German writers call *Weltschmerz*). Reality is most profoundly described for such a person by Virgil's immortal verse: '*Sunt lacrimae rerum et mentem mortalia tangunt*' ('Reality has a tearful dimension and life's transiency touches our souls').

James intends no negative judgement in his use of the term 'sick soul'. The 'healthy-minded soul' is of no more than equal valence. The terms describe two ways in which God-seekers evolve. The healthy-minded soul grows incrementally into holiness, whereas the sick soul is typically catapulted into sanctity by a profound conversion experience. As a sick soul, Paul saw the taint of sin everywhere and experienced Christ as his rescuer and redeemer. So it is to Paul, not to Jesus, that we can trace the headwaters of that mighty river in Christian theology called Original Sin. Different from the sins known to virtually all the classical religions, this Sin is a condition of our being, not a result of our choice. The seed planted in Paul becomes a tree watered by Augustine and nurtured by Christianity's great Reformers, especially Martin Luther and John Calvin.[6]

Sin and Redemption

Once humankind is understood as ineluctably entangled in this primordial and inherited Sin, alleviation of this condition must come from somewhere beyond the capacities of our human nature. Thus Christ's saving death, more than his example and teachings, become the focus of his message. And since only those aligned with this atoning death through faith and baptism can be saved, Christianity's exclusivism inexorably follows. The experience of Paul and his interpretation of the message of Jesus was not shared by all

Christians in the first century, nor should they be the only template of orthodoxy for Christians today. Cynthia Bourgeault, Episcopal priest and theologian, writes: 'Jesus was repositioned from *moshel meshalim* to mediator, and the spiritual journey was reframed from a quest for divinization to a rescue operation.'[7] No longer was the transformation of consciousness and conscience primary; being saved from Sin absorbed all other aspects of Christian identity. Jesus was no longer a Reminder of the divine mystery at the heart of our own being; he was now the Redeemer of a fallen humanity.

Emphasizing Jesus as Reminder, rather than Redeemer, has consequences for Jewish–Christian relations. First of all, if the focus is on the life and teachings of Jesus rather than his death, then the role Jews play in the story of Jesus' arrest and execution becomes less significant. Second, if Jesus called all human beings to recognize their own divine depth, then Jesus is not the only Reminder on the horizon. Ultimately this means that Buddhists are made whole and holy as Buddhists, Muslims as Muslims, and Jews as Jews. The exclusivism so prevalent in Paul's writings disappears. These two changes alone, if they had won the status of orthodoxy in place of Paul's teachings, would have led to a vastly different history of Jewish–Christian relations in the subsequent two thousand years. But it was Paul who won the victor's laurels and it was Paul's influence that shaped the only history Christianity was to write – at least to our own day.

Paul's three premises fall neatly into place. First, all are under the power of sin. Second, salvation from sin comes from the atoning sacrifice of Jesus. Third, only those with faith in that salvific action can be made whole and holy: '"Everyone is in the same predicament: since all are sinners falling short of God's glory, they are all made God-centred by the gift of God's grace. This comes about through Jeshu the Messiah, who is the redeemer put forward by God as an atonement sacrifice in his blood, made real for us by our faith" (Romans 3.22b–25).'[8] Alternative theologies have always existed but never prevailed; and thus Christian attitudes towards Jews and Judaism have largely been derived directly from these words of Paul.

In Paul's world, there is no access to God except through Jesus Christ. This applies to Jews and Gentiles alike. Thus, 'even today when the Torah is read, that veil covers their minds, and it is only by turning to the Lord that "the veil can be removed" (2 Corinthians 3.16).'[9] When visiting the cathedrals of Europe, I was often struck by the matching statues flanking the doorways: Church and Synagogue, two women: one reigning with crown and scepter; one with veiled eyes and holding broken tablets. The Hebrew Bible has become the 'Old' Testament (*testamentum* is the Latin word for *covenant*); without internal validity, it exists only as prophecy pointing to the fulfilment that will later be canonized as the 27 books of a 'New' Testament. Replacement theology, also known as supersessionism (literally, that which 'sits on' something else), has been born and continues to characterize much of Christian theology to our own day.

Matthew's Spin

The first of the 27 books of the Christian Testament is attributed to Matthew, though it is unlikely that the story is linked to the man of that name who appears in the narrative. The unknown author(s) of Matthew is using Mark's Gospel (he repeats over 95 per cent of it), along with a collection of sayings of Jesus conventionally called Q (from the German word for source, *Quelle*). This Gospel does not allow Jesus to be addressed as rabbi, since the Pharisees are now the rabbis; the Greek word for teacher, *didaskale*, is used instead. There are, however, two times when Jesus is called rabbi; both instances, however, come from the mouth of the traitor, Judas.[10] For the Gospel writer(s), Judas represents the rabbinic Jews who are the theological rivals of this community.

It is not only the rivalry with rabbinic Judaism that gives this Gospel an anti-Jewish spin. Written in Greek, this text can move through the entirety of the Roman Empire, calling people to this new faith. But having a felon as founder, one executed by a Roman official, opens few doors in the Roman world. Consequently, the Roman role in Jesus' arrest and execution must be downplayed. Pilate is whitewashed; he literally washes his hands of the whole affair in Matt. 27.24. In seesaw-like fashion, however, if the responsibility of Roman imperialism is denied, the burden of guilt has nowhere to fall but on Jesus' own people and thus is born the terrible lie that 'the Jews killed Jesus'. Matthew drives this point home by portraying the crowd of Jews gathered in front of the Roman headquarters in Jerusalem as condemning itself by crying out the infamous blood curse: 'His blood be on us and on our children' (Matt. 27.25). This was to haunt the next two thousand years of Christian history until the Catholic Church officially declared in 1965 that 'the Jews should not be represented as rejected by God or accursed'.[11]

By the time Matthew's Gospel was written sometime in the late 80s CE, the polemical struggle between rabbinic Jews and the followers of the Jesus Movement was intense. One can imagine the peace of the synagogue being broken on a Sabbath morning when representatives of rabbinic Judaism and representatives of the Jesus Movement clashed in argument, each side attempting to win other Jews to their respective hermeneutic. We hear an echo of this debate in Matt. 28.11–15. Matthew's community argues that their Messiah had risen because the tomb was empty; the rabbis would counter that a body can be stolen. The followers of Jesus would say that this was impossible since the tomb was guarded; the rabbis then asked why the guards didn't see the resurrection. The Jesus Movement representatives would say that they did indeed see Jesus rise from the dead but the Jewish priests bribed them to keep silent. The exchange ends with the Gospel writer stepping out of his story into his own time frame by saying: 'And this story is still told among the Jews to this day.'[12]

What is most insidious about this passage is the implication that the priests knew and believed the story of the guards that Jesus had indeed been raised from the dead. So they were not unbelievers, but believers. But if they were believers, why would they persist in their efforts to suppress the truth of the resurrection? There's only one possible answer. Because they were in league with Satan, the Hinderer, the fallen angel who from the beginning was committed to thwarting God's plans. So the Jews are not unbelievers; they are much worse than that. They are believers who have chosen to work with the devil to suppress the truth of Christianity. This piece of anti-Semitism will be woven into subsequent history and will have a profound effect on Christian attitudes towards Jews. Even in our time it is not uncommon for Jews to be asked to show their horns.[13]

Jews as the Evil-Other

The spin that grows from Paul to Matthew culminates in John, the last of the canonical Gospels. Here the term 'the Jews' is used over 70 times, almost always with a negative connotation. Jesus and his disciples are curiously separated from their identity as the Gospel describes how, after Jesus' death, 'the doors of the house where the disciples had met were locked for fear of the Jews' (John 20.19). But are the disciples not Jews as well? This strange wall of separation had been built before the first century CE ended. The Jews are not just others, like Hindus or Buddhists; they are '*the* other', as black to white, as night to day, as Satan to God. Jesus is portrayed as telling the Jewish leaders that their father is Satan: 'You are from your father the devil . . .' (John 8.44). This will be a major theme in the two-thousand-year history of Christian anti-Semitism, culminating with the Nazi slogan that whoever fights the Jews is indeed wrestling with the devil.[14]

The ABC of Anti-Semitism

With the close of the Christian canon, the ABC of anti-Semitism has become part and parcel of Christian identity. The Jews are (A) *accursed* since they rejected their Messiah and further committed deicide (killing God) in crucifying Jesus, who was both truly human and truly divine. They are (B) *blasphemous* since they secretly know the truth of Christianity and yet publicly deny it. They are (C) *contemptible* in their perfidy. It was not until 1958, during the pontificate of Pope John XXIII, that the official Holy Thursday liturgy was changed, no longer praying '*pro perfidis Judaeis*' (for the perfidious Jews).[15] They are (D) *diabolical* and will be associated with Satan for the next two thousand years. In Mel Gibson's viciously anti-Semitic film, *The Passion of the Christ*, devils move around freely among the homicidal Jews who gather in Pilate's courtyard, urging the benevolent Procurator (who even offers Jesus a glass of water) to crucify Jesus. And so it comes as no surprise that Jews are (E) *excluded* in Christian society: excluded from salvation; excluded from legal rights and any protection under the law; excluded from living outside of ghettos; and finally excluded from living at all, when the Nazi 'final solution' presses forward with ruthless logic on the path that began with Christianity's sacred texts.

Justin Martyr and Trypho the Jew

It was just about the time that the last books of the Christian Testament were being written (between 100 and 110 CE) that Justin was born in the city known today as Nablus in Samaria, the territory between Judaea to the south and the Galilee to the north. He was of Graeco-Roman ancestry and was educated as a Platonist. He was in Ephesus, on the west coast of Asia Minor (Turkey today) when he converted to Christianity at about the age of thirty. Shortly after this, the Jews rebelled against Roman occupation, an effort that was soundly put down by the Romans in 135 CE. It was during this period of Jewish militancy that he met Trypho, possibly the famous Rabbi Tarphon. His published *Dialogue with Trypho*, a lengthy work of over two hundred pages, was written when Justin was living in Rome, where he was eventually killed in one of the outbreaks of Roman persecution. It is thus that he is known in Christian history as Justin *Martyr*.[16]

The *Dialogue with Trypho* bridges the world of the Christian Testament and the world of the Church Fathers (the patristic age). In its pages we see the reactions of an educated Christian to Jews and Judaism. Replacement theology provides the foundation for Justin's argument: 'The law promulgated at Horeb is already obsolete, and was intended for you Jews only, whereas the law of which I speak is for all men. Now a later law in opposition to an older law abrogates the older, just as a later covenant voids an earlier one.'[17] Christians constitute the new Israel and the scriptures of the Jewish people can be rightly understood only as Christianity's Old Testament. 'We are the true spiritual Israel and the descendants of Judah, Jacob, Isaac, and Abraham.'[18] For Justin, it is indeed the Jews who killed Jesus: 'You crucified the only sinless and Just Man (through whose sufferings are healed all those who approach the Father through Him).'[19] The Jew has become the quintessential enemy of Christian truth and thus writing a tractate *Adversus Judaeos* (Against the Jews) would soon be a prerequisite for all aspiring Church Fathers.

Victim to Victor

Justin and other early Christian apologists could inveigh against the Jews theologically but were powerless to do anything to them politically. Christians had enough trouble themselves trying to survive the waves of persecution periodically emanating from imperial Rome. That all changed, however, in the early fourth century when Constantine declared Christianity a legitimate religion and co-opted the energies of the Church for his own political goals. With Christianity now on the ascendancy, the traditional religions (both the official Roman pantheon and the various popular cults) were driven into the countryside. *Paganus* means *rural* in Latin and thus these diverse religions were eventually included under the umbrella called 'paganism'.

What then was to be done with the Jews? Now that Christians had political power, poisonous polemics could become punitive policies. Should the Jews be killed, forcibly converted, or driven into exile? The views of the great Christian theologian Augustine (354–430 CE) prevailed and set the tone for Christian relationships to Jews for the next millennium. The Jews were not to be slaughtered; they were to be scattered. Living in a contemptible state among Christians, Jews would be an eternal sign of the truth of Christianity. And when Jesus returned, their conversion would be Christianity's final victory.[20] The Jewish philosopher Moses Mendelssohn wrote that without Augustine's 'lovely brainwave, we would have been exterminated long ago'.[21] The policy was not entirely 'lovely' but it did provide for survival, albeit with diminished status.

La Convivencia: 711–1492 CE

Christian hostility to Jews and Judaism was not unremitting. Moments of hope occasionally broke through the darkness of ignorance and persecution. One of those 'moments' lasted almost eight hundred years. The centre of this interreligious phenomenon was the city of Toledo, though it flourished throughout much of Spain. The bathhouses in Spain were the gathering places where Jews, Christians and Muslims met on common ground. And conversations begun in bathhouses ended up in the writings of scholars who borrowed freely from the ideas of their interfaith dialogical partners. The great thirteenth-century Christian theologian Thomas Aquinas quoted frequently both from the Jewish philosopher Maimonides and from the Muslim philosopher Avicenna. Despite such great promise, this wonderful interlude in a long history of persecution came to an abrupt end with the introduction of the Inquisition to Spain and the subsequent expulsion of Muslims and Jews from the Iberian Peninsula. Spanish Christians now sought blood purity, *limpieza de sangre*, a forerunner of the racial purity so highly prized by the later Nazis.

The Ghetto

Backlash movements of ignorance and repression almost inevitably followed times of dialogue and hope. Pope Paul IV found it unseemly that Jews 'whom God has condemned to eternal slavery because of their guilt' were found living in decent homes in the nice parts of town. Sometimes they even lived near churches. On occasion they were doing well enough to hire Christian servants. They even dressed like reputable citizens. All of this weakened the message that Jews were to convey by their diminished status, the message that they were forever cursed and meant to be contemptible in the sight of God and human beings alike. And so a papal statement was issued on 12 July 1555, requiring Jews to live on a single street or in a separate section of the city, an area with only one entrance, one gate whose key was in the keeping of a Christian.[22] Distinctive clothes, restricted civil rights, limited living space – the marginalization of the Jews was complete.

Lessing and Mendelssohn

Gotthold Ephraim Lessing was born in 1729 and died of a stroke in 1781. Philosopher and playwright, he believed in freedom of religious thought and religious tolerance. I always enjoy visiting his lovely residence in Wolffenbeutal. Today it is a museum but his gentle spirit still hovers over the house and grounds. Here was a man who, in an age when anti-Semitism was the air Europeans breathed, dared to write a play, *Nathan the Wise*, modelled on the famous Jewish philosopher Moses Mendelssohn (1729–86). Lessing regularly obtained the required legal permit, allowing Mendelssohn to leave the ghetto as a *Schutzjude* (a protected Jew) to attend philosophy meetings and gatherings of the arts. Escaping the poverty and degradation of the Dessau ghetto, Mendelssohn bested Immanuel Kant in a philosophical competition, translated the Hebrew Bible into German, and proved himself to be 'a revolution all by himself, rising by sheer talent to the heights of German cultural life'.[23]

Free . . . and Yet

In the wake of Napoleon's wars, Jews were allowed to emerge from the ghettos and enter civic life in the countries of Western Europe. The emancipation that Moses Mendelssohn had but a taste of by way of exception now became the norm. Overnight Jews were transformed from prisoners to guests in their respective host societies. They celebrated the enlightened thinking that led to their emancipation; and yet, clouds of ancient prejudice continued to glower menacingly above them. In 1894 a certain Captain

Alfred Dreyfus, the only Jew on the French general staff, was accused of spying for the Germans. After a secret military trial, he was found guilty and sentenced to life imprisonment on Devil's Island. Even though his innocence was later established, the military court reconfirmed its judgement of his guilt. Years passed until a civil court declared his innocence in July of 1906.[24] But it was too little too late. European Jews saw all too clearly that under the apparent tranquil waters of tolerance, currents of anti-Semitism were broiling.

With the rise of Adolph Hitler to power in Germany, two millennia of anti-Semitism reached their logical conclusion. The final solution was not that Jews live in contemptible circumstances in ghettos but that they not live at all. Only about 1 per cent of Europe's Christian leaders actively opposed this genocidal policy. Europeans had long been accustomed to Jews being deprived of rights, deprived of respect and dignity, deprived of life itself. Pope Pius XII saw himself as responsible for Catholics, but not for human beings outside of his flock. He worked for the safety of Jews who had converted to Roman Catholicism but showed little concern for Jews as Jews. By and large, he and Europe's other Christian leaders stood silently by as Jews were rounded up and sent to the death camps.[25]

In the Wake of the Holocaust

As the world absorbed the horrors of genocide on a scale never known in human history, some Christian individuals and groups began to awake from their long slumber, realizing their responsibility for a path that began with the letters of Paul and ended in the ovens of Auschwitz. The 'Declaration on the Relationship of the Church to Non-Christian Religions', voted on by some two thousand bishops at the Second Vatican Council, was officially promulgated by Pope Paul VI on 28 October 1965. It is an ambiguous document, reflecting a dawning awareness of Christian responsibility for Jewish suffering accompanied by a continued rhetoric of denial. The document does not reach that clarity of vision articulated by the theologian Rosemary Ruether when she boldly declared that the good news of Christianity has consistently been a bad news for Jews and that the essential credibility of Christianity, as well as its legitimate continuance, depends on changing that reality.[26] Nor does it challenge the essential thesis of replacement theology stating that it is only in Christ that Jews can ultimately be saved.

Like most of the documents of Vatican II, *Nostra Aetate* is a compromised text. Thomas Merton, monk and interreligious thinker, commented in a journal entry for 10 September 1964:

> Abraham Heschel has sent me a memo on the new Jewish Chapter at the Vatican Council. The new proposal is incredibly bad. All the meaning

> has been taken out of it. All the originality, all the light are gone and it has become a stuffy, pointless piece of formalism with the stupid addition that the Church is looking forward with hope to the union of Jews with herself . . .[27]

Anti-Semitism is indeed rejected but with a strange sense of disassociation in that it is condemned 'at any time and from any source'[28] but without the obvious recognition that a crucial 'time' was the two thousand years in which a large part of the Jewish community lived in 'Christian' Europe and a major 'source' was the very same ecclesiastical group now sitting in solemn session to ratify the document.

The Way Forward

A new path was opened when the United Church of Christ became the first major Protestant denomination in the United States to reject Christianity's traditional replacement theology. The document adopted on 30 June 1987 at a meeting in Cleveland, Ohio, included the recognition that the Christian Church has frequently 'denied God's continuing covenantal relationship with the Jewish people expressed in the faith of Judaism'.[29] After asking for God's forgiveness, the document then goes on to state explicitly that Christianity has not superseded Judaism. In other words, Christianity is not to be understood as the successor religion to Judaism. It is not a New Testament supplanting an Old Testament. All salvation is not through Jesus. God covenants with people in different ways: with Jews through the covenant of Sinai, with Christians through the covenant mediated by Jesus.

Following an honest act of contrition and a firm purpose of amendment, this rejection of supersessionisn and the consequent affirmation of a dual covenant theology are indispensable to the transformation of Christian attitudes to Jews and Judaism. Rosemary Ruether writes:

> The supersessionary pattern of Christian faith distorts both Jewish and Christian reality. We should think rather of Judaism and Christianity as parallel paths, flowing from common memories in Hebrew scripture, which are then reformulated into separate ways that lead two peoples to formulate the dialectic of past and future through different historical experiences. But the dilemma of foretaste and hope remains the same for both. For both live in the same reality of incompleted human existence itself.[30]

With these words, Jacob and Esau have at last embraced. The long years of strife can be acknowledged with repentance and forgiveness. There is hope now for a new future. '*Hinei ma tov ou ma naim shevet achim gam yachad.*'

'*Quam bonum et jucundum est habitare fratres in unum.*' 'How good and pleasant it is when brothers can sit down together in unity.' The opening verse of Psalm 133 – whether sung in Hebrew, chanted in Latin, or prayed in English – proclaims a shared experience of siblings finally finding a common ground where they can live and prosper in an atmosphere of trust, mutual understanding and peace.

And Yet . . .

Unfortunately, every movement forward generates a backlash. Fundamentalist Christianity continues to assert that people can be saved only by full acceptance of Jesus Christ as their Lord and Saviour. Mainline churches not embracing a dual covenant theology (such as the Roman Catholic Church) seek ways to include Jews and other non-Christians in the salvation available only through Jesus. Such church leaders speak of 'anonymous Christians' – people who sincerely seek to do God's will as Jews or members of other sacred traditions and are thereby included in the community of the saved anonymously, without knowing it. If Jesus is the unique incarnation of the divine, these churches argue, then this has no equivalent in other religions. Universalism inevitably stumbles on the dogmas supporting the long history of exclusivism.

No one can say where the future of these two faith communities lies or how long it will take for any of the visions of future to be achieved. Ultimately the path to the future will be determined by the ascendancy of one or other of the two theological models discussed earlier. In the 'Christ as Redeemer' model, Jesus is different from us in kind. He is a heavenly being, the Second Person of the Trinity, the Son of God, who came to this earth to die for the Sin under whose power humankind lay in bondage. His death constitutes his defining legacy and accessing that death provides humanity's only hope of salvation. In this model, Judaism can never be seen as an ally, an alternative covenantal path to God. If this model prevails, then the relations of Jews and Christians will largely replicate the history of the past two thousand years.

On the other hand, in the 'Christ as Reminder' model, Jesus is different from us in degree, not in kind. Every human being is an incarnation of God, though Jesus surpasses most in his level of transparency to his divine identity. Jesus' teachings, more than his death, define Christian existence. He opens up a way to God that complements the paths to the divine represented in countless other sacred traditions. Jews and Christians can be allies in their similarities and in their differences. Neither is to be defined in reference to the other; each is to be understood in its own integrity as a path to the holy.[31] If this model prevails, then another and radically different history will at last be written.

Study Questions

1 What would you consider to be the three most important factors in the development of Christian anti-Semitism?

2 Indicate three points in the shared history of Jews and Christians where a course of dialogue could have been chosen instead of a course of conflict?

3 Indicate three primary ways in which Jewish-Christian dialogue can improve today?

Further Reading

Braybrooke, Marcus, 2000, *Christian–Jewish Dialogue: The Next Steps*, London: SCM Press.

Carroll, James, 2001, *Constantine's Sword: The Church and the Jews*, Boston: Houghton Mifflin.

Eckardt, A. Roy, 1967, *Elder and Younger Brothers: The Encounter of Jews and Christians*, New York: Charles Scribner's Sons.

Flannery, Edward, 1985, *The Anguish of the Jews: Twenty-Three Centuries of Antisemitism*, New York: Paulist Press.

Jacob, Walter, 1974, *Christianity Through Jewish Eyes: The Quest for Common Ground*, Cincinnati: Hebrew Union College.

Miller, Ron, and Bernstein, Laura, 2005, *Healing the Jewish–Christian Rift: Growing Beyond Our Wounded History*, Woodstock: Skylight Paths.

Parkes, James, 1977, *The Conflict of the Church and the Synagogue: A Study in the Origins of Antisemitism*, New York: Atheneum Press.

Ruether, Rosemary Radford, 1974, *Faith and Fratricide: The Theological Roots of Anti-Semitism*, New York: Seabury Press.

World Council of Churches, 1988, *The Theology of the Churches and the Jewish People: Statements by the World Council of Churches and its Member Churches*, Geneva: WCC.

Notes

1 This is, for example, the central thesis of Alan Segal's classic work, *Rebecca's Children: Judaism and Christianity in the Roman World*, Cambridge MA: Harvard University Press, 1986.

2 For further discussion of the implications for Christian spirituality in this ancient text, refer to my book, Miller, Ron, 2004, *The Gospel of Thomas: A Guide to Spiritual Practice*, Woodstock: Skylight Paths.

3 *Shaul (Saul)* was his Hebrew name and *Paulus (Paul)* his Roman name. It was not uncommon then or now for Jews to have a Hebrew name used in the synagogue

and a secular name used in the larger society. It is a mistaken notion that Paul's name was changed from Saul to Paul at the time of his conversion. He always had both names.

4 Wills, Garry, 2006, *What Paul Meant*, New York: Viking, p. 10.

5 James, William, 1902, *The Varieties of Religious Experience*, New York: Longmans, Green and Co., p. 190.

6 I treat this topic in Miller, Ron, 2007, *The Sacred Writings of Paul: Selections Annotated and Explained*, Woodstock: Skylight Paths, both in the 'Introduction' and in the body of the text (most explicitly, pp. 18–19).

7 Bourgeault, Cynthia, 2003, *The Wisdom Way of Knowing: Reclaiming an Ancient Tradition to Awaken the Heart*, San Francisco: Jossey-Bass, p. 17.

8 This is my own translation from my book, *Sacred*, p. 29.

9 *Ibid*., p. 119.

10 The anti-Jewish spin of this Gospel is developed both in my translation and commentary on Matthew's Gospel, Miller, Ron, 2005, *The Hidden Gospel of Matthew*, Woodstock: Skylight Paths, and in the book on Matthew which I wrote with a Jewish colleague, Bernstein, Laura, 2006, *Healing the Jewish–Christian Rift: Growing Beyond Our Wounded History,* Woodstock: Skylight Paths.

11 This was in *Nostra Aetate*, the 'Declaration on the Relationship of the Church to Non-Christian Religions', promulgated on 28 October 1965, in Tanner, Norman (ed.), 1990, *Decrees of the Ecumenical Councils*, vol. 2, London and Washington, DC: Sheed & Ward and Georgetown University Press, pp. 970–1.

12 For an excellent treatment of other 'Jewish stories' found in rabbinic writings, see Schäfer, Peter, 2007, *Jesus in the Talmud*, Princeton: Princeton University Press.

13 One of my Jewish students visited a restaurant in Florida, where he was asking a waitress whether there was pork in a certain menu item. She was curious about his question, and when he told her that he was Jewish, she asked, 'Can I see them?' Several other of my Jewish students or colleagues have been asked this question, especially in the American South.

14 There is no better place to study this entire history than in the masterful work Carroll, James, 2001, *Constantine's Sword*, Boston: Houghton Mifflin Co.

15 The entire prayer read: 'Oremus et pro per perfidis Judaeis: ut Deus et Dominus noster auferat velamen de cordibus eorum; ut et ipsi agnoscant Jesum Christum Dominum nostrum.' Quoted from the *Missale Romanum* used in all Roman Catholic services. In English: 'Let us pray for the perfidious Jews, that our God and Lord will remove the veil from their hearts so that they will acknowledge Jesus Christ as their Lord.'

16 This background information, as well as all subsequent quotes from the dialogue, is taken from Falls, Thomas B. (ed.), 1948, *The Fathers of the Church*, vol. 6, Washington, DC: Catholic University of America Press.

17 *Ibid*., p. 164.

18 *Ibid*., p. 165.

19 *Ibid*., p. 173.

20 Carroll, *Constantine's*, pp. 215–19.

21 *Ibid*., p. 219. Cf. also, Saperstein, Marc, 1999, *Moments of Crisis in Jewish–Christian Relations*, London and Philadelphia: SCM Press and Trinity Press International.

22 Carroll, *Constantine's*, pp. 375ff.

23 Flannery, Edward, 1985, *The Anguish of the Jews*, New York: Paulist Press, p. 162.

24 *Ibid.*, pp. 185–9.

25 Carroll, *Constantine's*, pp. 523–35.

26 This is the overriding thesis of her excellent book, Ruether, Rosemary, 1974, *Faith and Fratricide: The Theological Roots of Anti-Semitism*, New York: Seabury Press.

27 Merton, Thomas, 1988, *A Vow of Conversation: Journals 1964–1965*, Stone, Naomi Burton (ed. and preface), New York: Farrar, Straus, Giroux, p. 76. A few months earlier, on 13 July 1964, Heschel had visited Merton in his monastery in Gethsemani, Kentucky. They spoke about one of the earlier and bolder proposals for a conciliar document, one that was discarded along the path of political compromise.

28 Tanner, *Decrees*, p. 971.

29 This was reported in the *New York Times* National News on Wednesday, 1 July 1987, in an article by Ari Goldman, entitled, 'Church Affirms Validity of Judaism', p. 8. This was subsequently published in the minutes of the Sixteenth General Synod of the United Church of Christ, 25–30 June 1987, pp. 67–8.

30 Ruether, Rosemary Radford, 1989, *Disputed Questions*, Maryknoll: Orbis, p. 71.

31 See the chapter on this theme, 'The Jewish–Christian Filter', in Race, Alan, 2001, *Interfaith Encounter*, London: SCM Press.

10

Islam: Jesus and Muhammad as Brothers

MARTIN BAUSCHKE[1]

Introduction

Christianity is considered to be the 'religion of love' and Islam to be the 'religion of peace'. However, both religions often enough during their history appeared not only in loving but also in unloving ways, not only by peacemaking but also by causing strife, and this not just within their own ranks but also in the way they faced one another. Nevertheless it is by no means the case that the entire common history of both Christians and Muslims was solely confrontational. There were and are times of peaceful coexistence, which were and are so unspectacular that we hardly or never hear of them in history books and newspapers.

Long periods of time, in Christian and Muslim history, resemble family conflicts. Obviously those closest to one another can fight best with each other; for they know exactly where and how they can hurt the other best. This is the reason why conflicts among siblings or with neighbours are worse than those between strangers, who happen to clash with one another. For this reason civil wars are more brutal than wars between different countries. Similarly, one could say that precisely because Christians and Muslims are close to one another, being religious (or rather monotheistic) brothers, so much worse were the dreadful wounds they inflicted upon each other. And by 'dreadful wounds' I do not only mean wounds from which blood flows, but also mutual theological injuries.

In what follows, I will briefly review the major Christian images of Islam in the past, and subsequently develop my own interpretation of Islam.

The Christian Views of Islam: Review of a Common History

The Christian View of Islam does not exist, for Christianity is as diverse as Islam. Concretely there are very different ideas of Muhammad, of the Qur'an and of 'Allah' that Christians developed throughout history. I distinguish five different types of Christian views of Islam (but there are certainly more):

Islam as a Christian heresy

Christianity was afraid of Islam right from the beginning because the very fact that there was another prophet *post Christum*, another Word of God after the New Testament, a new world religion after the Christian Church, was frightening. This put the Christian self-image – as the climax and ultimate point of God's revelation – radically into question. So, what can one do with a feared opponent? One ridicules him, one tries to deprive him of his dignity. This is exactly the strategy the teachers of the Church used. Thus the idea Christians had of Islam was distorted right from the beginning, and still is so frequently to this very day: marked by ignorance and prejudices.

For more than 1,000 years the judgement of John of Damascus (d. 750[2]) was seen as valid: Islam is no authentic religion, but only a Christian heresy, a diabolic distortion of Christianity. Muhammad was no real prophet, but a Christian heretic, a misguided monk and impostor from the Arab desert.[3] This interpretation of Islam was so widespread that Dante (d. 1321) in his 'Divine Comedy' (*La Divina Commedia*) naturally placed Muhammad in hell along with the Christian heretics.[4] The existence of Islam meant – psychologically speaking – a narcissistic offence to exclusivistic Christian self-assurance. Islam was only bearable while being theologically marginalized. Islam had been deprived of its claims. It could only be a Christian heresy. Muhammad could only be a pseudo-prophet on behalf of an Arab false god called 'Allah'. The Qur'an could only be a book full of lies, blasphemies and pseudo-revelations. For hundreds of years Islam was known to the Christian occident through a demonized and, at the same time, ridiculous caricature.

Further images of Islam, which were valid from the Middle Ages up to modern times, are:

- Being merely a Christian heresy, Muhammad, and the Qur'an, had not brought forward any new ideas, no progress such as Christianity (according to the same claim) had achieved in relation to Judaism and Jesus in comparison with Moses.
- It was believed that Muhammad was worshipped in the way Christ is in Christianity. This later marked, in missionary circles, the invention of the term 'Mohammedans' modelled on the term 'Christians'.
- Muhammad not only lets himself be worshipped as God, but abandons himself to indulgence and to all sorts of sexual vices, which the large number of his wives demonstrates.
- Islam is a violent religion, which right from the start – therefore with the deeds of Muhammad as commander – is spread by the use of 'fire and sword' and through 'Holy Wars'.

The fact that these Christian views have not yet become extinct, but on the contrary are virtually resuscitated, is shown by the controversial Muhammad caricatures, as well as by the lecture given by Pope Benedict XVI (in September 2006 in Regensburg, Germany). Measuring the spectacular worldwide consequences since the propagation of the first Crusade by Pope Urban II, 900 years ago, there has been no speech in the history of Christianity like that lecture of Benedict XVI. The Pope quoted the fourteenth-century Byzantine Emperor Manuel II Palaiologos: 'Show me what new ideas Muhammad has brought forward, and you shall only find bad and inhumane things, such as that he dictated that the faith he preaches of, is to be propagated by the sword.' It is hard to believe: 'Pope contra Muhammad' is no slogan from the age of the Crusades but from the present. It is the title of the 18 September issue, no. 38, 2006, of the German magazine *Der Spiegel*.

Islam as a hostile empire and the Antichrist

The theological depreciation of Islam goes, during the Middle Ages, along with a kind of upgrading of Islam as a military power, as a political threat. Theologically, Islam, being not more than a heresy, seemed to be ridiculous, but militarily, as a hostile empire, it was terrifying. In 1095 Pope Urban II (beatified in 1881), appealed in Clermont for the first Crusade against Islam. The Crusades deepened the abyss between Christianity and Islam. Bernard of Clairvaux (d. 1153 and beatified in 1174), nominated by the Pope as chief ideologist, staged, on his own account, another crusade 50 years later, with a sermon-campaign. The failure of this second crusade – measured by the number of the dead – can be compared with the catastrophes of Napoleon's and Hitler's Russian campaigns. Through the Crusades and the Reconquista in Spain (until 1492), a fair-minded and differentiated view of Islam in the Christian West, and a fair and differentiated view of Christianity in the Arab-Islamic world, had almost, with very few exceptions, become impossible.

Regarding the Protestant churches, Martin Luther's assessment of Islam, in particular, had a lasting impact on the Protestant attitude towards Muslims.[5] Luther believed the Qur'an to be the propagation of a religion of law and not of faith. While John of Damascus considered Islam to be the 'precursor (Gr. *pródromos*) of the Antichrist', Luther went a step further and identified Islam with the Antichrist itself. For Luther, Islam was as bad as the Roman Papacy: both were the devil's work and, in his opinion, the sign of the imminent last days: 'the Pope is the soul of the Antichrist, the Turk is the flesh of the Antichrist.'[6] To this very day, the anti-Islamic, and by the way also the anti-Jewish works of Luther, are hardly discussed critically in Protestant theology.[7]

Islam as a concern of mission and a spiritual enemy

In the eighteenth and nineteenth centuries there was a systematic Christian 'Mohamedan Mission'. The missionary confrontation with Islam was seen as the 'final battle between the Cross and the Crescent, carried out mainly in the Middle East and in India. The 1910 Edinburgh Missionary Conference, indeed, seemed to take a more unfavourable view towards Islam than the world's other major faiths, partly due to this sense of conflict, but takes a step forward in seeing points of contact, and believing that a sympathetic understanding of it should be gained.[8] Karl Barth, for many the greatest Christian theologian of the twentieth century, joined in the old anti-Islamic slogans, when he wrote: 'The God of Mohammed is an idol like all the other false gods.'[9] Today the medieval rhetoric about Islam as an anti-Christian, satanic power is still alive, primarily in some fundamentalist, charismatic and evangelical churches and parishes. Since the 1990s Islam has become their favourite bogeyman and they revel in conspiracy theories.

For example, at the Southern Baptist Convention, the largest Protestant denomination in the USA with its 16 million members, anti-Islamic agitation has been, ever since 9/11, highly distinctive. A range of well-known pastors participate in it, such as Jerry Vines, Jerry Falwell and Franklin Graham. For them, Christianity and Islam, Jesus and Muhammad, are 'perpetual enemies', because they represent different gods. 'Allah' is only a mask of Satan or of the Meccan moon god 'Hubal'. Christian extremists declared the zone between the tenth and the fortieth degrees of latitude – the core areas of Islam – the 'spiritual battlefield of the twenty-first century'. Islam is not only a concern anymore, but also a direct rival of the Christian mission – especially in Africa. Here Christian and Islamic fundamentalist preachers are fighting in a missionary duel, thus contributing to the destabilization of whole countries and nations.

Islam as a matter of academic studies

It was not until the Enlightenment, which shone brighter outside the Church than within, that some positive light was thrown on Islam. In the eighteenth and nineteenth centuries a number of scholars made an effort to re-evaluate Islam, the Qur'an and Muhammad, and to clear them from prejudices and clichés. For the first time in history, Islam was recognized as a civilizing intellectual power, and was seriously studied academically. Noted names are, for instance:

- the Dutchman Adrian Reland (d. 1718), Professor of Oriental Languages in Utrecht (*De Religione Muhammadica*, 1705),
- the English historian Edward Gibbon (d. 1794),

- the Scotsman Thomas Carlyle (d. 1881),
- and in Germany, Lessing (d. 1781), Goethe (d. 1832) and Friedrich Rückert (d. 1866), whose translation of the Qur'an is, to this day, the most beautiful in the German language.

These scholars, poets and thinkers have contributed to un-demonize Islam and to appreciate Muhammad as a 'donor of law', as a prophetical 'hero' and a statesman. In particular, they showed that Muhammad was no impostor, but that he acted in subjective truthfulness and credibility as a prophet. This enlightened esteem of Islam is only partially a Christian success, for the above-mentioned scholars were not really people of the Church – but perhaps had understood the spirit of Christ better than the Church itself. Modern Western studies of Islam emerged from these beginnings, and developed their own particular views and projections of Islam.[10] These have included two scholars with Christian backgrounds who, nevertheless, helped introduce a more positive account of Islam, Montgomery Watt and Wilfred Cantwell Smith. Watt believed that the Qur'an contained elements of both prophetic revelation, but also human production, and helped in his accounts of the life of Muhammad to introduce a more positive account of him than most previous ones.[11] Smith also believes that Christians should see the Qur'an as scriptural for Muslims,[12] and has been incredibly influential in the study of this tradition in the academy.

Islam as a partner of dialogue

Not all Christians encountered Islam with contempt, hate and violence. Among the few voices who already during the Middle Ages pleaded for the motto 'religious dialogue instead of religious wars', were four scholars, who were the most important proponents of peaceful communication between Christians and Muslims of their times:

1. Petrus Venerabilis, the Abbot of Cluny (d. 1156). He pleaded for a struggle with Islam by the word and not the sword of God. Due to his influence, the first translation ever of the Qur'an in Europe was made by the Englishman Robert of Ketton and published in 1143 – more than 500 years after Muhammad's death. This quite bad and manipulated Latin translation remained for the following five centuries the most widespread till the much better translation, also into Latin, by Ludovicus Marracci (d. 1700) appeared.[13]
2. Francis of Assisi, who travelled to Egypt to the Palace of Sultan Malik al-Kamil I (d. 1238), and also preached to him.
3. Ramon Lull, a Franciscan monk and mystic from Spain (d. 1316), who as a pacifist missionary – in line with his *via disputationis*, namely, con-

vincing the other through arguments – had various discussions with Muslims.

4 Cardinal Nicolaus from Kues (Cusanus, d. 1464), who like Ramon Lull dreamt of nationwide peace among religions. In view of the conquest of Constantinople by the Ottomans, Nicolaus argued in his work *De pace fidei* (1453) for a Council of Religions. He held that Judaism, Christianity and Islam coincide in their fundamental truths, but differ in their manifold rites and customs. In his *Cribratio Alkorani* ('Sight of the Qur'an', 1461) the Cardinal dealt especially with the *Qur'än* (the Latin translation of Ketton) and its Christology. He was better able to understand the Qur'an from its own point of view (*pia interpretatio*) than Martin Luther in his 'eisegesis'[14] of the Qur'an a hundred years later, who understood the Qur'an – especially concerning Jesus – from a dogmatic Christian point of view (*interpretatio Christiana*).

Following these 'Church fathers' of dialogue with Islam, the contemporary dialogue with Islam is mainly the domain of the Roman Catholic Church. The most influential theologians after the Second World War were Louis Massignon (d. 1962), Georges Anawati (d. 1994), and Kenneth Cragg (Anglican Church). With *Nostra Aetate*, the declaration of the Second Vatican Council on the relation towards non-Christian religions, proclaimed in 1965, a Copernican turn of Christianity regarding Islam was initiated. For the first time ever Islam is officially recognized as a respectable and, to some degree, theologically equal partner in dialogue, as one who shares theologically some common ground with the Church. The theological depreciation of Islam, which from the time of John of Damascus was common for 1200 years, had now been to a large extent withdrawn.

The key phrases of *Nostra Aetate* concerning Islam (no. 3) read as follows:

> The church has also a high regard for the Muslims. They worship God who is one, living and subsistent, merciful and almighty, the Creator of heaven and earth, who has also spoken to humanity. They endeavor to submit themselves without reserve to the hidden decrees of God, just as Abraham submitted himself to God's plan, to whose faith Muslims eagerly link their own. Although not acknowledging him as God, they venerate Jesus as a prophet; his virgin Mother they also honor, and even at times devoutly invoke. Further, they await the day of judgement and reward of God following the resurrection of the dead. For this reason they highly esteem an upright life and worship God, especially by way of prayer, alms-deeds and fasting.
>
> Over the centuries many quarrels and dissensions have arisen between Christians and Muslims. The sacred council now pleads with all to forget the past, and urges that a sincere effort be made to achieve mutual understanding . . .[15]

Although not mentioning Muhammad and the Qur'an, and not conceding Islam to be theologically on the very same level as the Church, this declaration was a turning-point for Roman Catholic relations with Islam.[16] The exclusivistic paradigm was abandoned: Islam was seen as a possible path of salvation and, to some extent, as communicating a true knowledge of God – measured, of course, against the supposed complete truth of the Christian faith (inclusivistic paradigm). Ever since 1967 the Pope has sent his annual greetings on the occasion of the feast of fast-breaking at the end of Ramadan. During his long pontificate John Paul II (1978–2005) made many friends in the Islamic world. He was a Pope of great gestures: the first Pope in history who entered a mosque (on 5 May 2001 in Damascus), a Pope who was not afraid to kiss the Qur'an in public – these are symbolic gestures which bring about more than scholarly words.[17] A serious dialogue between the Ecumenical Council of Churches and Islam began in 1969.[18] Although Christian–Muslim dialogue has become a kind of regular process today, its impact on public opinion is rather limited. As current scientific studies about the image of Islam in schoolbooks and the media confirm, a negative image of Islam is still fairly widespread.[19] Those who have perhaps done the most to spread a more positive view from both an academically knowledgeable and Christian perspective have been Kenneth Cragg and Hans Küng, both of whom believe we should see Muhammad as a prophet.[20]

My Christian View of Islam: Pillars of Understanding

What we need today is a confidence-building and peacemaking Christian theology of Islam and, correspondingly, an analogous Islamic theology of Christianity, where in both cases Christianity and Islam are – and must be seen – right from the start on the same theological eye-level. In other words: we need a Christian theology in which Muslims, even if they believe in God differently, are nevertheless seen as legitimate and thus can feel secure from Christian supersessionist claims. When will Christians and Muslims finally discover what unites them as monotheistic brothers? The 'flowers' of mutual esteem and trust in one another might germinate and blossom on the ground of a common faith and of similar beliefs. With that common basis and dealing with each other on the same eye-level – with these 'flowers' in our hands instead of weapons – it is easier to discuss our mistakes, misunderstandings and conflicts. In this spirit we need new bridge-builders between Christianity and Islam.

For me, the five pillars of understanding – in the double sense of communication and agreement – with Islam are:

1 The One God.
2 Abraham as an example of faith.

3 Jesus and Muhammad as brothers.
4 Common ethic.
5 Common prayer.

First pillar: the One God

A dialogue between Christians and Muslims is only sustainable if it is acknowledged that the God of the Christians and the God of the Muslims is one and the same God. It is not only the above-quoted passages of *Nostra Aetate* and *Lumen Gentium* of the Second Vatican Council that confess that both Christians and Muslims 'adore the one, merciful God' but already the Qur'an says so: 'our God and your God is One, and unto Him we surrender' (Sura 29.46).[21] Therefore Muslims confess that there is no mere God of the Muslims ('Allah') but that there is just One God being the 'Lord of the Worlds' (Sura 1.2) and being the God of the Christians (and the Jews) as well. Indeed, there is a great number of common statements of faith concerning that one God. Both Christians and Muslims believe in him/her

- as the living and eternal One;
- as the creator and conserver, as the king and the light of the world;
- as the loving power from whose hands we come and to whom we shall return;
- as the transcendent, hidden and secret One (*deus absconditus*); and at the same time
- as the self-revealer (*deus revelatus*), who has been speaking through the mouth and wonders of the prophets and the signs and wonders of the creation;
- as the merciful and helpful One towards human beings; and finally
- as the One who guides and fulfils history, who raises from the dead and is going to sit on the throne of judgement.

No matter what we call him/her (God, Allah, Higher Being, Father, Mother, the Merciful, and so on), it is the same One God, in whom Christians and Muslims (together with the Jews) believe, even if we might have different images of God or experiences with God. But these different images of God do not constitute different gods (as the fundamentalists in both religions maintain), for we find different images of, or experiences with, God already *within* each religion. The plurality of different images of God is a characteristic even of the Bible and the Qur'an. A God who would be partial, that is, only the God of Christians (against the Muslims) or, conversely, only the God of Muslims (against the Christians), would remain an idol – a distorted image of the living God, created by human beings in order to serve their particular interests as a group, functionalized and thus misused to support and justify their exclusivistic collective sentiments. Of course, there is no objective proof of God being one and the same in both religions, no more than there is proof of the sheer existence of this God. To speak of the one and same God is no abstract, theoretical point of view, rather a tangible, common experience of faith of those who practise Christian–Muslim dialogue.

Second pillar: Abraham as an example of faith

Judaism, Christianity and Islam, the three monotheistic religions, are also called the 'Abrahamic religions' because of the important role that Abraham plays in each one of them. There are many initiatives of dialogue between Jews, Christians and Muslims that call themselves 'Abrahamic'.[22] Abraham – together with his wives Sara and Hagar – is a wonderful model of faith in and devotion to the one God.[23] Abraham is the archetype of that kind of human being who, amidst an idol-worshipping environment, is seeking for the God who deserves his ultimate trust. Such a search justifies his exodus-existence. Abraham is a wanderer between the worlds, religions and cultures on his way to find God and to follow his/her promises. If we, as Christians in dialogue with Muslims, orientate ourselves on the example of Abraham, then we might also find the courage for another 'Exodus' or 'Hijra', to come irreversibly out of the cage of exclusivistic truth- and salvation-claims on both sides.

Something similar to the above discussion concerning the same One God perceived in different images, can be said about Abraham: the same example, but with different accentuations. Emphasizing common convictions does not exclude, but includes setting different priorities. Thus the three religions, including Judaism, each conceptualize a special profile for this patriarch. Jews mainly emphasize Abraham's unconditional obedience, his allegiance to the point of 'Isaac's binding' (Gen. 22). Christians refer especially, according to Paul, to the ultimate trust Abraham has in God's promise (Gal. 3.6ff.). Muslims see in Ibrahim (Abraham) above all a *Hanif*[24] (for example Sura 2.135) who recognized and avowed the one and only God, even before Jews, Christians or Muslims ever existed (Sura 21.5ff.; 37.83ff.); Ibrahim who restored and purified the Ka'ba in Mecca (Sura 2.125ff.). Such different accentuations don't need to speak against the nature of sister religions. The common basis is stressed by the Holy Scriptures themselves. In the Bible and in the Qur'an, Abraham is denominated with the same honorary title 'friend of God' (Isa. 41.8f.; James 2.23; Sura 4.125). This means for Christians and Muslims the chance to encounter one another in the spirit of Abraham, in a kind and friendly – even hospitable – way.

Third pillar: Jesus and Muhammad as brothers

Dialogue between Christians and Muslims is sustainable only if it is acknowledged that God wanted both religions as authentic ways to salvation. God revealed himself to both, Jesus and Muhammad! The Eternal Word of God – as Christians believe – became flesh in Jesus Christ (incarnation) and – as Muslims believe – it became *book* as Qur'an (inlibration). Our way to God is leading us across the way to the hearts of our believing brothers and sisters. For me, as a Christian, Jesus is 'the way (to God), the truth and the life' (cf. John 14.6). Nevertheless I am conceding that the Qur'an is the way to God, the truth and life for Muslims. And it is my hope that Muslims can make an analogous concession from their point of view. I am not looking for one-way statements but for reciprocal ones, and not merely for reciprocal tolerance but rather reciprocal acceptance; this is the consequence of the intellectual Golden Rule: granting the other the same right to be assured of his/her faith as to myself, independently of whether the other belongs to the same or another denomination or religion as I do.[25]

If Christianity and Islam are equal ways to God, then Jesus and Muhammad will become the two younger brothers of Moses, and the Bible and the Qur'an will become the second and third testaments of God, added to the first testament, the Torah. Personally I consider the discussion about Jesus to be a pillar of dialogue. For other than in Jewish–Christian dialogue, it can create a Christological bridge in Christian–Islamic dialogue. For Jews, Jesus does not play the same important role as for Muslims. Christians and Muslims believe in Jesus, although in different ways. The Qur'an is – apart from the New Testament – the only Holy Scripture of a world religion in which Jesus plays an important role. This is what makes Christian–Islamic dialogue special, for only in this case is it based, from both sides, on their Holy Scriptures.

Jesus, Mary's son, figures prominently in the Qur'an. Jesus does not only separate Christians from Muslims, but also unites them. A number of statements can be made about Jesus that find support from both Christians and Muslims. Of course there are also points on which Christians and Muslims cannot (and perhaps will never) agree, for example, the question of whether Jesus died on the cross, as Christians believe, or was saved from death, as many Muslims hold. However, after both sides have, for centuries, mainly gone about matters in controversial and polemical ways, mostly stressing the dogmatic difference of their opinions, nowadays in our multicultural society, it is time for both sides to discuss Jesus in such a way that a consensus which might be reached in some respects comes to the foreground.[26]

A Christological consensus between Christians and Muslims would be, first of all,

1 theocentric, emphasizing that Jesus, as a matter of fact (or biblical testimony), subordinated himself to the one God, as his Jewish 'ancestors' did, that he perceived himself as a 'servant' of God and mankind (Mark 10.45; Luke 22.27) and that he consistently differentiated himself from God, who is the only One to be called 'good' (Mark 10.18). Further, a Christological link between Christians and Muslims ought to be
2 prophetical, describing Jesus as God's prophet and teacher of wisdom. A Christian–Muslim Christology could have
3 a charismatic accentuation in which Jesus is described as a miracle healer, as a charismatic figure who is doing his powerful deeds and signs with the help of the Holy Spirit (Matt. 12.28; Sura 2.87; 2.253; 5.110). And finally, a Christological consensus between Christians and Muslims should be accentuated
4 metaphorically, speaking of Jesus as the 'Son of God' in symbolic language, not in any literal or ontological sense – but in the way Jesus himself used the title, for example, in the Sermon on the Mount: 'Blessed are the peacemakers, for they shall be called children of God' (Matt. 5.9). A short passage later Jesus says (Matt. 5.44): 'Love your enemies and pray for those who persecute you so that you may be children of your Father in heaven.' The term 'Son of God' is primarily an ethical not a physical or metaphysical title. It is a democratic and not an elitist title. Already some Muslim theologians, belonging to the Mu'tazilites in the ninth and tenth centuries, saw the analogy (Arab. *qiyas*) between the expression 'Son of God' for Jesus, the expression 'first born son' for Israel (Ex. 4.22) and the title 'friend of God' for Abraham in the Qur'an (Sura 4.125). There are liberal Muslim scholars of the past (for example, Ibn Qutayba, Sayyid Ahmad Khan) and in present times (for example, Mahmoud Ayoub, Ahmad von Denffer) who can accept the 'Son of God' title in this metaphorical sense.

Thus the dialogue about Jesus can inspire and enable Christians and Muslims to move forward to our common work of making peace. Suggesting and elaborating a 'Christological bridge' between Christians and Muslims means we should not discuss the title 'Son of God' merely from a dogmatic point of view (*Christo-Logy*), but we should come to an ethical competition (*imitatio Christi* as *Christo-Practice*). Do Christians and Muslims stand the test of being peacemakers and calling one another true 'sons and daughters of God'? Dogmatical correctness alone will not help, but rather doing the will of God, as Jesus himself says at the end of the Sermon on the Mount (Matt. 7.21).[27] Confessing 'the Lord' includes and means first of all the 'compassion and mercy in the hearts of those who are following Jesus' (Sura 57.27).

But dialogue is not only about Jesus. To me, as a Christian, it is of particular importance to converse also about Muhammad. First of all, we need to counteract the traditional demonizing of Muhammad through showing respect towards this younger brother of Christ.[28] Then it is necessary to accept the theological challenge of Muhammad's mission and acknowledge the dignity of the Qur'an as a revelation from God. I belong to those Christian theologians[29] who go beyond the mere phenomenological description of Muhammad as a 'prophet', and who also call for a theological recognition of Muhammad as God's Prophet. God in his/her sovereignty may reveal him-/herself somewhere else, through someone else rather than just through Moses or Jesus Christ, even if this new approach to mankind might disappoint and cross some of the expectations and self-conceptions of Jews and Christians.

When we speak about the prophethood of Muhammad, we are ultimately speaking about the Qur'an as an authentic word of God. 'The Call of the Minaret' (Kenneth Cragg, 1956) is to be taken as seriously by Christians as the call of the gospel of Jesus by Muslims. Within the tradition of Abraham I believe in a continuous revelation of God: it is manifold and also full of tensions and contradictions. But revelation has always been this way, within the Torah, within the Bible and within the Qur'an. I understand the mission of Jesus and of Muhammad, the revelation of the Word of God as incarnation and as inlibration as being complementary – such as light in physics, which behaves both as a wave and as a particle. Jesus and Muhammad are not doubles, but brothers with similarities and differences. Jesus' short public mission (up to three years) is complemented by the long mission of Muhammad (20 years). The kingdom of God is 'not of this world' (John 18.36) – nevertheless it is right in the centre of the world too. To follow God's will in life is not only a question of individual spirituality (*praxis pietatis*) but also a social, political and legal challenge for establishing societies with a just order. God does not only call believers out of the world (*ecclesia*), but rather places them as a viceroy (*khalifa*) into the world (Sura 2.30). The wandering preacher from Nazareth is complemented by the mediator, politician and commander from Mecca. Jesus, the suffering and murdered righteous in Jerusalem, is complemented by Muhammad, the suffering righteous in Mecca and in the end the victorious prophet in Medina. From our human point of view the merciful God sometimes seems to be powerless (the cross of Golgotha) and sometimes to be powerful (the purification of the Temple and the destruction of the idols in the Ka'ba[30]) when we look at what his/her messengers are doing or suffering.

Fourth pillar: common ethic

Beyond the question as to what theologically connects Christians and Muslims in their religious statements, another question arises which is possibly more important: What connects them ethically? It is a fact that both religions have common ideas about what their norms and values are. Both the gospel and the Qur'an stand in the ethical tradition of the Ten Commandments of the Torah. We find a common prophetical core ethic, rooted in Judaism, which unites, despite the differences, Jews, Christians and Muslims. It has a double accentuation – like the two foci of an ellipse: God and the neighbour. This common ethic is theonomic and social. The Abrahamic religions share the following directives:

1 respect for God alone (not to serve idols)
2 respect for parents
3 respect for life (not to kill)
4 respect for love and body (not to abuse sexuality)
5 respect for property (not to steal)
6 respect for the word (not to lie).

Moreover, Christianity and Islam – and many other religions – show a tendency to unite the numerous directives into one most significant commandment – known as the Golden Rule, which is testified in various forms throughout the world: 'What you do not wish done to yourself, do not do to others.' Jesus, in his Sermon on the Mount, accentuates the Golden Rule in its positive form (Matt. 7.12; Luke 6.31): 'In everything, do for others as you would have them do for you; for this is the law and the prophets.' An-Nawawi's collection of 40 *Ahadith qudsi* contains the saying of Muhammad: 'No one of you is a true believer until he desires for his brother that which he desires for himself.' The Golden Rule is the core of our ethical world heritage and at the same time the basis for humane behaviour, also among those secular Christians and Muslims who define their ethic in an autonomic way as self-commitment and not as divine (heteronomic) commandments 'from above'.

Fifth pillar: common prayer

The encounter between Christians and Muslims has an eminent spiritual dimension. Common prayer meetings are increasing worldwide, including Jews where possible. The overlapping of the calendar – Chanukkah, Advent and Ramadan – in past years intensified this new development. There are many occasions for common prayer meetings: services at school, interfaith weddings or pastoral care in hospital, prison and army. Christian–Muslim prayers for peace, in particular, form an important starting-point for dialogue, and at the same time counter the fundamentalist agitation in both religions.

When I am pleading for friendship and hospitality in the spirit of Abraham, here it becomes concrete: our common prayer is a form of spiritual hospitality. It is the offer to Christians and Muslims to be taken into the world of prayer of another Abrahamic religion, and in this way to experience God in a different manner, whether it might be surprisingly familiar or rather strange. Offering spiritual hospitality to one another means that we are taking the risk of making new experiences with the one God through praying together. Christians and Muslims can offer their prayers not only to God but also as a gift to one another, saying them separately or together – without ceasing to be Christians or Muslims. A hero is normally someone who defeats his enemy. A greater hero might be the one who makes, without weapons, his enemy his friend. But the greatest hero seems to be the one who prays together with his friend. I believe that the more Christians and Muslims pray together, the more we shall become a blessing to the world and a source of reconciliation among peoples.

I like to recall the prayer meetings for peace in Assisi (1986 and 2002) which Pope John Paul II held together with representatives of other religions, or more recently (2006) the joint quiet prayer of Pope Benedict XVI together with Imam Mustafa Cagrici in the Blue Mosque of Istanbul. It is also my own experience in common prayer meetings with Jews and Muslims: the common prayer does not only unite with God ('vertical' union) but also unites those who pray together ('horizontal' union). Common prayer creates a *unio mystica* in both directions. It opens my heart and my mind in such a way that the person praying at my side is not just any believer but my Abrahamic brother, my Abrahamic sister. The intellectual and the ethical Golden Rule transforms itself, at this point of dialogue, into a spiritual path, which incorporates the heads, the hands and the hearts of the Christians and Muslims involved.

As a result of these experiences I felt committed to publish the first 'Book of Common Prayer' in Germany, for Jews, Christians and Muslims.[31] It was published in co-operation with a rabbi and a female Muslim teacher of religion. A special edition with identical contents was printed simultaneously for pastoral care within the Federal Armed Forces, Christians and Muslims together from half of the world's population. If Christians and Muslims started speaking to one another, half of humankind would be in dialogue! Through dialogue both sister religions, Christianity and Islam, could finally overcome their family disputes – with the help of God.

Outlook: A Bridge into the Future?

In my own country, Germany, Islamophobia has grown considerably over recent years. For me, as a Protestant theologian, it is especially sad that my own church, the *Evangelische Kirche in Deutschland* (EKD), has supported this trend through its last official publication. In November 2006, the EKD published a text in which could be read the following words: 'Christians will hardly be able to set their hearts on a God as he is described in the

Qur'an and as he is honoured by Muslims.'[32] This caused an outcry among those who have tried for decades on both sides to build up Christian–Islamic dialogue. Many prominent Protestant theologians described these sentences as a scandal and were ashamed of being Protestant, if 'being Protestant' is defined by the publications of the EKD.[33] Does not the refrain, the *basso continuo* of the Qur'an's image of God go as follows: 'The merciful and the compassionate' (Arab *ar-rahman ar-rahim*)? Together, we Christians and Muslims stand or fall by God's compassion. If God does not show mercy to us, it counts for little when we respond, 'We are Christians indeed' or 'We are surely Muslims.' I want to counter the authors of the EKD publication with the following advice of Wilfred Cantwell Smith (d. 2000), one of the past century's most influential contributors to interfaith dialogue and the comparative study of religion: 'No-one should, in my view, have any views on any other aspect of interreligious questions until he or she has talked with members of the other communities; and preferably, not until he or she has friends among them.'[34]

However, in the midst of Islamophobic darkness there is now a glimpse of new hope. Earlier I mentioned that we need new bridge-builders between our religions. A bridge has been built towards the Christian world – coming not only from a single Islamic voice but even from an entire choir. At the Feast of Breaking the Fast (*Id al-Fitr*) in October 2007, 138 Islamic scholars sent an Open Letter to all Christian bishops, patriarchs and church leaders. The letter is titled *A Common Word Between Us and You.*[35] In the 1400-year-long history of Islamic–Christian relations we have never had such an initiative before! The scholars compare texts from the Qur'an and the Bible, and come up with the invitation: 'We as Muslims invite Christians to come together with us on the basis of what is common to us, which is also what is most essential to our faith and practice: the two commandments of love' – meaning the love of God and the love of one's neighbour. Let me cite further from this letter:

> Finding common ground between Muslims and Christians is not simply a matter of polite ecumenical dialogue between selected religious leaders. Christianity and Islam are the largest and second largest religions in the world and in history. Christians and Muslims reportedly make up over a third and over a fifth of humanity respectively. Together they comprise more than 55% of the world's population, making the relationship between these two religious communities the most important factor in contributing to meaningful peace around the world. If Muslims and Christians are not at peace, the world cannot be at peace . . . And to those who nevertheless relish conflict and destruction for their own sake or reckon that ultimately they stand to gain through them, we say that our very eternal souls are all also at stake if we fail sincerely to make every effort to join peace and come together in harmony.

In this Open Letter we hear a totally different voice than the one from the EKD's Protestant publication from Germany. This letter is exactly what I demanded above: a contribution to a confidence-building and peacemaking Islamic theology of Christianity. The Open Letter is a first stone of the bridge into a common future for Christians and Muslims. For these reasons, the letter has received much support from both Christian and Jewish scholars and church leaders. The pope, too, announced further meetings and talks. Despite all the agreement, however, I would like to raise the following questions with regard to the letter, questions that also concern Christians.

How far does love carry us?

Is the twofold love of God and of our neighbour really a sound common basis for dialogue if within both Christian and Islamic communities this love is often misapplied? If already Christians hate and kill other Christians, and if already Muslims hate and kill their fellow Muslims, why should they love and not hate or kill believers from other religions? Not only with respect to other religions, but already within the Christian religion and within the Islamic religion, the words from the Open Letter are true: 'Our very eternal souls are at stake if we fail to make peace.'

How do we handle the 'hawks' in our own religious communities?

A Christian–Islamic alliance for peace which is grounded in love is surely better capable of ensuring our common future than fundamentalist friend–enemy slogans, which can be heard on both sides and which have led to horrible deeds. Is the position advocated in the Open Letter acceptable to a majority in both of our religious communities? Can a reconciliatory attitude prevail against the irreconcilable hardliners on both sides? I agree with Karen Armstrong in her comment on the Open Letter: 'We must reclaim our traditions from the extremists. Unless the major faiths emphasize those teachings which insist upon the absolute holiness of the "other", they will fail the test of the twenty-first century.'[36] It is our common task today to develop a Christian–Muslim theology of reconciliation and friendship. But since on both sides we stand in competition to the theology of hate in extremist circles, any bridge to a common Christian–Muslim future is at the same time confronted with the challenge of an intra-religious dialogue which Muslims, and similarly Christians, have to conduct among their own communities.

What happens to the other halves of humankind?

I have pointed out that Christians and Muslims are already close to one another, being monotheistic communities, together with the Jews. But what happens in view of this monotheistic alliance to the remainder of the world, the other half of humankind, who do not believe in one God but many Gods, or in no God at all? Do we also show neighbourly love to them? Do they have human rights, too? And what happens to women? They constitute – in a different way – the other half of humankind as well. If I am correct, the Open Letter was exclusively written by male Islamic scholars. The Christian addressees – the church leaders – are overwhelmingly men, too. What contribution do the men owe to women, if we are to build bridges of peace and understanding in an equal manner? Or, do women have first to fight for this right in both religions? Do we hear their voice and do we take account of it? As long as men treat women in their own religions as 'second class human beings' – I talk explicitly of men in both religions – they will respect neither the men nor the women of other religions. The bridge to a peaceful future, to which this Open Letter makes some first important contributions, cannot be built without the women in our religious communities and without the secularists in our societies. Otherwise it will not stand for long.

Study Questions

1 In what sense, if at all, is it possible for Christians to recognize Muhammad as a prophet?

2 Is the doctrine of the Trinity necessarily an insuperable barrier for Christian–Muslim dialogue?

3 How might Christian theology respond to the traditional Islamic claim to represent the 'original religion'?

Further Reading

Bauschke, Martin, 2001, *Jesus im Koran* ('Jesus in the Qur'an'), Cologne, Weimar and Vienna: Böhlau Verlag (= 2007, *Jesus im Koran: Ein Schlüssel zum Dialog zwischen Christen und Muslimen* ('Jesus in the Qur'an: A Key to Dialogue between Christians and Muslims'), Erftstadt: Hohe Verlag).

Brown, Stuart, E. (compiled), 1989, *Meeting in Faith: Twenty Years of Christian–Muslim Conversations*, Geneva: World Council of Churches.

Cragg, Kenneth, 1984, *Muhammad and the Christian Response*, London: DLT.

Küng, Hans, 1985, *Christianity and the World Religions*, English trans. of *Christentum und Weltreligionen* (1985), London: Fount Paperbacks.

Küng, Hans, 2007, *Islam: Past, Present and Future*, Oxford: Oneworld.
Phipps, William E., 1996, *Muhammad and Jesus: A Comparison of the Prophets and Their Teachings*, London: SCM Press.
Watt, William Montgomery, 1998, *Muhammad's Mecca: History in the Qur'an*, new edn, Edinburgh: Edinburgh University Press.

Notes

1 This essay has been reproduced, with amendments and additional material, by kind permission of SCM Press, the author, and Perry Schmidt-Leukel and Lloyd Ridgeon, the editors of 2007, *Islam and Inter-Faith Relations: The Gerald Weisfeld Lectures 2006*, London: SCM Press.

2 The years in the text are following the Western calculation of time.

3 Johannes Damascenus, *De haeresibus*, ch. 100.

4 *Inferno*, ch. 28.

5 When the Ottomans stood at the gates of Vienna, his books *Vom Kriege wider die Türken* ('Of War against the Turks') and *Heerpredigt wider die Türken* ('Army Sermon against the Turks') were published (1529). In these, Luther gave each Christian soldier a good conscience; whoever fought against the Turks thus also fought against the 'enemy and blasphemer of Jesus Christ'. To shed the blood of a Turk was a deed obliging to God.

6 Weimar Edition (WA) *Tischreden*, vol. 1, p. 135, no. 330: 'Ego omnino puto papatum esse Antichristum, aut si quis vult addere Turcam, papa est spiritus Antichristi, et Turca est caro Antichristi.'

7 See Hagemann, Ludwig, 1998, *Martin Luther und der Islam*, Altenberge: Verlag für Christlich-Islamische Schrifttum; Wolf, C. U., 1941, 'Luther and Mohammedanism', *Muslim Word*, vol. 31, pp. 161–77.

8 1910, *World Missionary Conference, Edinburgh, 1910*, report no. IV: 'The Missionary Message in Relation to Non-Christian Religions', Edinburgh: Oliphant, Anderson & Ferrier, esp. pp. 122, 140, 142, 150. For commentary on this see, Hedges, Paul, 2001, *Preparation and Fulfilment: A History and Study of Fulfilment Theology in Modern British Thought in the Indian Context*, Bern: Peter Lang, pp. 256–60.

9 Barth, Karl, 1938, *Gotteserkenntnis und Gottesdienst nach reformatorischer Lehre*, Zollikon: Evangelischer Verlag, p. 57.

10 I am reminded of the 'Orientalism' debate that was initiated by Edward Said's book of 1978, *Orientalism*, New York: Pantheon.

11 Cf. (Qur'an) Watt, William Montgomery, 1969, *Islamic Revelation in the Modern World*, Edinburgh: Edinburgh University Press, and 1994, *Companion to the Qur'an*, Oxford: Oneworld (1st edn 1967); (Muhammad) Watt, William Montgomery, 1956, *Muhammad at Medina*, Oxford: Oxford University Press, and 1961, *Muhammad, Prophet and Statesman*, Oxford: Oxford University Press.

12 Smith, Wilfred Cantwell, 1992, 'Can Believers Share the Qur'an and the Bible as Word of God', in Gort ve diğerleri, J. D. (ed.), *On Sharing Religious Experience: Possibilities of Interfaith Mutuality*, Grand Rapids: Eerdmans.

13 *Alcorani Textus Universus* [. . .] *ex arabico idiomate in latinum translatus* [. . .] *auctore Ludovico Marraccio* (Padua, 1698).

14 That is, reading his views into the Qur'an in contrast to an 'exegesis' which attempts to spell out what is in the text.

15 *Nostra Aetate*, no. 3, in Flannery, Austin (ed.), 1996, *Vatican Council II. The Basic Sixteen Documents*, Northport and Dublin: Costello and Dominican Publications, p. 571.

16 Cf. also the Dogmatic Constitution on the Church (*Lumen Gentium*, 1964), no. 16: 'the plan of salvation also includes those who acknowledge the Creator, first among whom are the Muslims: they profess to hold the faith of Abraham, and together with us they adore the one, merciful God, who will judge humanity on the last day.' *Lumen Gentium*, in Flannery (ed.), *Vatican Council II*, pp. 21f.

17 Compared with John Paul II, the beginning of the pontificate of his successor Benedict XVI – the 'Professor Dr Pope' (*Der Spiegel*, no. 16 (April 2006)) – is quite disappointing with regard to Roman Catholic dialogue with Islam. Only Benedict XVI's visit to Turkey (autumn 2006) poured some oil on the troubled water of his Regensburg lecture. Apparently the Pope has now realized that the dialogue between Christians and Muslims does not only need 'head' but also plenty of 'heart'.

18 Brown, Stuart E. (compiled), 1989, *Meeting in Faith: Twenty Years of Christian–Muslim Conversations*, Geneva: World Council of Churches.

19 See for example, 2006, *Muslims in Europe: Discrimination and Islamophobia*, European Monitoring Center of Racism and Xenophobia (EUMC).

20 Cragg, Kenneth, 2000 [1956], *The Call of the Minaret*, Oxford: Oneworld; 1984, *Muhammad and the Christian*, London: DLT; Küng, Hans, 1985, *Christianity and the World Religions*, English trans. of *Christentum und Weltreligionen* (1985), London: Fount Paperbacks.

21 All quotations from the Qur'an, if not indicated otherwise, refer to Mohammed Marmaduke Pickthall (trans.), 2001, *The Meaning of The Glorious Qur'an*, Kuala Lumpur.

22 For example Abrahamic Houses, Abrahamic Feasts, national and international Abrahamic Fora. See Bauschke, Martin, 2001, *Internationale Recherche von Institutionen zum trilateralen Dialog von Juden, Christen und Muslimen*, Trialog und Zivilgesellschaft, vol. 1, Berlin: Maecenata-Verlag.

23 Cf. Bauschke, Martin, 2008, *Der Spiegel des Propheten. Abraham im Koran und im Islam* ('The mirror of the Prophet. Abraham in Qur'an and in Islam'), Frankfurt am Main: Lembeck Verlag.

24 According to Asad, Muhammad, 1993, *The Message of the QUR'AN*, Gibraltar: Dar al-Andalus, p. 28, footnote 110 to Sura 2.135, the term *hanif* describes the unitarian God-seekers of pre-Islamic times: 'Already in pre-Islamic times, this term had a definitely monotheistic connotation, and was used to describe a man who turned away from sin and worldliness and from all dubious beliefs, especially idol-worship.'

25 Cf. Hick, John, 1989, *An Interpretation of Religion*, London: Macmillan, p. 234: 'Nor can we reasonably claim that our own form of religious experience, together with that of the tradition of which we are a part, is veridical whilst the others are not . . . In acknowledging this we are obeying the intellectual Golden Rule of granting to others a premise on which we rely ourselves.'

26 Cf. Bauschke, Martin, 2001, *Jesus im Koran* ('Jesus in the Qur'an'), Cologne, Weimar, and Vienna: Böhlau (= 2007, *Jesus im Koran: Ein Schlüssel zum Dialog zwischen Christen und Muslimen* ('Jesus in the Qur'an: A Key to Dialogue between

Christians and Muslims'), Erftstadt: Hohe).

27 Cf. Sura 49.13; 'O mankind! We created you from a single (pair) of a male and a female, and made you into nations and tribes, that ye may know each other. Verily the most honoured of you in the sight of God is (he who is) the most righteous of you.' (Quotation from *The Holy Qur'an*. Text, translation and commentary by Abdullah YusufAli, Beirut, 1968.)

28 Cf. the hadith (saying of Muhammad), narrated by Abu Hurayra: 'Both in this world and in the Hereafter, I am the nearest of all the people to 'Isa (Jesus), the son of Maryam (Mary). The Prophets are paternal brothers; their mothers are different, but their religion is one.' Quotation from *Summarized Sahih Al-Bukhari Arab–English* (Riyadh, 1996), p. 680, no. 1437.

29 For example, Martin Forward, Notker Fúglister, John Hick, Bertold Klappert, Hans Küng, Reinhard Leuze, Paul Schwarzenau, Wilfred Cantwell Smith, Perry Schmidt-Leukel and Keith Ward.

30 The purification of the house of God to become a place of prayer instead of merchandise is the powerful mission of many prophets, according to the Qur'an prefigured by Ibrahim (Sura 2.125ff.) and followed by Jesus in Jerusalem and by Muhammad in Mecca.

31 Bauschke, Martin, Homolka, Walter, and Müller, Rabeya (eds), 2006, *Gemeinsam vor Gott. Gebete aus Judentum, Christentum und Islam*, Gütersloh: Gütersloher Verlaghaus (1st edn 2004).

32 *Klarheit und gute Nachbarschaft. Christen und Muslime in Deutschland. Eine Handreichung des Rates der EKD* ('Clarity and Good Neighbourhood; Christians and Muslims in Germany. A contribution from the Council of the EKD'), Hanover, 2006, p. 19.

33 Cf. the crucial reviews of the EKD resource: Micksch, Jürgen (ed.), 2007, *Evangelisch aus fundamentalem Grund. Wie sich die EKD gegen den Islam profiliert* ['Being Protestant from a Fundamentalist Viewpoint: How the EKD Positions Itself Against Islam'], Frankfurt am Main.

34 Smith, Wilfred Cantwell, 1991, 'Christian–Muslim Relations: The Theological Dimension', *Studies in Interreligious Dialogue*, vol. 1, pp. 8–24, at p. 8.

35 Cf. the official website: http://www.acommonword.com/. The following quotations in the main text relate to this website.

36 Karen Armstrong, 'Response to a Common Word'. Posted at: http://www.acommonword.com/index.php?page=responses&item=35. Accessed: 03/02/08.

Section B: Indic Traditions

11

Hinduism: We Are No Longer 'Frogs in the Well'

K. P. ALEAZ

This chapter begins by recalling briefly some trends in ecumenical responses to other faiths as a contextual preface to the main account of Christian responses to Hinduism. I shall then highlight the work of some nineteenth- and twentieth-century Christian theologians before drawing some conclusions.

Major Trends in Ecumenical Responses to Other Faiths

During the eighteenth and nineteenth centuries the Christian missionary attitude to other religions and cultures was marked by a spirit of certainty about the superiority of the gospel of Jesus Christ. At the Edinburgh World Missionary Conference of 1910 the missionaries who had come from lands of living faiths stated that in all lands the merely 'iconoclastic attitude' is condemned as radically unwise and unjust. The conference recognized the spirit of God working in the higher forms of other religions and affirmed that all religions disclose the elemental needs of the human soul, which Christianity alone could satisfy.[1] The fact that missionary as well as scholarly interest continued on the subject after the conference is evident from the writings of missionary theologians like J. N. Farquhar[2] and A. G. Hogg.[3]

The second meeting of the Missionary Conference, held at Jerusalem in 1928, thought that the enemy of the Christian mission was communism and secularism. The conference regarded other religions as allies of the Christian faith. Worship and reverence in Islam, sympathy over the world's sorrow in Buddhism, the moral order of Confucianism and the desire for contact with Ultimate Reality in Hinduism, and so on, were considered as 'rays of the same light'. The European continental missionaries and theologians were later critical of this view of the conference, but the Americans and the British supported it.[4]

A significant contribution came from the American Laymen's Report of 1932, *Rethinking Missions: A Laymen's Enquiry after a Hundred Years*, chiefly through W. E. Hocking,[5] according to whom the task of the missionary was to see the best in other religions. Hocking rejected the methods of 'radical displacement' and 'synthesis', and instead favoured the method of 'reconception'. The continental missionary theologians reacted against such a standpoint, and the clearest type of their reaction can be seen in Hendrik Kraemer,[6] who wrote *The Christian Message in a Non-Christian World* as the preparatory volume for the Third World Missionary Conference, held at Tambaram in 1938. According to Kraemer, God's self-disclosure in Jesus Christ is *sui generis*. His 'Biblical Realism' was influenced by Karl Barth and it stressed the absoluteness, finality and otherness of the gospel.

The Tambaram Conference more or less adopted the line of Kraemer's theology. In Christ alone is the full salvation which human beings need. Though values of deep religious experiences and great moral achievements may be found in other religions; though glimpses of God's light – as God did not leave Godself without witness in the world at any time – may also be found in other traditions, nevertheless all religious insight and experience, including that of Christians, has to be fully tested before God in Christ. Humans have been seeking God all through the ages, but often this seeking and longing have been misdirected. The Conference 'boldly' called people 'out' from world religions to the feet of Christ.

The 'Rethinking Group' of Indian theologians – P. Chenchiah, V. Chakkarai, and others – were highly critical of Kraemer and the Tambaram message, especially its standpoint of 'discontinuity' between the gospel and the religions. The convert of today should regard Hinduism as a spiritual mother. The Christian believer discovers the supreme value of Christ, not in spite of, but because of, Hinduism. Loyalty to Christ need not involve the surrender of a reverential attitude towards the Hindu heritage.[7]

Internationally, the debate continued throughout the 1940s and 1950s and the overall outcome was an open-minded approach to other religions and cultures. Though the relevance of the call for conversion to the Christian faith was affirmed, many theologians openly departed from the exclusive and authoritarian approach to other religions, and this paved the way for dialogue with other religions. According to the Fourth Assembly of the World Council of Churches, which met at Uppsala in 1968, the meeting with people of other faiths must lead to dialogue. In dialogue we share our common humanity. Dialogue for a Christian implies neither a denial of the uniqueness of Christ nor any loss of commitment to Christ.

Since the meeting of the Central Committee at Addis Ababa in 1971, dialogue with people of living faiths has been an integral part of the work of the World Council of Churches and was defined as 'witnessing to our deepest convictions and listening to those of our neighbours'.[8]

How do Christians theologically account for the diversity of the world's religious quest and commitment? What is the relation of the diversity of religious traditions to the mystery of the one Triune God? At both the Nairobi (1975) and the Vancouver (1983) assemblies of the WCC, dialogue became a controversial point primarily because of the implicit assumptions made in dialogue about the theological significance of other faiths. At Vancouver, for example, a major stream within the Assembly rejected the possibility of God's presence and activity in the religious life of people of other faiths. Eventually, however, a significant WCC ecumenical consultation in Baar, Switzerland, in 1990, produced the following consensus:

> We need to respect their religious convictions, different as these may be from our own, and to admire the things which God has accomplished and continues to accomplish in them through the Spirit. Inter-religious dialogue is therefore a 'two-way street'. Christians must enter into it in a spirit of openness prepared to receive from others, while on their part, they give witness of their own faith. Authentic dialogue opens both partners to a deeper conversion to the God who speaks to each through the other. Through the witness of others, we Christians can truly discover facets of the divine mystery which we have not yet seen or responded to. The practice of dialogue will thus result in the deepening of our own life of faith. We believe that walking together with people of other living faiths will bring us to a fuller understanding and experience of truth.[9]

Some Nineteenth-Century Christian Responses

In what follows I shall briefly outline the view of various significant figures in the Indian Christian response to Hinduism.

Krishna Mohun Banerjea

Krishna Mohun Banerjea (1813–85) was the first Protestant Christian to interpret Jesus Christ and Christianity in terms of Vedic thought.[10] In the 1860s his thought on the relation between Hinduism and Christianity underwent considerable changes, as he began to take a positive stance to Hinduism. The purpose of his book *The Arian Witness* [*sic*],[11] written in 1875, was to show the striking parallels between the Old Testament and the Vedas, and then to conclude that Christianity was the logical conclusion of Vedic Hinduism. The fundamental principles of the gospel were recognized and acknowledged both in theory and in practice by the Brahminical Arians of India. The original home of the Arians and Abraham was the same, namely Media. There are striking parallels between Hebrew and Sanskrit. There are parallels to the biblical creation stories in the Vedas. The legend of the Deluge is there in the Old Testament and *Satapatha Brahmana*.

The original sacrifice of the Vedas refers to the self-sacrifice of Prajapati, which foreshadowed the Cross of Jesus Christ. In the two Supplementary Essays,[12] and in the booklet *The Relation between Christianity and Hindu-*

ism (1881),[13] Banerjea further expounded the similarity between Hindu and Christian thought with respect to the understanding of sacrifice. The two theses of Banerjea were as follows:

> That the fundamental principles of Christian doctrine in relation to the salvation of the world find a remarkable counterpart in the Vedic principles of primitive Hinduism in relation to the destruction of sin, and the redemption of the sinner by the efficacy of Sacrifice, itself a figure of Prajapati, *the Lord and Saviour of the Creation, who had given himself up* as an offering for that purpose.
>
> That the meaning of *Prajapati*, an appellative, variously described as a Purusha begotten in the beginning, as *Viswakarma*, the creator of all, singularly coincides with the meaning of the names and offices of the historical reality *Jesus Christ*, and that no other person than Jesus of Nazareth has ever appeared in the world claiming the character and position of the self-sacrificing *Prajapati*, at the same time both mortal and immortal . . .[14]

Banerjea's exposition of Christ as the *True Prajapati* was an attempt to establish the fact that Christianity is not a foreign religion but rather the fulfilment of the Vedas. In fact 38 years before J. N. Farquhar it was Krishna Mohun Banerjea who was one of the first proponents of 'Fulfilment Theory' or inclusivism in Indian Christian theology of religions,[15] and without any of the negative criticisms of Hinduism that can be found in Farquhar's work. Also, some 84 years before Raimundo Panikkar,[16] K. M. Banerjea was the first person to hint at Prajapati as the 'unknown Christ of Hinduism' – again, without any negative criticisms of Vedanta as are found in Panikkar's thesis. Finally, 63 years before Kraemer proposed his theory of discontinuity between 'revelation' and 'religions'[17] Banerjea was expounding a theory of points of contact and continuity between Christianity and Hinduism.

H. A. Krishna Pillai

The thought of the Indian Christian poet H. A. Krishna Pillai, who had a conversion experience during the period 1857–9, shows that in understanding the work of Christ he was unable to find meaning in the ideas of expiation and juridical justification; rather, he interpreted Jesus as releasing precious life for humanity and making people his devotees.[18] Krishna Pillai was originally from the Vaishnava tradition, and Ramanuja's thought had influenced him. Hence he could understand salvation only as a recentring of one's relationship to God in such a way that the individual self becomes a focal point for the expression of the glory and love of the divine Self, which is human fulfilment.[19] When such a vision is applied to the interpretation of Christ, he believed, the result would be the emergence of something wholly new. As Christopher Duraisingh explains:

> Within such a theology, the role of Christ is not of one that mediates the propitiatory requirement to satisfy a righteous God. Rather, the mediatory potency of Christ is that of a potency of the most decisive paradigm case, classic instance, and unique manifestation in the plane of history of such a radical recentring and self-knowledge. Jesus' acknowledgement of the divine Self as his true Self was so complete and his recentring so maximal that in and through his life, death and continuing presence in the faith of the believing community a potency for the self-realization of the believer as centred in God, his only true self is released.[20]

A. S. Appasamy Pillai

A. S. Appasamy Pillai, who was born into an orthodox Hindu family in Tinnevelly in 1848, was baptized in 1871 and entered into a process of rediscovering Hinduism which gave him new insights into the Christian faith. In the *Rig Veda* he found an anticipation of Christianity, and hence it was for him akin to the Old Testament. The *Rig Veda* points to God as all-powerful, all-loving and all-merciful.[21] Through the teaching on *Hiranyagarbha*, it also prefigures Christ.[22] *Hiranyagarbha* the Golden Egg is for him the Golden Child who created everything and asked the question, 'To whom shall I sacrifice?' Thus according to him the germ of the doctrines of *logos* and atonement are found in the *Rig Veda*.[23]

A. S. Appasamy Pillai made use of Indian yoga techniques in Christian meditation and prayer. Through Shaiva Siddantic Yoga, he had the experience of receiving the Holy Spirit and gaining a clearer vision of Christ.[24] Later he practised Advaita Vedantic Yoga and recommended it for use by Christians, though without accepting the Vedantic philosophy as a whole.[25] On the basis of the revelation of Christ through yoga he tried to reinterpret the doctrines of the Trinity and the Logos. He experienced God as light, Spirit as Shakti and Christ as a spiritual body or a *Suksma Sarira* which reflects God.[26] He had the conviction that the Holy Spirit is working through yoga not only among Christians but also among Hindus.[27]

Brahmabandav Upadhyaya

The contributions of Brahmabandav Upadhyaya (1861–1907) to Indian theology lie in his interpretation of Trinity as *Sat-chit-anandam* (*Saccidan-*

anda) and Creation as *Maya*. It is the Upanishads and Shankara's writings which Upadhyaya takes as the basis for his explanation of the Vedantic concept Sat-chit-anandam. To speak of Brahman as Sat-chit-anandam means that Brahman knows Himself/Herself and from that self-knowledge proceeds His/Her eternal beatitude. Brahman is related of necessity only to the Infinite Image of His/Her own being, mirrored in the ocean of His/Her knowledge. This relation of Being (Sat) to Himself/Herself in self-knowledge (Chit) is one of perfect harmony and bliss (Anandam).[28] Upadhyaya then proclaimed that the Christian doctrine of God as Trinity is exactly the same as the Vedantic conception of Brahman as Sat-chit-anandam. The knowing Self is the Father, the known Self or the self-begotten by His knowledge is the Son; and the Holy Spirit is the Spirit of reciprocal love proceeding from the Father and the Son.[29]

Upadhyaya would point out that the revelation of God in Jesus Christ is further clarification of God conceived as Sat-chit-anandam. Only reason can know that self-existent Being is necessarily intelligent. But only revelation can tell us how self-existent Being's intelligence is satisfied within the term of its being, for revelation teaches us that the differentiating note in divine knowledge is the response of intelligence. Jesus Christ acknowledges responsively his eternal thought generation from the Father.[30] The relation between the Father and Jesus Christ is the revelation of the true relation between Sat and Chit as well as the revelation of Anandam, the result of that relation. And this revelation of the inner life of God is for humans to attain the goal of life, which is beatific vision, beholding God as God is eternally.

Regarding the doctrines of the human person, sin, fall, grace, atonement and salvation, Upadhyaya maintained the traditional Christian position and hence he tried to explain the traditional understanding of the person of Jesus Christ in terms of the Vedantic understanding of human nature also. According to Vedanta, human nature is composed of five sheaths or divisions (*kosa*), namely, physical (*annamaya*), vital (*pranmaya*), mental (*manomaya*), intellectual (*vijnanamaya*) and spiritual (*anandamaya*). In a human being these five sheaths are presided over by a created personality (*aham*). Jesus Christ is also composed of five sheaths, but in him the five sheaths are acted upon directly by the Logos-God instead of a created personality. The incarnation was thus accomplished by uniting humanity with divinity in the person of the Logos, and this incarnate God in human person we call Jesus Christ.[31]

Upadhyaya also interpreted the Christian doctrine of creation in terms of the Vedantic concept *Maya*. He pointed out that, according to Advaita Vedanta, the world originates by *vivarta*, a kind of communication which does not modify the communicator. *Vivarta* implies creation by will-causation (*sankalpa*). This is also the meaning of Maya, which signifies the will-power (*sankalpa*) of God. It means that creation is the result of the power (*shakti*) of the will (*sankalpa*) of God.[32] For Upadhyaya the term

Maya involves three truths: (a) God is not necessarily a creator; (b) creatures are non-beings, transformed as it were into being; (c) the transformation is caused by the mysterious power of the will of God. He then declared that this Vedantic doctrine of Maya, which explains creation, and the Christian doctrine of creation, are identical because, according to the Christian doctrine of creation, God does not create out of necessity but through the overflow of his perfections; creation has no being in and of itself but as the result of the divine will remains contingent.[33] Upadhyaya even said that the term Maya could express the meaning of the doctrine of creation in a far better way than the Latin root *creare*.

Some Twentieth-Century Responses to Hinduism

S. K. George

S. K. George (1900–60) and Manilal C. Parekh (1885–1967) espoused a version of pluralism in the theology of religions since the 1920s and 1930s respectively, and Stanley J. Samartha joined them in the 1990s.[34] For S. K. George the practice of redemptive suffering love manifested in the cross of Christ is the central principle of Christianity. Mahatma Gandhi's satyagraha movement was for him the cross in action and he joined it wholeheartedly in 1932, resigning a secure teaching job at Bishop's College, Calcutta.[35] Even prior to this, as a Bachelor of Divinity student of Bishop's College (1924–7), he had his doubts about the exclusive divinity of Christ. As early as 1937 S. K. George helped in organizing the All Kerala Inter-religious Students Fellowship, which tried to bring together students of various religions for mutual understanding and co-operation. The first conference of the Fellowship was held at Alwaye in May 1937 and adopted as its Aim and Basis the following:

> Amidst the conflicting claims made on behalf of different religions . . . we believe there is an urgent need for a full and free exchange of our differing religious experiences, in a spirit of mutual respect, appreciation and sympathy. We consider that for such mutual respect and sympathy to be real it is absolutely necessary that no member of the Fellowship should claim for his religion any exclusive and final possession of truth. We believe that such an interchange of experience will lead to:
>
> (a) An enrichment of one another's religious life;
> (b) Mutual respect, understanding and tolerance; and
> (c) Cooperation in purifying and strengthening the religious attitude of mind . . . from which our . . . problems have to be tackled.[36]

The Fellowship was to explore fully the value of all the different religious traditions and disciplines and present them for the benefit of all. But at the same time nobody in the Fellowship was to be persuaded to join another's religious belief and practice. To weaken the hold of the truth of any religion upon humankind was considered as a threat to religion itself; hence the Fellowship was to strive for the opposite. Those in the Fellowship were to help one another to understand and to live up to the best in all religions.

S. K. George held the conviction that the hope of world unity and human fellowship lies through interreligious co-operation. His desire was that the spirit of co-operation which he found among Christians would be established among the different religions as well.[37] In his view, the interreligious movement faces many misunderstandings. One charge is that it is syncretistic and will simply result in adding one or more new fancy religions to the already crowded world of religions. The clarification given by George in this context is:

> The interreligious movement does not aim at evolving a single universal religion for all mankind. That . . . is the dream of the militant missionary faiths, which would blot out all other religions. What inter-religionism stands for is the acceptance of the need and the fact of variety in religious experience, of diversity in man's approach towards and realization of the One Eternal Reality, which is the common object of religious quest throughout the ages. It admits the limitation of all human understanding of the Divine – even unique revelations are mediated through human channels – and is, therefore, humble and willing to accept light from various sources. It accepts the revelation through the spiritual geniuses of all mankind, and while it does not aim at, or believe in, evolving a uniformity of creed and conduct, it looks forward to a time when the spiritually minded of all religions will unite in the appreciation of all known truths and is welcoming fresh revelations from the unspent deep resources of God.[38]

The Fellowship of the Friends of Truth, which started in 1951 and whose secretary for the first seven years was S. K. George, functioned as an interreligious movement. According to George, the place of Jesus Christ in the Hindu religious heritage of India is as one of the *Ishta Devatas* or chosen or favourite deities. Hinduism readily grants such a place to Jesus Christ. As a disciple of Jesus, what is needed is the setting aside of the denial that other mediators between God and humans, other experiences of God's presence in the human heart, other *Ishta Devatas*, are valid. Such denials lie outside the positive experience of the Christian and therefore have no validity.[39]

Manilal C. Parekh

Manilal C. Parekh was born in a Jain home in Rajkot, Gujarat. He was introduced to Hindu Vaishnava Bhakti by his father. A serious illness helped him to experience theism. He came under the influence of the writings of Keshub Chunder Sen and served for some years as a *pracaraka* (evangelist) of the Church of the New Dispensation in Sindh and Bombay. The next stage in his pilgrimage was his growing interest in Christ, towards whom Keshub had so firmly pointed. The serious illness, tuberculosis, presented him with an opportunity to study the Bible and the *Vacanamrit* of Swami Narayana, the famous Gujarati Vaishnava religious and social reformer of the early nineteenth century. The study of Vaishnava Bhakti led him beyond the rationalism of the Brahmo Samaj to the conviction that God becomes incarnate, and this belief in turn pointed him to the Christ of the New Testament.[40]

Parekh was baptized, which he considered a spiritual matter only, in the Anglican Church in Bombay in 1918. He became disillusioned with the Westernization of the Indian Christian community and wanted a 'Hindu Church of Christ' free from Western influence. He now felt strongly that the new disciple of Christ should remain within his/her own community, witnessing from there. He drew a clear distinction between 'evangelism' – the proclamation of the gospel to individuals – and 'proselytism' by which he meant mass-conversion by dubious means. Like Brahmabandhav Upadhyaya (1861–1907) of Bengal, he made a distinction between *samaja dharma* (the social aspect of religion) and *moksha dharma* (the spiritual aspect). Christianity should be *moksha dharma* only.[41]

By the end of the 1930s, Parekh came to the final stage of his spiritual pilgrimage, namely *Bhagavata Dharma*. He conceived Bhagavata Dharma as a universal personal religion of devotion in which Christian devotion is one element among others, perhaps the central and organizing element. He used this term to describe a religion of personal *Bhakti*, which is seen at its clearest in Christianity and Vaishnavism, but is also seen in all other theistic faiths. He included in it Christianity, Judaism, Islam, Zoroastrianism and all the religions which believe in God. His bitter experiences in both Brahmo Samaj and the Christian Church eventually brought him to the conclusion that changing one's religion is undesirable, since it tends to lead to exclusiveness and communalism. For the New Harmony which he was evolving, he wanted a name that avoided the implication that one particular tradition had a monopoly of the truth, and this he found in Bhagavata Dharma.[42] Bhagavata Dharma truly represents a spirituality of pluralism.

Pandippedi Chenchiah

The convert of today, according to Pandippedi Chenchiah (1886–1959) of the Madras Rethinking Group that flourished in the first half of the twentieth century, regards Hinduism as a spiritual mother who has nurtured him or her in a sense of spiritual values. The disciple discovers the supreme value of Christ, not in spite of Hinduism but because Hinduism has taught the devotee how to discern spiritual greatness. Emancipation from double bondage, namely, to the traditions of Hinduism on the one hand, and to the traditions of Christianity on the other, opens up the freedom to study the question of the meaning and significance of Jesus untrammelled by doctrines and dogma, and to seek in the living forces of Hinduism a positive key to the still inaccessible spiritual riches deriving from Jesus.[43] The Christian is a new creation. The Holy Spirit is the new cosmic energy; the kingdom of God the new order; the children of God, the new type that Christ has inaugurated. The gospel is that God in Jesus has made a new creation. In Chenchiah's view human history has begun a new revolutionary chapter in Jesus. Christianity is not primarily a doctrine of salvation but the announcement of the advent of a new creative order in Jesus. The good news of Christianity is the birth of Jesus, and the challenge for the Christian is how to reproduce his impact. The Christian has to develop the Yoga of the Holy Spirit with a new *sadhana* of eternal life.[44] Today we have to realize Jesus as the head of a new world order; or as the creative expression of God's higher purposes with regard to human living.[45]

According to Chenchiah two categories of interpretation of Jesus, namely the juridical and the genetic or the creative, are possible. He rejects the former and accepts only the latter. In the juridical conception of Christianity the cross is understood as a sacrifice for the atonement for the sins of humankind. But as we accompany Jesus we never get 'the Kalighat' feeling of sacrifice: 'Neither in my studies of the Gospel, not even in my private devotion, can I capture the feeling that in Jesus I am in a temple where he is sacrificed for me to satisfy a terror inspiring deity. No Indian gets this feeling.'[46] We can never get to the heart of Christianity by the way of juridical theology. It is the creative aspect of Jesus, or the Holy Spirit as creative energy, that takes the Indian into the new 'given' in Jesus.[47]

The attempt to interpret Jesus exclusively in terms of justification by faith or reconciliation has resulted in the view that the ultimate effect of the ministry of our Lord was to *restore* humanity to its original condition, that is, to its primal stage before the alleged Fall. But for Chenchiah, the fact of Christ is the birth of a new order in creation. It is the emergence of life participating in the immortal nature of God beyond sin and death. In the company of Jesus we do not feel the gulf that separates God and humans. His own consciousness reveals the total lack of this sense of separation, and his teachings do not emphasize the awful gulf between God and humans. God and human persons have met in Jesus; and not merely met but fused into one. To be Christian is to gain this consciousness and this sense of harmonious blend with the divine. Jesus stands in relation to the human person as a new creation stands towards the old. He is the New Man; he is the first fruit of the new creation. Christianity brings into evolution the new Shakti of the Holy Spirit.[48] Jesus is never absolute, unapproachable and incomprehensible. He does not stand as the absolute to the human person. On this point, the Church has misconstrued the purposes of Jesus from the beginning: 'We have been always anxious to turn him into a God, place him over against us, and worship him. While he wanted to step out of God to be with us in fellowship, ours is a worship which militates against his fellowship.'[49]

A. J. Appasamy

In the view of A. J. Appasamy (1891–1975), Ramanuja realized with certainty that God is a personal being whose grace is sufficient for us. Also, out of love, God becomes incarnate in order to satisfy the human longing for God. Further, Ramanuja emphasizes the immanence of God, who is the inner ruler of the universe and souls. Just as the soul is within the body, controlling it and directing it, God is within the world of nature and of humans, ruling over these from the inner depths. God is immanent in the individual soul (*Tvam*) and is identical with Brahman who is the author of all creation (*Tat*). Ramanuja was the first to give a constructive and elaborate philosophical formulation for the doctrine of Bhakti. Ramanuja believed in a God endowed with the attributes of power, knowledge, love and bliss. For him Bhakti or love is the most effective to reach the divine, and even in the highest stage of the spiritual life individual souls continue to exist and derive their bliss from their intimate relation to the Ultimate Reality. Brahman's Being, Knowledge and Bliss are in relation to others and Brahman is not limited to the attributes. Bhakti involves us in the continuous recollection of God, which is also characterized by vision (*darsana*) and meditation (*dhyana*).[50]

As these doctrines of Ramanuja make an unfailing appeal to the heart of India, in the light of them Appasamy has suggested a different line of enquiry for Christology in India. The farewell discourses of John 13–17 have to be made the focus for Christology, where the phrase 'abide in me and I in You' becomes the Christian *mahavakya* expressing the intimate relationship between Christ and the believer. Christian faith is communion with Jesus who lived on this earth long ago and who now, as the eternal Christ, dwells in the depth of the human heart. The living Christ continues to do in one human heart after another what the Jesus of history accomplished in Palestine.[51] Appasamy also thought that fundamentally the Hindu doctrine of *Avatara* is akin to the Christian doctrine of incarnation. But he also reminds us that when speaking of Jesus as *Avatara*, we should also bear in mind the distinctiveness that he is the incarnation of the whole Being of God for all time, and that he came to redeem sinful humanity. For Appasamy, the identity between Jesus and the Father was one of will and not of essential nature. Further, we may note that he has interrelated Ramanuja's doctrine of the Indwelling God (*Antaryamin*) or the Inner Ruler with the Christian understanding of the Holy Spirit.[52]

Swami Abhishiktananda

Swami Abhishiktananda (1910–73) has interpreted Jesus Christ as *Cit* in the context of his interpretation of Trinity as *Saccidananda*. While Brahmabandhav Upadhyaya holds that with regard to the concept of Supreme Being the Advaitic and Christian doctrines are identical, Abhishiktananda would point out that a reinterpretation of the Hindu concept *Saccidananda* is necessary to make it Christian. The Hindu experience of *Saccidananda* should be remoulded to attain the Christian experience of *Saccidananda*, and once that is actualized the renewed experience of *Saccidananda* would be the Trinitarian culmination of Advaitic experience.[53]

In the view of Abhishiktananda, when the Advaitic *Saccidananda* is considered in the light of the Christian experience of God as Trinity it gives the impression of being essentially monistic.[54] Because of the Advaitic understanding of Being as monad, Advaita faces the antinomy and paradox of created being. However, the revelation of the Trinitarian understanding of God in Jesus Christ is purported to be the solution to the paradox of created being, as Jesus Christ is the revelation that 'Being is communion'.[55] Hence creation can be understood as the 'expansion' of God's inner self-manifestation. In the very mystery of the Trinitarian God, the human person discovers him- or herself as a unique and irreplaceable manifestaton of God's Being and love.[56]

Abhishiktananda explains the Hindu Advaitic experience of *Saccidananda* as follows:[57] a person realizes Being, *Sat*, as him- or herself as well as infinitely beyond the self. A person *is*, and knows that he or she *is*. When pure self-awareness is sufficiently realized, the whole of one's being is flooded with an inexpressible sense of completion, peace, joy and fullness and this is what the Hindu tradition calls *Ananda*. Thus if one descends into the successive depths of one's true self, the awareness of being and joy in being, then finally nothing will be left but the self, the only one, infinitely alone – Being, Awareness and Bliss, *Saccidananda*.

The claim of Abhishiktananda was that in Jesus Christ we get a different picture.[58] In the relationship between Jesus Christ and God the Father there is the expression of oneness as well as the distinct face-to-face relationship. In awakening to himself at the centre of his being, Jesus realized his oneness with the Father. And because he is pre-eminently the representative 'Son of Man', humanity shares in everything that he does and all that he achieves. Moreover, the Holy Spirit is the expression of the mystery of the non-duality of the Father and the Son, as well as the expression of the mystery of the non-duality of the whole of humanity and the Father actualized in and through the Son. Thus in Christian *Saccidananda*, that is to say, in Trinity, Being (*Sat*) opens itself at its very source to give birth eternally to the Son and in him to countless creatures, each of which in its own way will for ever manifest and celebrate the infinite love and mercy of God. According to Christian *Saccidananda*, self-awareness (*Cit*) comes to be only when there is mutual giving and receiving between the Father and the Son and between the Father and the whole of humanity in Jesus Christ, for the *I* only awakes to itself in a *thou*. And according to Christian *Saccidananda*, joy (*ananda*) is present because of the reciprocal love between the Father and the Son, God and the human person, and one person and another.

The spiritual diary of Swami Abhishiktananda, now available in English, more or less shows that the transformation Advaitic experience, awakening in him as early as 1952, was to stay throughout his life. Although, through his books *Saccidananda* and *Hindu–Christian Meeting Point*, he projected externally an inclusivist position, there was a second internal Abhishiktananda – a Vedantin-Christian Abhishiktananda – according to whom it is the Christian Trinitarian experience which has to be remoulded in terms of Advaitic experience.[59] We should also note that towards the end of his life Abhishiktananda could experience the saving Christ only as pure self-awareness, going beyond religious distinctions.[60] His work has been continued by Bede Griffiths, who has developed thinking in the area of Hindu–Christian dialogue and theology, and has done much to make it known outside of India.[61]

Raimundo Panikkar

According to Raimundo Panikkar, the role of *Ishvara* in Vedanta corresponds functionally to the role of Christ in Christian thought.[62] If we start with the historicity of Christ, essential though that may be, we are liable to fail to grasp that Ishvara is the unknown Christ of Hinduism.[63] In Vedanta, the concept Ishvara is one which is put forward to explain the problem of the relation between Brahman and world. But the concept Ishvara cannot solve the problem satisfactorily. In Shankara's philosophy, the distinction between Brahman and Ishvara is overstressed in order to safeguard the absolute purity of the former.[64] In Ramanuja's Visistadvaita, on the other hand, it is the identity between Brahman and Ishvara which is overstressed in order to retain the reality of the world. According to Panikkar, only Christ can be the true link between the World and God. The Ishvara of Panikkar's interpretation is really 'human' without ceasing to be 'divine', and it points towards a reality which not only connects the two poles of God and the world, but which 'is' the two poles without permitting them to coalesce. In Christian language this interpretation of Ishvara points towards the mystery of Christ.[65] In other words, Panikkar is reinterpreting the Vedantin concept of Ishvara so that it becomes the already formulated traditional Christian understanding of Christ.

Of course it is also true that, by the name 'Christ', Panikkar now means more than Jesus of Nazareth, even though Jesus is the manifestation of Christ for the Christian. Christ is the supername. The Christic principle is for him the centre of reality, as seen by the Christian tradition in a theanthropocosmic vision. Though the Christic principle is still central for him, Panikkar is today more positive and open to other faiths, more or less moving away from inclusivism to pluralism.[66]

Negative Approaches: P. D. Devanandan and Surjit Singh

There have been some Indian Christian thinkers who were negative in their approach to Hinduism, and P. D. Devanandan and Surjit Singh may be taken as their representatives. P. D. Devanandan (1901–62) held the view that the classical Hindu Vedantic theology is incapable of giving an ideological basis for the new anthropology emerging in independent India[67] and that the revelation of God in Jesus Christ provides the solution. Part of the answer is found in the doctrine of the incarnation: it was of revolutionary significance for the world when God assumed human form. If God is personally and purposefully involved in real life then this provides a meaningful ideological basis for human service (*diakonia*), for it signals that God's redemptive power is at work in the world, liberating the individual and renewing human society. Individuals can enter into creative relationship in community due to their being bound together as persons in relation to the Person.[68] The lack of emphasis on the sinful nature of the human person, as well as an over-emphasis on the gulf between the transcendental Being and karma-samsara-life are the characteristic limitations of Hinduism, according to Devanandan.[69] Alternative to Hinduism is the view which it accepts that the human person is sinful, that God is actively involved in world history and that God's redemptive plan is cosmic in its scope.[70]

In Surjit Singh's view, the values at stake in Advaita Vedanta are of personality, history and time. It is confusing to call God personal in the Advaita system. Also, according to Advaita, the individuality of a person is ultimately absorbed in the Absolute.[71] Hence Surjit Singh wishes to safeguard the reality of the human personality, world history, and the flux of time, by recapturing the New Testament significance of the person and work of Jesus Christ. Christian thought has maintained that the God–human person is an eternal fact, and this preserves the importance of both human nature and historical existence. Ultimate reality is not only divine but also divine–human. If some determinate aspects of the Real are involved and grounded in the actual, then the features of the actual are preserved in the Real beyond the cosmic process. It means that individuality, in so far as it aligns itself with the pattern of Ultimate Reality, will be affirmed and preserved.[72]

The divine–human relation in Jesus Christ has the characteristics of involvement, interaction, interpenetration and a new paradigm.[73] This divine–human relation in Jesus demonstrates the capacity for relationship within the inner structure of God; God is Saguna, personal. It shows the working of God both in an individual human person and also in socio-historical communities and groups. Moreover, Christ – through his experience of death and resurrection – is the foundation which enables the human movement from estrangement from God, self and the world, to reconciliation with God, self and the world.[74]

Pluralistic Inclusivism

The present author's Christian thought in relation to Indian philosophy, especially Shankara's Advaita Vedanta, and which spreads over the 1990s to the present, is a practical demonstration of an Indian dialogical theology in terms of a perspective which can be termed 'Pluralistic Inclusivism'. This embraces the relational convergence of religions as well as recognizing the emergence of the new in Christian thought, and conceives all of the religious experiences of the world as the common property of humanity.[75] Our Indian hermeneutical context, a major factor of which is Advaita Vedanta, decides the shape of theology. I have tried to make the content of the revelation of God in Jesus truly pluralistic by elaborating the contributions of Shankara's Advaita Vedanta in relation to it.[76] I hold that there is a possibility of understanding the person of Jesus as the extrinsic denominator (*upadhi*) of Brahman, the name and form (*namarupa*) of Brahman, the effect (*karya*) of Brahman, as well as the reflection (*abhasa*) and delimitation (*ghatakasah*) of Brahman.[77] There is also the possibility of interpreting the function of Jesus as re-presenting the all-pervasive (*sarvagatatvam*), illuminating (*jyothi*) and unifying (*ekikrtya*) power of the Supreme Atman; as the Witness (*saksi*) and Self of all (*sarvatma*); as re-presenting the Supreme Brahman as Pure Consciousness (*prajnanaghanam*); and as re-presenting the ever-present scope for (*nityasiddhasvabhavam*) human liberation.[78]

I have also elaborated an Indian Christian epistemology in terms of the six *pramanas* (sources of valid knowledge) of Indian philosophy, namely, perception, inference, scripture, comparison, postulation and non-cognition. If scripture (*sabda*) can be classified under revelation, the other five *pramanas* come under reason and there is an integral relationship between reason and revelation in Indian epistemology and consequently in Indian Christian thought. Perception (*pratyaksa*) proclaims the integral relation between humans, nature and the Innermost Reality (Atman), and which roots theology in day-to-day experiences. Inference (*anumana*) challenges us to identify the invariable concomitances (*vyaptis*) in Christian theological discussion in terms of the present-day Indian context.

I have also suggested how Advaita Vedanta can dynamically enrich the development of Eastern Christian theology. The insight that Brahman/Atman pervades, illumines and unifies all reality – including levels and layers of the human personality as well as the whole of creation – enables Eastern Christian theology to arrive at new insights regarding the energies of God through which God is knowable and through which deification is actualized. The divine willing, the ideas of created things, the *logoi* (words), are expressions of the energies of God and not the divine essence. The Advaita Vedantic view that before creation this universe pre-existed in Brahman as potential seed (*bijashaktih*) and undifferentiated name and form (*avyakrtanamarupa*) clarifies the understanding of creation expressed through the energies of God. The *neti neti* negative theology of Advaita, together with the experience of Brahman/Atman as the subject and knower of all and everything which cannot be known, enables Eastern Christian theology to develop its apophatic theology. The Orthodox conception of 'deification' is enriched through Advaitic insights. Deification can be interpreted in terms of the implantation (*mayah*) of the Atman in the five human sheaths, or in terms of the pervasion of the Atman in the total human personality. The luminous Atman (*atmajyotih*) imparts lustre to the intellect and all other organs, thus effecting deification. Brahman/Atman unifies everything and everyone in his or her homogeneity (*ekarasata*) and the result is again deification. Awareness that Brahman/Atman is reflected at all the levels of our personality lends new vigour to the interpretation of the human person as created in the image of God, a factor stressed by Orthodox Christian thought.[79]

Conclusion

The Missionary Conferences of the early twentieth century struggled to respond to the challenge of the relationship between Christian faith and other faiths, and the Tambaram Conference of 1938 upheld the standpoint of 'discontinuity' between the concepts of 'revelation' and 'religion'. The Madras Rethinking Group opposed such a perspective and asserted that, because of Hinduism, the convert from that religion is able to arrive at new meanings regarding the person and function of Jesus Christ. Pandippedi Chenchiah explained that a new creation has begun with the birth of Jesus and we are incorporated into it through the power of the Holy Spirit. God and humans have united in Christ and we should affirm this without any Barthian nervousness going beyond the atonement theories. Before Chenchiah, H. A. Krishna Pillai, who was rooted in a Hindu Bhakti background, and who moved beyond notions of expiation and juridical justification, celebrated the meaning and impact of Jesus in terms of a radical recentring of life in God. The present author has also interpreted the function of Jesus in terms of Advaitic experience, such that he re-presents before human beings and the whole of creation the all-pervasive, illuminative and unifying power of the Supreme Atman. In the thought of Brahmabandav Upadhyaya, again we can identify new creative theological insights emerging in terms of a Vedantic interpretation of Trinity as *Saccidananda* and Creation as Maya. All of these thinkers were upholding the creative perspective of Pluralistic Inclusivism in the theology of religions.

In their response to Hinduism I have considered two prominent Indian thinkers, S. K. George and Manilal C. Parekh, who upheld Pluralism in the theology of religions as early as the 1920s and 1930s. Decades before the World Council of Churches or the Roman Catholic Church arrived at the idea of dialogue with people of other faiths, S. K. George was organizing the All Kerala Inter-religious Fellowship. He was of the view that we should not deny other mediators between God and human beings, other experiences of God's presence in the human heart, and the validity of other *Ishta Devatas*. Manilal C. Parekh conceived Bhagavata Dharma as a universal personal religion of devotion in which Christian devotion is one element among others, though perhaps the central and organizing element. Bhagavata Dharma truly represents a spirituality of pluralism.

Krishna Mohan Banerjea was a pioneer inclusivist, interpreting Jesus Christ as the True Prajapati as early as 1875. A. S. Appasamy Pillai conceived the techniques of Shaiva Siddantic, as well as Advaita Vedantic, Yoga as helpful in Christian experience. A. J. Appasamy presented an understanding of Christ in the light of the Bhakti philosophy of Ramanuja. Abhishiktananda held the view that the Hindu experience of *Saccidananda* should be remoulded to attain the Christian experience of *Saccidananda*, which would be the Trinitarian culmination of Advaitic experience. Raimundo Panikkar is of the view that the role of Ishvara in Vedanta corresponds functionally to the role of Christ in Christian thought. It is not Ishvara but Christ who can be a proper link between the world and God, Christ who transcends Christianity and is the centre of reality in a theanthropocosmic vision. All these thinkers, to some extent, represent the school of Inclusivism in the theology of religions.

Also, we find a few Exclusivists who rejected Hinduism. For example Paul D. Devanandan thought that Hindu Vedantic theology cannot yield an ideological basis for the new Indian anthropology; only the revelation of God in Jesus can achieve what is necessary. In the view of Surjit Singh, the values at stake in Advaita Vedanta are of personality, of history and time, all of which can be restored by recapturing the New Testament significance of the person and work of Christ.

But we must realize that overall Christian responses to Hinduism have been positive, encouraging and rewarding. Learning from the past, it is hoped that we may in future take a perspective regarding the reception of Hinduism by transcending the perspectives of either Reinterpretation or Rejection.

Study Questions

1 Is it possible to absorb at least a little of the faith experience of your Hindu neighbour with empathy? In the light of it how might you reconceive your own faith experience?

2 How do you think God is working among Hindus? Is it possible for a Christian to participate in the work of God among the Hindus, upholding the liberative resources of Hinduism to counter the forces of evil and oppression?

3 How useful do you think the attempts of such figures as Upadhyaya and Abhishiktananda to see *Saccidananda* as an India analogue to the Trinity have been? Does the reoccurrence of the idea in more contemporary figures, such as Bede Griffiths, suggest it is important to a Christian understanding of Hinduism?

Further Reading

Abhishiktananda, Swami, 1974, *Saccidananda: A Christian Approach to Advaitic Experience*, Delhi: ISPCK.

Aleaz, K. P., 1997, *An Indian Jesus from Sankara's Thought*, Calcutta: Punthi Pustak.

Aleaz, K. P., 2005, *Christian Responses to Indian Philosophy*, Kolkata: Punthi Pustak.

Appasamy, A. J., 1970, *The Theology of Hindu Bhakti*, Madras: CLS.

Baago, Kaj, 1969, *Pioneers of Indigenous Christianity*, Madras and Bangalore: CLS/CISRS.

Devanandan, P. D., 1959, *The Gospel and Renascent Hinduism*, London: SCM Press.

Panikkar, Raimundo, 1981, *The Unknown Christ of Hinduism*, London: DLT.

Notes

1 Chandran, J. R., 1981, 'Christianity and World Religions – The Ecumenical Discussion', *Indian Journal of Theology*, vol. 30, nos. 3 and 4, pp. 186–7.

2 Farquhar, J. N., 1913, *The Crown of Hinduism*, London: Oxford University Press; 1917, *Gita and the Gospel*, 3rd edn, Madras: CLS.

3 Hogg, A. G., 1909, *Karma and Redemption: An Essay toward the Interpretation of Hinduism and the Re-statement of Christianity*, London: CLS; 1947, *The Christian Message to the Hindu*, Duff Missionary Lectures for 1945 on the Challenge of the Gospel in India, London: SCM Press.

4 Chandran, 'Christianity', p. 191.

5 Hocking, William Ernest, 1940, *Living Religions and a World Faith*, New York: Macmillan.

6 Kraemer, Hendrik, 1938, *The Christian Message in a Non-Christian World*, London: Edinburgh House Press; 1961, *Religion and the Christian Faith*, London: Lutterworth Press.

7 Job, G. V., *et al.*, 1938, *Rethinking Christianity in India*, Madras: A. N. Sundarisanam.

8 *Ibid.*, p. 16.

9 WCC, 1990, 'Baar Statement', *Current Dialogue*, vol. 18, p. 7.

10 For K. M. Banerjea's life and thought: Aleaz, K. P. (ed.), 1999, *From Exclusivism to Inclusivism: The Theological Writings of Krishna Mohun Banerjea (1813–1885)*, Delhi: ISPCK; Philip, T. V., 1982, *Krishna Mohan Banerjea: Christian Apologist*, Madras and Bangalore: CLS and CISRS.

11 Cf. Banerjea, K. M., 1975, *The Arian Witness*, London: Thacker Spink & Co.

12 Banerjea, K. M., 1880, *The Arian Witness: Supplementary Essays*, London: Thacker Spink & Co.

13 Banerjea, K. M., 1881, *The Relation between Christianity and Hinduism*, Calcutta: Oxford Mission Press.

14 Banerjea, K. M., 1969, 'Selected Writing', in Baago, Kaj, *Pioneers of Indigenous Christianity*, Madras and Bangalore: CLS and CISRS, p. 98.

15 See Hedges, Paul, 2001, *Preparation and Fulfilment: A History and Study of Fulfilment Theology in Modern British Thought in the Indian Context*, Bern: Peter Lang, pp. 51–87, 137–54.

16 Panikkar, Raimundo, 1964, *The Unknown Christ of Hinduism*, London: Darton, Longman & Todd (rev. and enl. edn. 1981).

17 Kraemer, *Christian*.

18 Hudson, D. D., 1972, 'Hindu and Christian Theological Parallels in the Conversion of H. A. Krishna Pillai 1857–1859', *Journal of the American Academy of Religion*, vol. 40, pp. 196–205.

19 Duraisingh, Christopher, 1982, 'Reflection on Theological Hermeneutics in the Indian Context', *Indian Journal of Theology*, vol. 31, nos. 3 and 4, pp. 271–5.

20 *Ibid.*, p. 273.

21 Appasamy Pillai, A. S., 1924, *Fifty Years' Pilgrimage of a Convert*, London: CMS, pp. 89–92.

22 *Hiranyagarbha* is the golden egg or golden womb that appears as the source of all things in Vedic legend, and is sometimes identified with *Brahma* as the supreme deity [eds].

23 *Ibid.*, pp. 92–4. Cf. *Rig Veda* 10.121.

24 Appasamy Pillai, A. S., 1926, *The Use of Yoga in Prayer*, Madras: CLS, pp. 10–13.

25 *Ibid.*, p. 17.

26 Appasamy Pillai published two pamphlets: *The Eternal Divine Son* and *The Divine Birth of the Eternal Son*. Cf. Appasamy, A. J., 1924, *An Indian Interpretation of Christianity*, Madras: CLS, pp. 4–8.

27 Appasamy Pillai, *Fifty*, pp. 97ff.

28 Upadhyaya, B., 1898, 'A Vedantic Parable', *Sophia*, vol. 5, no. 8, p. 119; 1900, 'Being', *Sophia*, vol. 1, no. 7, p. 7; 1900, 'Notes', *Sophia*, vol. 1, no. 2.

29 Upadhyaya, B., 1898, 'An Exposition of Catholic Belief as Compared with the Vedanta', *Sophia*, vol. 5, no. 1, p. 11; 1898, 'Our New Canticle', *Sophia*, vol. 5, no. 10, p. 146; 1897, 'Hinduism and Christianity as Compared by Mrs. Bezant', *Sophia*, vol. 4, no. 2, p. 8; 1900, 'Question and Answers', *Sophia*, vol. 1, no. 11, p.7.

30 Summary of the lecture by Upadhyaya: 1897, 'Hinduism, Theosophy and Christianity', *Sophia*, vol. 4, no. 12, pp. 2, 4–5; 1901, 'The Incarnate Logos', *The Twentieth Century*, vol. 1, no. 1, pp. 6–7; 1901, 'Christ's Claim to Attention', *The Twentieth Century*, vol. 1, no. 5, pp. 115–16.

31 Upadhyaya, B., 'Incarnate', pp. 6–8; 1900, 'Notes', *Sophia*, vol. 1, no. 4, pp. 6–7.

32 Cf. Upadhyaya, B., 1900, 'Maya', *Sophia*, vol. 1, no. 18, pp. 6–7.

33 Cf. Upadhyaya, B., 1899, 'The True Doctrine of Maya', *Sophia*, vol. 6, no. 2, pp. 226–8; 1900, 'Vedantism and Christianity', *Sophia*, vol. 1, nos. 15 and 16, p. 6.

34 Samartha, S. J., 1992, *One Christ Many Religions*, Bangalore: Sathri.

35 Aleaz, K. P., 2000, 'S. K. George: A Pioneer Pluralist and Dalit Theologian', *Bangalore Theological Forum*, vol. 32, no. 1, pp. 91–111; George, S. K., 1947, *Gandhi's Challenge to Christianity*, 2nd edn, Ahmedabad: Navajivan.

36 *Ibid.*, p. 80.

37 *Ibid.*, p. 52.

38 *Ibid.*, pp. 53–4.

39 *Ibid.*, p. 48; George, S. K., 1959–60, 'Christianity in Independent India', in *S. K. George Souvenir*, *FFT Quarterly*, vol. 7, nos. 1 and 2, p. 37.

40 Boyd, R. H. S. (ed.), 1974, *Manilal C. Parekh 1885–1967, Dhanjibhai Fakirbhai 1895–1967: A Selection*, Madras: CLS.

41 Aleaz, K. P., 2001, *Religions in Christian Theology*, Kolkata: Punthi Pustak, pp. 95–6.

42 *Ibid.*, p. 97. Cf. Parekh, Manilal C., 1953, *A Hindu Portrait of Jesus Christ*, Rajkot: Sri Bhagavata Dharma Mission; 1947, *Christian Proselytism in India – A Great and Growing Menace*, Rajkot: Sri Bhagavata Dharma Mission.

43 Chenchiah, P., 1938, 'Jesus and Non-Christian Faiths', in G. V. Job, *et al.* (eds), *Rethinking Christianity in India*, Madras: A. N. Sundarisanam, p. 49.

44 *Ibid.*, p. 60.

45 Chenchiah, P., 1938, 'The Christian Message in a Non-Christian World: A Review of Dr. Kraemer's Book', in Job, *Rethinking*, 'Appendix', p. 19.

46 Job, *Rethinking*, p. 22.

47 Job, *Rethinking*, pp. 22–3.

48 Job, *Rethinking*, pp. 42–3.

49 Job, *Rethinking*, pp. 16–17.

50 Cf. Appasamy, A. J., 1970, *The Theology of Hindu Bhakti*, Madras: CLS.

51 Appasamy, A. J., 1952, 'Christological Reconstruction and Ramanuja's Philosophy', *The International Review of Missions*, vol. 41, no. 162, pp. 170–6.

52 Appasamy, A. J., 1942, *The Gospel and India's Heritage*, London and Madras: SPCK, pp. 256–8, 75–93.

53 Swami Abhishiktananda, 1974, *Saccidananda: A Christian Approach to Advaitic Experience*, Delhi: ISPCK; 1969, *Hindu–Christian Meeting Point: Within the Cave of the Heart*, Bombay and Bangalore: Institute of Indian Culture and CISRS.

54 Abhishiktananda, *Saccidananda*, pp. 43, 174.

55 *Ibid*., pp. 98, 103, 109, 117, 135.

56 *Ibid*., pp. 103–4, 124, 130; Abhishiktananda, *Hindu–Christian*, p. 84; 1967, *Prayer*, Delhi: ISPCK, p. 3.

57 Abhishiktananda, *Saccidananda*, pp. 167–70.

58 *Ibid*., pp. 79–80, 82, 88, 91, 95, 97, 98, 176–9, 184–5; Abhishiktananda, *Meeting Point*, pp. xvi, 80, 96–7.

59 Panikkar, Raimundo (ed.), 1998, 'Abhishiktananda: Ascent to the Depth of the "Heart"', in *The Spiritual Diary (1948–1973) of Swami Abhishiktananda (Dom H. Le Saux), A Selection*, Fleming, David, and Stuart, James (trans.), Delhi: ISPCK, pp. 63, 73, 109, 124, 268, 388.

60 Stuart, James, 1989, *Swami Abhishiktananda: His Life Told Through His Letters*, Delhi: ISPCK, pp. 293, 294, 305, 306, 317, 318, 321, 329, 342, 346, 348, 350, 353.

61 Griffiths, Bede, 1983, *The Marriage of East and West*, London: Fount; 1987, *Return to the Centre*, London: Fount.

62 Panikkar, Raimundo, 1981, *The Unknown Christ of Hinduism: Towards an Ecumenical Christophany*, rev. and enlarged edn, London: Darton, Longman & Todd, p. 164.

63 Panikkar, 1968, *Unknown*, reprint, p. 137.

64 *Ibid*., pp. 125, 128, 129.

65 Panikkar, 1981, *Unknown*, pp. 159–60.

66 Panikkar, Raimundo, 1987, 'The Jordan, the Tiber, and the Ganges: Three Kairological Moments of Christic Self-consciousness', in Hick, John, and Knitter, Paul F. (eds), *The Myth of Christian Uniqueness: Toward a Pluralistic Theology of Religions*, Maryknoll: Orbis, pp. 92, 113–14; 1973, 'The Meaning of Christ's Name in Universal Economy of Salvation', in Pathrapankal, Joseph (ed.), *Service and Salvation, Nagpur Theological Conference on Evangelization*, Bangalore: TPI, pp. 258–9, 262–3; 1991, 'Indian Christian Theology of Religious Pluralism from the Perspective of Interculturation', in Pathil, Kuncheria (ed.), *Religious Pluralism: An Indian Christian Perspective*, Delhi: ISPCK, p. 292.

67 Devanandan, P. D., 1950, *The Concept of Maya: An Essay in Historical Survey of the Hindu Theory of the World (with special reference to the Vedanta)*, London: Lutterworth Press, p. 227.

68 Devanandan, P. D., 1958, *The Gospel and the Hindu Intellectual: A Christian Approach*, Bangalore: CISRS, pp. 23–7; 1959, *The Gospel and Renascent Hinduism*, IMC Research Pamphlets no. 8, London: SCM Press, pp. 57–9; Devanandan, Nalini, and Thomas, M. M. (eds), 1964, *Preparation for Dialogue: A Collection of Essays*

on Hinduism and Christianity in New India, Devanandan Memorial Volume no. 2, Bangalore: CISRS, pp. 39–40, 164–8.

69 Devanandan, *Preparation*, p. 38.

70 *Ibid.*, p. 170; Devanandan, P. D., 1961, *Christian Concern in Hinduism*, Bangalore: CISRS, p. xi.

71 Singh, Surjit, 1961, *Christology and Personality*, Philadelphia: Westminster Press, pp. 19, 139, 140, 141, 143–51, 151–8.

72 *Ibid.*, pp. 155, 158, 159, 162–3.

73 Singh, Surjit, 1981, *A Philosophy of Integral Relation (Samyagdarsna)*, Indian Christian Thought Series, no. 15, Madras and Bangalore: CLS and CISRS, pp. 32–4.

74 *Ibid.*, pp. 34–5, 39.

75 Pluralistic Inclusivism is a perspective in the theology of religions that holds each religious faith to be pluralistically inclusive. That is, on the one hand each living faith is truly pluralistic in relation to other faiths and on the other hand each is inclusivist such that each is fulfilled in and through the contributions of other living faiths. Cf. Aleaz, K. P., 1990, 'Religious Pluralism and Christian Witness: A Biblical-Theological Analysis', *Bangalore Theological Forum*, vol. 21, no. 4, and vol. 22, no. 1, pp. 48–67; 1993, *Harmony of Religion: The Relevance of Swami Vivekananda*, Calcutta: Punthi Pustak, pp. 154–65; 1998, *Theology of Religions: Birmingham Papers and Other Essays*, Calcutta: Moumita, pp. 168–99.

76 For a detailed study on Shankara's thought, see Aleaz, K. P., 1996, *The Relevance of Relation in Sankara's Advaita Vedanta*, Delhi: Kant.

77 Aleaz, K. P., 1997, *An Indian Jesus from Sankara's Thought*, Calcutta: Punthi Pustak, pp. 33–102.

78 *Ibid.*, pp. 105–62.

79 Cf. Aleaz, K. P., 2000, *A Convergence of Advaita Vedanta and Eastern Christian Thought*, Delhi: ISPCK.

12

Buddhism: Two Essential Movements of the Human Spirit?

ELIZABETH J. HARRIS

Introduction

At his enlightenment, Buddhists believe that the historical Buddha, Siddhartha Gautama, awoke to Truth. He saw what undergirds the cosmos, just as numerous other Buddhas had done in previous aeons of time. He then taught for over 40 years, beginning a new movement within the religious landscape of north-east India in the fifth century BCE.[1] After his death the movement spread across north India, into what is now Pakistan and then into Central Asia. By the first century CE, it was travelling along the Silk Road to China. In the fourth century it reached Korea, and in the sixth century, Japan. It also spread south. It was formally adopted in the north-west of Sri Lanka in the third century BCE and from Sri Lanka spread to Burma, Thailand, Cambodia and Indonesia.[2] It was not until the seventh century CE that it crossed the Himalayas into Tibet.

Northern India in the fifth century BCE was undergoing social, economic and religious change. Fortified cities were growing; social patterns were shifting. Conflict between rival kingdoms, and between these kingdoms and independent republics, caused periodic wars. And there was vigorous debate about the meaning of life. Broadly speaking, there were two main religious groupings: a brahminical tradition that placed emphasis on correct ritual and sacrifice and a 'wanderer' tradition of spiritual seeker/teachers, who left family commitments to pursue freedom for the soul or insight into truth and who drew groups of supporters around them. The Buddha and his followers were part of the latter. Each group within this religious patchwork had to gain patronage from lay people in order to survive, leading to inevitable competition.

What the Buddha 'saw' at his enlightenment, therefore, had to be earthed through debate with other religious groups. Early Buddhism, in fact, cannot be understood properly unless its debates with Brahminism and other 'wanderer' traditions – the followers of Mahāvīra, for instance, from whom today's Jains developed – are taken into account.[3]

The Buddha's core message was: 'The way you see the world is wrong. If you want to bring an end to the pain and unsatisfactoriness in your life, change the way you see and act.' So, in a context where some Brahmins stressed that correct religious ritual was necessary for a harmonious society, the Buddha encouraged his disciples to uproot greed and hatred from their minds through meditation and the practice of loving kindness. Where the followers of Mahāvīra taught that every action (*karma*), even involuntary ones, had a positive or negative fruit that had to be worn away through austerities, the Buddha taught that it was the motivation that was important. Volition was action. So killing an insect could only have negative fruit if the killing was intended. Asceticism was pointless if not accompanied with work on the mind and the heart. Then, in a society stratified by caste, the Buddha taught that people should be judged by their deeds not their birth.

After the Buddha's death, the debates continued, both within the Buddhist community and with groups outside it. Within Buddhism, between 80 and 90 years after the death of the Buddha, the first major division occurred, over monastic discipline rather than doctrine. Others followed. Then, between the first century BCE and the second century CE, some new discourses (Pāli *sutta*; Sanskrit *sutras*), attributed to the Buddha, appeared in India, probably within Buddhist monastic communities, around which what is now called Mahayana Buddhism grew – a movement that built on older teachings about compassion and emptiness, but offered Buddhism a new goal and vision.[4]

As Buddhism spread out of India, further change came as it encountered the religious practices of the countries it reached. Rarely did Buddhist 'missionaries' condemn these practices outright, preferring co-option or co-existence. So the gods and spirits of nature religions were made servants of the Buddha, and what Peter Harvey has called 'an open frontier' was established with traditions such as Confucianism, Daoism and Shinto.[5] The result is that Buddhism in Sri Lanka appears different from Buddhism in Japan, and Buddhism in China is different from Buddhism in Tibet. Further changes occurred as Buddhists adapted and responded to European domination of Asia from the sixteenth to twentieth centuries, and again when Buddhism became a religion of Europe and America in the twentieth century.

Christian encounters with Buddhism, therefore, have been diverse, conditioned by geographical, cultural and historical factors. This chapter will take a contextual approach. First, it will look at the history of Christian–Buddhist relations beginning with the early years of Christianity and the claim that Buddhism influenced Christianity at source. Then, using Japan, Sri Lanka, Burma and Britain as examples, it will turn to later centuries and to three tendencies that have surfaced again and again in Christian–Buddhist relations: adaptation to the point of fusion; demarcation and polemic; sympathetic observation.[6] Lastly, it will turn to themes and theories within the last 60 years of Christian–Buddhist relations.

Looking at History

Since the nineteenth century, when Buddhist texts became more easily available in the West, the assertion has periodically been made that Buddhism must have influenced Christianity because of the number of parallels between the stories of Jesus in the Gospels and those of the Buddha; or, conversely, that Christianity influenced the development of Buddhism in its Mahayana form. For instance, Simeon's prophecy in Luke 2.25–35 has a striking resemblance to the story of Asita, a wise man who, according to the biographies developed after the Buddha's death, predicted that Prince Siddhartha would become a Buddha and grieves that he will not be alive to hear him teach.[7] As early as 1914, however, Richard Garbe concluded that only a few narratives connected with Jesus, and perhaps the phrase 'wheel of births' in James 3.6, could possibly have had a link, however tenuous, with Buddhism.[8]

Attempts to prove a link between Christianity and Buddhism did not stop after Garbe's work. The evidence has been inconclusive and some of the data offered has been absurdly speculative. Some sort of influence, however, cannot be ruled out. After all, communication between the Mediterranean world and north-western India began with the campaigns of Alexander the Great in the third century BCE, and by c. 200 CE there were Christian communities in north-west India.[9] Perry Schmidt-Leukel believes that the most convincing evidence is for Indian influence on the mystical philosophy of Neoplatonism, which in turn influenced Jewish, Christian and Muslim mysticism, although he stresses that 'all these considerations remain speculative'.[10]

One of the earliest documented Christian recognitions of Buddhism, however, was by Clement of Alexandria (c. 150–c. 215), who wrote something like the following: 'Among the Indians, some follow the instructions of the Buddha, whom they have honoured as a god because of his unusual holiness.'[11] We do not know whether this was based on encounter with Indian Buddhists in Alexandria, but it is possible.

The Tendency towards Fusion

Adaptation to the point of fusion may have started as early as the third century CE with Mani, an Iranian brought up in a Jewish–Christian community and the founder of Manichaeism. He is believed to have preached in India in about 242 and eventually to have brought the Buddha into his creed. It was the Silk Road, however, stretching from Antioch to Beijing, which led to the most remarkable early example of this tendency – in missionaries from the Church of the East (sometimes called the Nestorian Church),[12] when they settled among the Buddhists and Daoists of China, for instance after the monk Alopen arrived in today's Xian in central China in 635 CE.

The missionary methods of the Church of the East were very different from those adopted by Western Christianity in later centuries. As Martin Palmer points out, the Church of the East developed 'an Eastern version of the Christ story and of Christianity',[13] and, in China, sought to communicate this through the spirituality of Daoism and Buddhism. What Palmer calls a 'Taoist Christianity' resulted. Light was thrown on its spirituality when scrolls that spoke of Jesus the Messiah were found among the massive cache of religious manuscripts, mainly Buddhist and Daoist, uncovered at the end of the nineteenth century in a cave in Dunhuang, on the Silk Road.[14]

There is also other evidence of this fusion. The Church of the East sometimes depicted the cross resting on a lotus flower, an important Buddhist symbol of purity. Christian figures have also been found in Buddhist caves in eastern Turkestan, now the Xinjiang autonomous region of China.[15]

'Taoist Christianity' in China did not survive as a separate religion, and the knowledge of Chinese Buddhism and Daoism gained by the Church of the East does not seem to have been passed on to other parts of the Christian family. It was certainly not transmitted to the Western Church, which had little knowledge of Buddhism at this time or into the medieval period, save for occasional references in the writings of explorers and missionaries who reached Buddhist lands, such as the Flemish Franciscan William of Rubrück (c. 1215–c. 1270) and Marco Polo (c. 1254–1324). The situation was compounded by the growth of Muslim empires in Central Asia, which created a barrier between the West and the East. In spite of this, via Arabic and Greek sources, the tendency towards adaptation and fusion can be seen in the appearance, by the medieval period, of a christianized Buddha in the list of saints in the Roman Catholic Church – St Josaphat (a corruption of *bodhisattva*), the son of an Indian King, Josaphat, so the story went, was protected from all evil by his father. He was converted to Christianity through Barlaam (a possible corruption of *bhagavān* or venerable one, another name of the Buddha) and eventually renounced the world as an ascetic. He was added to the Roman martyrology in the sixteenth century, his feast day being 27 November.

In the West, in the nineteenth century, the tendency reappeared, mixed with a heavy dose of romanticism, when some writers with Christian roots encountered the Buddha biography. Edwin Arnold's poem, *The Light of Asia* (1879) had a profound effect on England and other countries in its portrayal of the historical Buddha as a hero who sacrificed *eros*, romantic love, for *agape* (self-sacrificial love for the good of the world).

The Tendency towards Demarcation and Polemic

At the same time as the Church of the East was developing a Daoist Christianity influenced by Buddhism, some Syrian and Persian Christians were stressing the differences between Christianity and Buddhism, such as those surrounding creation or the constitution of the human body – the tendency towards demarcation and polemic.[16] In Europe, this tendency began at the time of European expansionism in the sixteenth and seventeenth centuries, reaching its peak after the birth of independent evangelical missionary societies in Britain in the 1790s. Europe's first in-depth encounter with Buddhism was therefore undergirded by the arrogance that flowed from imperial power.

To illustrate what happened, Sri Lanka and occasionally Burma will be taken as examples. In 1505, the Portuguese reached Sri Lanka and gradually extended their power over the island until they were in control of a belt of land that stretched right around the coast. Sri Lankan Buddhists remember them today for their destruction of Buddhist temples. A large mural depicting the Portuguese hacking down the Kelaniya temple, a pilgrimage site with political importance, hangs on the wall of the rebuilt temple, reminding pilgrims of past 'Christian' aggression. Some Portuguese also wrote about Buddhism. One of the most detailed accounts was written by Fernao De Queyroz (1617–88), a Portuguese Jesuit who lived in India for 53 years. In a massive work completed in 1686, but not published until long afterwards,[17] he wrote:

> The fact is the Devil has forestalled everything . . . if we preach to those of further India and of Ceylon (for this Sect has disappeared from many parts of India wherein it began), they reply that their Buddum or their Fo or their Xaka also took the shape of a man, though he was an eternal being . . .[18]

De Queyroz, therefore, was convinced that Buddhism was false and had to give way to Christianity. If the two religions possessed similarities, it was because the devil was preventing non-Christians from seeing Christianity's truth.

In the Dutch period that followed from the 1660s, Buddhists learnt to show outward acceptance of Christianity while continuing to go to their nearest *vihāra* (lit. living place, a place where Buddhist monks live), as everyone working in government service under the Dutch in Sri Lanka had to be baptized. The demarcation of Buddhism from Christianity, therefore, continued under the Dutch, although some Europeans sought a more objective understanding of Buddhism at this time.

The British were the next dominant power in Sri Lanka, arriving in the 1790s, bringing British soldiers, civil servants, planters and evangelical Christian missionaries to the island. It was the missionaries, and some civil servants who sympathized with them, who perpetuated the tendency to polemic. Some engaged in a form of dialogue with Buddhists in a wish to know, to categorize and to understand what they sought to undermine. Others studied the Sinhala and Pāli languages in order to master Buddhism's holy texts. By the end of the nineteenth century, the missionary representation of Buddhism condemned the religion as atheistic, pessimistic and morally corrupt – a religion of darkness. Against the background of positive interest in Buddhism in the West, some also pointed to the difference between textual Buddhism and the popular Buddhism of the villagers, with its belief in gods and demons. Of the Buddhist transcendent reality, *nirvāna*, for instance, the Methodist missionary Robert Spence Hardy (1803–68) could write, in one of his later, more polemical works:

> These are the characteristics of nirwána. That which is void, that has not existence, no continuance, neither birth nor death, that is subject to neither cause nor effect, and that possesses none of the essentialities of being, must be the cessation of existence, nihilism, or non-entity. Thus dark is the pall thrown by ignorant man over his own destiny; but the thought is too sad to be dwelt upon, and we turn away from its painful associations.[19]

From Constance Gordon Cumming (1837–1924), aristocratic traveller and sympathizer with the Anglican Church Missionary Society, came this:

> The Buddhist Gospel of Misery teaches that all is vanity and all is suffering, and that complete cessation of craving for existence is the only cessation of suffering, and therefore the one thing to strive after.[20]

Others, such as the Oxford-educated bishop of Colombo, Reginald Stephen Copleston (1845–1925), could admit that much within Buddhism was praiseworthy but, in his major book, *Buddhism Primitive in Magadha and Ceylon* (1892), nevertheless presented it as an anti-intellectual religion that encouraged its followers to develop disgust towards life.[21] A Buddhist could later say of him that he would 'fully and freely admire the luxuriance of the leaves and the flowers, only to deliberately lay the axe at the very root of the tree'.[22] Of the same ilk was Bishop Bigandet, in Rangoon, who, like Copleston, combined affirmation with a cut to the root. In the Preface to the first edition of *The Life or Legend of Gaudama*, he wrote this:

> Though based upon capital and revolting errors, Buddhism teaches a surprising number of the finest precepts and purest moral truths. From the abyss of its almost unfathomable darkness it sends forth rays of the brightest hue.[23]

One of the consequences of this European Christian encounter with Buddhism was Buddhist revival. Archival evidence suggests that Buddhist monks in Sri Lanka at first sought peaceful coexistence with Christian missionaries from Britain. When it became obvious that this was the last thing the missionaries wanted, the Buddhists rose in defence of their religion.[24] The tragedy for Christian–Buddhist relations was that their defence was predicated on condemnation of Christianity. Eventually the accusations that the missionaries threw at Buddhism were all thrown back at Christianity. For instance, at a debate between Christians and Buddhists, held in 1873 at Panadura, the Buddhist contender, the Venerable Mohoṭṭivattē Guṇānanda, sought to prove, using biblical quotes, that the object of Christian worship was, in fact, a devil.[25]

Sympathetic Observation and Academic Study

To Christians, however, who showed no contempt towards Buddhism, Buddhists were lavish in their openness and courtesy. Willem Falck, one of the Dutch Governors, was one of these.[26] So also was Robert Knox (1641–1720), who, although a British prisoner between 1660 and 1679 in the Kandyan Kingdom – the part of Sri Lanka that remained independent until 1815 – received much hospitality from those he lived among. Knox's account of his experience, published in 1681, gives a detailed and not unsympathetic account of popular Buddhism.[27] He praised the way Buddhists gave to the monks, refused to harm animals, were generous to the poor and to foreigners, and possessed sobriety, charity and truthfulness. 'It is accounted religion to be *just* and *sober* and *chaste* and *true*, and to be endowed with other virtues, as we do account it,' he claimed.[28]

Some British Christian civil servants consciously sought to contest the missionaries. George Turnour (1799–1843), translator of one of the most important ancient historical chronicles of Sri Lanka, the *Mahāvaṃsa*, was one. Robert Childers (1838–76), compiler of an influential Pali Dictionary, and Thomas William Rhys Davids (1843–1922), founder of the Pali Text Society in 1881, were others.[29] Less well known is John Frederick Dickson, who came to Sri Lanka in 1859 as a civil servant, learnt Pāli and explored Buddhism in practice, particularly the ceremonies connected with the monastic community. He wrote this about the life of the Buddhist people:

> It [Buddhism] lives enshrined in the hearts of a pious, simple and kindly people; it leads them through a life of charity to a peaceful deathbed such as most Christians may envy. Having conquered desire, they enjoy a repose which cannot be disturbed.[30]

To the missionaries, he declared:

> It is a religion such as this, older than Christianity by many centuries, that certain missionary societies seek to subvert by means of agents of imperfect education, married, ordained indeed, but in their regard for their own comfort and for domestic luxury, anything but what a missionary should be. Is it a matter of wonder that they have no success? The Buddhist seeks not to make converts, but he will not be converted – certainly not by men who in education and in self-denial compare unfavourably with the celibate Buddhist monks and with the celibate priests of the Church of Rome.[31]

In Burma, which came under full British control only in 1885, worthy of note are the sensitive and surprisingly accurate words of Francis Buchanan (1762–1829), an employee of the East India Company, who published a compilation of writings on Buddhism as early as 1799.[32]

The Twentieth and Twenty-First Centuries: Themes and Theories

The missionaries who travelled to countries such as Sri Lanka and Burma adopted a no-compromise attitude towards Buddhism. Converts to Christianity had to reject their former beliefs completely and utterly. Theirs was a stereotypically exclusivist viewpoint. It is an approach that has continued to the present in some Christian writings.

The scholarly approach seen in Robert Childers, who entered in-depth dialogue with Buddhist scholar monks in Sri Lanka, has also continued, as has the romantic, inclusivist interest that Arnold's poem generated. In fact, Buddhist–Christian relationships in the twentieth and twenty-first centuries both continued and contested what came before. New patterns of fusion, demarcation and sympathetic observation arose.

The following themes in Christian–Buddhist relationships will be taken as case studies to draw out what has most excited and challenged Christians in their relationship with Buddhism in the last hundred years:

- Silence as a place of meeting.
- Redressing the polemic of the past.
- A dialogue of social engagement.
- Reconciling and interrogating differences through dialogue.

Silence as a Place of Meeting

At the turn of the nineteenth century, a new Buddhist movement was beginning in Japan, which was to lead to the founding of the Kyoto School. Key to this was Nishida Kitarō (1870–1945), who sought to reconcile

Mahayana Buddhism, particularly its concept of emptiness or no-thingness, with Christian-influenced Western philosophy as seen in Hegel and Kant. Hegel believed that when human beings came to full awareness of themselves, they saw themselves as pure or absolute Spirit, which he linked with the consciousness of God. Kitarō paralleled this with a Mahāyāna Buddhist idea, largely from the Zen tradition: that there is a place of absolute nothingness, realizable through meditation, which is the place of salvation. It was a place where duality broke down and where nothingness became fullness. Some members of the school were actually willing to use the word God, not as Supreme Being, but as absolute being in absolute nothingness.

The Kyoto School became central in the development of Zen as a system in which Christians could immerse themselves without losing their identities as Christians; for parallels could be made between the place where nothingness became fullness and God (the latter as seen through the lens of apophatic theology, which stresses the inadequacy of language to say anything about God, except through negatives). With such parallels, one could be truly Christian and yet practise Zen. Two pioneers of Zen for Christians were Jesuits: H. M. Enomiya Lasalle, a German, and J. Kachiri Kadowaki.[33] Others have followed, for instance Elaine MacInnes, Catholic nun and Zen Master – her book on Zen for Christians has gone through several editions – and Pierre de Béthune, Belgian monk and pioneer of intermonastic dialogue.[34] In the United States, Christianity's early dialogue with Buddhism was much influenced by the Kyoto School. D. T. Suzuki (1870–1966), one of the key people in the transmission of Zen to the West, was a friend of Kitarō's.

Many but not all of the Christians who immersed themselves in Zen were monastics. Parallel to the effect of the Kyoto School on Christian encounter with Buddhism was the development of intermonastic dialogue, which offered another place of meeting through silence. Encounter between Buddhist and Christian monastics may go back to the early years of Christian monasticism, as Buddhism stretched into Central Asia and met Eastern Christian traditions. Formal intermonastic dialogue, however, started only in the twentieth century. Thomas Merton (1915–68), a Trappist monk, was the pioneer. His call was for an international, interreligious monastic encounter. He died tragically in Bangkok at a meeting of 'L'Aide à l'implantation monastique' (AIM), an international network of groups involved in Buddhist–Christian intermonastic dialogue. But his vision did not die. Two series of Spiritual Exchanges started, one between European and Zen monks and nuns; the other between Tibetan monks and nuns and American Christian monastics. Committees for intermonastic dialogue were set up to pioneer this, the first two in America and France. Now, intermonastic dialogue is present in almost every part of the world, with the regular production of newsletters and books.[35]

The Spiritual Exchanges benefited both Christians and Buddhists, but an asymmetry has been present. On the whole, Christians, as the initiators of this dialogue, have benefited more. On the Buddhist side, there has been surprise that Christianity has possessed such depth. Venerable Karma Pema Tsultrim, for instance, a nun born in Sikkim, wrote this of her experience of nunneries in America:

> I feel really fortunate to have been allowed to share in the monastic life and spirituality of the Benedictines of Annunciation Priory. I have learned much through seeing and experiencing their mode of life, a blend of prayer to God and service to others. I recognize many similarities between Buddhism and Christianity, and that there is also a depth in Christianity which I had not suspected.[36]

The writings of the German Dominican Meister Eckhart (1260–1328), the Spanish Carmelite St John of the Cross (1542–91) and the more contemporary British mystic Evelyn Underhill (1875–1941) have also appealed to some Buddhists.

The Christian response has been more effusive, touching on the very heart of Buddhist doctrine. Thomas Merton, already experienced in Christian–Buddhist intermonastic dialogue, could write this after experiencing the colossal images of the Buddha carved into rock at the Gal Vihara in Polonnaruwa in Sri Lanka, 'The rock, all matter, is charged with *dharmakāya*[37] . . . everything is emptiness and everything is compassion.'[38]

Peter Bowe of Douai Abbey near Reading in England wrote this when reflecting on his 20 years of intermonastic and interfaith dialogue:

> At the early morning meditation of an interfaith retreat about ten years ago at Amaravati, a Theravada monastery in Britain, we were seated together before a large, golden image of the Buddha. I felt I was seated before Christ, and yet for a moment I had the clear intuition that the figure of the Buddha and the figure of the Christ were overlapping. Do the Buddha, the Purusha and the cosmic Christ in some indefinable way overlap? I do not know, but I hope they do.[39]

He went on to say that, although being open to other faiths does not mean syncretism or sinking differences, it does mean avoiding judging which is the best or superior faith.

Moving wider than the Christian practice of Zen and intermonastic dialogue, some Christians, lay and ordained, have been attracted by other Buddhist methods of meditation. Two methods central to Theravāda Buddhism and some Mahayana forms are *samatha* or tranquillity meditation and *vipassanā* or insight meditation. In *samatha*, the meditator concentrates on an object such as the breath to concentrate the mind and gain a one-pointedness that can lead to states of higher consciousness. In *vipassanā* the meditator aims at insight into the nature of existence. One form of *vipassanā* involves giving 'bare attention' to what arises in the mind and the heart. For Buddhists, it can lead to seeing how real the three characteristics of existence are: impermanence, unsatisfactoriness and non-self. For when the mind and heart are watched, it becomes obvious that thoughts and feelings forever change and cannot be controlled. They are completely impermanent. And if they are impermanent, where is the self? Even where Christians have found the doctrine of non-self difficult, some have still valued *vipassanā* as a way of gaining greater awareness into how their minds work – how negative responses, for instance, based on selfishness, greed and hatred, arise. *Vipassanā* can open a window on to what lies deep within the human person. Buddhist meditation techniques have complemented Christian prayer:

> Where I most clearly discovered complementarity between Buddhism and Christianity was in the experience of meditation. Meditation in the Theravāda Buddhist tradition is a mental culture. It is rooted in the conviction that the cause of our dis-ease, the cause of the world's fatal love affair with greed and hatred, lies in our minds. Buddhist meditation is a journey towards discernment, if we may use a Christian word – discernment of the ways in which our minds and hearts have been conditioned since birth. Of course Christianity has its aids towards this goal. But Buddhism has taught me just how much work on the mind is necessary, and it has also given me a method that works.[40]

Redressing the Polemic of the Past

In 1969, Tissa Balasuriya, OMI, a Sri Lankan Roman Catholic priest and liberation theologian, in an article published in a major newspaper, publicly expressed sorrow for the past failure of the Church to relate well to Buddhists and called on Catholics to live in sincere respect towards them.[41] It did not gain the response he expected. For as well as expressing sorrow for the past, he claimed that he believed the Buddha was in communion with God. This inclusivist statement touched a raw nerve among Sri Lankan Buddhists, because it projected on to Buddhism a Christian category that they did not want to own. For some Buddhists, this revealed the ongoing arrogance of Christians. A lively exchange of letters in the press resulted. Balasuriya's letter, however, was a significant attempt to redress the past.

Balasuriya was one of a group of Sri Lankan Christian priests, who, aware that Buddhists had inherited a mistrust of Christianity from the colonial past, began to chart a new path for Christian–Buddhist relationships. Yohan Devananda, influenced by the Indian Christian ashram movement, started a Christian community in 1957 called Devasaranaramaya, with a spirituality intended to be in harmony with Buddhist culture. Meditation, vegetarianism and simplicity of lifestyle were practised, and links were made with local Buddhist temples. The publication to mark its first ten years stated this at the very beginning:

> St John, in the fourth Gospel, calls that light (the Light of Christ) 'the real light that lightens every man'. By this he means that it is not a light that is confined to a particular people, a particular place, or a particular age, but illuminates the whole of mankind.
>
> So Christians may expect to find the truth or at least part of it wherever they go. They may gladly acknowledge it and serve it wherever they find it. We may, for instance, rejoice unaffectedly at the contribution of the Buddha, the Dharma and the Sangha, to the spiritual nurture of Lanka through the centuries, and make common cause with our Buddhist brethren in diverse fields of service.[42]

Lynn de Silva was a Methodist minister who learnt Pāli and became an eminent scholar of Buddhism. At the same time as Devananda was setting up the ashram, he was calling for an intellectual, courteous dialogue with Buddhists about the differences and similarities between the two religions, and he helped to set up a centre in Colombo to make this possible – now called the Ecumenical Centre for Study and Dialogue. His books exploring the two religions are still authoritative, written in Sinhala and English, tackling questions such as the problem of the self in Buddhism and Christianity.[43]

Two others must also be mentioned: Aloysius Pieris, SJ (b. 1934) and Michael Rodrigo, OMI (1927–87). A chapter such as this cannot do justice to them. Both completed doctorates in Buddhist Studies. Both immersed themselves in Buddhism and called others to do so. Pieris was, in fact, the first Christian to obtain a Ph.D. in Buddhism at a Sri Lankan university. His first call to Christians in Sri Lanka was that they should immerse themselves in the waters of Asian spirituality and Asian poverty in order to be truly Christian. He spoke of a church humble enough 'to be baptized by its precursors in the Jordan of Asia and bold enough to be baptized by oppressive systems on the cross of Asian poverty'.[44] From this flowed a waterfall of other insights and hundreds of articles. His conviction continues to be that Buddhism and Christianity are two essential movements of the human spirit. They have different core experiences – self-sacrificial love in Christianity, and wisdom or awakening in Buddhism – but need each other as mutual correctives. In this situation, he has stressed, interreligious dialogue is not a luxury but a necessity if the oppressed in society are to be liberated.[45]

Rodrigo, in his early fifties, chose to settle in Alukalavita, an entirely Buddhist village in the south of Sri Lanka, where there was considerable mistrust of Christianity because of colonial history. He set up a small community, whose aim was not to create a church but to change the attitudes of the Buddhists towards Christianity, by being a supportive presence among the people. After almost seven years of devoted service, he was shot, in October 1987, as he was saying Mass. His killers have never been named, but they were not of the village. By the time he died, he had succeeded: the view of the villagers towards Christianity had changed from mistrust to trust.[46] Among his words about the relationship between Buddhism and Christianity were these:

> Buddhism and Christianity must grow together. This demands a radical self-emptying. The *kenosis* of the Jesus Community of today, drawn from Jesus' self-emptying must be matched with the selflessness, *anatta* of the Buddha sasana community of today as closely as possible, for unless there is this basic human trait operative in religion and society, there is no truly human.[47]

A Dialogue of Social Engagement

Buddhism is not a religion of social withdrawal. It places loving kindness and compassion at the centre. It has nurtured a theory of governance that stresses the need for social justice and has inspired remarkable acts of political witness. The first encounter some Westerners may have had with Buddhism was seeing Venerable Thich Quang Duc burning himself to death at a downtown crossroads in Saigon on 11 June 1963 in protest against the repression of Buddhism under the Diem regime.[48] In Sri Lanka, Venerable Walpola Rahula started a vigorous debate in the monastic community when, in 1946, he wrote, *Bhikṣuvagē Urumaya* (*The Heritage of the Bhikkhu*), which argued that it was the duty of monks to liberate their country, nation and religion.[49]

Buddhism sees the world as shot through with greed, hatred and ignorance. To quote one Pāli text, it is 'smothered, enveloped, tangled like a ball of thread, covered as with blight, twisted up like a grass-rope' with craving, *taṇhā*.[50] Except for some spiritually advanced people who can choose their rebirth, all humans find themselves in this world, according to Buddhism, because their minds and hearts are not free of the craving that causes injustice, oppression and violence. All Buddhists would add, though, that this same human birth is a precious opportunity to root out these poisons. Some would go further and say that working on oneself is not enough by itself, addressing what causes suffering in others is necessary.

A resonance is present between this view of the world and the Christian insight that most humans are alienated from God because of their self-centredness. Yet, some Christians have not seen this, feeling a sense of alienation from the perceived individualism of Buddhism. For in the mid-twentieth century, a stereotype of Buddhism as a passive religion, concerned only with withdrawal from the world, circulated. 'Where was the cutting edge in a violent world?' 'Where was the passion to change the world?' some Christians asked. The image of a tortured Jesus on the cross was more challenging in an unjust world than the peaceful face of the Buddha.

Other Christians, however, have found common cause with those Buddhists who have challenged a purely individualistic interpretation of their faith. Sulak Sivaraksa (b. 1933), a Siamese Buddhist (he refuses to call himself Thai), has been one of these. He has consistently argued for the social dimension of Buddhism. When interviewed for the BBC, recalling his time in Britain as a student, he shared this:

> In Britain, I joined the Buddhist Society formed by Mr Christmas Humphreys and he said that western Buddhists must be concerned only about personal transformation. Let the Christians deal with society. Let the politicians deal with society. I felt this was escapism, not Buddhism – or certainly not the whole aspect of Buddhism. When I came home, I was very concerned about this.[51]

Sulak Sivaraksa together with Thich Nhat Hanh (b. 1926), a Vietnamese Buddhist monk and Zen master, founded the International Network of Engaged Buddhists in 1989. Thich Nhat Hanh has always recognized a debt to Christianity. As Sivaraksa, he also travelled to the West – to America at the time of the Vietnam War, sponsored by the Fellowship of Reconciliation. Political conditions meant that he could not return. In America, Western Christians such as Thomas Merton, Daniel Berrigan and Martin Luther King were profoundly influenced by him, and influenced him in return. Nhat Hanh wrote of them later: 'These were, in fact, the Americans I found it easiest to communicate with.'[52]

Christian feminists such as Rosemary Radford Ruether have also found common cause with Buddhist feminists. In 1999, in Ohio, Ruether co-presented a workshop on religious feminism and the future of the planet with the Buddhist feminist Rita Gross. They had known each other for some time and engaged in a structured dialogue on the oppressive and liberating aspects of religion. Neither was afraid to be self-critical; neither was afraid to speak about painful personal experiences of religion.[53]

Reconciling and Interrogating Differences Through Dialogue

In some areas of doctrine and belief, Christianity and Buddhism may seem poles apart. Buddhism does not place a creating and sustaining God at the centre, most Buddhists claiming that Buddhism is non-theistic. In many forms of Buddhism, rebirth is central, as is the conviction that liberation comes through personal effort, not through the actions of another. But how deep are the differences? Do the touching points outweigh them? In the last half-century, a variety of formal dialogues have addressed these questions.

De Silva has already been mentioned in his search for an intellectual dialogue in Sri Lanka in the 1960s and 1970s. In Japan, a similar institution to the one founded by de Silva was founded in 1976, the Nanzan Institute for Religion and Culture. Then, in 1980, the East West Religions Project began at the University of Hawai'i Department of Religion, championed by the Buddhist scholar David Chappell (1940–2004). International Buddhist–Christian conferences followed: Honolulu (1980), Hawai'i (1984), Berkeley (1987). Inspired by these, regional initiatives arose, such as the Japan Society for Buddhist–Christian Studies and the well-known North American Buddhist–Christian theological encounter group under Masao Abe of the Kyoto School and John Cobb, Jr. The 1987 Conference gave birth to the Society for Buddhist–Christian Studies, which aimed to facilitate worldwide Buddhist–Christian dialogue. About every four years it continues to hold an international conference on a theme that is wide enough to generate diverse discussions and presentations. It also publishes an excellent annual journal, *Buddhist–Christian Studies*, as well as occasional books.

Europe developed parallel initiatives. Voies de L'Orient (Ways of the East) was founded in Belgium in 1980 to educate Christians about the spirituality of Indian religious traditions, including Buddhism. In February 1996, a meeting of European Christians involved in the study of Buddhism was organized by the Revd Gerhard Köberlin at the mission academy of the University of Hamburg. This resulted in the formation of a European Network for Christian Studies of Buddhism, which then became the European Network of Buddhist–Christian Studies. The Network through its biennial conferences has chosen to focus on specific themes, particularly those where Buddhism and Christianity would appear to differ, such as the significance of Jesus and creation.[54] In addition to these collective initiatives, individuals such as James Fredericks and Robert Elinor have struggled to find paradigms for comparison and contrast, Fredericks through 'comparative theology' and Elinor through drawing parallels in the representation of the Buddha and Jesus through iconography.[55]

Concluding Thoughts

The historical part of this chapter identified three tendencies in Christian–Buddhist relationships: adaptation to the point of fusion – an inclusivist tendency; demarcation and polemic – an exclusivist tendency; and sympathetic observation. Each offers a way of dealing with difference. All three tendencies continued into the twentieth and twenty-first centuries. As the case studies that have been given show, however, other ways of dealing with difference emerged. Five are particularly significant: affirmation and respect for both touching points and differences; the use of Buddhist beliefs and practices to throw light on Christianity; recognition of Buddhism and Christianity as two essential and complementary movements of the human spirit; seeing the Buddha and the Christ as inflections of one archetype; the conviction that the apparent differences between Christianity and Buddhism can be lessened through dialogue.

The first is rooted in the belief that an injustice is done to Buddhism and Christianity if differences are not recognized. Respect must be given to the fact that most Christians do not believe in rebirth and that most Buddhists do, and that a creator God is central to Christianity but is not to Buddhism. However, in this case, as Peter Bowe pointed out, difference is not taken as proof that Christianity is superior. Belief in God does not make Christianity the superior religion. Belief in rebirth does not make Buddhism superior. The differences simply exist, in dialogue with one another. Some would add that the similarities between the two religions can make them seem less important. The fact, for instance, that both religions stress that selfishness must be eradicated for liberation or salvation to come, or that compassion is central, can override the significance of differences. Others might say that the existence of difference can in itself be creative. It can be a chance for each religion to interrogate itself in the light of the other. The Buddhist concept on non-self, for example, can help Christians understand better what Christianity teaches about the soul.

Similar to the latter is the second way, which is sometimes called comparative theology. James Fredericks has pioneered it in the field of Buddhism. In his book *Buddhists and Christians: Through Comparative Theology to Solidarity*, he takes the Buddhist concept of emptiness as developed by Nāgārjuna, a key philosopher in the development of Mahayana, to throw light on what Aquinas meant when he said that God was incomprehensible. Buddhism, therefore, becomes a resource for Christianity. Dialogue becomes the praxis out of which a revision of Christian theological self-understanding is possible.[56]

The third is seen in the writings of Aloysius Pieris and Michael Rodrigo. Buddhism and Christianity need one another. They are different but complementary and can help each religion to be truly itself. Pieris might go so far as to say that they are stronger together than apart, especially in contexts where the poor need to be empowered. The difference between Pieris and Rodrigo, and Fredericks, is that Buddhism is not seen merely as a resource for the development of Christian theology but as a vital part in the creation of a society liberated from greed and oppression.

The fourth is illustrated in Elinor's book, *Buddha and Christ: Images of Wholeness*, which argues, though looking at depictions of the Buddha and Christ in art, that the Buddha and Jesus are two masks of one transcendental reality or local inflections of a universal archetype. Differences are overlooked and some of the comparisons made are strained, but the argument is a moving one.

The fifth way of dealing with difference is shown in the writings of the pluralist theologian Perry Schmidt-Leukel. Both the Buddha and Jesus are mediators of transcendent reality, according to Schmidt-Leukel. But, since Reality must ultimately be One, Buddhism and Christianity must meet in this one reality. Differences between the two religions exist but can be overcome, if both religions interrogate themselves in the light of the other, and are willing to move towards each other through negotiation and compromise, growing in wisdom in the process.

The five approaches touch and diverge. All of them lie in stark contrast to the exclusivist view that would deny Buddhism salvific value.

These approaches to difference have been undergirded in the last century by two relatively new phenomena: passing over in order to come back and hyphenated identity. The first is an option for immersion. A conscious decision is taken to 'pass over' into another religion by sitting at the feet of teachers of that religion, allowing one's own religious identity to go into hibernation. Aloysius Pieris did this when he was a young priest, living anonymously in a Buddhist monastery. Some of his disciples have followed his example. Most have 'come back' to Christianity, not to exactly the same place – that rarely happens – but with an ability to see the Christian message with new, more creative eyes. Some who have 'passed over', however, have so identified with Buddhism that a single religious identity is no longer possible. The only way forward is to become a Christian-Buddhist or a Buddhist-Christian. This has happened more frequently with Christians who have encountered Zen than other forms of Buddhism.

What will happen within Christian–Buddhist relationships in the future is difficult to predict. The author of this chapter believes, with Aloysius Pieris, that Buddhism can help Christianity be truly itself, and that Christianity may be able to help Buddhism be truly itself. They both represent essential movements within the human spirit. Their meeting is exciting and necessary. The differences between them should not be seen as a threat to the identity of each but as an opportunity for each to give to the other. The differences, though, will probably remain as will the paradoxes connected with them – that is until all of us can see with eyes unclouded by our conditioned humanness.

Study Questions

1. In what ways do the worldviews of Christianity and Buddhism touch each other and in what ways do they conflict? To what extent can the differences between the two religions lead to creative dialogue?
2. What is the purpose of meditation in Buddhism? How far can Buddhist meditation techniques be used by people of other religions?

3 Critically explore the view of Elinor that the Buddha and Jesus are 'two masks of one transcendental reality'.

Further Reading

Fredericks, James L., 2004, *Buddhists and Christians: Through Comparative Theology to Solidarity*, Maryknoll: Orbis.

Gross, Rita M., and Muck, Terry C. (eds), 2000, *Buddhists Talk about Jesus; Christians Talk about the Buddha*, London and New York: Continuum.

Harris, Elizabeth, 2006, *Theravada Buddhism and the British Encounter*, New York: RoutledgeCurzon.

Lai, Whalen, and Bruck, Michael von, 2000, *Christianity and Buddhism: A Multi-Cultural History of Their Dialogue*, Maryknoll: Orbis.

Mitchell, Donald W., and Wiseman, James, OSB (eds), 1999, *The Gethsemani Encounter: A Dialogue on the Spiritual Life by Buddhist and Christian Monastics*, London and New York: Continuum.

Pieris, Aloysius, SJ, 1988, *Love Meets Wisdom: A Christian Experience of Buddhism*, Maryknoll: Orbis.

Schmidt-Leukel, Perry (ed.), 2005, *Buddhism and Christianity in Dialogue: The Gerald Weisfeld Lectures 2004*, London: SCM Press.

Notes

1 Some traditional datings place the Buddha in the sixth century BCE. Twentieth-century research by scholars such as Heinz Bechert and Richard Gombrich has placed him in the fifth century.

2 The reign of the Indian Mauryan King, Asoka (c. 268–239 BCE), is particularly significant. Asoka used the ethics of Buddhism to govern his large empire and sent Buddhist missionaries throughout India, to Sri Lanka and probably to what is now Shan State in Burma.

3 See Gombrich, Richard, 2005, *How Buddhism Began: The Conditioned Genesis of the Early Teachings*, 2nd edn, London: Routledge.

4 A good account of the development of Mahāyāna thought can be found in Williams, Paul, with Tribe, Anthony, 2000, *Buddhist Thought: A Complete Introduction to the Indian Tradition*, London and New York: Routledge, pp. 96–111.

5 Harvey, Peter, 2001, *Buddhism*, London and New York: Continuum, p. 4.

6 I have taken the first two categories from Michael von Brück, in Lai, Whalen, and von Brück, Michael, 2001, *Christianity and Buddhism: A Multi-Cultural History of Their Dialogue*, Maryknoll: Orbis, p. 10. To his two tendencies, I would add a third – sympathetic observation for the purpose of gaining knowledge.

7 This is found in the *Buddhacarita*, a poem written by Aśvaghosa in the second century CE: Canto I, v. 62.

8 See Schmidt-Leukel, Perry, 2005, *Buddhism and Christianity in Dialogue: The Gerald Weisfeld Lectures 2004*, London: SCM Press, p. 2, where he refers to Garbe,

R., 1914, *Indien und das Christentum: Eine Untersuchung religionsgeschichtlicher Zusammenhänge*, Tübingen: J. C. B. Mohr.

9 See Lai and von Brück, *Christianity*, p. 9.

10 Schmidt-Leukel, *Buddhism*, p. 3.

11 His *Stromateis* 1.71.6 quoted in Lai and von Brück, *Christianity*, p. 9n.

12 The heartland of this Church was in what is now Iraq, Iran and Afghanistan, although it stretched to the borders of India and Tibet.

13 Palmer, Martin, 2001, *The Jesus Sutras: Rediscovering the Lost Religion of Taoist Christianity*, London: Judy Piatkus, p. 96.

14 See the International Dunhuang Project; contact the Project at The British Library, 96 Euston Road, London NW1 2DB, or go to http://idp.bl.uk.

15 See Fleming, Kenneth, 2002, *Asian Christian Theologians in Dialogue with Buddhism*, Bern: Peter Lang, p. 40–1.

16 Lai and von Brück, *Christianity*, p. 10.

17 One of the first translations in English was, De Queyroz, 1930 (1688), *The Temporal and Spiritual Conquest of Ceylon*, vol. 1, Perera, S. G. (trans.), Colombo: Government Printer, 1930.

18 De Queyroz, *Temporal*, p. 141.

19 Spence Hardy, Robert, 1866, *The Legends and Theories of the Buddhists Compared with History and Science*, London: Williams and Norgate, p. 174.

20 Cumming, Constance F. Gordon, 1892, *Two Happy Years in Ceylon*, 2 vols, London: William Blackwood and Sons, vol. 2, p. 418, quoted in Harris, Elizabeth, 2006, *Theravada Buddhism and the British Encounter*, New York: RoutledgeCurzon, p. 114.

21 Copleston, Reginald S., 1892, *Buddhism Primitive and Present in Magadha and Ceylon*, London: Longmans, Green and Co. See Harris, *Theravada*, pp. 125–38.

22 Harris, *Theravada*, p. 127, quoting from '"Bishop Copleston on Buddhism": A Review from a Sinhalese Buddhist', *The Buddhist* (Colombo), 17 March 1893, pp. 81–3.

23 Bigandet, P., 1880, *The Life or Legend of Gaudama: The Buddha of the Burmese*, 3rd edn, London: Trubner & Co., p. ix.

24 Accounts of this can be found in Malalgoda, Kitsiri, 1976, *Buddhism in Sinhalese Society 1750–1900: A Study of Religious Revival and Change*, Berkeley: University of California Press; Young, R. F., and Somaratne, G. P. V., 1996, *Vain Debates: The Buddhist–Christian Controversies of Nineteenth Century Ceylon*, publications of the De Nobili Research Library, vol. 23, Vienna: University of Vienna; Harris, *Theravada*.

25 The best analysis of the period of debates is Young and Somaratne, *Vain*.

26 He was Governor of the maritime provinces from 1765 to 1785 and sent questionnaires on Buddhism to prominent monks. See Harris, *Theravada*, p. 171.

27 Knox, Robert, 1681, *An Historical Relation of the Island of Ceylon in the East Indies*, London: Robert Chiswell. Modern editions, including an enlarged edition with additions Knox made after the first publication, have been published by Tisara Prakasakayo in Dehiwala, Sri Lanka.

28 Knox, *Historical*, p. 85.

29 See Harris, *Theravada*, pp. 117–38, for surveys of Rhys Davids' and Childers' contribution to Buddhist studies.

30 Dickson, J. F., 1889, 'Ceylon', *The Illustrated English Magazine* (October),

p. 24, quoted in Harris, *Theravada*, p. 120.

31 See Harris, *Theravada*, p. 1.

32 Buchanan, Francis, 1799, 'On the Religion and Literature of the Burmas', *Asiatick Researches*, vol. 6, pp. 136–308.

33 See Lasalle, Hugo M. Enomiya, 1993, *The Practice of Zen Meditation*, London: Thorsons.

34 See MacInnes, Elaine, 1997, *Light Sitting in Light*, New York: HarperCollins, which was an updated version of an earlier book, *Zen for Christians*; and, de Béthune, Pierre-François, OSB, 2002, *By Faith and Hospitality: The Monastic Tradition as a Model for Interreligious Encounter*, Groves, Mary (trans.), Leominster: Gracewing.

35 Information from the Committees for Monastic Interreligious Dialogue can be found on: www.dimmid.org.

36 *DIM/MID International Bulletin*, 1997.

37 The Truth Body of the Buddha – one of the three bodies of the Buddha in Mahāyāna Buddhism.

38 Quoted from Thomas Merton's *Asian Journal* in Harris, Elizabeth, 1994, *A Journey into Buddhism*, Bodhi Leaf 134, Kandy: Buddhist Publication Society, p. 22.

39 Bowe, Peter, OSB, 2003, 'Deepening Roots of Faith', in *Monastic Experiences of Interreligious Dialogue: 25th Anniversary of the DIM/MID Commissions 1978–2003*, Commissions pour le Dialogue Interreligieux Monastique (DIM) and the Monastic Interreligious Dialogue Commissions (MID), p. 22.

40 Harris, Elizabeth J., 2002, 'The Beginning of Something Being Broken: The Cost of Crossing Spiritual Boundaries', in *Spirituality Across Borders*, *The Way Supplement*, vol. 104, pp. 6–17, at p. 16.

41 Balasuriya, Tissa, 1969, 'Buddhism and Christianity', *Ceylon Daily News*, 24 May.

42 Devasaranaramaya, 1967, *If They Had Met: Devasaranaramaya – The First Ten Years 1957–1967*, Colombo: Wesley Press, p. 3.

43 See de Silva, Lynn, 1968, *Reincarnation in Buddhist and Christian Thought*, Colombo: Christian Literature Society of Ceylon; 1974, *Buddhism: Beliefs and Practices in Sri Lanka*, Colombo: Wesley Press; 1975, *The Problem of the Self in Buddhism and Christianity*, Colombo: Study Centre for Religion and Society.

44 Pieris, Aloysius, SJ, 1988, *Love Meets Wisdom: A Christian Experience of Buddhism*, Maryknoll: Orbis, p. 41.

45 Several collections of Pieris's articles have been published. See n. 44, and also: 1988, *An Asian Theology of Liberation*, Edinburgh: T & T Clark; 1996, *Fire and Water: Basic Issues in Asian Buddhism and Christianity*, Maryknoll: Orbis.

46 Rodrigo told the story of this in: 1993, 'The Hope of Liberation Lessens Man's Inhumanity: A Contribution to Dialogue and Village Level', in Sugirtharajah, R. S. (ed.), *Asian Faces of Jesus*, London: SCM Press, pp. 189–210.

47 'Fr Michael's Rodrigo's Mission in his Own Words', in *Fr Michael Rodrigo: Prophet, Priest and Martyr*, Colombo: Christian Workers' Fellowship, p. 16.

48 See King, Sallie, 2000, 'They Who Burned Themselves for Peace: Quaker and Buddhist Self-Immolators during the Vietnam War', *Buddhist–Christian Studies*, vol. 20, pp. 127–50.

49 For a translation of this see, Rahula, Walpola, 1974, *The Heritage of the Bhikkhu*, Wellampitiya, Sri Lanka: Godage.

50 From the *Aṅguttara Nikāya* of the *Sutta Piṭaka* in the Pāli Canon: ii 213.

51 From the tape of an interview with Sulak Sivaraksa in December 1995, in preparation for a 1996 BBC World Service series on Buddhism, reproduced in Harris, Elizabeth J., 1998, *What Buddhists Believe*, Oxford: Oneworld, p. 100.

52 Hanh, Thich Nhat, 1995, *Living Buddha, Living Christ*, London: Rider, p. 4.

53 Gross, Rita M., and Ruether, Rosemary Radford, 2001, *Religious Feminism and the Future of the Planet: A Buddhist–Christian Conversation*, London and New York: Continuum.

54 See Schmidt-Leukel, Perry (ed.), 2006, *Buddhism, Christianity and the Question of Creation: Karmic or Divine?*, Aldershot: Ashgate.

55 See Fredericks, James L., 2004, *Buddhists and Christians: Through Comparative Theology to Solidarity,* Maryknoll: Orbis; Elinor, Robert, 2000, *Buddha and Christ: Images of Wholeness*, New York: Weatherhill.

56 Fredericks, *Buddhists*, p. 106.

13

Sikhism: From Competition to Co-operation

JOHN PARRY

Introduction

The task of considering a theology of religions in the light of the dialogue with the Sikh faith-tradition is somewhat difficult, since a history of the encounter of Sikhs and Christians is yet to be published. There is a further difficulty in that the number of writers who have contributed to a Christian understanding of Sikhism is small. I propose, therefore, to give a brief outline of the encounter before exploring the theological stances taken by both Western missionaries and Indian Christians.

It would seem that the first account of a meeting between Sikhs and Christians was an exceptionally short comment from Bhai Gurdas (1558–1637), who wrote of the Jesuits present at the court of the Mogul Emperor, Akbar:

> *Isai* (Christians) *Musai* (Jews) *haimaim* (self-centred) *hairane* (confused).[1]

Thus, the opening impressions did not augur for good relationships.

By the mid-1830s, Protestant missions had been established in the Punjab, first by the American Presbyterians and later by the Church Missionary Society (CMS). Sikhs were seen as 'a people who had discarded the idolatry of Hinduism and broken, in some measure, the bonds of caste, and, therefore might be considered to be in a favourable state to be influenced by the preaching of missionaries'.[2] Elsewhere, comments by Elijah Swift, the Americans' mission society secretary, indicated that conversion was the name of the game but not without an indication of his respect for the Sikhs and their lifestyle.

It was among missionaries of the CMS, however, that were to be found clergy who chose to study the faith in greater depth, though sometimes to the dismay of their colleagues who thought such studies should only be undertaken 'as far as leisure permits'. The predominant attitude was that one had to recognize 'the truth of Christianity and the fundamental error of other systems'. 'We ought to rely much on the authentic declarations of inspired truth . . .'[3]

Struggling to be Positive towards Sikhism

By 1862 one CMS missionary, William Keene, had made an attempt to study Sikhism and written a short essay, mainly cribbed from J. D. Cunningham's *A History of the Sikhs*.[4] The title of his essay, 'The Sikhs: All that Can Be Said About Them from a Missionary Point of View', illustrates Keene's conviction of the need to present the Christian faith in the light of the beliefs of his hearers. He acknowledged the deep desire of Guru Nanak to find freedom 'from every earth-born trammel', but maintained that it is 'the Son (who) makes you free'. Like Cunningham, he portrayed Guru Nanak as one who rejected the then current practices of Hinduism, and followed that by a relatively positive presentation of Sikhism: their understanding of the Godhead; their rejection of 'idolatry' and caste; liberation through grace; and, finally, God's forgiveness and the futility of an outward show of religiosity through ceremonial ablutions. He carefully drew a distinction between iconoclastic Sikhism as a reforming faith and 'the gross errors of the popular Hindu belief' in which people 'prostrate (themselves) before senseless stone, and believe the Divine Being to be in such idols'.

Years before J. N. Farquhar (1861–1929) and his colleagues were to suggest Christianity as the fulfilment of other faiths, Keene suggested that such teaching is 'all in favour of the Christian missionary'. Further he pointed out that the Sikh scriptures, *Guru Granth Sahib*, abounded in passages which struck common accord with Christian belief and asked if, like the teaching of Moses and the prophets which was designed by God to prepare the Jewish people, the teaching of Nanak might prepare Sikhs 'for the reception of Christianity'.

CMS did themselves no favours in terms of the establishment of good relations between Sikhs and Christians through their employment in the 1850s and 1860s of Ernest Trumpp, a German Lutheran minister whose arrogance and academic posturing is recalled to this day by Sikh scholars. He had been employed as a linguist to help in the work of providing grammars and dictionaries of modern Indian languages but was also involved in an attempted translation of the *Guru Grant-Sahib*. In the company of Sikh *Granthis* Trumpp explained to the *Granthis* that he knew Sanskrit better than they did (even though the text of the Sikh scriptures is based on the common language of the sixteenth century in the Punjab) and then lit up a cigar as he read the copy of the *Guru Granth Sahib* which lay on a table before him. 'Tobacco being an abomination to the Sikhs, the priests fled in consternation, and left Dr Trumpp to plume himself on his display of learning and originality.'[5]

Beyond Fulfilment Theory

It was, therefore, a distinct contrast to have Edward Guilford arrive in Tarn Taran to answer Keene's call for someone to specialize in evangelization among the Sikhs in the villages of the Punjab. It was the very fact that he lived in close proximity to the Sikhs that forced him not to make any outright rejection of their faith. This may be illustrated by the description he wrote of what was labelled by a CMS Headquarters secretary as a 'strange prayer meeting for rain'. In it he recounts what amounts to a multifaith meeting in which Christians, Sikhs, Muslims, Hindus and members of the so-called 'outcaste' community took part, with most offering prayer. Whereas competitive prayer was rife in an attempt to demonstrate the power of one's faith, akin to Elijah and the prophets of Baal, this account, and other writing from Guilford, indicate a man with genuine respect for people of other faith. In his brief introduction to Sikhism, he portrays Guru Nanak as one who provided a *preparatio evangelica* for the Christian missionary through what he called 'gems which may be got from Guru Nanak's teaching':

- The Fatherhood, the love, the mercy, and the justice of God.
- The brotherhood of man [*sic*].
- The necessity of obedience to the inward divine voice.
- The unerring working of divine justice.
- The necessity of a divine Teacher.
- The existence of One who can put away sin.
- The folly and sin of idolatry.[6]

Indicative of his understanding was his conviction that 'the *Shabad* (Word) of the *Granth* is in truth no other than the Eternal Logos'.[7]

A colleague of Guilford was Pandit Walji Bhai, who published *Hari Charitra* or *Comparison Between the Ad Granth and the Bible*.[8] He claimed that Guru Nanak was in reality a Christian who presented Jesus Christ in the Sikh scriptures as *Hari*, the saviour of humankind, the True Teacher.

In the 1920s the greater part of missionary work in the Punjab was among the so-called 'outcaste' or Dalit groups. However, not only Christians, but Sikhs also, were engaged in attempts to attract followers from the same social groups. Sikhism was receiving new converts since it offered a rise in social status without the disadvantage of possible persecution for leaving the Indian tradition.[9] Thus by this time Sikhs and Christians saw each other as competitors. Since most missionaries were involved with the 'mass movement' of Dalits to Christianity, few gave themselves to an attempt to understand the Sikhs. There was one major exception. Clinton Loehlin was an American Presbyterian missionary who must be regarded as playing a most significant role in bringing about an atmosphere of mutual understanding and an appreciation of dialogue between people of the two faiths. He went to the Punjab in 1923 as a Princeton graduate and from then until his retirement 44 years later worked in various parts of the Punjab.

Loehlin's later working life coincided with that of many who contributed to the SCM 'Christian Presence' series, and much of his nature reflects their philosophy.[10] While his work in the Punjab started in the 1920s, his most significant contributions were made after Indian Independence in 1947 when the Church recognized that it existed in a new situation in which the Christian faith was to be distinguished from its past with its association with Western political, economic and cultural aggression. Likewise, in deep humility, many Christians were able to recognize that God had not left 'himself without witness' so that one could approach other faiths in the expectation that the love of God could be discovered in and through others. Though one may disagree with one's partners in dialogue one has to respect their faith and integrity. In his editorial Introduction to William Stewart's *India's Religious Frontier*, Max Warren writes: 'We have to try to sit where they sit, to enter sympathetically into the pains and griefs and joys of their history and see how (they) have determined the premises of their argument. We have, in a word, to be "present" with them.'[11] Loehlin's manner was a fine example of this approach, to the extent that he won many friends among, and was trusted by, the Sikh community and was asked to preach in the Golden Temple.

His period of work covered the time of Independence when millions of people were displaced. But the very evils which were inherent in Partition also brought a new impetus for reconciliation. Since the 1880s when the mass movements of 'outcastes' were searching for a more meaningful place in society, both Sikhs and Christians had tried to attract them into their respective folds. The year 1947 saw many Christians actively supporting Sikh refugees from Pakistan through the work of the mission hospitals. There were, of course, some Christians who continued to maintain old rivalries, but Loehlin was convinced that hostility could not be the attitude Christians should take. He rejected aloofness or separation and wrote of the discontinuity inherent in some of the attitudes of the Tambaram Conference of 1938 that this 'attitude breeds communalism, which is rampant in India. Its dangers were dramatized in the Partition rioting of 1947. Enough of it.'[12]

In Loehlin one sees a missionary who has taken a step beyond the 'fulfilment' theory to an attitude of co-operation. He recognized that some Sikhs may see Christ as a 'True Guru', the 'Sinless Incarnation' but also had to acknowledge the failure of the Church: 'Where is the Sermon on the Mount fulfilled in the Christian Church? With the Sikhs, at any rate, who judge by the fruit of the tree, and who even might claim that Sikhism is the fulfilment of Christianity, being later in time, we might as well abandon fulfilment as an immediate approach, however much we may believe in it as the culmination of all history.'[13] Taking his lead from his friend Archer,[14] a Yale Professor, Loehlin was convinced of the need to venture into the field of co-operation, not knowing what the future would be but leaving that 'in the hands of him whose Will both faiths acknowledge to be the supreme guide in life'.[15] Given that both faiths emphasize the working out of God's purpose within history, Loehlin suggested that the Christian's emphasis must be on a kingdom-centred theology. 'Surely a realm', he wrote, 'where brotherhood, justice and love predominate will appeal to those who daily pray, "Help us to meet those beloved in whose fellowship Thy Name may come to mind . . . By Thy favour may there be welfare for all".'[16]

Indian Christian Voices

Among post-Independence Indian Christians, three evangelical writers have presented Sikhism in a positive, if unfulfilled, light. K.V. Paul Pillai writes of Sikhism as 'one of the most dynamic of all Indian religions . . . (which) comes nearer than all other religions to the concept of one God who reveals Himself through His prophets'.[17] In a similar vein the Inayat Khan[18] attempts to show that similarities between the faiths do exist and considers the purpose of his booklet to be that of proving this to be the case by references to the scriptures of both faiths. E. Ahmad-Shah[19] holds Sikhism in a similarly positive light and, like Pandit Walji Bhai in the last century, he attempts to find references to Christ in the *Guru Granth Sahib*.

Among Indian Christian academics, two figures stand out. Anand Spencer taught in the Punjabi University in Patiala. His Ph.D. thesis gives an indication of his stance. He wrote on the comparison of the Punjabi concept of *shabad* (Word) and Logos, and draws out significant parallels in terms of the Word as divine Word; pre-existent entity; as an idea, eternal, everlasting, pure and as truth, life and light; as power, creative, sustaining, destroying, healing, blessing and cursing; as a vehicle of revelation; as the means and end of salvation; as being of God and as message of God; as teacher or Guru; as divine entity; as Scripture; in relation to worship and devotion; and, finally, he contrasts the Christian understanding, and Sikh rejection, of the Word as divine incarnation in a single human being.

His thesis posits the idea that the concept of the Word should take one beyond the confines of Christian dogma to an understanding of something far wider and more universal:

> The Word represents truth and is not confined to cultural, geographical or traditional boundaries. It does not belong to Christianity or Sikhism as such; it belongs to God. The Word or truth is no one's monopoly. Religions are expressions of a certain comprehension (experience) of the same Reality. But Reality remains transtemporal, above space and time. The Word being Divine Reality is not the exclusive possession of any one religious tradition. It is universal in nature.[20]

Thus, suggests Spencer, there can be no firmer basis for dialogue between the two faiths since a dialogue which takes the 'Word' as a starting point is grounded in mutual understanding. Anticipating objections to this from a Christian perspective he suggests, 'The Bible says, "The word of God is not bound," which clearly indicates that the revelation of God is not bound to any single tradition.'[21] This is not to suggest that in his analysis of the 'Word' he overlooks differences that exist between the faiths, primarily regarding the Sikh rejection of incarnation.[22] Notwithstanding this, dialogue is possible and that on a deep level, for 'A Sikh who believes in God and also in the theology of the *Sabad* is already an "Imago Dei", and he has thus every right to be listened to by a Christian. He is a fellow believer, a fellow pilgrim to the same sacred destiny.'[23] In taking such a step, the Christian, Spencer suggests, will be able to see the presence of the Word beyond Christian confines:

> to see the larger Christ in the universal and cosmic setting. Consequently, he is enabled to broaden the meaning of his faith (and) include his Sikh partner not as 'other' but as a fellow participant and sharer in the same heritage . . . A feeling of *ananyatva* 'un-otherness' . . . begins to emerge. One realises one's essential relatedness to the other.[24]

Yet Spencer is no easy-going syncretist, since he indicates that while Christianity and Sikhism meet in Word or *Shabad* 'they uphold the tenets of their own faith and remain faithful and loyal to their beliefs and convictions'.[25]

Spencer's work takes further the encounter of Christians and Sikhs. The experience of co-operation between members of both faiths is extended from the practicalities of nation-building and the creation of good communal relations to a deeper spiritual search, made possible because, as Spencer suggests, there is a mutually understood basis for theological dialogue in terms of the *Shabad*/Word.

While in recent years James Massey has written considerably on Dalit issues, he is also one of the few Presbyters of the Church of North India to gain a qualification as a *gyani* (a Sikh religious expert). One of his early works in Panjabi was *Masihat: ik Parichay* (Christianity: An Introduction). It is both an apologetic to Sikhs and an attempt to encourage Punjabi Christians to take seriously their literary heritage since it is through this that they can actually learn about their own faith through that of people of other faith. He writes of parallel beliefs, the exploration of which will enhance and deepen faith. Unlike many of his fellow Indian Christians, Massey makes no attempt to find the 'hidden' Christ within the *Guru Granth Sahib*. That is not his task. His genius is in terms of his presentation of the gospel in terms of his own Punjabi cultural milieu, finding parallels but pointing out differences between Christianity and Sikhism. Like Spencer, Massey's work is not by nature syncretistic but a matter of inculturation.

In the Sikh Diaspora

Sikhs are an adventurous people, to be found in many parts of the world, with the result that Sikh studies are pursued in various parts of the Sikh diaspora. In the United Kingdom two people stand out as pioneers of Christian and Sikh co-operation and understanding. They are Owen Cole and the late Piara Singh Sambhi. Together they produced *Sikhism and Christianity: A Comparative Study*.[26] The comparison of theologies of two differing faiths is a task fraught with difficulties. There is the temptation to draw superficial parallels of belief; the problem of finding adequate English equivalents for Panjabi theological words; the need to find ways of remaining faithful to, and reflecting, the differing methods of theological reflection and the near impossibility of finding definitive statements about the faiths. Cole and Sambhi attempted to overcome these problems as they dealt with such issues as the background from which the two faiths emerged; God; Jesus and the Gurus; spiritual liberation and salvation; the scriptures; worship; personal devotion; ceremonies; authority; ethics; and, finally, attitudes to other religions.

In doing so they make no attempt to establish the superiority or otherwise of one faith over the other; rather the book reflects a dialogue in which those who are involved explore not only the partner's faith but their own and in so doing deepen the theological search for understanding of the dealings of God with humanity.

Jesus Revered in Sikhism

I am aware that in the attempt to establish one's own theology or theologies of religions I have been influenced by my experience alongside Sikh friends as we have explored faith together, whether this has been in terms of close friends in Southall (UK) or colleagues in India. In Delhi I was moved in discussion with Mr Justice Pritam Singh Safeer. Enthralled by Jesus, he spoke movingly of his belief that 'once you are on the path He is always with you'. This was particularly so for him during a period of great suffering. In one of his poems[27] he describes the shadow-like half-creatures who torment the human frame bringing with them depression and fear, yet from Palestine two thousand years ago comes the figure of Christ who takes on that same suffering.

In a second poem[28] he writes of a fleeting glance, like lightning, of Christ in Majesty, when his heart felt a burning, searing impact, which was to be his own crucifixion. Here is a man who seems to live with Christ, yet this Christ figure is as much his, as a Sikh, as he is the Church's. Here is the 'unbound'[29] Christ of a Sikh, universal in nature, adored.

Such a universal figure is also to be found in the work of Gopal Singh, who was invited to address the Vancouver Assembly of the World Council of Churches. It was there that he reminded participants that Jesus is no stranger to the peoples of the East, whatever their faith:

> 'Will you be shocked,' he asked, 'if I told you that He was an eastern man, poor like the most of us here and a manual worker all His life? He neither had blonde hair, nor blue eyes as you have painted Him to be, and He spoke neither English, nor French, nor German, nor Spanish – the four official languages of the WCC at this Holy Assembly. Perhaps, He was a black, but had the necessary IQ and the moral authority to shake the world through the centuries. We in the East recognised Him – three wise men of the East – at His very birth as the Son of God, along with a wonder-struck star that stood above Him in awakened silence and refused to move as He had seen a sight he had never seen before. You recognised Him not even after He was crucified, but only after He rose from the dead – and then, too, three centuries later when Rome accepted Christianity. But we in India accepted Him in 67 AD, when St. Thomas, the Apostle, landed on the shores of Kerala in South India.'[30]

It was Gopal Singh who was later to write an epic poem about the figure of Jesus Christ: *The Man Who Never Died*.[31] The poem is self-evidently based on the life and death of Jesus Christ, yet running through it is a vein of Sikh thought, philosophy and theological perspective. While many of the scenes portrayed, the teaching given and the theological affirmations made may remind the reader of the biblical narrative of Christ, nevertheless there is a deeper meaning to be gleaned which is more in keeping with the faith and worldview of the poem's author.

Even the very title can be off-putting for the Christian reader,[32] since the immediate perception one has is that the crucifixion is denied. This is actually not the case, as further reading of the poem would show. Rather, the title is in the light of the Sikh scripture which indicates that nothing that dies is worthy of worship.[33] A further illustration of the representation of the Christ figure via a Sikh framework is to be found in the depiction of the discussion Jesus has with the woman at the well in Samaria (John 4). Here Gopal Singh cleverly recasts the story in Sikh terms by suggesting that the five husbands represent the five evil forces which, according to Sikh philosophy, constantly assail the human frame. Thus on denying she has a husband, Gopal Singh has Jesus say:

> . . . you've had
> five husbands – Ego, Wrath, Envy, Infatuation
> and Greed . . .

Further he goes on to indicate that in accordance with Sikh theology she must escape the round of birth, death and rebirth and find her liberation:

But now what you live with,
– Time –
is not your husband.[34]

Liberation, says Gopal Singh, becomes possible through God's grace, but not through any easy piety or effortless claims. In keeping with the nature of the Sikh experience he has the Christ figure claim:

A new life has to be delivered through ME, and so,
like a mother,
I must suffer awhile.[35]

Salvation is possible only in a tragic world.[36]

This, he writes, is at the heart of the Cross, through which in this poem comes the goal of faith, the immortality of humanity reunited with God:

God lives, for nothing dies in the
realm of God. For while man lives
in the past and present, God lives
with the ever-fresh splendour of
TOMORROW.[37]

But he said unto those that believe
that nothing dies in the realm of God –

neither seed nor drop, nor dust, nor man.

Only the past dies or the present,
but the future lives for ever.

And I'm the future of man.[38]

It is in the light of encounters with my Sikh colleagues, whether in terms of discussion together or in the reading of material such as this, that I am influenced in my understanding of the theology of religions. I am torn by a number of issues: by my own faith in the nature of new life that comes through following the way of Jesus Christ and the loyalty I feel I must maintain; by the depth of faith, as trust in God, that is evidenced by my Sikh colleagues; by the very spirituality that they demonstrate through their lives; by the remarkable nature of new insights I have gained as a result of long discussions – to name but a few issues. My experience is not unique and to an extent parallels that of many of the Christians I have mentioned above. I would suggest that in the encounter of Sikhs and Christians one can trace the development of various theologies of religions which have been held often in the light of the experience of dialogue.

Different Models

In the early period of missionary work those American Presbyterians were sent on their way with the explicit task of conversion. After all, an alternative faith to the 'charlatan' Nanak was needed for he 'adopt(ed) the common method of pretended visions and miraculous endowments . . . and confirm(ed his) arguments by the power of his miracles'.[39] It was obvious that little or nothing was known about Guru Nanak, who firmly rejected the practice of miracles: 'I have no miracle to display save the miracle of the True Name.'[40] Here among the Christian missionaries of the time was an exclusivist stance which sees little of value in the other faith. Nothing other than a painful conversion will do. It was this mindset that motivated so many CMS missionaries also, yet as time went on some came to experience a tension between their evangelical fervour and their appreciation of certain elements of the Sikh faith. Keene was one such person. He was certainly no inclusivist, but one gathers the impression of a man who did not fit in easily with the expectations and attitudes of his colleagues. His was in the form of a 'replacement' model, if one may borrow from Paul F. Knitter's vocabulary,[41] though there are shades of a burgeoning fulfilment understanding in some of his writings. I am left with a question which cannot be resolved, and that is with regard to the extent to which peer pressure prevented him from a further positive theology of the Sikh faith.

In both Walji Bhai and Guilford one detects a fulfilment model. It is evident that close contact with members of the Sikh community, together with familiarity of the text of Sikh scripture, enabled these men to look beyond the exclusivism of some of their peers towards recognition of the seeds of the Word present in the faith of their interlocutors. Herein is a particularly significant matter in that no theology of religion can be simply a theology of religion as system *per se* – in our case, it must take into account the faith of the individual Sikh.

I would turn to those who worked with Sikhs in the second half of the twentieth century to discover examples of what we might call pluralism, but following Knitter, I will use the term mutual accountability.[42] In Clinton Loehlin we have an American missionary whose daily life was an encounter with Sikh friends. He chose to examine the *Granth* of Guru Gobind Singh for his Ph.D., and the scriptures of the Sikhs were also the subject of a much appreciated book which ran to three editions, thanks to remarkable sales among the Sikh community. In retirement he helped the Sikh community in California to establish a *Gurdwara*. The consequence was that here was a man whose own faith as a Christian was profoundly challenged, enhanced and deepened.

We see two Presbyters of the Church of North India – James Massey and Godwin Singh – similarly exploring Sikh theology to the advantage of their own, the latter in terms of his study of the concept of grace within the Sikh faith. Here we are on the move from mutuality to acceptance,[43] affirming the other's faith distinctiveness, accepting and respecting difference. While these two scholars represent the fruit of the encounter in India, Owen Cole and the late Piara Singh Sambhi, in the UK, opened up both Sikh studies and an appreciation of the 'other', while maintaining the integrity of their own faiths characteristically in their jointly written book: *Sikhism and Christianity: A Comparative Study*.

Continuing the Journey Together

So let me proceed to what is not really a conclusion. Considering theologies of religions, and in terms of my own response to the encounter with the Sikh community, I find myself oscillating between the mutual accountability and acceptance. I am challenged and my faith is enhanced by questions posed by my Sikh colleagues. Let me try to outline some of the issues which have struck me.

As Sikhs and Christians we have explored together in scripture studies a variety of concepts – the *Shabad*/Word; the grace of God; the centrality of Scripture; living to God's glory; the nature of God's self-manifestation, and so on. The response of those of both faiths has been so much in line with my upbringing in the Reformed traditions that it has made me face up to what I really believe; how I might speak of these things to my colleagues of the Sikh faith and what it is that is particularly distinctive of my own faith, indeed how distinctive is it?

I am also being challenged to consider that it is not the religious traditions themselves that bring salvation but a believer's attitude of mind, the rejection of self-centredness, the openness to others in service and, above all, the reliance on the grace of God that is of the essence. Sikhism has within its scriptures the words of Guru Amar Das (*Guru Granth Sahib*, p. 853): 'O Lord, this world is burning, save it by whatever means you choose.' It constitutes in the Sikh mind a recognition that God is able to use whichever religious path because those paths are means to an end and not the end in themselves. A little modesty on the part of the Christian, for whom the vulnerability of the Cross should be a dominant matter, may lead to a more suitable response to other faiths.

That leads to the nature of the Christ and, in particular, the matter of the 'unbound' Christ, a figure beyond the proprietorial claims of the Church. Further exploration of Gopal Singh's figure of *The Man Who Never Died* is presently vital, but for the time being it leads me to a recognition that I cannot easily dismiss Singh's presentation at the end of his poem that liberation comes only through the pain of human suffering even to the extent of physical death, so that the soul of humanity is reunited with the divine.

How far from the Kingdom is Justice Pritam Singh Safeer? In his definition of his brothers and sisters, Jesus names those who do the will of God (Matt. 12.50). Is this man who feels that Jesus walks by his side and that he liberated him from great suffering labouring under total misapprehension? But I must also ask if our preoccupation with the figure of Christ means that we fail to recognize that Jesus Christ pointed beyond himself to the *basileia* of God – to God's *shalom*, God's commonwealth. Ravidas speaks of the 'City of No Sorrows' (*Guru Granth Sahib*, p. 345), a fascinating eschatological vision that has so many parallels with the New Jerusalem of John's vision. How do we respond to this? Is it an illusion? Is it the same vision cast in another mould? Do we actually have the capacity to answer those questions?

I am further challenged by an insight from Clinton Loehlin: that Sikhs are not moved by theological prowess but by the practical application of the faith. Must not any theology of religions not only be a matter of cerebral reflection but have practical consequences also? Finally, I am also challenged in one further way, in a way which means that my conclusion must be that I cannot but be 'faithfully agnostic' (to borrow David Lochhead's term[44]) with regard to excessive claims about my own faith. In other words, I must ask if we have so domesticated and institutionalized our traditions that we have failed to grasp the immensity of the vision that people like Guru Nanak and Jesus of Nazareth had of life under the sovereignty of God.

Study Questions

1 What 'points of contact' are seen to exist between Sikhism and Christianity? What significance has been and/or should be given to these?

2 How might mutual reflection on 'the man who never died' be theologically significant for Christian understandings both of Sikhism and of internal Christological understanding?

3 Sikhism is a (relatively) young and small religion, which has often adopted an open and tolerant attitude to surrounding faith communities. How do you think this impacts on Christianity's approach to this faith? Can Christianity learn from its experience and example?

Further Reading

Cole, W. Owen, and Sambhi, Piara Singh, 1993, *Sikhism and Christianity: A Comparative Study*, Basingstoke: Macmillan.

McLeod, W. Hugh, 2004, *Sikhs and Sikhism*, comprising: *Guru Nanak and the Sikh*

Religion, Early Sikh Tradition, The Evolution of the Sikh Community, Who is a Sikh?, Oxford: Oxford University Press.
Tatla, Darshan Singh, 1999, *The Sikh Diaspora*, London: UCL Press.
Tatla, Darshan Singh, and Singh, Gurharpal, 2006, *Sikhs in Britain: The Making of a Community*, London: Zed Books.
UNESCO, 1973, *The Sacred Writings of the Sikhs*, London: Allen and Unwin.

Notes

1 Bhai Gurdas, *Var* 38.1.

2 Newton, John, 1886, *Historical sketches of the India missions of the Presbyterian Church in the United States of America, known as the Lodiana, the Farrukhabad and the Kolhapur Missions: from the beginning of the work, in 1834, to the time of its fiftieth anniversary, in 1884*, or *History of American Presbyterian Missions in India*, Allahabad: Allahabad Mission Press, p. 4.

3 Report of the Missionary Conference, 3–5 January 1855, in CMS archives CI1 o/7/1.

4 Cunningham published his work in 1849. He was an army officer who made it his duty to study and describe the faith of the Sikh soldiers who were to be under his command.

5 Macauliffe, M. A., 1991, 'The Holy Scriptures of the Sikhs', *Asiatic Quarterly Review* (October).

6 Guilford, Edward, 1915, *Sikhism*, London: Lay Reader's Headquarters.

7 *Ibid.*, p. 28.

8 Lodiana Mission Press, 1893.

9 Barrier, N. Gerald, 1970, *The Sikhs and Their Literature*, Delhi: Manohar, p. xxxii.

10 For example, William Stewart; Kenneth Cragg; George Appleton; Raymond Hammer; Peter Schneider.

11 Stewart, William, 1964, *India's Religious Frontier*, London: SCM Press, p. 15.

12 Loehlin, C. H., 1966, *The Christian Approach to the Sikh*, London: Edinburgh House Press, p. 71.

13 *Ibid.*, p. 72.

14 In July 1918 Archer wrote in his diary: 'I am very excited over the big idea that came through last night, *Inter-Religious Cooperation* as a field of Christian activity . . . it (the idea) has now broken on me with tremendous power.'

15 Loehlin, *Christian*, p. 73.

16 *Ibid.*, p. 74.

17 Paul Pillai, K. V., 1978, *India's Search for the Unknown Christ*, New Delhi: Fazl, p. 93.

18 Khan, Inayat, c. 1961, *SHABAD in Christianity and Sikhism*, pub. by author, Ferozepore Cantt., p. 1.

19 Ahmad-Shah, E., n.d., *Sikhism and Christian Faith*, Lucknow: Lucknow Publishing House.

20 Spencer, 1979, unpublished Ph.D. thesis, Punjabi University, Patiala, p. 343.

21 *Ibid.*, p. 344, quoting 2 Tim. 2.9.

22 *Ibid.*, p. 313.

23 *Ibid.*, p. 355.

24 *Ibid.*, p. 358. For many Christians this would be a dangerous and unacceptable theology, but it is a challenge which interfaith dialogue lays before those who participate.

25 *Ibid.*, p. 363.

26 Cole, W. Owen, and Singh Sambhi, Piara, 1993, *Sikhism and Christianity: A Comparative Study*, London: Macmillan.

27 'These indistinguishable shadows . . .' – a handwritten document.

28 'Someone came for a moment'.

29 Here one may borrow a term from Samartha, S. J., 1974, *The Hindu Response to the Unbound Christ*, Madras: CLS.

30 Singh, Gopal, 1983, 'A Sikh Scholar Speaks to the World Church', *The North India Churchman*, vol. 12, no. 2, p. 3.

31 Singh, Gopal, 1987, *The Man Who Never Died*, New Delhi: World Book Centre.

32 I first found a copy of *The Man Who Never Died* on a remainder stand in Southall Broadway, but rejected the book on the discovery that it seemed to bear little or no resemblance to the figure of Jesus Christ as understood during my initial theological education.

33 See *Guru Granth Sahib*, p. 237.

34 John 4.7–26; Gopal Singh, *Man*, p. 32.

35 *Ibid.*, p. 61.

36 *Ibid.*, p. 73.

37 *Ibid.*, p. 41.

38 *Ibid.*, p. 77.

39 Farewell address by Dr Elijah P. Swift, 29 October 1834.

40 Bhai Gurdas, *Var* 1.43.

41 Knitter, Paul F., 2002, *Introducing Theologies of Religions*, Maryknoll: Orbis, especially ch. 1. I have adopted Knitter's terminology here since I believe it represents a more accurate reflection of Keene's understanding at this point. Keene would not have subscribed to the term 'inclusivism' *per se*.

42 Knitter terms one of his categories 'The Mutuality Model', *Introducing*, Part III.

43 Another of Knitter's categories is 'The Acceptance Model', *Introducing*, Part IV.

44 Lochhead, David, 1988, *The Dialogical Imperative: A Christian Reflection on Interfaith Encounter*, London: SCM Press.

Section C: Chinese Traditions

14

Chinese Religions: Negotiating Cultural and Religious Identities

PAN-CHIU LAI

Introduction

The term 'Chinese religions' conventionally refers to the 'three-teachings' (*san jiao*[1]) of China, namely Confucianism, Daoism (Taoism) and Buddhism. However, 'Chinese religions' is actually an ambiguous concept because the meanings of both 'Chinese' and 'religions' are multivalent.

With regard to the term 'religion', whether Confucianism is a religion remains a controversial issue. Though some scholars endeavour to demonstrate the 'religious dimension' of Confucianism, many others prefer to identify Confucianism primarily as an ethical or philosophical system, rather than a religion. The dispute reflects the diversity of definitions of religion, but also the complicated history and contemporary phenomenon of Confucianism. In pre-modern China, Confucianism was associated with the official cult as well as the veneration of ancestors and thus functioned as a civil religion. However, in the contemporary world, without an independent religious institution with its own distinct community of believers or practitioners, Confucianism appears more as a school of philosophy than a religion. Other than Confucianism, one has to consider whether Chinese popular religion, which reflects the local culture and incorporates elements from Buddhism, Daoism and even Confucianism, should also be included. In addition to popular beliefs, including astrology and *feng-shui*, one has to consider also whether ancestor worship and official worship, which includes worship at local level and the imperial worship officiated by the Emperor as the priest, is to be classified as religion.

The term 'Chinese' is ambivalent with regard to its reference, especially when applied to religions. First, it may mean the religions that originated from China. In this sense Chinese Buddhism is not included. Second, it may mean the most dominant religions in China or the religions bearing the characteristics of Chinese culture. In this sense, Chinese Buddhism should be included. Third, it may also mean the religions which have some sort of recognizable presence in China or have attracted a considerable number of followers in China. In this sense, Chinese religions might include Christianity and even Islam. Due to this kind of ambiguity, some scholars talk about 'Chinese religion' with Christianity and Islam being omitted,[2] whereas many others prefer to discuss 'Chinese religions' with Christianity and Islam being included.[3]

Given the context of this book, which focuses on Christian approaches to other religions, this chapter will adopt the conventional usage and focus on Christian attitudes towards Confucianism, Daoism and Chinese Buddhism. Other 'Chinese' religions will be mentioned when necessary.

Historical Discussion

Christianity began to face the problem of its relationship with Chinese religions since the arrival of missionaries of Assyrian Christianity during the seventh century. One of the Christian monks was even involved in the translation of Buddhist texts. Based on the existing documents, one can find the borrowing of terms used by Daoism and Buddhism. However, since these could be simply terms commonly used at that time, and the Christian missionaries also employed many transliterations when translating their texts into Chinese, it is by no means easy to detect their attitudes towards Buddhism, Confucianism and Daoism.

The first well-articulated Christian position on Chinese religions was proposed by Matteo Ricci (1552–1610), probably the best-known Jesuit missionary to China. When the Catholic missionaries reached China, they first dressed like Buddhist monks. Afterwards, upon realizing that the most welcome people in China were the Confucian scholars, rather than the Buddhist monks, the Jesuits decided to adopt the Confucian lifestyle and etiquette, circa 1595. This change of outlook was merely part of their missionary strategy, which was based on a general policy of accommodation towards Chinese culture.[4]

This general policy of accommodation, widely adopted among the Jesuits, did not imply an uncritical acceptance of all the aspects and elements of Chinese religions. When putting this general policy into practice, Ricci endeavoured to 'discover', if not 'invent', the ancient Chinese religious tradition, which was embodied in the ancient Chinese texts before Confucius. In *The True Meaning of the Lord of Heaven* (1604), as well as refuting Buddhism, Ricci attempted to argue that this ancient Chinese religious tradition, which was succeeded by classical Confucianism, was derived from natural reason and compatible with the monotheistic Christian tradition. By and large, the classical Confucian texts indicate that the ancient Chinese did have some knowledge of God probably due to natural revelation and reason. Accordingly, the Heaven (*tian*) mentioned in ancient Chinese texts,

Ricci attempted to argue, is the Christian God. The crucial point which Ricci endeavoured to drive home was that classical Confucianism was monotheistic, or, at least, theistic, whereas contemporary Neo-Confucianism, under the influence of idolatrous Buddhism and Daoism, became atheistic. Accordingly, when attempting to understand Confucianism, one should reject the interpretations made by the Confucians of the Song (960–1279) and Ming (1368–1644) dynasties and go back to the original ancient texts of classical Confucianism. In this way, one might then find that Christianity and Confucianism do not contradict each other.

Ricci and his followers attempted to present Confucianism as a rational, humanistic, ethical system and Chinese culture as an ancient, civilized and ordered culture. Many of the moral teachings of Confucianism were acceptable for Christians. Some Catholic missionaries even attempted to prove that the rise of Chinese civilization was after the flood of Noah and inherited the biblical tradition. Ricci's strategy was to supplement Confucianism and to replace Buddhism. With the supplement from Christianity, together with the elimination of the influence from Buddhism and Daoism, Chinese culture, represented by Confucianism as its mainstream, was expected to be purified and restored to its original purity and thus fulfilled.

Under the influence of Ricci, many Europeans assumed that Confucianism was mainly a social teaching or a natural theology, which could be employed by Christianity as a preparation for the gospel. Gottfried Wilhelm von Leibniz (1646–1716), who assumed that there was a natural theology in the Chinese tradition, even suggested inviting Chinese missionaries to Europe to teach the people about the use and practice of natural theology, just as the Europeans sent missionaries to China to teach the people there about revelatory theology.[5]

The approach championed by Ricci was challenged by Niccolò Longobardo (1565–1655). In his *Traité sur quelques points de la religion des Chinois*, which was quoted by several persons involved in the Chinese Rites Controversy, Longobardo offered an alternative approach to the Chinese religions. Unlike Ricci, Longobardo tended to accept the contemporary Confucian scholars' interpretation of the ancient Chinese texts. Accordingly, Longobardo regarded the ancient Chinese philosophers as merely ancient Gentile philosophers. As the ancient Chinese tradition was against theism, it was ridiculous to talk about Chinese natural theology. For Longobardo, one should not accommodate the Christian faith to the Chinese, who will simply take the accommodation made as the vindication of the superiority of Chinese culture and reinforce their cultural pride.[6]

The divergence between these two approaches to the Chinese religions emerged during the Rites Controversy, which mainly concerned three issues:

1 Whether to translate the term *Deus* (God) into *tian* (Heaven) and *shangdi* (High Lord), two terms found in the Chinese classics.
2 Whether to take part in the ceremonies honouring Confucius and the veneration of ancestors.
3 Whether to participate in the community festivals in honour of non-Christian divinities.[7]

Whereas some Catholic missionaries understood these as religious rituals and thus to be forbidden as idolatry, Ricci suggested that they were merely civil activities and Chinese Christians should be allowed to take part. Underlying the controversy are the differences between the two understandings of, and attitudes towards, the Chinese religions, especially Confucianism.

The Catholic missionaries talked very little about Daoism; their prime target of criticism was Buddhism, which had also launched its counter-attack against Catholicism. Their disputes covered a wide range of topics, including: the existence and nature of God; the distinction between the Creator and the creature vs. the equality and unity of all things; the origin of the world (Christian doctrine of creation vs. Buddhist concept of dependent co-arising); whether human nature is good or bad; immortality of the soul; human destiny, including the concepts of final judgement, reincarnation, pure land, hell; and so forth.[8]

Unlike the missionaries, who tended to consider their approaches to the Chinese religions from the perspective of missionary strategy, Chinese Christians had to consider the Chinese religions as part of their own cultural heritage. In fact, many of them had been influenced by the three religions before their conversion to Christianity. It is thus rather natural that their attitudes towards the Chinese religions could be quite different from the missionaries coming from the West. For example, Yang Ting-yun (1562–1627), one of the three pillars of the Catholic Church in China, had been attracted to Buddhism before his conversion to Catholicism, and he continued to identity himself as a 'Confucian' even after his conversion to Catholicism. For him, there should be no irreconcilable conflict between Christianity and Confucianism. Many of his interpretations of Catholicism bore the characteristics of Confucianism.[9]

Many of the Protestant missionaries, arriving in China during the nineteenth century onwards, viewed Confucianism in a way quite similar to that of Matteo Ricci. Some of them, including particularly James Legge (1814–97), appreciated positively the Confucian classics and devoted their time to studying the Chinese classics and even became professional Sinologists. However, significantly different from the Catholic missionaries, who aimed at converting the literati first and focused on the religion and culture of the intellectuals, many of the Protestant missionaries had opportunities to make contacts with the popular aspects of Chinese religions. Unlike some of the Western scholars, whose understandings of Chinese religions were based mainly on the classical texts being translated, many Protestant missionaries had opportunities to observe the actual religious practices in China at that time. Probably due, at least in part, to their presuppositions of the superiority of Western civilization, their observations reinforced their pre-understandings or impressions that the Chinese religions, particularly the popular Chinese religion(s), were basically idolatry and superstition.[10]

At a missionary conference held in Shanghai in 1877, a Protestant missionary working in Shanghai known as Revd Dr Yates, criticized the superstitious practice of ancestral worship and *feng-shui*. He said:

> As a system, ancestral worship is tenfold more potent for keeping the people in darkness, than all the idols in the land, not connected with it. Its essence is *feng-shui* – that intangible, but all powerful weapon which is wielded by high and low, against changes in established customs and practices, and which is the great bar to progress and civilization.[11]

For Yates, ancestral worship is not only worship of the dead, but also the 'principal religion of the Chinese'[12] constituting a major obstacle for the Chinese converting into Christianity.[13] He came to the conclusion that it was impossible for Christianity to accommodate. In his own words:

> To supplement Christianity, and thereby make it more acceptable to the Chinese, by allowing, or conniving at *any* of the custom practiced in the worship of the dead, *is to yield everything*. . . . The end desired by us all, can be accomplished by nothing short of regeneration – a change that consists in a complete renovation of heart and life by the Grace of God; by a complete turning from all superstition, all former objects of worship and fear, and through the merits of Christ's death and resurrection, trusting alone in the living and true God. . . . The Gospel of Our Lord Jesus Christ, then is the *only* antidote for the woes of China.[14]

It is important to note that Yates's attitude towards the Chinese religions was not only shaped by the influence of modern Western culture and his theological background, but also his understanding and observation of the actual practice of popular aspects of ancestral worship, especially its hindrance for the Chinese becoming Christians.

With regard to Buddhism and Daoism, many of the missionaries, even those appreciative towards their philosophies, were critical towards 'their popular aspects'. For example, in his address 'Buddhism and Tauism in Their Popular Aspects' to the missionary conference mentioned above, Revd J. Edkins commented that the Buddhism he saw at his own time was focused on the magical efficacy of prayer and the law of moral retribution rather than the beautiful moral precepts of early Buddhism. The centrality of the doctrine of nirvana was replaced by the longing for rebirth in the Western

Heaven (Pure Land). Similarly the contemporary Daoists were not philosophers or alchemists, but magical healers, exorcists and professional prayers for rain.[15] For Edkins, the Daoist religion was particularly responsible for those dangerous superstitions.[16] He urged:

> Every man [*sic*], whether a Christian or not, ought on moral grounds and on the greatest happiness principle itself, if he thinks that it is a safer basis, to desire the extinction of a religious system which encourages dangerous and lying delusions.[17]

Edkins' evaluation of Buddhism was slightly less negative for he found some positive elements in Buddhism, including the 'structural' similarities between Buddhism and Christianity in their devotion to a saviour. He commented:

> Then as to the effects of Buddhism it may be said to have been good in some respects. It bears a consistent testimony to the vanity of the world, and the essential and immense superiority of soul purity to earthly grandeur. But in founding on this a monastic institute it has followed a wrong plan and failed to attain the purity desired. It teaches the need of a personal Redeemer to rescue from the moral evils attendant on our present existence. But this redeemer is a Buddha or a Bodhisattva, a man or being possessing none of the powers attributed to him. Among the prominent and most pernicious evils for which the popular Buddhism of the present day is responsible is idolatry. It is an enormous evil that Buddhism has placed the Buddhas and Bodhisattvas in the position in the reverence of the people that ought to be held only by the Creator and Father of the world.[18]

Edkins' comments reflected not only his Western bias for science, but also his Protestant bias against monasticism. Edkins concluded:

> Our great contest as Christian missionaries is with Confucianism. There is found the intellect, the thought, the literature, the heart of the nation. But we have also a preliminary struggle with Buddhism and Tauism. These constitute three mighty fortresses erected by satanic art to impede the progress of Christianity. Confucianism is the citadel of the enemy raising its battlements high into the clouds and manned by multitudes who are animated by a belief in their superiority and their invincible strength. The taking of this fortress is the conclusion of the war. But Buddhism and Tauism each represents a fortress which must also be captured and destroyed. So far as argument and intellect are concerned these fortresses are weakly manned. But think of the numbers, the millions on millions, who are deceived by these superstitions, and held fast by chains of spiritual darkness.[19]

Timothy Richard

Unlike many of his fellow Christian missionaries, who despised or ignored Chinese Buddhism and other Chinese religions, assuming that Buddhism was a dying religion and constituted no contest to Christianity, Timothy Richard (1845–1919), a famous Baptist missionary, endeavoured to build up relationships with leaders of different religions in China. Through his personal encounter with the Buddhists in China, especially the famous Buddhist reformer Yang Wen-hui (1837–1911), Richard believed that Buddhism was on its upturn and was full of life, even though the actual situation of Buddhism was still in disarray at that time.[20]

What Richard deeply appreciated was not Buddhism in general, early Buddhism, nor Theravada Buddhism, but Mahayana Buddhism, which flourished mainly in China and Japan. What impressed Richard most remained what he found in the Mahayana Buddhist texts – a gospel of grace comparable to that of Christianity.

Richard spent a lot of time studying Chinese Buddhism and translating some Buddhist texts, including *The Awakening of Faith* and *The Essence of the Lotus Scripture* (a synopsis of the Lotus Sutra), into English, which formed the major contents of his *New Testament of Higher Buddhism* (1910). As the title of the book implies, it is Richard's assumption that, as the New Testament is superior to the Old Testament, Mahayana Buddhism is higher than preceding forms of Buddhism. Referring to Mahayana Buddhism, Richard wrote:

> In Buddhism we see two wondrous developments – first, Atheism into Theism; and secondly, the development of that Theism into a Monotheistic Trinity in Unity.[21]

This Trinity, according to Richard's understanding, consists of *Amitābha* (pinyin: *Omitofo*) in the centre, *Ta Shih Chih* (pinyin: *Dashizhi*; the Great Mighty One; *Mahasthāma*) on his right and *Kwan-yin* (pinyin: *Guanyin*; *Kuan-yin*; *Avalokiteśvara*) on his left.[22] For Richard, corresponding to Christ was the *Ta Shih Chih* who 'becomes incarnate', sometimes represented by an image of *Mileh Fo* (pinyin: *Milofo*; the Buddhist Messiah; *Maitreya*) and 'can put an end to the Karma chain of endless births and deaths caused by sin, by removing sin altogether, without needing a single re-birth, but go straight to the Pure Land of Paradise, and live for ever there'.[23] Richard further suggested that the one corresponding to the Holy Spirit was Kwan-yin, as the 'Hearer of the world's prayer' as well as 'the one who looks down upon human suffering and is the Inspirer of men and woman to save their fellows'.[24] Other than the triune character of the object of worship, Richard also highlighted that: 'Both the Christians and the Buddhists regard their chief object of worship as divine and full of compassion for human suffering.'[25]

The most striking parallel with Christianity, according to Richard, remains the Pure Land School of Mahayana Buddhism, which stresses the following:

1 Help from God to save oneself and others from suffering.
2 Communion with God, which gave the highest ecstatic rest to the soul.
3 Partaking of the nature of God by new birth, as to become Divine and Immortal oneself.[26]

Summarizing the Christian character of Mahayana Buddhism, Richard exclaimed that, 'its theology is Christian in everything almost but its nomenclature'.[27] He further declared:

> If it be, as it is more and more believed, that the Mahayana Faith is not Buddhism, properly so-called, but an Asiatic form of the same gospel of our Lord and Saviour Jesus Christ, in Buddhistic nomenclature, differing from the Old Buddhism just as the New Testament differs from the Old, then it commands a world-wide interest, for in it we find an adaptation of Christianity to ancient thought in Asia, and the deepest bond of union between the different races of the East and the West, namely the bond of a common religion.[28]

Richard was particularly impressed by the 'wonderful similarity' between the Lotus Sutra and the Christian gospels.[29] He even called the Lotus Sutra 'a Fifth Gospel', 'Faith Gospel' or simply 'the Lotus Gospel'[30] for he found that the teaching of the Lotus Sutra was, 'the same teaching as in the Gospel of St. John in regard to Life, Light, and Love, a teaching which forms a wonderful bridge crossing the chasm between Eastern and Western religion and civilization'.[31]

Richard was knowledgeable about the theological tradition of fulfilment theology, which identifies other religions as preparations for the gospel and considered it part of Christian mission to serve as a purifier of Buddhism, helping it to separate the doctrines of the New Buddhism from the Old Buddhism.[32] Richard significantly differed from this theological tradition by making the fulfilment relationship mutual rather than unilateral. He wrote:

> It is also getting clearer each year that different truths, wherever found, cannot be antagonistic. They do not neutralize, but *complement each other*; they do not destroy, but *fulfill one another.*[33]

Richard also clearly stated that the objectives of his translation of the synopsis of the Lotus Sutra were not simply to show 'the strongest bond of union between East and West'.[34] There were two further objectives. One is 'the Unity of all religion'. What Richard endeavoured to achieve was that 'there shall be *One religion* in the future, and that one will contain what is truest and best in all past religions which reveal the Divine in them'.[35] The other one was to 'strengthen the forces struggling against the selfish materialism of this age by the united efforts for the promotion of universal good-will, by all the children of God of every race'.[36] What Richard particularly looked for was the revival of 'the great Renunciation of all ascetics, whether Christian or non-Christian', because 'the materialists become more materialistic than ever'.[37] In other words, Richard's translation of the Buddhist texts into English had its practical purpose: 'producing brotherhood amongst men [*sic*] of different religions'.[38] It was Richard's expectation that through discovering their similarities, Buddhists and Christians would reach a situation where they 'no longer feared each other as foes, but helped each other as friends'.[39]

For Richard, the ultimate aim of missionary work is the establishment of the kingdom of God on earth rather than the salvation of individual souls. This missionary vision includes not only the unity of religion, but also the co-operation of Christians and non-Christians for the well-being of all the people on earth, especially establishing justice and peace on earth for the poor and the oppressed.[40] It is interesting to note that Richard's approach to dialogue with Buddhists is reminiscent of Paul Knitter.[41]

Richard's endeavours in dialogue with Chinese Buddhism had inspired William E. Soothill (1861–1935), who became a famous Sinologist, and Karl Ludvig Reichelt (1877–1952), who became the founder of Tao Fong Shan, which continues the work of Buddhist–Christian dialogue until today.

John C. H. Wu

John C. H. Wu (1899–1986) was one of the most famous Chinese Catholics during his life. He had been trained in classical Chinese as well as English literature, was very successful in the legal profession, and had lived a very sensual life (including frequenting infamous places and taking a concubine) before being baptized a Catholic in 1937. Wu, whose spiritual journey was quite similar to that of St Augustine, also gave an autobiographical account of his religious journey in his *Beyond East and West*. Wu wrote:

> Far be it from me to assert that my cultural and spiritual heritage was on a par with the Old Testament. What I do assert is that, in an analogical way, the three religions of China served as my tutors, bringing me to Christ, so that I might find justification in faith (Gal. 3.24).[42]

For Wu, Confucius was a theist rather than an agnostic and his greatness lies in his childlike attitude towards 'Heaven', which is synonymous with

'God'.[43] Due to the influence of Confucius' followers, Confucianism became more humanistic and even pantheistic.[44] For Chinese Christians, it is thus not necessary to abandon Confucianism, because the Confucian emphasis on filial piety remains very beneficial to Christian spirituality:

> The idea of filial piety is so deep-rooted in the Chinese mind that when a Chinese becomes a Christian he naturally would apply it to his relations with God. To him the imitation of Christ means the imitation of His supreme filial piety toward His Father Who is also our Father.[45]

However, what Wu treasures most is perhaps Daoism rather than Confucianism.

Wu agrees with John Monsterleet's comment on his own spiritual life: 'A disciple of Confucius for moral truth, he turns more to Lao Tzu for mystic truth, and the mystic in him surpasses the moralist.'[46] With regard to the value of Daoism, Wu summarizes his view as follows:

> The significance of time is to evoke Eternity; that of voyaging is to evoke the Home; that of knowledge is to evoke Ignorance; that of science and art is to evoke Mystery; that of longevity is to evoke the Evanescence of life; that of all human greatness is to evoke Humility; that of complexities and subtilities [*sic*] is to evoke Simplicity; that of the many is to evoke the One; that of war is to evoke Peace; that of the cosmos is to evoke the Beyond. It is not the voyage that causes harm; but to lose oneself in the voyage so as to forget one's destination is a target indeed.[47]

While Monsignor Fulton Sheen comments on Wu:

> Although in his generosity he was ready to give up his pagan cultural heritage, he found out that none of it that was good was lost to him now that he was a Catholic. On the contrary, it was uplifted and complemented. Indebtedness to life became indebtedness to God for His graces, filial piety was made stronger because it had its source in filial piety to God and His Mother. Confucian moralism and Taoist contemplativeness were marvelously balanced and he could be even more Chinese because he was a Catholic.[48]

With regard to Buddhism, what Wu admires most is not the Buddha's teaching, but his personality. For Wu, the Buddha was 'more a moral teacher than a religious teacher'.[49] The Buddha had no knowledge of divine grace, but as a prince who sacrificed all the luxuries in order to search for the Truth with a view to setting himself and others free, the Buddha remains admirable. Even though Wu did not think that the Buddha successfully found the Truth, he still regarded the Buddha as a foreshadowing of Christ.[50] Wu acknowledged his indebtedness to Buddhism in three respects. First, he had inherited from Buddhism an intense longing for the 'Other Shore', which for Wu was but another name and a faint foreshadowing of the kingdom of God which is within us. Second, Buddhism had disposed his mind for the appreciation of the biblical passages concerning 'vanity of vanities' from Ecclesiastes. Third, Buddhism, particularly the Ch'an school of Buddhism, taught him the importance of direct personal experience in the matters of spiritual life.[51]

Wu proudly admits, 'Since I became a Catholic, all the wisdom of the East is grist to my mill.'[52] Wu even proclaims that Christianity is the only really possible synthesis between East and West.[53] He suggested that Gautama Buddha, Confucius, Lao Zi (Lao Tzu), and so on, in the East, together with Socrates, Plato, Aristotle, and others, in the West, were heralds who sowed the 'seeds of the logos' in human hearts before the Word of God was made flesh:[54]

> Their doctrines, it is true, are not mixed with errors, and even where they were not erroneous they were inadequate and left the human mind at an *impasse*. But this very *impasse* underlined the necessity of the Revelation; while the grains of truth that they contained and shared in common were faint intimations of the Gospel, in whose light alone we can perceive their real significance.[55]

It is apparent that Wu's attitude towards Chinese religions came very near to inclusivism. But it is important to note that his approach was to take them as part of his cultural and religious heritage rather than living partners in actual dialogue. Furthermore, his account of the Chinese religions is quite selective – concentrating on the 'valuable' elements appreciated by Wu himself and overlooking the 'popular' aspects of these religions which were the primary target of the criticism launched by many Western missionaries. Wu's case is by no means unique or isolated. Another famous example is Lin Yu-tang (1895–1976).[56] There are many other Chinese Christian intellectuals who continued to find spiritual inspiration from the Chinese religions even after their conversion to Christianity. For them, the dialogue between Christianity and Chinese religions is primarily, borrowing Raimundo Panikkar's term, an 'intra-religious' rather than 'inter-religious' dialogue,[57] for they tended to inherit both traditions.

Xu Xongshi

From the Protestant side, Xu Xongshi (1900–99), also known as Princeton Hsu, offers a distinctive approach to the Chinese religions. When Xu was a Baptist minister in mainland China, especially during the 1930s and 1940s, he attempted to use concepts from Chinese religions to interpret Christian faith in order to indigenize Christianity. He even adopted a very Buddhist pen name for publication – '*Zhaoliu jushi*', in which the term '*jushi*' usually refers to a lay Buddhist. Without definitely denying or affirming the salvific validity of the Chinese religions, Xu emphasized that there were also truths in Chinese religions. Xu believed that God's Spirit, which is present universally, is also present in all human beings and brings people of different religions to enlightenment. In other words, Christianity and the Chinese religions have the same spiritual origin in God's Spirit.[58] It is thus not necessary for Chinese Christians to abandon Buddhism, Confucianism and Daoism. On the contrary, it is legitimate and desirable for Christians to reinterpret Christian faith through Chinese religious concepts, because Confucian theory of morality and ethics, Buddhist spirituality and Daoist concepts of non-action (*wu-wei*) are all beneficial to the development of Christian theology.[59]

Other than his detailed expositions on the similarities and complementarities between Christianity and Buddhism, Xu also reinterpreted the major Christian doctrines of God, Christ, the Holy Spirit, and so forth, from a Buddhist perspective, including employing the Buddhist concept of skilful means (upāya-kauśalya) and the method of laddering (pariṣaṇḍa) to explain the salvation of Christ. The basic idea is that as different people have different capacities for understanding, Christ has to employ different methods and preach in different ways, skilfully, in order to help people of different capacities understand the truth step by step. In this process, all human beings are able to attain the Hinayana level of salvation, but after they are reborn in Christ, they will be able to attain the Mahayana stage of salvation.[60]

After his migration to Hong Kong in 1957, Xu's position on the Chinese religions became more and more exclusive. When comparing Christianity with the Chinese religions, Xu's emphasis shifted from their similarities to their dissimilarities. He further explicitly stated that Buddhism, Confucianism and Daoism were merely part of human culture and could not save human souls, which could be saved by the gospel of Jesus Christ alone. For him, it is no longer necessary for a Chinese Christian to embrace the Chinese religious traditions.[61] However, with these changes, Xu continued to conduct his 'comparative theology', comparing the distinctive characteristics and relative strengths of the doctrines of different religions. The method he employs is quite similar to the method of doctrinal classification originated in Buddhism and adopted in the historical disputes among the three Chinese religions. For example, Xu suggests that there are three kinds of love in this world: affection for one's parents; benevolence towards people; and, kindness towards (living) things (referring to Mencius VII. A. 45). Other than emphasizing that God is the ultimate origin of love, Xu can freely admit that the attachment to parents is best expounded in Confucianism, benevolence towards the people in Christianity, and sparing with things in Buddhism.[62]

Xu's positions on the Chinese religions, including his inclusivist position in his early thought,[63] and his exclusivist position in his late thought, might not differ in substance from the comparable approaches in the Western theological tradition. However, he did offer some distinctly Chinese, as well as Buddhist, formulations to these approaches – not only in terms of the theology of religions, but also in comparative theology.

Contemporary and Theoretical Discussion

Contemporary and theoretical discussions on Christian approaches towards Chinese religions have been shaped to a certain extent by the discussion of the theology of religions concerning exclusivism, inclusivism, pluralism, and so on, which originated in Western theological circles.

At the grassroot level, many Chinese Christians take a very exclusivist attitude towards Chinese religions.[64] Among contemporary Chinese scholars of Christianity, a few argue for an exclusivist attitude. For example, Liu Xiao-feng, based on his assessment of the decline of the influence of traditional Chinese culture on the contemporary Chinese, and his rather one-sided reading of Karl Barth's theory of religion as unbelief, emphasizes the contradiction between Christianity and other religions and disregards the significance of the Chinese religions for Christian theology.[65] In sharp contrast to this robust rejection of the Chinese religions, one will also find voices from the other end of the spectrum. Wang Zhi-cheng, who has translated a lot of books by John Hick, Paul F. Knitter, Raimundo Panikkar, and others, and introduced their thought to the academia of mainland China, suggests that, as the world religions are entering into the Second Axial period, religions should take a thoroughly pluralistic attitude towards other religions.[66]

In addition to these discussions, shaped by Western theological approaches, there are also discussions shaped by Chinese Christians' concern for theological indigenization and cultural identities. From time to time, Chinese Christian attitudes towards the Chinese religions are mixed with problems concerning Christianity and Chinese culture. They seem concerned more with particular questions related to Christianity and Chinese religions, rather than the general theological questions concerning religious pluralism. When discussing the reformulation of Christian faith in an indigenous Chinese way, some Chinese Christians considered the possibility of replacing the Old Testament with the Chinese religious classics in order to form the Chinese Christian Bible. Some others have even attempted to argue for a positive appreciation of syncretism, which is expected to be able to affirm the use of local cultural and religious sources in Christian theology.[67]

Apart from issues related to the theology of religions, dual identity is one of the issues raised when discussing questions concerning Christianity and

Chinese religions. Whereas it is rather common for the Chinese to embrace two or more religious traditions, it is less common for Christians, especially those in the West, to do so. The question for Chinese Christians is whether they can and should be, say, Confucian-Christians, Buddhist-Christians or Daoist-Christians. A related question is how they evaluate religious syncretism, which is rather common in China. There are many religious groups advocating the idea of the unity of the three religions (Buddhism, Confucianism and Daoism), or even five religions (adding Christianity and Islam). Is it necessary for Christianity to reject all the elements from the Chinese religions? Is it possible for Chinese Christians to reinterpret Christian faith with the terminologies of the Chinese religions, which are also closely related to Chinese philosophy? The question becomes more complicated when considering that the Chinese religions, though relatively less prominent in contemporary Chinese culture, play a vital role in the Chinese cultural heritage. Will a total rejection of the Chinese religions imply a total rejection of Chinese culture?

Hans Küng, in his comprehensive discussion with Julia Ching on the Chinese religions, suggests that cultural and ethical dual citizenship are acceptable and even desirable, but not dual citizenship in faith.[68] John Berthrong, a participant of Christian–Confucian dialogue, is sceptical on the issue and expects that even though Christians and Confucians may learn from each other through dialogue, Christians will remain Christians and Confucians will remain Confucians.[69] However, Robert C. Neville, an advocate of 'Boston Confucianism' and another participant of Christian–Confucian dialogue, while admitting that any person affirming multiple religious identities has to be ready to defend the compatibility of the multiple traditions, declares that:

> Boston Confucianism, especially in its members who are also Christians, is deeply committed to multiple religious identity, and to the serious and faithful conversation that can test its limits.[70]

Neville himself has conducted experiments in doing comparative theology involving Christianity, Confucianism and Daoism.[71] There are many other Christian theologians who find useful resources from the Chinese religious traditions, for example the concept of Dao (Tao) in the *Dao De Jing* (*Tao Te Ching*).[72] Other than Confucianism and Daoism, resources from Chinese Buddhism, especially those from the *Tian-tai* (*Tien Tai*) and *Hua-yan* (*Hua-yen*) schools, are also employed by some Chinese Christian theologians in their experiments in comparative theology.[73] Other than these rather theological or philosophical discussions, some Christians also find the Chinese religions important resources for the enrichment of Christian spirituality.[74] Without articulating a formal theology of religions, these discussions or experiments may practically have implied that they are leaning to a dialogical rather than an exclusive attitude. In fact, there is a significant increase of comparative studies of, and even dialogues between, Christianity and the Chinese religions in recent years.

Criticism of Thought in the Area and Conclusion

Among Chinese Christian intellectuals, those who take a wholesale condemnation or an indiscriminative pluralistic affirmation of the salvific value of the Chinese religions are relatively rare. If one accepts the typology of exclusivism, inclusivism and pluralism, the most dominant is perhaps inclusivism, especially fulfilment theology. This may have been due to its being open for a discriminative as well as critical approach to deal with the different aspects of Chinese religions. This approach may allow Chinese Christians to uphold their religious (Christian) and cultural (Chinese) identities at the same time. On the one hand, this approach allows Chinese Christians to accept the value of their cultural heritage or at least part of it. On the other hand, this can help them to affirm why they are Christians.

When surveying Christian attitudes towards Chinese religions, various factors have affected them. One factor is the particular aspect(s) of Chinese religions focused on. 'Chinese religions' is a vague and ambiguous term which may refer to a very wide range of religious phenomena. In fact, Küng's theological responses to the Chinese religions differ from one religion to another, and within religions. While he highly praises the Confucian humanistic ethics, which seems to concur with his own proposal for a Global Ethic, he criticizes the static and hierarchical worldview related to Confucianism.[75] Similarly, a Christian may very much appreciate the philosophy of Daoism, but despise the popular ritual of Daoism. It is thus rather difficult to generalize and neatly classify one's overall attitude towards the 'Chinese religions'. It seems to be natural and appropriate for a Christian to accept some aspects of Chinese religions and reject other aspects. One may even query whether it is responsible to indiscriminately accept or reject another religion as a whole,[76] not to say Chinese religions as a complicated 'religious river system'.[77] The complexity of the Chinese case may raise a more general question for the contemporary debate in the theology of religions. Can the Chinese religions be recognized as equally valid ways to salvation among other world religions? Are all the Chinese religions 'world religions'? What are the criteria? Is it necessary to have a clearly defined theology of religions in order to have dialogue and co-operation with people of other religions?

Study Questions

1 What are the theological and non theological factors affecting Christians' attitudes towards the Chinese religions?

2 Is it possible for one to have dual identity in both Christianity and a Chinese religion, for example being a Confucian-Christian? How about a Buddhist-Christian?

3 Is it necessary and desirable for Chinese Christians to reject their Chinese cultural and religious traditions entirely?

4 Is syncretism necessarily bad?

Further Reading

Berthrong, John, 1994, *All Under Heaven: Transforming Paradigms in Confucian–Christian Dialogue*, Albany: SUNY Press.

Covell, Ralph R., 1986, *Confucius, The Buddha, and Christ: A History of the Gospel in Chinese*, Maryknoll: Orbis.

Gernet, Jacques, 1985, *China and the Christian Impact: A Conflict of Cultures*, ET, Cambridge: Cambridge University Press.

Küng, Hans, and Ching, Julia, 1993, *Christianity and Chinese Religions*, ET, London: SCM Press.

Neville, Robert C., 1991, *Behind the Masks of God: An Essay Toward Comparative Theology*, Albany: SUNY Press.

Reinders, Eric, 2004, *Borrowed Gods and Foreign Bodies: Christian Missionaries Imagine Chinese Religion*, Berkeley: University of California Press.

Notes

1 Chinese terms given are in pinyin unless another term is used by a particular figure or a different version of the name is in common usage. Pinyin and other usages will be given in parentheses, except in the case of personal or place names where a non-pinyin format is the accepted standard, for example Tao Fong Shan.

2 For example, Thompson, Laurence G., 1989, *Chinese Religion: An Introduction*, 4th edn, Belmont: Wadsworth.

3 For example, Smith, D. Howard, 1968, *Chinese Religions*, London: Weidenfeld and Nicolson; also, Ching, Julia, 1993, *Chinese Religions*, London: Macmillan.

4 Standaert, Nicholas (ed.), 2001, *Handbook of Christianity in China*, vol. 1: *635–1800*, Leiden: Brill, pp. 310–11.

5 Mungello, David E., 1977, *Leibniz and Confucianism: The Search for Accord*, Honolulu: University of Hawaii Press.

6 Li, Wenchao, 2006, 'Niccolò Longobardo and his *Traité sur quelques points*

de la religion des Chinois', *Sino-Christian Studies: An International Journal of Bible, Theology and Philosophy*, vol. 1, pp. 159–84 (in Chinese with English abstract).

7 Standaert (ed.), *Handbook*, pp. 680–5.

8 Chung, Andrew K., 2004, 'The Dialogic Encounter between Christian and Buddhist Thought in Late Ming and Early Qing China', *Ching Feng*, n.s. vol. 5.1, pp. 65–91; also Jacques Gernet, 1985, *China and the Christian Impact: A Conflict of Cultures*, ET, Cambridge: Cambridge University Press.

9 Standaert, Nicholas, 1988, *Yang Tingyun, Confucian and Christian in Late Ming China*, Leiden: E. J. Brill.

10 Reinders, Eric, 2004, *Borrowed Gods and Foreign Bodies: Christian Missionaries Imagine Chinese Religion*, Berkeley: University of California Press, p. 7.

11 Dr Yates, 1878, 'Ancestral Worship', in *Records of the General Conference of the Protestant Missionaries of China, held at Shanghai, May 10–24, 1877*, Shanghai: Presbyterian Press, p. 368.

12 *Ibid.*, p. 368.

13 *Ibid.*, pp. 381–2.

14 *Ibid.*, pp. 386–7.

15 Edkins, J., 1878, 'Buddhism and Tauism [*sic*] in Their Popular Aspects', in *Records of the General Conference of the Protestant Missionaries of China, held at Shanghai, May 10–24, 1877*, Shanghai: Presbyterian Press, pp. 65–6.

16 *Ibid.*, p. 70.

17 *Ibid.*, p. 70.

18 *Ibid.*, pp. 70–1.

19 *Ibid.*, p. 72.

20 Richard, Timothy, 1910, *The New Testament of Higher Buddhism*, Edinburgh: T&T Clark, pp. 135–6.

21 *Ibid.*, p. 12.

22 *Ibid.*, pp. 12–13.

23 *Ibid.*, pp. 14–15.

24 *Ibid.*, pp. 15–23.

25 *Ibid.*, p. 23.

26 *Ibid.*, p. 26.

27 *Ibid.*, p. 27.

28 *Ibid.*, p. 29.

29 *Ibid.*, p. 129.

30 *Ibid.*, pp. 129, 134, 138.

31 *Ibid.*, p. 2.

32 *Ibid.*, pp. 131, 134–5.

33 *Ibid.*, p. 49, emphasis added.

34 *Ibid.*, p. 141.

35 *Ibid.*, p. 142.

36 *Ibid.*, p. 142.

37 *Ibid.*, p. 143.

38 *Ibid.*, p. 147.

39 *Ibid.*, p. 49.

40 *Ibid.*, pp. 35–6.

41 See, Knitter, Paul F., 1995, *One Earth Many Religions: Multifaith Dialogue and Global Responsibility*, Maryknoll: Orbis.

42 Wu, John C. H., 1951, *Beyond East and West*, New York: Sheed and Ward, p. 150.

43 *Ibid.*, pp. 151–3.

44 *Ibid.*, pp. 153–4.

45 *Ibid.*, p. 156.

46 *Ibid.*, p. 171.

47 *Ibid.*, p. 171.

48 *Ibid.*, pp. 149–50.

49 *Ibid.*, p. 175.

50 *Ibid.*, p. 175.

51 *Ibid.*, p. 185.

52 *Ibid.*, p. 185.

53 Wu, John C. H., 1965, *Chinese Humanism and Christian Spirituality: Essays of John C. H. Wu*, Sih, Paul K. T. (ed.), Jamaica, NY: St John's University Press, pp. 157–71.

54 *Ibid.*, p. 157.

55 *Ibid.*, p. 158.

56 Lin, Yu-tang, 1959, *From Pagan to Christian*, Cleveland: World Publisher.

57 Panikkar, Raimundo, 1978, *The Intra-religious Dialogue*, New York: Paulist Press.

58 Ho, Hing-cheong, 2005, 'Reinterpreting Christianity Buddhistically: Xu Songshi's Indigenous Theology', *Ching Feng*, n.s. vol. 6.1, pp. 105–9.

59 Lai, Pan-chiu, and So, Yuen-tai, 2004, 'Migration, Theology and Religious Identity: Christianity and Chinese Culture in the Life and Thought of Xu Songshi', *Asia Journal of Theology*, vol. 18.2, pp. 325–7.

60 Ho, 'Reinterpreting', pp. 100–4.

61 Lai and So, 'Migration', pp. 329–35.

62 Lai, Pan-chiu, 1997, 'Chinese Religions and the History of Salvation: A Theological Perspective', *Ching Feng*, vol. 40.1, pp. 29–30.

63 Ho, 'Reinterpreting', pp. 110–11.

64 Lai, Pan-chiu, 1999, 'Hong Kong Christians' Attitudes towards Chinese Religions', *Studies in World Christianity*, vol. 5.1, pp. 22–5.

65 Lai, Pan-chiu, 2001, 'Barth's Theology of Religion and the Asian Context of Religious Pluralism', *Asia Journal of Theology*, vol. 15.2, p. 261.

66 Wang, Zhi-cheng, 2005, *Towards the Second Axial Age*, Beijing: Zhongjiao Wenhua Chubanshe (in Chinese).

67 Lai, 'Hong Kong', pp. 25–8.

68 Küng, Hans, and Ching, Julia, 1993, *Christianity and Chinese Religions*, London: SCM Press, pp. 273–83.

69 Berthrong, John, 1994, *All Under Heaven: Transforming Paradigms in Confucian–Christian Dialogue*, Albany: SUNY Press, p. 182.

70 Neville, Robert C., 2000, *Boston Confucianism*, Albany: SUNY Press, pp. 208–9.

71 Neville, Robert C., 1991, *Behind the Masks of God: An Essay Toward Comparative Theology*, Albany: SUNY Press; also, 1982, *The Tao and the Daimon: Segments of a Religious Inquiry*, Albany: SUNY Press.

72 For example, Kim, Heup Young, 2001, *Christ and the Tao*, Hong Kong: Christian Conference of Asia; also, Hieromonk Damascene, 2002, *Christ the Eternal Tao*, 3rd edn, Platina: Valaam Books.

73 For example, Lai, Pan-chiu, 2006, 'Barth's Doctrines of Sin and Humanity in Buddhist Perspective', *Studies in Inter-religious Studies*, vol. 16.1, pp. 41–58; also, 2004, 'Doctrine of the Trinity, Christology and Hua-yen Buddhism', *Ching Feng*, n.s. vol. 5.2, pp. 203–25.

74 For example, Tam, Ekman P. C., 2002, *Christian Contemplation and Chinese Zen-Taoism: A Study of Thomas Merton's Writings*, Hong Kong: Tao Fong Shan Christian Centre.

75 Küng and Ching, *Christianity*, p. 122.

76 Lai, 'Chinese', pp. 15–40.

77 Küng and Ching, *Christianity*, pp. xi–xix.

Section D: Further Traditions

15

Indigenous Religions: Lessons of History and Challenges for the Future

GARRY W. TROMPF

Introduction

There are over 7,000 small-scale traditional societies on planet Earth. About a third of these lie around and across the vast Pacific Ocean – where territorially limited yet distinct linguistic and cultural complexes have been sitting side-by-side in curious separateness and typical enmity for untold generations. Malekula, an island of Vanuatu, contains more traditional language diversity in a confined space than anywhere else on earth; and Papua New Guinea is home to over 750 different tongues and tribal life-ways, the greatest number of any contemporary nation. If these cases from Melanesian contexts put a frightening demand on our scholarly knowledge of the human condition,[1] matters are made worse by surrounding regions. On the broad eastern side of Melanesia are the scattered cultures of Polynesia and Micronesia. To the south-west lies Australia, traditional home of over 500 peoples, and to the west are the islands and peninsulas of South-east Asia. Indonesia, which has West Papua (or Irian Jaya) and thus part of the Melanesian zone to complicate matters, hosts over 740 localized cultures (in Sulawesi, Borneo, and so on), the Philippines around 175 (famously those on Luzon) and Malaysia over 140 (including tribes along the peninsula highlands). In Asia, India houses over 1,500 tribal societies, making it facile just to consider her traditionally 'Hindu'; in the Eurasian north groupings stretching from the Lapps in Scandinavia to the Ainu in Japan have to be counted; while across a broad middle band of Asia, from the Bedouins of north-western Arabia, through Central Asia and western China on as far as Taiwan's Aboriginals, a host of commonly forgotten indigenous 'pockets' need their 'minority voices' heard. In black Africa, almost 2,000 peoples are conventionally demarcated; and in the Americas, indigenous peoples from the Inuit in the far north to the Fuegians, farthest south, make up as many as 600 discrete 'pre-Columbian' cultures.

The most crucial characteristic of small-scale traditional societies is that they lack the instruments for a securely centralized polity (or what would now be commonly taken as conditions for 'statehood'). Their smallness, then, may be typical, but not essential, for some linguistically related tribes can expand very widely (as the Bantu did, 3000 BCE–500 CE) without being a united front. The epithet 'primitive' has been applied to these small-scale societies, but this is an 'inferiorizing' descriptor, even though it is better than previous depreciative usages, such as 'savage' and 'lower races'. 'Primal' and/or 'First Peoples' are not unjustifiable captions, if by these is meant the kind of societies that have pre-existed and been absorbed by larger political unities – empires, nations, or states. But 'primal' has already begun to be *démodé*, and is less resilient than the appellations 'indigenous', even 'tribal'. Societies so named can build cities (as the west African Yoruba have), and yet *civitas* is often presumed the very opposite of primary modes of life (hunting and foraging, herding and planting). Our spectrum of possibilities for the myriad of such societies must therefore be broadened. We can hardly work on the premise that smaller-scale traditional societies lacked government; it is just that the greater number of them, as culturo-linguistic complexes, were acephalous, or without a headship over and above tribal or clan leaders. When they did possess an overall rulership, even kingship, their position was usually 'fragile', whether because of being highly dependent on sensitive inter-tribal agreements (as in equatorial Africa), or because genuine control over separate entities (many islands) was hard to achieve (as in the Hawaiian Islands). In any case, religious life, whether or not a priestly caste pertained, was highly localized, with a distinctive focus on the land 'held' by small social units – on the fecundity of its ground, animals and women, and on manly defence for its nominal integrity.

Upon cursory investigation, peoples of all the above-mentioned regions and social conditions have been recipients of Christian missionary messages and activities. Starting from the *jinn*-venerating north-west Arabian pastoral nomads, who at Wadi Ram and Petra constructed the first churches of 'indigenous tribal peoples' as we define them – and who have baulked at Islam since its emergence – down to the last-contacted isolated groups in Irian Jaya and Amazonia, the Christian faith has had its airing, appeal and frequent acceptance. One may fairly claim that Christianity's growth as a 'global' religion over the last two centuries is especially due to the widespread welcome given it among the remaining 'small fry' of the religious world. The largest mass movement of religious change during the last century, indeed, was the 'Christianization' of black Africa (with Islam in serious competition for the same broad constituency), and for an outstanding case of a whole new regional identity being secured as a consequence of mission labours, one looks immediately to Oceania (or the Pacific Islands). Christians have not made as much significant headway in zones where the other 'great religious traditions' had been well established – growth in South Korea (in reaction to a decadent Buddhism) and south India (in rejection of the caste system) being notable exceptions. But Christian work among tribal peoples has by now, at the turn into the new millennium, produced hundreds of autonomous national churches (let alone the thousands of independent ones, for which southern Africa is renowned).

The purpose of this chapter is to discuss the relationship between Christianity and indigenous religions as a contemporary issue. The matter is rather delicate, because, in our world of vast disparities of values and outlook, there are quite contrary opinions and accusations bandied around that require both clarification and mature response.

The image of Christian missionary work, for a start, varies from place to place. In secular Western discourse there is a veritable mix of voices. Some speak stridently against it – as insidious interference with peoples' freedoms – but with bare knowledge of what occurs on the ground in the relevant (typically Third World or 'Two-Thirds-South') contexts; and others hold working assumptions that clash with those of missionaries 'in the field'. A middle position weighs up pros and cons, or assesses 'relative damage' by missions; while a common secular positioning accepts missionization of tribal peoples as a necessary stage (later to be left behind), because the implanting of a universal outlook is necessary for nation-building and the transcendence of small-group loyalties. Within Western and other foreign Christian outlooks, a spectrum runs from views that external missionary activity should wind down, sooner or later, across to tight-knit conservative approaches with no other concern but mission (even as I have found to the point of training highland Papua New Guineans to reconvert backsliders in America!). The great bulk of Christian churches are of course committed to mission, but points of debate are now very widely aired as to whether approaches to the conversion of indigenous people have been too often misguided, and thus whether previous mistakes can be avoided.

To reiterate, however, there are currently many millions of Christians in or from indigenous contexts. Whatever we may conclude about missions, the phenomenon of 'indigenous Christianities' has to be reckoned with in its own right, and it is now much less a matter of thinking through 'foreigner/indigenous relations' than the relationships that exist between indigenous Christians and homegrown traditional life-ways. Indeed, apart from who has final oversight over any given set of flocks (whether expatriate or national), almost every contemporary indigenous religious sphere is now being addressed by Christians born in its own ambit, old dependencies on Western or extraneous judgements falling into recess. Perhaps many of the same old problems will affect the newer autonomous churches as they did the older missions – questions (often linguistic ones) about the levels of understanding among the mass of the faithful, or nominalism, so-called 'syncretisms' and new religious movements, persisting traditionalism and neo-traditionalism, post-Christian resentments among educated élites, and social pressures bringing new configurations of conflict (with modern weaponry). But the shift has been undeniably towards intra-indigenous religious relations (including dialogue), and the centre of attention is now on local Christian initiatives – on the role of national clergy, on home-grown styles of mission, and also on the emergence of indigenous (especially critical indigenous) theologies. As a reflection of these decolonizing trends, the role of outsiders is more and more reduced to a facilitation of local leadership and material support.

The academic disciplines of missiology, historical theology, the sociology and/or anthropology of religion, peace studies, and so on, serve to elucidate the key issues we are introducing,[2] and provoke rethinking about 'Christian/indigenous relationships' right around the globe. Using them in this small compass, one can only address what has happened and is going on with broad brushstrokes and judicious examples, to get one's bearing at the turn into the third millennium and help develop a useful interfaith platform for furthering and enriching ongoing interchanges. Combining my expertise in critical scholarship with a Christian ecumenism, I will proceed by summarizing the historical record of relations between Christianity and indigenous traditions, representing them 'without fear' between positions of malice and favouritism in search of a realistic assessment. Then I shall turn to the business of a new or preferred agenda for this relationship, combining missiological and theological insights with my sense of social reality.

Bearing the Weight of a Questionable Past

At this juncture in time, it is probably necessary to ask some hard questions as to whether the whole process of Christianizing indigenous peoples was a series of tragic mistakes, or whether it brought more problems than it solved, or left a dismal rather than positive legacy. From a certain point of view, such questions might be considered absurd or irrelevant, because we just have to be reconciled with the way things have turned out and work for the better with what is placed before us. There are strong positions around, though, ready to accentuate the negativities. In the tradition of anti-religious Colonel Ingersoll, worldwide missionization spells the expansion of consolidated religion, allegedly spawning more conflict and clerical duping among humankind. Strong protagonists for a non-Christian faith, moreover, would be expected to express disappointment that it was not Buddhism or Islam that secured the converts where Christians did; and, prolonging a long-lasting habit of mind, a fundamentalist Protestant might deem every successfully founded Catholic mission a victory for idolatry and Satan. With such dragons of polemic at large, hopefully we can keep our balance, negotiating the chasm between wilful antagonism and apology with a fair-minded, if very briskly drawn characterization of missionary

Christianity among 'the indigenes'. We shall divide our materials under the dual subheadings of 'Social' and 'Ideo-cultural'.

Social

It remains undeniable that the post-Columbian globalization of Christian (including missionary) presence has been dependent on European conquests. By 1900 Westerners were the virtual masters of the earth, and, where colonial outposts were planted, marking pacification of an area, mission work was typically carried out in the vicinity. This is not to deny that missionaries could be classic pioneers – Marquette before any foreign government between the Great Lakes, Livingstone to Nyasaland, Chalmers to Papua, and so on – but only to make a safe generalization. Indigenous peoples almost ubiquitously valued male warriorhood; they put up a fight, and military subjugation in some form or other had to occur for the current borders of world polities to exist as they do today. In the changes many people were killed and doughty indigenous defenders were common victims of superior firepower.

Signalling settlement into a peaceable way of life were church buildings, acting as sanctuaries, often between tribal borderlands, where inter-group fighting was rejected and rituals and sermons connected local congregations to the wider world of 'true worship'. Unfortunately in some regions of Western expansion the takeover was more devastating than in others. At the bitter end of conquest, remnants of indigenes were confined to reservations, often far from their original homelands (as in North America and Australia, with Canada's Inuit and the Northern Territory's Arnhem Land being the only saving, exceptional and vast enclaves to impede 'the Great White Flood'). In such circumstances social demoralization was rampant, and, in the Australian Aboriginal case especially, psycho-social dislocation devastating, because people were utterly tied to their land, understanding themselves to be conceived via some part of it before birth. In other places subjugation meant virtual enslavement, as with the Hottentots of South Africa (especially under Dutch settlers); and obviously the European slave trade is an horrific part of the tale, over 4 million persons being displaced to face a grinding existence on plantations, mostly across the Atlantic.[3] Christian believers of one shade or another were embroiled in all this, some unthinking, some 'doing their job', some utterly disturbed, some resistant.

In many cases the presence of Westerners (including missionaries) among indigenous peoples spelt susceptibility to introduced diseases. 'The Great Dying', or the transmission of pathogens (smallpox, measles, malaria) by the Iberian *conquista* of the Americas, decimated millions, and because epidemics were inevitably sped up by 'the profligate use of Indian labor' to procure gold, such irresponsibility, when coupled with military onslaughts, can be read as a sixteenth-century 'holocaust'.[4] Through the far-flung Pacific Islands, Polynesia in particular, such collective contagions (including venereal diseases) are known well enough, as exemplified from the publicized life of a Calvinist missionary to the Hawaiian Islands, Hiram Bingham, helpless and abashed as many new converts died around him (in 1826). Missions have been more involved than any other institution in history thus far in bringing a wide range of previously localized people into contact with each other, fostering intermarriage, freeing social relations between men and women, and internationalizing education. All this has borne health costs. The first Australian Aboriginal theologians, trained by the Benedictines in Spain, both died of Western illnesses there in the early 1850s.[5] Even with the best contemporary epidemiology, high degrees of social breakdown in Africa, within countries where both Christianity and modernization are strong together, make it more difficult to stem the HIV/AIDS scourge.

Christian missionary activity has been complicit in the process of modernization, entailing massive social change and the imposed 'trappings of civilization'. Hundreds of indigenous societies have been exposed to modes of production, industrial organization and machine technology totally foreign to them. Missions have often been generators of new communities (English-model 'villages' replacing scattered hamlets, as Terence Ranger noticed of British Africa), and they also trained villagers into a new skilled workforce, ready to set out for cities and be paid by money (as early twentieth-century 'industrial missions' illustrate). By this point in time, all the old forms of social organization have been undermined by the imposition of new political economies and the spreading tentacles of capitalism or foreign investment, and missions have prepared their constituents for these realities, encouraging new institutional life and leadership structures (first of all in local churches), educating for a world order of numbers and non-traditional concepts, inculcating new modes of behaviour (usually preferring modern to traditional dress or undress, for instance), and accepting the human right of social mobility (primarily between the village and a source of financial income). In short, missionary activity, if not in entirely unqualified ways, has facilitated development and wealth creation sought by colonial and then new national governments. If church politics has generally been in favour of decolonization and national determination, this involves commitment to modernization that relegates indigenous traditional life to a secondary consideration. And modernity has many (frequently shanty-town) victims in the Third World.

Competition between missions has produced more divisions in local cultures, regions and nations than would seem socially desirable. Thus even disputes within the Catholic Church (between Franciscans, Dominicans and Jesuits, for instance, in Latin America), let alone energies to 'get in ahead of the others' by Catholics, Protestants and such sectaries as Adventists or Jehovah's Witnesses, only exacerbated internal conflicts among tribes.

Tribal leaders could play off one missionary side against another, perhaps manoeuvring for the presence of a mission station. Histories of confusion over the Truth commonly followed.

The mission station model produced dependency on outsiders and lessened chances of Christian initiatives by local people. In the modern world, the mission station remains a 'permanent fixture' among indigenous peoples, bespeaking an historic conditioning of outside influences and an expectation that local groups should 'grow the same tree that had been planted'. Such stations over the centuries have marked outposts of civilization, empires and nations (even special enclaves of a Western nationhood, as German or French stations within a British colony or newly independent Anglophone country exemplify). They become effective service-points of a European offering to a needy world, and consequently tend to generate admiration for patterns of church life from the outside world. Local innovations in organization, liturgy and architecture can consequently be dampened. In cases where people are recurrently on the move – I think of Australian Aboriginals – such stations are inevitably opposed to traditional mores. In any case, 'the station paradigm' apparently runs against the biblical model of planting and then moving on, even if continuing to communicate or occasionally revisiting (as in the Pauline example).[6]

Ideo-cultural

As a missionary faith, the Christian tradition bears with it the inherent presumption of its own religious superiority. Its message is best and the truest; what its disseminators find in not-yet-converted societies will therefore immediately fall under a transcendent judgement, and be preconceived as inferior and in need of elevation. With indigenous societies this 'inferiorization' can easily be accentuated: they ostensibly lack 'civilization', they are commonly wracked by internal violence, and their eerie masks, effigies and bloody sacrifices can quickly evoke the response of 'idolatry', 'paganism', 'fetishism', 'superstition', and (somewhat better) 'animism'. For newcomer bearers of the gospel it has not been dialogue suggesting itself, but the need for help, or the triumphant shining of Light to overcome savage Darkness.[7]

Part of this problematic is that, within the dissonant messages of the religious world, Christianity among other 'salvation religions' may also be charged with raising new questions that were not 'natural' to 'more natural' religions. Most small traditional belief systems assume life after death, with everybody (or all but the 'unlucky') destined for the same place, a replication of life in the sky, let us say, or some 'happy hunting ground'. Salvation religions raise new questions about the state of one's mortal/immortal soul, and pose the choice between heaven and hell, and in Christianity's preaching (in a unique emphasis) men and women have been called to face a state of inward sinfulness that no previous set of initiations required them to discern. Indigenous peoples' variegated behavioural modes unfortunately have given more reason for being deemed sinful, potentially undercutting cultural self-confidence.

As would-be bearers of light, Christian missioners stand accused of having been insensitive to local cultures, indeed to have dismantled, even 'destroyed' smaller cultures, their subversive effect worse whenever they could not disengage the gospel message from their own Western cultural baggage. The tendency is linked to the general problem of paternalism or supererogated benevolence in colonial contexts ('Watch us, we know how to do it best'), with its resulting over-dependency of 'natives' upon their 'superiors', and a common culturo-religious mimicry of 'whiteman's fashion', as Melanesians would put it. At the same time, many missionary personnel have simply lacked training (or unbiased instruction) in the anthropology of religion, so relevant to an understanding of indigenous religions. All this entails the lessening of interest in any traditional group's resources – its botanical, dietary and medicinal repertory, to illustrate – that could keep it healthier (possibly even permit disclosure of esoteric knowledge vital for all humanity!).

In earlier days any serious attention to 'strange' or spatially confined vernacular languages was not thought helpful in establishing a wider Christian society. In Latin America, and by extension the Philippines, many opportunities were sadly missed to overcome the 'foreignness' of the new message, and Spanish became the linguistic tool by which both political and religious authorities controlled subdued peoples.[8] The worst scenarios saw the burning of pre-Christian books (those of the Maya, for instance, under Franciscan Diego de Landa), followed by the Spanish Inquisition. That said, in much later (post-Second World War) days, there was a Protestant evangelistic rush to translate the Bible into every tongue (in the light of Mark 13.10), and this automatically meant a massive amount of labour among tribal peoples. Yet the work was often done without ethnological background knowledge, and with only a rare (but necessary) concern to seek out and translate local 'oral texts' as *praeparationes Evangelii*.

Protagonists and supporters of Christian missions can be said to have wielded subtly coercive 'pastoral power', so that their indigenous listeners, belonging to highly vulnerable 'small fry' in the world of religions, have not been in the best position to make a genuine individual choice about changing their beliefs. A number of aspects immediately come to mind here – a common bossiness among missionaries, for one, reflecting frustration over the slow pace of activity, or even having to become a 'colonial' – perhaps a European seminarian's last choice! Before the gospel can be instilled, moreover, the prescriptive aspects of the Bible, such as the Ten Commandments (that can also be tied in pastorally with the laying down of the law by secular administrative officials), lend themselves to missionary 'impositions of will from on high'.[9]

The collective mentality of tribal peoples has meant that group pressure on individual change has been particularly heavy, and can be deployed in missionization through the conversion of leaders. On the other hand, missionary theorists like the German Lutheran Christian Keysser (at work in New Guinea 1889–1920) have maintained that, for the sake of continuing social cohesion, it is better for whole tribes to enter the new order consensually for a preferred collective well-being. A debate about this issue has recurred in one guise or another, with vociferous conservative Protestants insisting on the individual 'change of heart', scorning superficial mass conversion – under the Jesuit, Francis Xavier, for instance, who sprinkled holy water on the sweaty throngs of Ambon (1546–7).

Any account of Christianity's relationships with indigenous peoples, and any hope of extending, healing and deepening them, must honour and meet the challenges of this past. Before conceiving a basis for improving relationships, then, we should make a realistic assessment as to where historical events have taken us. Comparatively speaking, all civilizations affected by Christianity have turned out to be the most self-critical, because the Faith's ambiguous relationship with politics has always thrown up prophets to expose those bent on exploiting religion in their own interests. Discerning between high ideal and distortion, these critics have spotted 'the schemers of this world', as the hymnist John Newton once called them. Or assessments of the past should make use of powerful judgements from the past – from the defender of the American Indians Las Casas to the liberation theologian Gustavo Gutiérrez, to encapsulate them – thereby both facing up to old weaknesses and horrors while standing in positive-minded solidarity with those who point beyond the morass. A new spirit of social criticism, moreover, can deter commentators from rampant reification ('Christianity does this', 'Catholicism that', and the like), clarifying that conceptual colligations actually do nothing at all, but only individual agencies. And even then we must learn who gives and who has to follow orders, and how to read chains of responsibility and social role-playing. Epitomizing the range of possibilities within this *problématique*, just ponder the extraordinary deeds of the Jesuit Pedro Claver, as he bound the wounds and kissed the sores of West African slaves disgorged on the wharf at Cartagena, Columbia (starting in 1615), before a non-plussed ship's chaplain (let alone its officers), who just wanted to thank God for a safe journey across treacherous seas.[10] Who do we look to, to represent a tradition, the great inspirers, or sad products of compromising systems?

Whatever shadows cover the past, the enormous datum remains: thousands, indeed the majority of indigenous peoples have embraced Christianity. It is as if, in the terms of the pioneer social scientist Giambattista Vico, Providence showed itself despite countless human mistakes. And it now becomes tantamount to insulting millions of interesting individual strugglers to suggest that their embracing of the new faith has somehow been vitiated by human frailty, whether by imputing too much external coercive power to the evangelists, or too much gullibility to the gospel's recipients. Indigenous Christians, largely belonging to the less privileged parts of the current world system, can stand erect as a crucial and vital component of a complex world faith, for they found in the message borne to them something far more important than was conceived by most of their colonizers, indeed more precious than the homelands they tragically lost. Broadly speaking, they saw through imperialism and its systems, and, whatever they made of individual missionaries or missions, they valued the gospel to the point that a whole range of new nations depend on 'Christian values' for socio-spiritual survival and (especially in Africa, north-eastern India, and Melanesia) as an antidote to civil and tribal conflict. In the percolation of Christian insights across these many lands, moreover, due acknowledgements must be granted to indigenous 'labourers in the vineyard'. It is absurd to ascribe all that has happened to 'expatriate' figures, since by now the amount of creative ecclesiology – consider the thousands of African independent churches – and cutting-edge theology in indigenous contexts bespeak the indigenous contribution to world Christianity.

Addressing the Present and Future

The dawn of the third millennium portends a great New Day in the relationship between Christianity and First Peoples. On the basis of principles laid down by the World Council of Churches, the Vatican, and United Nations protocols, an ever-widening respect for indigenous societies, including their autochthonous bodies of knowledge, their persisting marks of cultural identity and their native spiritual propensities, should be welcomed. Where such societies have embraced a larger religious tradition – and Christianity, Islam and Buddhism are the major missionary cases in point – grafting processes or symbioses are to be encouraged that heal the wounds of prior conflict within traditional contexts (as well as any post-contact traumas) yet also foster positive distinctive aspects of the old culturo-religious life that are continuing and/or recoverable. Conversion from smaller to larger 'faiths' is unhealthy if the roots have been cut off or badly damaged. And where indigenous life-ways persist in vulnerable circumstances, within reservation systems or affected by heavy urbanization or rapid modernization (especially monetization), important pastoral work is needed to cushion people from exploitation, and to help internal stresses and strains of already ravaged groups.

Complementing our preceding approach (toward the past), we shall provide a platform for contemporary and future relations between Christians and indigenous peoples along both social and ideo-cultural lines. While positions vary over preferred theological professions of Christian truth, over the best manner of presenting the gospel, and over choices whether or not to extend missionization (*Mission oder Demission*, as the German Catholic radical Richard Friedl poses it[11]), here I gather up today's hardiest missiological threads to present them as a working consensus for current times.

Social

The Christian churches must be committed to the decolonization of regions inhabited by indigenous people who desire autonomy (as in West Papua, New Caledonia, French Polynesia), to secure and ratify honourable treaties for indigenes in countries (such as Australia, New Zealand, USA) where the long-term history of immigration has far outstripped the original populations, and to uphold the highest principles of justice and reconciliation where decolonization is being completed (as in South Africa, or Zimbabwe). And where, under persisting colonialism or neo-colonial pressures, indigenous peoples are subject to genocidal (and automatically ethnocidal) actions or policies, the churches must never let go of their prophetic role to protect human rights and insist on justice. Take Amazonia: as the rainforest has been devastated over the last century by loggers, miners and planters, one tribe on average has been wiped out every two years, often by massacre, in the name of gold and recklessly opening frontiers for exploitation. If 7,000 Nambiquara west Brazilian Indians were counted in 1915, only 530 remain today, indicating the heightened rate of tribal extinction, with Amazonians now reduced to only 215 groups in contrast to an original thousand or more. Here frontier missions are absolutely necessary to prevent atrocities and advocate land rights. They are usually the only institutions that can provide reparation for survivor groups and the 'disinherited', and continuous care to overcome neglect and ill-health in the wake of social decimation.[12] But any vestige of past horrors that recur in Latin America – from alleged Jesuit kidnapping of Hikbatsa children for education, to the Protestant Charismatic and Guatemalan President Efraín Montt's background complicity in massacres of the Maya (early 1980s) – call for fearless advocacy of prophetic justice.

To uphold this stance, liberation theologies are central to provide the dual witness – against exploitation and for a full redemption (that is, including physical salvation). Given dire straits, both church and theology require to be interlocked in social application. Hazardous work can be involved, reconciling parties after racist rule (South Africa) or bloodbaths (Rwanda), or facilitating negotiations between pro-government forces and resistance fighters to protect vulnerable tribal peoples (from pacifist Baptists in Nagaland, North India, to the mixed Catholic/traditionalist T'Boli of southern Mindanao, Philippines).

The churches are called to be agitants for the integral work of both bodily and spiritual security among indigenous peoples. By now it is a byword that the smaller peoples of the planet have taught us immeasurably important truths about survival against environmental odds (let alone against outside inflictions borne through expansionism and migration). Repertories of plant lore and traditional medicine helped solve countless everyday problems within particular eco-systems: just consider *saw palmetto*, curated by Floridan Everglades Indians, with properties now universally acclaimed for prostate protection. Kinship mechanisms within 'solidary groups' (phratries, totem memberships, tribes, clans, lineages, bands) played their part, not just as identity markers, but as means of mutual support – a given group, for instance, keeping a custodial role over food sources of others. Christians need to learn how inherited mechanisms shore up overall survival potential and general health of local communities, so that introduced components of knowledge – inoculations, dietary instructions, schooling – can be made to complement rather than cancel out pre-existing resources of benefit. There will have to be ongoing processes of discernment, of course, as to which inheritances are beneficial or not, often to be sorted out on a case-by-case basis. No Christian worker could be criticized for applying methods of strong persuasion to stop tribal fighting (in the Papua New Guinea highlands, for example), even if it may still be the firmest means of securing tribal solidarity. Or for dissuading western Tanzanian mothers from feeding newborns on one breast only (it being a long-inured taboo to do otherwise) because infant mortality rates are so high as a result.[13]

To combine preaching Christian messages with either confirming or bringing instruments of social value, we may stress, is not to be despised, and separating them is wrong-headed. The 1974 Evangelical Lausanne Covenant affirms this, much evangelical mission theology now persuasively stressing the gospel call to an integrative view of life – a 'heavenly rule' – in which bodily and spiritual life in both individuals and communities is nurtured.[14] Never has this been more necessary than in the case of tribal societies. Huge disparities in life possibilities exist between the fully capitalized West and the underdeveloped, poverty-wracked Third World. Life expectancies in countries like Lesotho and Swaziland (old South African 'homelands') and nations neighbouring South Africa are on average under 39 years, with HIV/AIDS rampant. There Christians and traditionalist Africans live side-by-side, desperate for mutual support, and the best available healing resources (traditionalist, indigenous Christian, and foreign) are needed.[15]

Given their inner communal strength, and the lessons they teach in moderating human needs, the Christian churches are challenged to mediate between satisfying local (typically rural) lifestyles and modernization (which under transnational investment and internationally funded national projects has attained almost apocalyptic proportions, and which motivates individual desires for 'the Cargo' – such internationally marked commodities as radios, refrigerators and cars – into manic consumerism). Traditional small-scale groups are commonly imaged as standing in the way of progress, especially when large projects (mining, damming) may be the only means by which new national governments could pay off debts to the World Bank or satisfy requirements of fast-growing urban centres. Moreover, the pressures of the World Bank's 'structural adjustment policies' to deregulate national markets and allow the free circulation of foreign capital damages subsistence economies, forcing their members to find money (and therefore look for work in cities, as has been a common pattern for the last century) rather than 'live simply but in dignity' in village-type contexts.[16] A new pressure falls on financially well-off churches to provide preferable alternatives to inappropriate development, particularly through using NGOs. If the latter can sometimes be criticized for abetting local church causes, this is because their projects are best implemented by local church leaders, who can in any case use overseas aid intended for *all* needy souls, as a means of bringing Christians, traditionalists and members of other faiths into a healing, non-(or less) privileging relationship.[17] Theologically, a 'wider hermeneutic' than normal is required here, one 'in many modes' to provide Christian 'hope in [people's] active transition', sensitive to both anthropological background and the sociology of change.[18]

In view of their splintered past may the churches find inspiration in the solidarity of the new tribe of the 'New Israel' in the New Testament and in the comparable communality of life in traditional tribal religions. Already indigenous Christians have undone the competing activities of introduced missions in their own special ways. One is through a grassroots ecumenism operating at local and regional levels where historic differences are glossed over by acknowledged multi-pronged co-operation in different areas of large, needy fields. Such a 'sharing of the harvest' or working ecumenicity between the mainline churches can have its limits, of course, where sectarian Protestant churches (Adventists, Witnesses, Pentecostals) are perceived to 'steal sheep' from older established parishes. Another means of undoing old competitions is to outdo them by creating very many independent, often local and novelly titled churches to tackle indigenous pressures on Christianity with a 'free hand' – to express tribal-type solidarity, for example, or to treat earth sacramentally (as in Africa). Such independencies are rife in urban South Africa, Botswana and beyond, not only showing up among African Americans in turn (witness downtown Miami), but much further afield (as in Melanesia). At the inter-ecclesial level the former mission-founding churches are called to foster ecumenical theology, dialogue and co-operation, even (as with David Barrett's secretariat in Nairobi) creating possibilities for the myriad independencies to speak to each other and the wider Church. Meanwhile new opportunities are arising for the indigenous leadership of the largest denominations to offer an ecumenical (and as a result more tolerant) Christian presence among First Peoples, neither duplicating old European bigotries nor over-accommodating tribalist *mentalités* found in independent churches.

Prior presumptions about the necessity of bearing outside guidance to indigenous peoples, whether they are converting or still traditionalist, should by now be replaced by mature initiatives of inculturation. Missiologically, in- or enculturation denotes the healthy relationship between the biblical outlook and any culture. It allows an enabling, through an even-handed interaction between proclaimers and listeners, for the gospel to be received as the fulfilment, not a destroying agent, of culture, even while discernment is encouraged to reveal how Christ redeems from the false idols and pretensions of human 'cultural effort'. In the Protestant theologian Richard Niebuhr's terms, inculturation affirms first how Christ is 'for Culture' as a feeling after the divine (cf. Acts 17.27) while waiting to see what is in need of change – under the criterion of the love this same Christ has shown. Many Catholic documents prepared under the late Pope John Paul II have systematized the inculturative agenda, and among his important emphases is empowerment of the local church, and in particular its laity, to develop a rich communal life that interweaves traditional social intricacies with redemptive insights of *Missio Dei*.[19]

Ideo-cultural

The widespread presence of Christian adherents among peoples retaining autochthonous beliefs, and perhaps seeking to synthesize tradition and Christianity, calls for dialogue (including dialogical theology), and for confidence in humility rather than straining to replace the presumed 'superior' by the 'inferior'. Doubtless a danger lurks that 'new Christians' will perpetuate the old-fashioned fervour to eliminate heathen darkness before divine light, yet it remains true that many members of indigenous churches have lived through and experienced traditional ways and can make more meaningful comparisons between Christian and indigenous faiths that are not like 'the whiteman's knee-jerk reactions'. In any case, it is now especially their challenge to whittle away at remnants of paternalism in prior church atmospheres, to unload the Church of its burden of association with racist and inferiorizing tendencies, more patiently handle those caught between tradition and Christianity, and, hardest of all, to live out relationships between the genders that transcend common attitudes in many (but admittedly not all) traditional societies in which female voices have been belittled or women treated as male possessions.

The Christian churches can no longer maintain insensitivity towards indigenous belief-systems when so much positivity has been revealed about them, and thus new theologies of accommodation require developing. The amount of skilful anthropological and religious studies research carried out among indigenous peoples during the twentieth century has revealed subtleties and complexities of thought unimagined without proper language facility. Nuances of myth, and the intricate relations between narrative, song and ritual, have been uncovered for many and varied Aboriginal and Oceanic groups. The strength of ancient monotheistic tendencies in African traditional religion has been held high for contemplation, and honoured in ecclesiastical circles (as for example in John Paul II's *Ecclesia in Africa* (1995)).[20] The stress on being in a community of both the living and the dead in indigenous societies recalls for the churches the hoary question – aired before in the Chinese rites controversy – as to whether veneration of the dead conflicts with the Christian faith, and whether the ancestors' stories (even carved poles reflecting them, as among west Canada's Nootka or Irian Jaya's Asmat) can ever sit beside the Old Testament as liturgical preparations for the gospel. A much deeper interreligious sharing of the riches within both Christian and First Peoples' spiritualities is waiting to happen, to honour the many different paths into the divine Ambience (even, some now argue, by way of shamanism).[21]

Many indigenous theological minds now set the missiological agenda for their respective contexts. Because most were trained under expatriates, initial reactions to such theologians have been to rate them low beside the highly conceptualist, systematic exponents of the Christian faith in Western halls of learning, as though they rely more on 'story materials' than discursive *modi operandi*. However, not only have the ablest of these theologians 'won their spurs' internationally, but shifts within the theological arena in favour of the narrational have also widened their readership. The globalization of information about human crises (epidemics, famine, war and refugees) has necessitated a heeding of 'voices from the edge' (on the rims of comfort zones, but in the centre of troubles). When these thinkers reach international forums, recounting their extraordinary trials becomes very powerful. Female voices are telling: as with the Bible expositions of the Ghanaian Mercy Yamoah-Odudoye working out of the World Council of Churches, or the Tasmanian Aboriginal (*Palawan*) womanist theologian Lee Miena Skye stunning her audience to silence at the 2004 Parliament of the World's Religions when she disclosed the plight of her people and the effects of Aboriginal women's deep Christian/indigenous spirituality for salvaging disintegrating communities.[22]

The Christian churches present among indigenous communities are urged to shed all associations of lordly, 'parental' power and rely on the prophetic Word of justice, and not only for the care of despairing humans but also for the oppressed earth itself. Using this affirmation as the gateway to a conclusion, I suspect, in all realism, that no one can wish away residual paternalisms or an inbred sense that tribal (in some persisting parlances 'primitive') societies have still got more to learn from so-called *hautes civilisations* like those in the West. But the dawn of the third millennium calls for new reckonings. Highly urbanized and consumptive societies such as those found in Europe, North America and Australia have been despoiling the earth since the Second Industrial Revolution (1880s on), and they can no longer be sure of having the means to rectify the damage they continue to cause. Traditional peoples represent one preferable paradigm for the future, one of simplicity, reciprocity and a self-sufficient smallness that has been lauded in Western thought from the Anarchist Peter Kropotkin to the hard-nosed economist E. F. Schumacher. In all this the wisdom of the traditional elders should be allowed to speak to the world, and to be honestly mediated through the churches. Small peoples have suffered much. They can speak to everyone, as it were, from the Cross. They can shame us into action to improve life on earth as the necessary teachers of those who thought they could take over the world and leave an unholy mess. In any case, when one shares the tough, survivalist life of a small people, inhaling the smoke that rises through the floor-poles to keep the mosquitoes away, drawing out sweet witchetty grubs from hot coals, but above all experiencing beside excited flames the mysteries of indigenous story and life-way from its best custodians,[23] one hears the Gospel of the Earth. It is time for Christians to be willing learners at the feet of 'the natives'. As the French Reformed Protestant missionary Maurice Leenhardt admitted nearly a century ago, upon returning to become Professor of Anthropology at the Sorbonne, perhaps the Melanesians had taught him more than he thought he could give to them.[24]

Once two richly robed pilgrims knocked on my Sydney door, and upon facing me they fell to the floor and kissed 'the ground' before me. I was startled and embarrassed, urging them to rise, and insisting I was hardly worthy of such treatment. But they abruptly reassured me: they were two members of a Nigerian independent church, the Brotherhood of the Cross and Star, bearing a simple message to 'Love God, love your fellow human being; and love the Earth.' How my heart responded to this adapted gospel, with the call to love by a Jewish rabbi – who himself relayed the beauteous depths of his own tradition in a revelatory new way – in symphony with the cry of the earth, with its awe and richness, and the extraordinary array of peoples closest to it.[25]

Study Questions

1 What are the major difficulties in generalizing about the historical and contemporary relationship between Christianity and indigenous cultures?

2 If there have been many problems in Christian–indigenous encounters and relations, how would you account for the continuing acceptance of the Christian message among 'First Peoples'?

3 Are missionaries inevitably caught up in trying to impose a presumptively 'superior' religion on implicitly 'inferior' peoples?

4 Should emissaries of the Christian way of life now focus more on helping indigenous peoples to meet their material needs and solve social justice problems rather than stressing evangelization and church membership?

Further Reading

Allen, Roland, 1968, *Missionary Methods, St. Paul's or Ours?*, London: Lutterworth.

Parratt, John (ed.), 1987, *A Reader in African Christian Theology*, London: SPCK.

Samone, Frank A. (ed.), 1985, *Missionaries and Anthropologists*, part II, Studies of Third World Societies, vol. 26, Williamsburg: College of William and Mary.

Shaw, R. Daniel, and Van Engen, Charles E., 2003, *Communicating God's Word in a Complex World: God's Truth or Hocus Pocus?*, Lanham, New York and Oxford: Rowan and Littlefield.

Tinker, George E., 1993, *Missionary Conquest: The Gospel and Native American Cultural Genocide*, Minneapolis: Augsburg Fortress.

Trompf, Garry W. (ed.), 1987, *The Gospel is Not Western: Black Theologies from the Southwest Pacific*, Maryknoll: Orbis.

Tucker, Ruth A., 1983, *From Jerusalem to Irian Jaya: A Biographical History of Christian Missions*, Grand Rapids: Academie Books.

Whiteman, Darrell L. (ed.), 1985, *Missionaries, Anthropologists and Cultural Change*, part I, Studies of Third World Societies, vol. 25, Williamsburg: College of William and Mary.

Notes

1 See Trompf, G. W., with Tomasetti, Friedegard, 2006, *Religions of Melanesia: A Bibliographic Survey*, London: Praeger.

2 See, for example, Jongeneel, Jan, 1986, *Missiologie*, vol. 1, The Hague: Boekencentrum, ch. 5.

3 Pattel-Gray, Anne, 1998, *The Great White Flood*, Oxford: Oxford University Press (Australian Aboriginals); Warneck, Gustav, 1883, *Modern Missions and Culture*, Smith, T. (trans.), Edinburgh: James Gemmel, pp. 179, 314–19 (Africa).

4 Wolf, Eric, 1982, *Europe and the People Without History*, Berkeley: University of California Press, p. 133.

5 Pattel-Gray, Anne, and Trompf, G. W., 1993, 'Styles of Aboriginal and Melanesian Theology', *International Review of Mission*, vol. 82, no. 326, p. 173.

6 Especially, Allen, Roland, 1927, *The Establishment of the Church in the Mission Field*, London: World Dominion Press. For historical background, Williams, Peter, 1990, *The Ideal of a Self-Governing Church*, Leiden: Brill.

7 See also, May, J. D'A., 2003, *Transcendence and Violence: The Encounter of Buddhist, Christian and Primal Traditions*, London: Continuum, pp. 32–41. For this key issue, see also the piece by Gustav Warneck in the Reader which accompanies this volume.

8 Storch, Tanya (ed.), 2005, *Religions and Missionaries around the Pacific*, Aldershot: Ashgate, pp. xx–xxi.

9 Cf. King, Noel, and Fieder, Klaus (eds), 1991, *Robin Lamburn – From a Missionary's Notebook*, Saarbrücken: Breitenbach, p. 91; Trompf, G. W., 1994, *Payback*, Cambridge: Cambridge University Press, p. 309 (using Michel Foucault).

10 Thomas, Hugh, 1997, *The Slave Trade*, London: Picador, p. 433.

11 Friedl, Richard, 1982, *Mission oder Demission: Konturen einer lebendigen, weil missionarischen Gemeinde*, Freiburg, Switzerland: Universitätsverlag Freiburg.

12 Peacock, James, *et al.*, 1996, 'Missionaries, Anthropologists and Human Rights', *Missiology*, vol. 24, no. 2, Special Issue.

13 Of introductory value: Hiebert, Paul, and Hiebert, Frances, 1987, *Case Studies in Mission*, Grand Rapids: Baker.

14 Lundström, Klas, 2006, *Gospel and Culture*, Uppsala: Swedish Institute of Mission Research, p. 281 (citing Lausanne).

15 Auna, Ade, 1987, 'The Church's Healing Ministry', in Parratt, John (ed.), *A Reader in African Christian Theology*, London: SPCK, pp. 110–16.

16 Balm, Grégoire, 2001, 'Spiritualité et développement économique', *Laval Théologique et Philosophique*, vol. 57, no. 1, p. 267.

17 Bornstein, Erica, 2005, *The Spirit of Development*, Stanford: Stanford University Press, chs 4–6.

18 Blaser, Klauspeter, 1992, 'Neuere Missionstheologie', *Verkuendigung und Forschung*, vol. 37, no. 2, pp. 21–2.

19 See Bowie, Fiona, 1999, 'The Inculturation Debate in Africa', *Studies in World Christianity*, vol. 5, no. 1, pp. 67–92; Bieniek, Janusz, 2007, 'Evangelisation as the Practical Mission of the Church', in Trompf, G. W. (ed.), *Melanesian Religions and Christianity*, Madang: DWU Press, ch. 4.

20 Cf. also Oborji, Frances, 2002, 'Revelation in African Traditional Religion: The Theological Approach since Vatican II', *Euntes docete*, vol. 55, no. 3, pp. 68–78.

21 For example Yule, Sandy, 2005, *The Burning Mirror*, Delhi: ISPCK.

22 Yamoah-Odudoye, Mercy Amba, esp. 2000, *Introducing African Women's Theology*, Maryknoll: Orbis; Skye, Lee Miena, 2007, *Kerygmatics of the New Millennium*, Delhi: ISPCK. Cf. the series Voices from the Edge, Raúl Fernández-Calienes and Trompf, G. W. (eds), Delhi: ISPCK.

23 That is, while being fully aware of touristic representations of cultures, and (with sadness) of inevitably 'fake' presentations of them (after cultural decimations).

24 On Leenhardt, see Clifford, James, 1982, *Person and Myth*, Berkeley: University of California Press.

25 My thanks for helpful criticism during the preparation of this essay are offered to my colleague Dr Friedegard Tomasetti.

16

New Religious Movements: Dialogues Beyond Stereotypes and Labels

J. GORDON MELTON

Introduction

Through the last half of the twentieth century, observers documented a notable increase in religious pluralism in the West, spearheaded by the appearance of hundreds of new religions that fell far outside of the Christian religious consensus that had dominated society for many centuries. Interestingly enough, the first recognition that something was happening occurred in Japan. At the end of the Second World War, a new constitution that included provisions delineating an American-style religious freedom was imposed on the country. Within a very few decades, hundreds of new religions emerged and a set of older religions that had been suppressed under the previous Meiji Regime were reborn with a renewed vigour. By the 1960s, books about the 'new religions of Japan' spread word of the phenomena globally.[1]

Then in 1965, the United States radically revised its immigration laws that had for almost a century blocked immigration from Asia. Through the next decade, a wave of Asian teacher/missionaries from a spectrum of Asian religions took up residence in the United States, ready to recruit followers from the general population. They discovered American society somewhat in turmoil from the coming of age of the baby-boom generation. A generation of young adults, finding integration into mainstream society somewhere between difficult and impossible, tried a variety of alternatives that included communal living, experimentation with mood-altering drugs, and flirtation with different religious perspectives. Observers saw a wave of 'new religious consciousness' sweeping the younger generations. Some welcomed it as an antidote to spiritually dead churches while others reacted with horror at the emergence of primitive paganism.[2]

As some of the more colourful and controversial of the 'new religions' that first became known in their North American setting began to appear on the streets of European cities, European scholars took notice of the emerging pluralism across the continent. Initially blaming it on America in general and California in particular, they soon realized that the new religions of Europe had emerged quite independently of America. Their growth had gone largely unnoticed as it had occurred gradually, beginning in the 1950s following the Chinese Revolution and Indian independence. The increase in diversity had happened so slowly that it had not been recognized until it reached a critical mass during the 1970s.[3] Still more were alerted to the existence of the new religions by the death of the members of the Peoples Temple in 1978.[4]

By the end of the 1970s, a reactionary movement to the growth of the new religions had already developed, and the Jonestown event occasioned its spread. By the early 1980s, an international network aimed at countering the presence of what were seen as 'destructive cults' was in place across North America and Europe. Initially, this cult awareness network consisted largely of people upset with youthful family members who had joined one of the new religions and some psychologists who saw a potential danger in the new groups, but they quickly sought allies among the media, law enforcement agencies and the legal professions, anyone whom they felt could assist them in demanding government intervention to suppress the new religions. As government action developed very slowly, the anti-cult groups adopted alternative means. In North America, families often utilized a process of deprogramming that involved forcefully detaining and pressuring individual group members to leave the group.

The growth of the anti-cult movement and especially the practice of deprogramming attracted a number of scholars, motivated by the debate over brainwashing, to the study of new religions. At the end of the 1970s, several psychologists, most notably Margaret Singer, suggested that the new religions, the cults, were engaged in a subtle but powerful technique with recruits that led to their losing their free will and joining the new religions against their own best interest. Singer called it coercive persuasion, but it was popularly termed brainwashing. Such a loss of the ability to choose to leave the group justified the radical intervention of deprogramming even if it meant the overriding of government guarantees of religious liberty.

In Europe, the debate took a different course, with cult awareness advocates arguing that those people (mostly young adults) who joined the new religions had in effect dropped out of society and were on their way to becoming a socially irrelevant (and hence irresponsible) segment of the population.[5] The loss of so many people needed to maintain the social fabric, the advocates argued, justified the government's action to suppress them.

Through the 1980s and 1990s, religious scholars and social scientists devoted a considerable amount of energy to the study of new religions (also termed New Religious Movements or NRMs) and debate on their possible destructive influences.[6] The result of that debate was a general consensus that the brainwashing hypothesis was baseless. That opinion was underscored in 1987 when the American Psychological Association rejected a lengthy report written by Margaret Singer and some of her psychological colleagues that attempted to make the case for intervention among members of cults that practised coercive persuasion. At about the same time, the American Sociological Association and the Society for the Scientific Study of Religion released statements that concurred. Based upon these documents, beginning in 1990, the American courts began to reject any discussion of brainwashing.[7] These rulings led to the abandonment of coercive deprogramming by the cult awareness organizations.

In Europe, the fears of the 1970s over the possible loss of a generation of young people to society proved unfounded, and the older arguments about the dangers of 'youth religion' fell by the wayside. However, just as the brainwashing hypothesis was abandoned in North America, now termed 'mental manipulation', it found new life in Europe – finding increased support after several violent incidents concerning NRMs in the 1990s, especially the murder/suicides of members of the Solar Temple in Switzerland (1994). Through the decade, a number of countries involved in the European Union issued reports, those of France and Belgium being the most negative and those of Sweden and Germany the more positive. While some support of the brainwashing hypothesis remains in Europe, since the end of the century, its popularity has noticeably waned.

The New Age Movement

While the debate over NRMs was being pursued,[8] a second phenomenon appeared on the scene – the New Age movement. Birthed in several independent Theosophical centres in England in the 1970s, the movement spread rapidly and by the beginning of the 1980s was visible throughout the Western world. Observers quickly recognized it as a revival of older Spiritualist/esoteric/occult themes that had been present in the culture for centuries, but were somewhat baffled by its decentralized movemental organization. NRM scholars were initially taken aback by New Age assertions that they were spiritual but not religions, and puzzled at how the loosely organized New Age groupings fitted into the larger development of new religions, most of which seemed to form rather tightly knit organizations.

Gradually, however, the significance of the New Age became evident, even as it was dying. The New Age emerged as a revitalization movement of the older occult community, now recast as a millennial movement with a vital additional component of transforming spirituality. The occult, now generally called Western Esotericism, had been present as a minority tradition in the West for centuries, but in the 1970s a new generation of leaders proposed the imminent arrival of a New Age of light and love (wisdom and peace) that would be characterized by the ready availability of a host of transformative tools (channelling, psychic healing, divination, astrology, crystals, body work therapies, alternative healing disciplines). Personal transformation would provide not only healing for the body, mind and spirit of individuals, but the abandonment of our dysfunctional society.

Almost everyone involved in the formative stages of the New Age movement was also involved in one of its definitive practices – channelling. Channels, known as mediums in Spiritualism, were special people who possessed the ability to contact various spirit entities, most often a spiritually advanced teacher. Channelling became the means of establishing the movement's authority and of injecting fresh ideas into the community. It would become one of the most enduring (and studied) aspects of the New Age movement.[9]

Recast as the New Age, the small older esoteric communities grew exponentially. In the United States in a matter of two decades, the number of adherents went from several hundred thousand to several millions. The most visible (and permanent) element of the new movement was the host of New Age bookstores and publishers that emerged in the 1970s. A generation later, they remain as the most vital points for the dissemination of esoteric belief. As could be expected, the movement provoked a wide range of reaction, from ridicule[10] and extreme hostility[11] to empathetic support.[12]

Then at the beginning of the 1990s, the movement underwent a significant change as most of the leadership abandoned the millennial aspect of their belief while concluding that the benefits of the spectrum of transformative tools and the spirituality they undergirded were worth all that had occurred. Though they were in effect abandoning the 'New Age', they would continue as spiritual change agents. In the wake of this change, talk of the New Age has all but disappeared, replaced by a more modest hope for the transformative movement's continued expansion.[13] Under a variety of names, the community of people attentive to the transformative tools has continued.[14]

The emergence of the New Age also called together a new generation of scholars, only a minority of whom were involved in the larger discussions of NRMs, but who were ready to give their primary attention to the Esoteric tradition.[15] Taking their lead from Antoine Faivre, who held a chair in Esoteric studies at the Sorbonne, these scholars began the process of defining and highlighting Western Esotericism as a continuing if at times broken and dissenting tradition in Western religious thought beginning with ancient Gnosticism and as known today by its prominent modern components – Rosicrucianism, Freemasonry, Swedenborgianism, Spiritualism, Christian Science and New Thought, Theosophy, ceremonial magic, and most recently, Wicca and Neo-Paganism. Western Esotericism has been relatively unnoticed through the centuries as a separate tradition due to the persecution it faced from the religious establishment and the several mechanisms it developed to survive. The suppressive action of state and church was so severe at times as to threaten Esotericism's very existence. In reaction, Esotericists articulated their position as 'mystical' Christianity, and since the eighteenth century they often organized as non-religious (but spiritual) fraternal groups such as Freemasonry.

Toward a Definition

The brief introduction to the world of new religions and the New Age begins to get at the continuing problem of understanding and even defining those groups covered by the terms. Unlike Buddhists or Muslims, for example, the new religions do not form a community that shares a history or a set of symbols, beliefs and practices. If anything, collectively they embody the extreme diversity of the contemporary religious world. It is also the case that while Hindus or Zoroastrians proudly use that self-designation, no 'new religion' uses that term in its own self-description, and no Esoteric group uses the term New Age any more (and many never did). 'New Age' and 'new religion' are the terms of outsider observers and critics. In fact, the term 'new religion' originally became popular in the West as a scholarly alternative to the older term 'cult' (and in Europe 'sect'), which in popular usage had acquired too many derogatory connotations.

The problem is easily seen in the many Eastern groups that surfaced in the West in the 1970s. High on the list of 'new religions' was the International Society for Krishna Consciousness (ISKCON, the Hare Krishna movement). ISKCON always insisted that it was a Vaishnava Hindu organization but went through a period of controversy as it grew as a popular devotional movement drawing its basic membership from non-Asians. However, as its Asian membership grew, it has been able to integrate more easily into the growing Asian Hindu community in the West and has since the 1990s made a concerted (and to some extent successful) effort to be seen as a Hindu group, not another new religion.

Scholars have generally taken one of three approaches to defining the world of new religions. Some, most notably Eileen Barker, have emphasized the 'new' element in new religions,[16] suggesting that NRMs are basically distinct in that they are either newly formed religions (such as the Church of Scientology) or older religions that have opened operations in a new cultural environment (Asian religions growing a non-Asian membership in the West). Barker emphasizes that we have much to learn from first-generation groups (and from there transition to a second and third generation). They provide, for example, much information about the beginnings of the older religions.

Other scholars have emphasized the overall social positioning of new religions and the fact that some NRMs (Jehovah's Witnesses, Theosophy, Christian Science) have retained their designation as a 'new religion' for a century or more.[17] Developing his understanding from the old church–sect–cult trichotomy popularized in the 1950s, the sociologist David Bromley suggests that new religions are those groups, many of which are relatively new organizations, that lack both social and cultural alignments in the culture in which they exist. The new religions are alienated from the dominant religious leadership and lack allies in the political community to an extent that they have trouble accessing those social elements that embody power in any given society. They also dissent in key elements of belief and/or practice to the point that they are alienated from the dominant religious culture of the society in which they operate.[18]

Still other scholars emphasize the new religions' dissent from the dominant pattern of acceptable religious life in a society. In the Christian West, a number of new religions are groups that have denied what many consider essential Christian beliefs, most notably the Trinity and the divinity of Jesus.[19] Others advocate new forms of behaviour that the majority find beyond their ability to tolerate – high-pressure evangelism, involvement in illegal or violent activity, or sexual promiscuity. Non-Christian religions attain their status as new religions when they begin to operate outside of their accepted ethnic communities. While no one assigns the status of new religion to Japanese Buddhists, Punjabi Sikhs, or Turkish Muslims, the same cannot be said of the Soka Gakkai, the 3HO Sikh Dharma, or the Nation of Islam.

Most of the NRMs are Western representatives of the older and larger religious traditions, and generally think of themselves as Hindus, Buddhists, Sikhs or Muslims, but for different reasons do not fit well within the representative Asian or Middle Eastern communities. The Indian groups built around a single charismatic guru have almost been a definition for some of 'cult'. Possibly half of the new religions represent new forms of Christianity or Judaism. For a spectrum of reasons they have not found recognition from the larger Christian and Jewish communities. Some NRMs reject key beliefs at the heart of their tradition; others propose innovative and controversial practices. A very few, the Unification Church being the most prominent example, present a new synthesis of several older belief systems.

These different approaches to new religions lead directly to the New Age. The Western Esoteric tradition, certainly in its modern incarnations since the seventeenth century, has always been a minority and socially alienated part of Western society. It has regularly been suppressed and denounced as the 'occult' and only began to gain some recognition in its 'non-religious' aspect in the nineteenth century as Freemasonry aligned with some of the democratic movements that created the modern Western European democratic states. It also found a new intellectual life as leading thinkers discarded its older naive supernaturalism and developed a more sophisticated philosophy utilizing modern science (Mesmerism, evolutionary biology, depth psychology, quantum mechanics).

The groups that make up the present Esoteric community form possibly the most important segment of the total of what might be termed 'new religions'. In terms of the number of groups and individuals involved, the community of Esoteric believers constitutes over half of the 'new religions' phenomenon. In the United States, polls show some 6 to 9 million (2–3 per cent of the population) are regularly involved in Esoteric activities (more than the total community of Buddhists, Hindus and Muslims combined), and if one measures the more popular parts of New Age belief such as astrology or reincarnation or the practice of meditation, the figures jump sharply upward. Figures for different European nations are even higher.

The Neo-Pagan community has become a unique addition to Western Esotericism.[20] While drawing heavily on Western Esoteric beliefs and practices, Wiccans and Neo-Pagans also see themselves as part of a global reassertion of pre-modern indigenous or ethno-linguistic religions which would include Native American, traditional African, Afro-Caribbean and Asian shamanistic religions. Once seen as a disappearing part of the religious landscape, these traditional religions have made a remarkable recovery since the end of colonialism, and Pagan revivalist groups are now evident throughout the West. In addition, representatives of the surviving traditional religious communities from Africa, Asia and the Americas have now moved to establish worshipping centres among immigrants in the West. A survey of new religions must of necessity include groups such as the African Theological Archministry based in South Carolina, who have built the village of Oyotunji, where they seek to recover their Yoruban heritage.

Dialogue

Interfaith dialogue between Christians and representatives of the new religions has been quite rare. Through the late twentieth century, the cult awareness movement was quite successful in branding the new religions as destructive cults worthy of broad disdain. Paralleling the cult awareness movement has been an even larger Christian-based counter-cult movement which grew out of the American fundamentalist movement of the 1920s. Spearheaded by Walter R. Martin (1928–89), this movement expanded significantly in the 1960s and 1970s. Martin and his successors have complained that the cults are a basic threat to Christianity as they exist only to lure Christians from their faith into a false religion. The most ignoble of the new religions are seemingly Christian churches that have revived the old heresies from the era of the great church councils that hammered out Christian orthodoxy in the fourth to eighth centuries. Additional NRMs are bringing the false religions of Hinduism, Buddhism and the other world religions to our doorstep. Most Evangelicals believe that our only relationship to these groups should be one of evangelical endeavour. As the number of groups has grown and some have become relatively successful, some Christian counter-cult leaders[21] have also adopted the brainwashing hypothesis and called for government action against the new religions.

While the majority of Christian literature against the cults/new religions has emanated from the more conservative wing of Protestantism, representatives of Roman Catholicism, Eastern Orthodoxy and liberal Protestantism have contributed their share.[22] The larger denominations often produced only a modest amount of material, but coming with a denominational imprimatur or from a denominational publishing house, it assumed a role as representing the group's policy. Often such literature was the result of dialogue on other fronts, the most notable case being the publication by Fortress Press, an official publishing house of the Evangelical Lutheran Church in America, a prominent supporter of Jewish–Christian dialogue, of *Prison or Paradise: The New Religious Cults*, written by two prominent American Jewish leaders.[23]

The Roman Catholic Church, which in the wake of Vatican II established a Pontifical Council for Interreligious Dialogue, has pursued one of the most active programmes of interfaith dialogue with Buddhists, Hindus, Jews, Muslims and representatives of Native American and African Traditional Religions. The council has also developed a concern around new religions, but as its Coordinator for Attention to New Religious Movements and Sects noted, the intention of the Council has been 'not so much to have dialogue with representatives from these new groups as to study and prepare papers with a view to pastoral action'.[24] Over the last 20 years the Council has published a series of items on new religions, actually some of the more perceptive responses to the presence of so many new religions by any Christian bodies, but none that shows any sign of initiating even minimal dialogical activity.[25]

In 1993, Francis Cardinal Arinze, then head of the Pontifical Council for Interreligious Dialogue, attended the conference sponsored by the Center for Studies on New Religions (CESNUR), the largest annual gathering of new religions scholars, and spoke on 'Is the Dialogue with NRMs Possible?' This is the only such paper to be delivered by a Vatican leader of his status at an international conference to date. Within limits, Arinze acknowledged that dialogue was both possible and desirable, but the Church would be reluctant to enter it with groups that either viciously attack the Roman Catholic Church or engage in sheep-stealing outside the rules of normal civility. Possible models for dialogue are the quiet conversations that have occurred between some church leaders in Japan and several of the more prominent of the Japanese new religions.

The reluctance of the Catholic Church to begin dialogue with new religions derives from two basic perceptions. First, the Church has felt the presence of the movement of Eastern religions into the Western Catholic countries and saw the popular spread of Zen and other forms of meditation within religious orders and among the laity.[26] It eventually reacted strongly to both, along with the most popular New Age activity – astrology.[27] Second, while some ideas of the Western Esoteric tradition command a large popular audience, the major groups remain quite small compared, for example, with the representative communities of Buddhist or Muslim groups. There is a sense that any dialogue with new religions would be uneven. By recognizing the new religions as possible dialogical partners, the Church would be granting them a status that they have not yet earned.[28] In his 1993 presentation, Cardinal Arinze also showed concern about and obvious annoyance with smaller religious groups that wanted to use a dialogue merely to have a media event – a chance to be photographed with the pope or a Vatican official that they could later circulate as evidence of their legitimacy.[29]

The Orthodox Church has been uniformly opposed to any dialogue with new religions, and different Orthodox bishops have written books attacking the 'cults'. Liberal Protestant groups have promulgated few statements on the new religions, though on occasion, like the Lutherans, they have stood by as their publishing houses have issued anti-cult books. They have also made little effort to respond to any overtures for dialogue. The most positive response from the liberal Protestant community derived from a conference sponsored by the World Council of Churches in 1986,[30] which like the Roman Catholic efforts included no representatives of the groups under discussion.

Evangelical churches have persistently attacked the cults, seeing them as competitors who have wooed members away. Some of the larger evangelical groups, most notably the Southern Baptists, have funded apologetic efforts to produce material refuting the teachings of the new religions while defending Christian truth, while the small groups have been supportive of the many Christian counter-cult apologetic ministries. As the twenty-first century begins, some former leaders of the evangelical counter-cult movement have separated themselves from the older approach (and especially the shrill rhetoric with which it was so often associated) and attempted to find a more pastoral approach to new religions that honours their integrity and, while retaining an emphasis on evangelism, seeks a more effective way to communicate with the believers of other faiths.[31]

Dialogical Initiative

While attempts at dialogue between Christians and representatives of the new religions have been rare, a few have occurred. The most notable and long-standing dialogue has been that initiated in the 1970s by the Unification Church. For several decades, the Unification Church held a variety of highly publicized conferences in which leaders from key fields of endeavour (science, the media, government) were brought together to talk about issues that the church founder Sun Myung Moon considered important. Among those issues was the healing of the division of Christianity. The formal name of the church, the Holy Spirit Association for the Unification of World Christianity, suggested Moon's belief that his movement would be a focal point around which Christian leaders could come together. To this end Moon supported the graduate education of some of his more promising members, a cadre of which had by the end of the 1980s assumed roles in the church's hierarchy and on its seminary faculty.

During the 1980s, he found some Christian scholars and ministers who were willing at least to consider his unifying ideas (along with a parallel interfaith programme for uniting all the religions). A series of dialogical session produced a set of books with papers by Christians and Unificationists.[32] In the end, these produced little visible fruit.

The dialogue sessions were criticized as less than true dialogues, in that all the expenses were paid for by the Unification Church. Many dismissed them as little more than church propaganda. Additionally, those who participated were often criticized by their Christian colleagues for supporting a cult operation. The sociologist and Catholic priest Joseph Fichter, for example, was active in conversations with Unificationists whom he admired for their stance on sexuality. He received considerable criticism from his colleagues after publishing favourable opinions of Moon's teachings.[33] In the 1990s, the dialogues with Christian scholars were superseded by what were seen by Unification Church leaders as more productive meetings with Christian pastors, and these have continued to the present.

In the 1990s, the International Society for Krishna Consciousness made a concerted effort to change its 'cult' image that included dialogue with its most severe critics in the cult awareness movement, attempts to integrate itself with the larger world of Hinduism in both India and the West, and opening a dialogue with some responsive Christian scholars. The possibility of these efforts bearing fruit rested on the movement's development of a trained leadership and the first elements of an intelligentsia. All three efforts have been productive, with the cult awareness people backing away from their highly critical stance, the emergence of a cordial relationship with many Hindu leaders, and a basis for future development of Christian–ISKCON relations being laid in a series of papers that probed issues of similarities and differences.[34]

In addition to the very pointed dialogue between Christian scholars and the Unification Church and ISKCON, there have been reports of a few attempts at holding dialogue sessions at which a variety of diverse NRMs have attended. These have been less productive. Informal reports from such efforts have catalogued all the problems at sustaining such gatherings beyond a meeting or two. Most have been initiated following an immediate crisis that one group experienced, and initial discussions often centred on the discrimination that the attending groups had encountered over the years. Rather than dialogue, most groups use such gatherings to present their group while making little effort to listen and respond to others. Highly critical and blunt responses to other groups often proved destructive, the more so if offered prior to building a foundation of trust and initial good will. (One such session attended by this author in the 1990s was killed when some feminist attendees responded to a presentation by a Jewish rabbi by changing the subject and attacking him over the issue of circumcision.)

Such Christian–New Religions gatherings have also been hampered by the different levels of sophistication manifested between Christian representatives, who tended to have graduate degrees, including special training in theology, as opposed to many new religious groups whose leadership has not been college graduates and who are trained only in the tradition they represent. These sessions find it difficult to escape a certain aura of condescension. The relative success of the Unification and ISKCON dialogues derives from their being a meeting of equals.

While many new religions have shown little interest in dialogue, the emerging Wiccan–Neo-Pagan movement has expressed some interest and has through the 1990s developed a community of scholars. They are, however, hindered by their association with 'witchcraft' and hence all the baggage that term carries in Western culture, and to a lesser extent their approach to sexuality, which is considerably more liberal than that of the great majority of Christians and Christian leaders. During the final years of Pope John Paul II's pontificate, a group of Pagan leaders attempted to approach the Vatican based upon the several speeches the pope had delivered in which he apologized for the past sins of the Catholic Church. Believing themselves the contemporary heirs of the medieval witches, the Pagans believed that they had an issue from which dialogue could begin. They prepared a packet of material, which was hand-delivered to the offices of the Pontifical Council for Interreligious Dialogue and mailed a copy to Pope John Paul. They received no response.

Problems and Prospects

The idea of interfaith dialogue is relatively new, though its beginnings are often traced to the 1893 World Parliament of Religions held in Chicago. The present global interest in dialogue was, arguably, the product of the Second World War: more positively as a response to the many contacts between Christians and those of other faiths during and immediately after the war; and, more negatively, as a realization of the horrendous events of the Holocaust. The present era began, however, with the initiative that grew out of Vatican II. The most productive era of interfaith dialogue is thus just now entering its second generation.[35] It is not surprising that such dialogue has been focused on those larger and older international religious communities that command the allegiances of the great majority of humankind.

During this time, the new religions have emerged (and additional new religions are being founded every year) and assumed their place on the world stage. Like the smaller of the older religions (such as Shinto, Sikhism, Sant Mat, Zoroastrianism) and the various surviving indigenous religions, the new religions are now claiming their rights to recognition as partners in the human quest for spirituality, enlightenment and salvation. On the one hand, they ask not to be judged by the sins of their past for which they have repented and attempted to make restitution (as the churches have done relative to colonialism, racism, the Holocaust, and recent scandals over child abuse). On the other hand, the great majority of new religions have now existed for multiple decades in peace with their communities which they offer as demonstration that any fears expressed about them in the 1970s and 1980s were unfounded. As a whole, they have a record no worse, if no better, than that of the older religious communities.

Meanwhile some problems with building a dialogue between Christians and the new religions remain. The Unification Church, ISKCON, several of the older Japanese new religions (Soka Gakkai, Tenrikyo) and the Neo-Pagan community are very much in the minority in their development of an academically trained leadership, in many cases having adopted a view that such training at best is distracting for the ministry and at worst destructive of spirituality. Some of the older new religions, most notably the Swedenborgians and the New Thought churches, have developed graduate schools, but they are in the minority. No colleges exist for Spiritualists, not to mention the average New Ager, or the majority of the newer Eastern groups.

However, given the gains that have been made by ecumenical and interfaith dialogue in reducing the tensions between religious groups, it can be assumed that, in a proper context, further encounters and dialogue between Christians and the new religions and the Western Esoteric community can also yield some positive results. Initially, those in dialogue will have to overcome strongly entrenched stereotypes. Many members of the new religions and the New Age have left the older churches in which they were raised for a new faith, while many members of the older churches believe that the new religions are threatening or at best collectivities of shallow spirituality. Working through initial stereotypes is no small task, as those who led the way in the last generation of dialogue could testify.

Those who wish to engage the new religions in dialogue must also overcome the problem of gaining at least a modest amount of knowledge about the spectrum of religious life in the world, a daunting task given the range of religious life and the number of different religious communities that presently exist. However, learning and dialogue can go on hand in hand, and as long as dialoguers are willing to continue their personal self-education throughout their life, most challenges can be met and overcome. And those who take up the task of building relationships with the new religions can know that they are pioneers and will have the long-term rewards of those who spend their life exploring new territory.

Study Questions

1 How does including new religions and the New Age as dialogical partners alter our picture of the larger religious community?

2 What obstacles – theological and practical – stand in the way of including new religions and New Age groups in interfaith dialogue?

3 How would you go about preparing yourself to talk to adherents of new religions and the New Age?

Further Reading

Clarke, Peter, 2005, *New Religions in Global Perspective*, London: Routledge.

Fergusion, Duncan S., 1992, *New Age Spirituality: An Assessment*, Philadelphia: Westminster Press.

Hexham, Irving, Rost, Stephen, and Morehead, John W. II, 2004, *Encountering New Religious Movements: A Holistic Evangelical Approach*, Grand Rapids: Kregel Academic and Professional.

Johnson, Philip, DiZerega, Gus, and Morehead, John W., 2008, *Beyond the Burning Times: A Pagan and Christian in Dialogue*, Oxford: Lion Hudson.

Saliba, John A., 1999, *Christian Responses to the New Age Movement: A Critical Assessment*, London: Cassell.

Siegler, Elijah T., 2006, *New Religious Movements*, Englewood Cliffs: Prentice-Hall.

Notes

1 Thomsen, Harry, 1963, *The New Religions of Japan*, Rutland: Charles E. Tuttle; McFarland, H. Neill, 1967, *The Rush Hour of the Gods*, New York: Macmillan; Shimazono, Susumu, 2004, *From Salvation to Spirituality: Popular Religious Movements in Modern Japan*, Melbourne: Trans Pacific Press.

2 Nelson, G. K., 1969, *Spiritualism and Society*, New York: Schocken Books; Needleman, Jacob, 1979, *The New Religions*, New York: E. P. Dutton; Wuthnow, Robert, 1976, *The Consciousness Reformation*, Berkeley: University of California Press.

3 Barker, Eileen, 1989, *New Religious Movements: A Practical Introduction*, London: HMSO; Coleman, John, and Baum, Gregory, 1983, *New Religious Movements*, Edinburgh and New York: T&T Clark and Seabury Press; Gallagher, Eugene V., and Ashcraft, W. Michael, 2006, *Introduction to New and Alternative Religions in America*, 5 vols, Westport: Greenwood Press; Melton, J. Gordon, and Moore, Robert, 1982, *The Cult Experience*, New York: Pilgrim Press.

4 The Peoples Temple was a Californian religious group who set up Jonestown,

a short-lived agricultural commune established in north-western Guyana. Jonestown became internationally notorious in 1978, when nearly its whole population died in a mass murder-suicide orchestrated by their leader, Jim Jones. Jonestown's population was about one thousand, once it was fully established, and the bulk of Jones's followers had moved to it, but most of them lived there for under a year. In November 1978, the United States Congressman Leo Ryan, accompanied by reporters and a delegation of concerned relatives of Peoples Temple members, visited Jonestown to investigate allegations of abuses there. The visit ended in the murders of Ryan and four others by members of the Peoples Temple, shot at the Port Kaituma airstrip as they were about to fly out. That evening, 18 November, Jones led his followers in their mass murder-suicide. Somewhat over 900 men, women and children perished, Jones among them.

5 Beckford, James A., 1985, *Cult Controversies: The Societal Response to the New Religious Movements*, London: Tavistock.

6 Robbins, Thomas, and Anthony, Dick, 1980, 'The Limits of "Coercive Persuasion" as an Explanation for Conversion to Authoritarian Sects', *Political Psychology*, vol. 2, no. 22, pp. 22–37; Richardson, James T., and Bromley, David G. (eds), 1983, *The Brainwashing/Deprogramming Controversy*, Lewiston: Edwin Mellen Press; Anthony, Dick, 1989, 'Religious Movements and "Brainwashing" Litigation: Evaluating Key Testimony', in Robbins, Thomas, and Anthony, Dick (eds), *In Gods We Trust: New Patterns of Religious Pluralism in America*, 2nd edn, New Brunswick: Transaction Press, pp. 295–344; Richardson, James T., 1993, 'A Social Psychological Critique of "Brainwashing" Claims about Recruitment to New Religions', in Bromley, David G., and Hadden, Jeffrey K. (eds), *The Handbook of Cults and Sects in America*, Religion and the Social Order, vol. 3 (Part B), Greenwich: JAI Press.

7 Melton, J. Gordon, 2000, 'Brainwashing and the Cults: The Rise and Fall of a Theory', in Melton, J. Gordon, and Introvigne, Massimo (eds), *Gehirnwäsche und Secten. Interdisziplinäre*, Annäherungen, Marburg, Germany: Dialogonal-Verlag. Posted at http://www.cesnur.org/testi/melton.htm.

8 Clarke, Peter, 2005, *New Religions in Global Perspective*, London: Routledge; Davis, Derek H., and Hankins, Barry (eds), 2002, *New Religious Movements and Religious Liberty in America*, Waco: J. M. Dawson Institute of Church–State Studies; Dawson, Lorne L., 1998, *Comprehending Cults: The Sociology of New Religious Movements*, Toronto: Oxford University Press; Jenkins, Philip, 2000, *Mystics and Messiahs: Cults and New Religions in American History*, Oxford: Oxford University Press.

9 Hastings, Arthur, 1991, *With the Tongues of Men and Angels*, Fort Worth: Holt, Rinehart & Winston; Klimo, Jon, 1987, *Channeling: Investigation on Receiving Information from Paranormal Sources*, Los Angeles: Jeremy P. Tarcher; Brown, Michael F., 1997, *The Channeling Zone: American Spirituality in an Anxious Age*, Cambridge, MA: Harvard University Press.

10 Kilham, Chris, 1988, *In Search of the New Age*, Rochester: Destiny Books.

11 Basil, Robert (ed.), 1988, *Not Necessarily the New Age*, Buffalo: Prometheus Press; Martin, Walter, 1989, *The New Age Cult*, Minneapolis: Bethany House.

12 Bloom, William (ed.), 1991, *The New Age: An Anthology of Essential Writing*, London: Rider.

13 Redfield, James, 1994, *The Celestine Prophecy*, New York: Warner Books.

14 Introvigne, Massimo, 2000, *New Age and Next Age* (in Italian), Casale Monferrato: Piemme.

15 Judah, J. Stillson, 1967, *The History and Philosophy of the Metaphysical Movements in America*, Philadelphia: Westminster Press; Faivre, Antoine, 2000, *Theosophy, Imagination, Tradition: Studies in Western Esotericism*, Albany: SUNY Press; Godwin, Joscelyn, 1994, *The Theosophical Enlightenment*, Albany: SUNY Press; Hanegraaff, Wouter J., 1996, *New Age Religion and Western Culture: Esotericism in the Mirror of Secular Thought*, Leiden: Brill; Hanegraaff, Wouter J., with Faivre, Antoine, Broek, Roelof Van Den, and Brach, Jean-Pierre (eds), 2005, *Dictionary of Gnosis and Western Esotericism*, 2 vols, Leiden: Brill; Rothstein, Mikael (ed.), 2001, *New Age Religion and Globalization*, Aarhus, Denmark: Aarhus University Press.

16 Barker, Eileen, 2004, 'What Are We Studying? A Sociological Case for Keeping the "Nova"', *Nova Religio: The Journal of Alternative and Emergent Religion*, vol. 8, no. 1, pp. 88–102.

17 Nelson, *Spiritualism*.

18 Melton, J. Gordon, 2007, 'Introducing and Defining the Concept of a New Religion', in Bromley, David G. (ed.), *Teaching New Religious Movements*, New York: Oxford University Press, pp. 29–40.

19 Rhodes, Ron, 2001, *The Challenge of the Cults and New Religions*, Grand Rapids: Zondervan.

20 Pike, Sarah M., 2004, *New Age and Neopagan Religions in America*, New York: Columbia University Press; Berger, Helen A., 2005, *Witchcraft and Magic: Contemporary North America*, Philadelphia: University of Pennsylvania Press; Harvey, Graham, 1997, *Contemporary Paganism: Listening People, Speaking Earth*, New York: New York University Press; Hutton, Ronald, 1999, *The Triumph of the Moon: A History of Modern Pagan Witchcraft*, Oxford: Oxford University Press.

21 Martin, Paul R., 1993, *Cult Proofing Your Kids*, Grand Rapids: Zondervan.

22 Saliba, John A., 1995, 'The New Religious Movements in Theological Perspective', in Saliba, John A., *Perspectives on New Religious Movements*, London: Geoffrey Chapman, pp. 167–97.

23 Rudin, James, and Rudin, Marcia, 1980, *Prison or Paradise: The New Religious Cults*, Minneapolis: Fortress Press.

24 Gonçalves, Theresa, 1999, 'Report on the Activities of the PCID: Attention to Sects and New Religious Movements', *Pro Dialogo* (Vatican City), vol. 101, p. 220.

25 The primary Vatican document on new religions is 'The Challenge of the Sects or New Religious Movements: A Pastoral Approach' (1991). Posted at: http://www.cesnur.org/2004/arinze_en.htm.

26 The primary document on meditation practices has been the 'Letter to the Bishops of the Catholic Church on Some Aspects of Christian Meditation' released in 1989 by the Congregation for the Doctrine of the Faith (rather than the Council for Interreligious Dialogue) and signed by, then, Cardinal Josef Ratzinger (now Pope Benedict XVI). Posted at: http://www.ourladyswarriors.org/zen.htm.

27 The most recent statement on the New Age Movement is: Pontifical Council for Culture, Pontifical Council for Interreligious Dialogue, 2003, *Jesus Christ the Bearer of the Water of Life: A Christian Reflection on the 'New Age'*, Vatican City: Vatican. Posted at: http://www.vatican.va/roman_curia/pontifical_councils/interelg/documents/rc_pc_interelg_doc_20030203_new-age_en.html.

28 Saliba, John A., 1993, 'Dialogue with the New Religious Movements: Issues and Prospects', *Journal of Ecumenical Studies*, vol. 30, pp. 61–80; 1999, *Christian Responses to the New Age Movement: A Critical Assessment*, London: Cassell.

29 In recent years, a major obstacle to Roman Catholic dialogue with the new religions has been created by the so-called Milingo affair. In 2001, the Zambian Roman Catholic Archbishop Emmanuel Milingo participated in one of the mass weddings arranged by Revd Sun Myung Moon and was married to a Korean Unificationist. The embarrassment caused by the wedding has been multiplied by the former Cardinal's subsequently launching a movement against priestly celibacy. The Milingo affair was seen by many as a specific anti-Catholic effort by the Unification Church.

30 Brockway, Allan R., and J. Paul Rajashekar (eds), 1987, *Religious Movements and the Churches*, Geneva: WCC.

31 Hexham, Irving, Rost, Stephen, and Morehead, John, II (eds), 2004, *Encountering New Religious Movements: A Holistic Evangelical Approach*, Grand Rapids: Kregel; Clifford, Ross, and Johnson, Philip, 2003, *Jesus and the Gods of the New Age*, Oxford: Lion.

32 Bryant, Darrol, and Hodges, Susan (eds), 1978, *Exploring Unification Theology*, New York: Rose of Sharon Press; Quebedeaux, Richard, and Sawatsky, Rodney (eds), 1979, *Evangelical–Unification Dialogue*, New York: Rose of Sharon Press.

33 Fichter, Joseph, 1985, *The Holy Family of Father Moon*, Kansas City: Leaven Press.

34 Cracknell, Kenneth, 2000, 'ISKCON and Interfaith Dialogue', *ISKCON Communications Journal*, vol. 8, no. 1. Posted at: http://www.iskcon.com/icj/8_1/cracknel.html.

35 Braybrooke, Marcus, 1980, *Inter-Faith Organizations, 1893–1979: An Historical Directory*, Lewiston: Edwin Mellen Press.

Index

References to words, names and terms in this index do not necessarily denote a reference to that precise term, i.e. references to Vedanta cover 'Vedantic', 'Vedantin', etc.